Teaching the Neglected "R"

Teaching
the Neglected "R"

Rethinking Writing Instruction
in Secondary Classrooms

Edited by
Thomas Newkirk & Richard Kent

HEINEMANN
Portsmouth, NH

Heinemann
A division of Reed Elsevier Inc.
361 Hanover Street
Portsmouth, NH 03801–3912
www.heinemann.com

Offices and agents throughout the world

The editors and publisher wish to thank those who have generously given permission to reprint borrowed material:

Excerpt from "Valentine" from *Mean Time* by Carol Ann Duffy. Copyright © 1993. Published by Anvil Press Poetry. Reprinted with permission of the publisher.

"Wanna Hear a Poem" by Stephen Colman from *Burning Down the House: Selected Poems from the Nuyorican Poets Café's National Poetry Slam Champions* by Roger Bonair-Agard, Stephen Colman, Guy LeCharles Gonzalez, and Alix Olson. Copyright © 2000. Published by Soft Skull Press. Reprinted with permission of the publisher.

Library of Congress Cataloging-in-Publication Data
Teaching the neglected R : rethinking writing instruction in secondary
classrooms / edited by Thomas Newkirk & Richard Kent.
        p. cm.
  Includes bibliographical references.
  ISBN-10: 0-325-00987-2
  ISBN-13: 978-0-325-00987-2
  1. English language—Composition and exercises—Study and
teaching (Secondary). 2. English language—Rhetoric—Study and
teaching (Secondary). 3. Report writing—Study and teaching (Secondary).
I. Newkirk, Thomas.   II. Kent, Richard.

PE1404.T3967 2007
808'.0420712—dc22   2007025643

Editor: Lisa Luedeke
Production management: Appingo Publishing Services
Production coordination: Vicki Kasabian
Cover design: Night & Day Design
Editors' cover photo: Dawn Pendergrass
Typesetter: Appingo Publishing Services
Manufacturing: Steve Bernier

Printed in the United States of America on acid-free paper
11 10 09 08 07 EB 1 2 3 4 5

In memory of
Donald M. Murray
1924–2006

Contents

Preface

When we first met to discuss the possibilities of *Teaching the Neglected "R,"* we turned to well established writing teachers whose scholarship and classroom practices had weathered the effects of educational tides. We also agreed that the collection would benefit from new voices in the field—teachers and writers whose practices reach well into this new century. To our good fortune, and yours, we landed both.

This new century welcomes a lively and far-reaching emphasis on writing and writing instruction. This awareness has even garnered support from our legislators in Washington, with the formation of a national commission. *The Neglected "R,"* the first report to Congress from The National Commission on Writing, presented bold facts and a road map into this new century with recommendations such as "[t]he amount of time students spend writing (and the scale of financial resources devoted to writing) should be at least doubled" (2003, 4). Further, the opening of the Commission's executive summary asserts

> American education will never realize its potential as an engine of opportunity and economic growth until a writing revolution puts language and communication in their proper place in the classroom. Writing is how students connect the dots in their knowledge. Although many models of effective ways to teach writing exist, both the teaching and practice of writing are increasingly shortchanged throughout the school and college years. Writing, always time-consuming for student and teacher, is today hard-pressed in the American classroom. Of the three "Rs," writing is clearly the most neglected.

This book is the result of hundreds of email discussions, hours of conversations, and one memorable twenty-six-hour immersion at Rich's home in the western mountains of Maine. Our book's collaborators offered many lessons that fed our discussions and pushed us to examine our own teaching practices. Just as we were feeling truly challenged by this book, by the startling realities facing this century's teachers, and by the examining and reexamining of our own practices and those of our collaborators (and perhaps feeling a bit ill equipped), our friend and mentor the late Don Murray reassured us with the opening words of his chapter, "One of the many gifts of the writing craft is that our apprenticeship never ends."

You will finish reading this volume with questions and, we believe, many ideas. We have featured the authors' biographies at the front of each chapter so that you will seek out their other works to help answer your questions and to fuel your imagination. And when you discover one of your own teaching practices that truly engages your students, we urge you to share your work with school colleagues, in a professional journal, or at a conference. As teachers, we gather strength by sharing our stories.

Back in the spring of 2003, Tom consented to a phone interview with students in one of Rich's doctoral seminars. The title of the course was "Coming to Know James Britton,

Theory and Practice." Both of us had known Mr. Britton, the language and learning scholar from England. Tom's dissertation featured Britton; Rich had studied in Mr. Britton's final course at the Bread Loaf School of English.

Near the end of the conference call one of Rich's students asked, "So, when it comes to writing instruction in the secondary classroom, what's the number one priority, Tom?"

A moment of silence and then a chuckle: "Have 'em write a lot."

All of us, veteran teachers and fourth-year university interns alike, have felt besieged at times as writing teachers. Whether conferring with one reluctant writer or managing 185 wired teenagers a day as they create digital life stories in space-age programs, our lives as teachers of writing can be a chaotic adventure of people and their individual processes.

Tom's response above may seem glib, but honestly, it gets to the heart of both of our teaching practices. We suggest that you take a step back and identify, in plain terms, your own central beliefs about writing and the teaching of writing. Start with yourself, your words, and your own writing process.

To help in your self-study, we offer the "NCTE Beliefs about the Teaching of Writing" from the Writing Study Group of the National Council of Teachers of English (2004):

1. Everyone has the capacity to write, writing can be taught, and teachers can help students become better writers.
2. People learn to write by writing.
3. Writing is a process.
4. Writing is a tool for thinking.
5. Writing grows out of many different purposes.
6. Conventions of finished and edited texts are important to readers and therefore to writers.
7. Writing and reading are related.
8. Writing has a complex relationship to talk.
9. Literate practices are embedded in complicated social relationships.
10. Composing occurs in different modalities and technologies.
11. Assessment of writing involves complex, informed, human judgment.

We would like to add a twelfth belief to this list: that teaching writing—as difficult and time-consuming as it is—can reconnect us with the reasons we joined the profession. One reason, of course, is the special privilege of entering into the lives and passions of our students through their writing. In effect, we ask, "Well, what is it like?" and they respond, "It's like this." We have both been sustained, and humbled, by these extraordinary acts of trust.

Thomas Newkirk
University of New Hampshire

Rich Kent
University of Maine

Acknowledgments

We thank the following students who reviewed the second edition of *To Compose: Teaching Writing in High School and College*. Their reviews convinced us that it was time for a new book: Susan Anderson, Tina Birolini, Natalie Cahill, Dan Caragher, Matt Carrington, Erin Crangle, Justin DeLuca, Bridget Griffin-Bales, Jim Grobecker, Jenn McArdle, Meredith McCarthy, Beth Mitchell, Ashley Stach, Andy Vaughan, Ashley Walton, Kristen Wiggin, Ben Zink, Jacqueline Evans, Mark Gosztila, Stephanie Ouimette, Jen Partridge, Laura Ritchie, James Smith, and Scott Taylor.

In addition, we thank Sabina Foote and Anne Wood for their assistance.

As always, the Heinemann staff led by Lisa Luedeke has been superb. Vicki Kasabian did an expert job with the design of the book, and Belinda Thresher carefully ushered the book through the last stages of production.

Teaching the Neglected "R"

1

Looking Back to Look Forward

Thomas Newkirk

Thomas Newkirk is director of the New Hampshire Literacy Institutes and professor of English at the University of New Hampshire. Before teaching at the university level he taught high school in Boston, and he continues to work with high school English teachers. He has written and edited numerous books and essays about literacy, including The Performance of Self in Student Writing, *which won the David Russell Award from the National Council of Teachers of English. His most recent work is* Misreading Masculinity, *which was featured in a PBS production of Michael Thompson's* Raising Cain.

We are in a period of unprecedented technological change that calls into question traditional ways of teaching writing. A whole new set of skills will be needed for students competing globally in the "flat world" of the twenty-first century. And the traditional organization of school itself—grading, taking subjects, the schedule of the day—will need to be changed. The very nature of writing is being transformed at a breathless rate...

I had actually planned to start this introduction with something futuristic like this, some projection of the great changes, driven by new technologies that will fundamentally alter the way we teach writing. It is exciting, after all, to imagine the time we live in as a crucial turning point in educational history. But before I indulged, I thought it might be useful to look backward, to sample the ideas of educators in my shoes at the beginning of the twentieth century who were trying to chart a new direction for teaching writing in high schools. So I spent several hours in the basement of the University of New Hampshire library with the journal *School Review*, which began publication in 1893 out of the University of Chicago, then a driving force in progressive education (John Dewey was a regular contributor). What, I asked myself, were these writers arguing for? What were they arguing against? And how relevant were these arguments for teaching in classrooms today?

This historical excursion can help us to get our bearings, to quiet for a moment the noise of futuristic rhetoric; by looking backward we can begin to sort out those permanent principles of writing instruction that have held up for centuries and the ways in which these princi-ples need to be adapted in contemporary education. As I read through the brittle, yellowed pages of *School Review*, I was struck by the common ground I shared with the writers, and by the similarity of the obstacles that writing teachers then and now must deal with. It occurred to me that the challenge of the twenty-first century is likely to resemble the challenge of the twentieth: to cut through the sheer curricular clutter that causes us to lose sight of the real goal of writing instruction—to truly engage students in purposeful acts of composing.

What Is Writing/What Is English

By the time these articles were being written, English had become established as a subject, though reformers still often had to argue against the classical focus on Latin and claims that classical languages were superior at instilling "mental discipline." But, as Samuel Thurber writes in 1894, "He who to-day claims a large place for English in a course of secondary studies finds himself wholly in harmony with the spirit of the times" (468). Writing a little more than a generation after the end of the Civil War, Thurber argued that instruction in English contributes to the formation of an American identity—"the aim of secondary Eng-lish is to bring the individual mind into the closest possible touch and sympathy with the national mind" (471). This sense of national identity (and by extension racial identity) necessitated a focus on written expression in English and an Anglo-American canon of lit-erature. The debate about what constituted "English" was also active (for example, Speech Communication broke off from English in the early twentieth century to become its own subject). Yet it is clear from these articles that writing was considered the central activity of the English class, or at the very least co-equal with reading literature; in fact, one of the major functions of reading literature was to provide models for writing. Adams Sherman Hill used *English* as almost synonymous with *writing* in his 1885 essay "English in the Schools," which appeared in *Harper's Magazine*.

If there is a key word for these educators it was *habit*, used in a similar way to *fluency* in contemporary instruction. In his widely read psychology text, William James devoted an entire chapter to habit, which he saw as essential to mental and character formation:

> The more of the details of our daily life we can hand over to the effortless custody of automa-tism, the more our higher powers will be set free for their proper work. There is no more mis-erable human being than one in whom nothing is habitual but indecision. (1961, 11–12)

F. A. Barbour built his pedagogy around this concept in his 1898 essay. He quotes F. W. Newman, the brother of Cardinal Newman: "No one will write well who has made a study of such matters when he sits down to write. All must previously have become an ingrained habit, *perhaps without his being aware of it*" (500). Writing instruction that focused on gram-mar, rules, and usage was worse than ineffective—it actually created a self-consciousness that interfered with writing.

> Young people do not learn to write well by trying to apply rules of any text-book to their writ-ing, but *unconsciously* rather. Good writing, like good speech, must become a matter of habit, a sort of second nature; it is to be acquired only by having good models in reading; by long continued practice upon subjects that interest the writer; and finally by the kindly, encourag-ing, and authoritative criticism of an efficient corps of teachers. (502)

Yet one senses that this stripped down conception of writing instruction faced considerable obstacles in its day (as it does in ours).

One obstacle was a college examination system that turned the writing class into test preparation; teachers lost their sense of agency and choice as they bent their instruction to "the dictation of authority" as represented in "the examination machinery." Many of the examination prompts—as well as traditional writing topics—frequently required young writers to comment on moral issues, leading to a "falseness of tone" as they attempted to philosophize on these issues. Barbour notes that they typically began by stating that "such and such a virtue" was "one of the greatest blessings we enjoy." He goes on to claim that effective, engaged writing can only come when students can choose topics relevant to their lives and interests:

> If ever any spontaneity, freshness, life, power are to find their way into written pages of our high-school boys and girls, it will be when they write on subjects in which they take a natural and lively interest, subjects suggested by their investigations, their imagination, their reading,— subjects, finally, on which they have grown more or less eager to express their thoughts. (503)

Louise Bacorn similarly notes that engagement can only occur when the writer owns the writing situation:

> When the student is the originator and owner of the situation, then it is his to deal with as he likes; it is his child, he naturally has the most tender and enduring interest in it. (1901, 299)

Or this from Adams Sherman Hill:

> To the extent that a young writer works with a purpose to say something of his own, what he writes will have freshness, and will inspire interest in his subject and in him. To the extent that he fails to put himself into his work, he becomes what is known as a hack writer, a mere beast of burden, who serves as the common carrier for the thoughts of other men. (1885, 132)

Barbour quotes the great turn-of-the-century nature writer John Burroughs on the absolute importance of the emotional connection between writer and topic: "I must feel the thing first, and then I can say it; I must love the subject upon which I write, it must adhere to me, and for the time being become a part of me" (509).

To teach in this way, however, posed logistical problems that were also discussed in journal articles. The very first article in the first issue of *English Journal*, published in 1912, was titled "Can Good Composition Teaching Be Done Under the Current Conditions?" The first word, the first sentence, the first paragraph of the article was the single word, *No*. The sheer number of students to be taught by the English teacher meant that this intimate personal form of instruction placed a huge burden on English teachers. Seventy years later, Ted Sizer would write his classic, *Horace's Compromise*, to describe exactly this dilemma.

I could continue to quote from these century-old articles, but I hope by now my point has been made. The basic principles of effective writing instruction were clearly articulated long before Don Murray or Peter Elbow began describing the writing process; in fact, Quintilian had them right when he was teaching the children of Roman emperors. I'll wager that the major challenge of twenty-first century writing instruction will be similar to the challenge of twentieth-century writing instruction or first-century writing instruction—that is, to resist the forces that pull us away from genuinely helping students to engage in writing. The teaching of writing is difficult because there are so many institutional, commercial, and political forces that pull teachers away from the work that needs to be done. These can be as trivial as the fire codes that prohibited Rich from putting posters on the walls and from hanging student-made mobiles from the ceiling (I mean, has there ever been a case of a cinderblock-and-linoleum school set on fire by posters?).

Normal Schooling

For all the focus on reform of schools, I still believe there is an image of "normal schooling" that is implanted in the minds of administrators, parents, and the general public. In my second year of teaching in a terribly deprived urban school in Boston's Roxbury district, I worked hard to find books that students could and would read—and I had some success. One day a group of students (thankfully not mine) started a small riot, pounding on lockers and yelling for students to leave the building. My class of tenth graders was reading, actually reading, Steinbeck's *Of Mice and Men*. As the pounding and yelling continued, they kept at it—a wonderful tribute, I thought, to them, to Steinbeck, and to me. Suddenly, the headmaster, frustrated by his inability to halt the riot, poked his head in my door and said, "Mr. Newkirk, will you begin *teaching*!"

I've thought about that moment often. What my headmaster saw in that moment did not match an image of instruction that he took as normal. To fit that image I would have needed to be at the front of the classroom talking, passing on information that students would be held responsible for; it would lead to a test that would create grades. Students would be listening and taking notes. At times in this school, the teaching was almost a parody of this model: the head of the history department put notes on the board, which students copied, then on Friday he gave an open notebook test for which students copied their notes to answer the test questions. But this double-copying passed as instruction because it looked like teaching.

Technology and the Internet do not automatically work to alter this expectation for normal education; in fact, technology can reinforce it. For example, schools are increasingly purchasing software that enables teachers to post grades so that they can be accessible to parents. Parents using these systems will expect to see, for each subject, a string of numerical or letter grades, lots of them. Systems like this, however well-intended, may work against teachers who want to engage a student in long-term writing projects, who want to use narrative forms of evaluation, or who want to delay the grading of writing until the student has produced a body of work. Good writing teachers will try to finesse these expectations, I'm sure, but my point is that the system itself is built on the model of normal schooling.

Educational products can also reinforce the gravitational draw toward normal schooling. Indeed, the textbook is often seen as the center of a curriculum—which is viewed as a march through the textbook. To teach a writing class, it follows that you need a writing textbook, often with worksheets, a handbook, a spelling program, a vocabulary program, a book of writing prompts, and at the higher levels, a reader. These products, in turn, shape instruction; they promise to lift the burden of planning from the teacher's shoulders, they are created by experts (so they say), and they provide an orderly pattern of work and assessment. Not coincidentally, they are also turn a profit for commercial publishers. Yet it has always seemed to me that the content of writing is minimal; the major goals could be written on the back of an envelope, and unless someone is selling envelopes, the writing class should not be a big commercial market. The tools (that is, the materials) can easily become the masters.

There are other aspects of normal schooling I could mention. The concept of coverage can prevent in-depth work on writing projects. I recently reviewed my own state's standards and came across this objective for sixth-grade social studies (bear in mind that this is one of many for that one subject):

> Demonstrate a basic understanding of the origin, development, and distinctive characteristics of major ancient, classical, and agrarian civilizations including: Mesopotamian, Ancient Hebrew, Egyptian, Nubian (Kush), Greek, Roman, Gupta Indian, Han Chinese, Islamic, Byzantine, Olmec, Mayan, Aztec, and Incan Civilizations. (New Hampshire State Frameworks, Social Studies, 18)

This list verges on parody, but it reflects the tendency of learning objectives to proliferate; after all, they are usually committee documents that reflect the varied priorities of committee members. But the effect on instruction can be a compulsion to rush, to move on; rather than focusing the energy of instruction, curricular lists like this one only disperse it.

Writing instruction—and instruction in general—also suffers from the pernicious confusion of standards with standardization. The thinking goes something like this: if every teacher is doing the same thing, there is an equality in the educational product because students in every class are getting the same thing. In a fuzzy way, it is all about fairness. To be sure, some agreement about goals makes sense. One of my daughter's middle school teachers, for example, once admitted that he was not good at teaching writing, so he didn't do it. I could barely keep from asking, "You can make that choice?" But a healthy—and I would argue—fair system allows teachers to use their passions, temperaments, and particular skills to create writing programs that they own. A fair system is one in which every teacher is working to his or her top potential, even if that instruction varies—as it will—from class to class. The argument about choice in writing can be applied to teaching. We can paraphrase Adams Sherman Hill: to the extent that teachers fail to put themselves into their work, they become beasts of burden, who serve as common carriers for the plans of others.

My point in all this is not that good writing instruction cannot be accomplished in secondary schools—it can. The chapters in this book show it can be done. But I want to suggest that there are deeply conservative trends in public schooling, that exist at an almost instinctive level (in images as I've argued), that can work against thoughtful writing instruction. It has been said that if a physician from 1900 visited a modern-day hospital, he would be stunned by the changes; but if an English teacher from 1900 visited a school today, he or she would feel strangely at home. It is naïve to imagine that these conservative forces will magically disappear in the twenty-first century, or that technology itself will make them obsolete. As Larry Cuban and David Tyack point out in their splendid book, *Tinkering Toward Utopia*, the twentieth century saw immense technological change—radio, television, movies, the telephone, the slide projector—all of which failed to transform the dominance of normal schooling.

Dealing with Failure

This book provides close-up looks at wonderful innovations in writing instruction: it shows how we might introduce new genres of writing like digital storytelling; it shows how writing can enter the community through service learning; it helps us imagine how we can reimagine what the essay is; it offers guidance for teaching students whose first language is not English; it revisits the writing conference and components of the writing process; and much more. Collectively these chapters demonstrate that there is more to teaching than normal schooling and the inevitable five-paragraph theme on what a wonderful man Atticus Finch is.

I'd like to end this introduction with a topic we don't address—failure and the temperament teachers need to deal with it. Failure, it seems to me, is such an integral part of teaching that it's simply dishonest to pretend it doesn't exist, or that it doesn't have the potential to sap the confidence of teachers.

There's a story about the outstanding professional golfer, Ben Crenshaw, who would sometimes play with the varsity golfers at his alma mater, the University of Texas. Both Crenshaw and his UT partner bogeyed one hole, each missing a short putt for par. On the way to the next hole, the varsity golfer said, "I hope you don't mind my asking, but what's the difference between your game and mine?"

Crenshaw paused, then answered, "You know that bogey you just had. Is that bothering you?"

"Well, yeah."

"Well, it's not bothering me. That's the difference."

Crenshaw was not saying that the bogey didn't matter to him, only that he could process this small failure without feeling discouragement or frustration that would carry on to the next hole. He could make a technical adjustment, if need be, but emotionally he remained on an even keel.

Failure is an integral part of teaching. It happens to some degree, every day, every class—a discussion that falls flat, workshop groups that don't stay on task, the student with great writing potential who doesn't try no matter what we do, the lesson that works wonderfully in second period but bombs in sixth period. When I began teaching in 1970, in an inner city Boston school, I was woefully underprepared, and failure was about all I experienced. I know in the pit of my stomach what it feels to try to maintain a sense of being a teacher in the face of unremitting difficulty. I know how easy it is to fall into a deadly cycle—failure leads to discouragement which leads to more failure, and perhaps ultimately to emotional disengagement, to going through the motions. Sadly, it happens.

From hard experience, from mistakes I have made, and from my work with teachers over almost three decades, I've come to some conclusions about ways of processing failure. One of the tendencies of late middle age (besides always forgetting where you parked your car) is the perpetual feeling that you have advice to give—which is what I will do.

Failure is inevitable   There is simply no way that everything will work as planned, even for the most effective teacher. In this regard, it is important to have a realistic idea of what success looks like. It is a trap to imagine the successful teacher as profoundly charismatic, almost from another planet. Their students are never bored, never stare out the window, never digress to talk about what they saw on TV the night before. The writing of these students is not only better than that of your students; the students in these classes write better than you do. It's a little like the teenage girl who feels bad about herself because she can't look like the models in the slick magazines she buys. Well, the model doesn't even look like the model; photographs, as we know, are digitally enhanced. She's a fantasy, and often an unhealthy one.

When I have visited the classes of excellent teachers, I am struck by the small things that make up this excellence—the exact pacing, the sense of having a clear purpose for the class, the appropriate and interesting selection of examples, the precision of explanations, and often a kind of slowness that creates a comfort level. Like most skillful performances, there is an economy, a lack of clutter. The teaching is thoughtful but not magical. It is crucial for all teachers, and particularly beginning teachers, to spend time in these classes; otherwise it is so easy to imagine these successful teachers as perfection itself.

Process failure in a technical way One of my favorite quotes is by Marvin Minsky, an MIT innovator in cognitive science and artificial intelligence. He writes:

> Thinking is a process, and if your thinking does something you don't want it to, you should be able to say something microscopic and analytic about it, and not something enveloping and evaluating about yourself as a learner. The important thing in refining your thought is to try to depersonalize your interior; it may be all right to deal with other people in a vague global way—by having "attitudes" toward them, but it is devastating if this is the way you deal with yourself. (Quoted in Bernstein 1981, 122)

This advice applies as well to teaching as it does to thinking. When something doesn't work in teaching, there is, for most people, an inevitable sense of emotional disappointment. But the sooner we "depersonalize the interior" and think about the problem in a "microscopic and analytic way," the sooner we learn from the experience and perhaps make changes. What exactly went wrong? Were the instructions unclear? Was the timing off? Did I rush things? Why was James so distracted today? Should students have come to response groups with something written? Or was it just an off day for everyone (we all have them)? This kind of problem-solving can draw us away from the kind of self-accusatory thinking—doubting your ability to teach—that can be so painful and debilitating.

Cherish small victories In my first year of teaching, I sometimes staggered out of the building at the end of a day feeling completely spent. Nothing had prepared me for this kind of fatigue. On some days I'd reward myself with a hot fudge sundae at Brigham's and try to review the day. "Something must have gone right," I would try to tell myself. And usually something did—maybe one reluctant student who seemed a little more willing to work, the ninth graders who liked it when I read *Manchild in the Promised Land*, the journal one of my ninth graders, Keith Fields, kept on his own and let me read (I still have a copy of it). It kept me going.

It may be that our view of success is distorted by the movies. I know that in the early 1970s there were all those films where a teacher would meet a resistant class, and triumphantly, totally win them over. This may happen, but my guess is that excellence usually has a different look. It consists of the accumulation of small victories and the ability of the teacher to recognize and celebrate them.

You need a team As teachers we can close our doors and try to deal with the complexities of teaching on our own. But this solitude can be punishing. My wise brother once explained to me his philosophy of coping with the emotional demand of his complex life; he established a nationwide company from scratch, had disagreements with the IRS that cost hundreds of thousands of dollars, suffered a painful divorce, and like most members of our family, was subject to bouts of depression. The secret, he said, is that everyone needs a team. "It's like NASCAR. You have to have all these people behind you that you count on. You just can't do it by yourself. It's too hard, too complex. There's no great virtue in toughing it out."

Seeking help and offering help should be part of the natural fabric of social groups because self-sufficiency is a myth. Teaching is just too demanding to go it alone.

Part of this team is, of course, one's immediate family, but we need professional friends as well. Recent studies of friendship patterns in the United States show that we are less likely these days to have close friends outside the family as compared to previous generations. Beginning teachers often feel there is an awkward age gap that separates them from experienced teachers (older teachers also can feel that awkwardness). I believe that efforts to bridge that awkwardness pay off; it is important for beginning teachers to enter the social life of the school, attending baby showers, retirement dinners, attending conferences with experienced teachers, and participating in the wonderful writing project sites across the country.

I can't say that I followed this advice when I began teaching, maybe through a combination of arrogance and shyness, but there was one older man, Tom Giachetto, a mechanical drawing teacher, who reached out to me. He lived on the North Shore and his route home took him close to my apartment on Beacon Hill. As we weaved though traffic on Storrow Drive, we'd talk about students we had in common. I had such a difficult time reading student behavior, determining what was disruptive—what I should let go, what I should laugh at—and he helped me sort things out. "He's really a good kid. He just gets frustrated easily—you have to get to him fast." This was the kind of advice I needed desperately. We came to the spot where Storrow Drive met Charles Street, and he stopped to let me off (at the absolutely most dangerous stopping point in Boston). Each ride was a great lesson about teaching, and the funny thing is, I don't even think he was aware that he was teaching. He was just giving me a ride home.

Since coming to New Hampshire in 1977, I have regularly hiked Mt. Chocorua, a stunning mountain on the southern edge of the Whites. As I approach the trailheads on Route 16, I pass the summer home of William James, the great American psychologist and a leading proponent of pragmatism. From that home he had a wonderful view of the mountain and could easily walk out his front door to the same trails that I hike—Piper, Hammond, Liberty. I like the idea of walking the same ground that he walked a century ago. And I continue to be inspired by the vision of knowing what he and other American pragmatists developed in the latter part of the twentieth century. Much of this introduction is right out of their playbook.

Rich and I were even tempted to begin this collection with an epigram from one of James' most famous students, Gertrude Stein: "There ain't no answer. There ain't gonna be any answer. There never has been an answer. That's the answer." The pragmatists rejected the belief in permanent truths, in big ideologies, in dogma and tradition, in top-down mandates that presumed to dictate behavior in particular situations. All of these had to be put to the test of actual experience. It's a restless philosophy—we never arrive, we're always moving. There "ain't no answer" that we can accept once and for all. Pragmatism requires of us all an alertness to the situations we are in and a willingness to change. James expressed this view indelibly in a letter he wrote on June 7, 1899:

> I am against bigness and greatness in all their forms, and with the invisible and molecular moral forces that work from individual to individual, stealing in through the crannies of the world like so many soft rootlets, or like the capillary oozing of water…The bigger the unit you deal with, the hollower, the more brutal, the more mendacious is the life displayed. So I am against all big organizations as such, national ones first and foremost; against all big successes

and big results; and in favor of the eternal forces of truth which always work in the individual and immediately unsuccessful ways, underdogs always, till history comes, after they are long dead, and puts them on the top. (Quoted in Menand 2001, 372)

Bigness is even more a force in education today. Big reforms. Big textbooks. Big research. Big business. Yet I suspect real, lasting change will occur on a small scale, in the "crannies" of the educational system, in the micro-experiments of the teaching day. That, I suspect, will be the challenge of the twenty-first century.

Works Cited

Bacorn, Louise. 1901. "The Assignment of Essay Subjects." *School Review* 9: 298–309.

Barbour, F. A. 1898. "English Composition in High School." *School Review* 6: 500–13.

Bernstein, Jeremy. 1981. "Profiles: Marvin Minsky." *The New Yorker* (December 14): 50–128.

Hill, A. S. 1885. "English in Schools." *Harper's Magazine* 71: 122–33.

Hopkins, Edwin. 1912. "Can Good Composition Teaching Be Done Under the Current Conditions?" *English Journal* 1: 1.

James, William. 1961. *Psychology: The Briefer Course.* Notre Dame, IN: University of Notre Dame Press.

Menand, Louis. 2001. *The Metaphysical Club: A Story of Ideas in America.* New York: Farrar, Straus, and Giroux.

New Hampshire State Frameworks. Social Studies. http://www.ed.state.nh.us/Curriculum Frameworks/k-126.htm.

Thurber, Samuel. 1894. "English in Secondary Schools: Some Considerations as to Its Aims and Its Needs." *School Review* 2: 468–78.

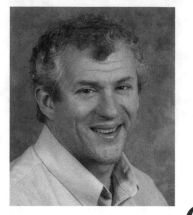

2

Thoughts on the Twenty-First Century Classroom

An Interview with Jeffrey D. Wilhelm

Jeffrey D. Wilhelm is a professor of English education at Boise State University, where he also directs the Boise State Writing Project and serves as the in-service director for a national demonstration site project in content-area literacy. He previously taught middle and high school for fifteen years. A past winner of the Promising Researcher Award from the National Council of Teachers of English and a current member of the editorial board for Voices from the Middle, *Jeff has authored and coauthored many books, including* Reading Don't Fix No Chevys, Strategic Reading, Imagining to Learn, *and* Going with the Flow.

How has your thinking about teaching writing changed over the last fifteen or so years? What practices and thoughts did you used to have that you've changed?
There are two major changes. The first change is a response to our current situation in schools and the problem with information-driven teaching and testing. As a result of this emphasis, kids have lost the essential gift of time. Students now need more time to immerse themselves in curricular topics, more time to read, write, and reflect; they need more informal writing, they need more exploration, and they need to do things that really matter to them—or to explicitly see how what they are doing in school can and does matter out in the world. When I refer to informal writing, I mean writing that is used to explore and express, writing that is for trying things out, for bricolage, for practice that is risk free, where taking chances is encouraged and rewarded. I'd challenge anyone to identify anything they ever learned of any significance—from kissing, to cooking, to kayaking—that they got right the first time. If we want kids to be better writers, we have to take time to model, to mentor their practice in journals and drafts, to assist them, to rehearse both ideas and techniques, to revise and respond to each other. This is what real writers do, and what

we now do in school so often does not meet the correspondence concept by reflecting and meeting the real writer test, or real reader, real ethicist, or real whatever we are trying to teach and learn test. Not only does this undermine true learning and understanding, it makes kids feel disconnected and cynical about school and what we do there.

The second change concerns explicit instruction. I think that there is a widespread notion that if you just get kids reading or get them writing a lot, they'll become better readers and writers. I've become convinced that this is absolutely not the case. They'll get better at reading and writing the kinds of things they already know how to read and write. I'm not saying that's insignificant, but if I want my students to be good writers and readers of argument, or even of specific arguments like arguments of policy, then there are very specific demands that are placed on them by the conventions of those kinds of texts. I'm going to need to explicitly assist them to learn those conventions and to use them in meaningful ways. The same is true of classification, extended definition, and specific kinds of narrative. As students go through school, narrative is rarely straightforward; it is often subverted through irony or unreliable narrators or other kinds of devices . . . kids are unlikely to learn how to deal with these kinds of sophisticated demands—as readers or writers—on their own. They need to be given experience with these writerly moves, to be taught specifically how to use and respond to them. These are great intellectual tools that students rarely master because they are not taught to master them nor given the requisite opportunity to practice and use them in real contexts. I've begun to think very hard about what is involved in the particular kinds of writing tasks that I ask my kids to do, and how can I assist them, through exploratory and informal writing, to get the stuff to write about and then put it in a form that is both conventional—meeting the expectations of the discipline—and that does intellectual work that is both personally meaningful and socially significant.

Can you say more about the kind of explicit teaching students need?
Part of it is to teach a variety of genres and to actually teach the conventions and demands of that genre, to get kids to reflect on what kind of work each genre does and ask themselves, what do I have to do to make my text fit that genre, or how can I subvert it in some way for a particular purpose? One of the things that George Hillocks points out is that you very rarely see a genre in a pure form. Arguments embed definitions, descriptions, and classifications; narratives embed descriptions, definitions, tangential narratives, and much more. We have to understand that genre is a messy thing, but kids need to understand the heart of the matter about each genre, i.e., why do people write and read arguments, lyric poems, ironic monologues, and the like. They also need to understand the heart of the matter about particular tools and devices.

Let's take the example of character in narrative. What's the heart of the matter with character? It's how they respond to the pressures that are put upon them. If we could just teach kids that, they'd be more engaged with reading and writing about characters, and they would write much better stories and fables. Setting, what is important about setting? What is the heart of the matter? It's how the setting constrains or encourages the characters' actions. If you taught students that, they wouldn't use weak settings that do no work for the reader. I challenge teachers to think about what the heart of the matter is. So often in school we teach that setting is when and where a story takes place. This does no work and misses the point about setting.

Let's use another example from argument. What is a persuasive claim supposed to do? What does it look like? Students can employ a simple plus-minus-interesting test, an idea from Edward DeBono and my friend Michael Smith. To introduce it, the teacher states a claim: "All cars should be yellow." Are there any plusses? Any minuses? Are there any interesting things that might evolve? If you don't have plusses and minuses, you don't have an arguable claim. It is something either everybody agrees with or nobody agrees with. And if the claim does not also bring up interesting insights or angles the reader hasn't thought of before, then it's not going to be interesting to write or read. This PMI test is a heuristic, or a problem solving repertoire, that gets at the essence of a particular tool like claim writing in argument.

We need to help students get to the heart of the matter for any convention we teach. Once they know the rules, their purposes, how they work, and what work they do, then they can bend and transform the conventions, but you have to know the rules of the game before you can break them. The point, I think, is that we must help students inquire into how language works so they can achieve deep understanding. With understanding comes the capacity to extend, apply, transform, and revise the tools you have learned. In general, I don't think we do a very good job of that in school. Kids learn a lot of *what* and not very much *how, why, when*, or *where*. Information isn't very exciting or important until you start to purposefully use it in real situations. So in effect, our teaching misses the point because we don't teach how what is learned really matters in the kids' lives, in the here and now, and in the real world beyond school.

When you consider high school literacy practices, what changes would you like to see in the twenty-first century?
First, I'd like to see a reorganization of curriculum around problems because that is how disciplines are organized. That is why disciplines were invented, to address particular kinds of problems and issues. So, for example, instead of teaching To *Kill a Mockingbird* as a textual artifact, teach it in the context of the question "What are civil rights and how do you protect them?" I have taught several texts using this essential question and a lot of sub-questions came out of that, like "Where do rights come from?" and "How do you best promote them?" and "What threatens them?" and that kind of thing. Now, these are problems that social scientists and historians work on. It is a problem that legislators work on. It's a problem in the real world. It's a problem that kids work on: have you ever met a ninth grader who didn't think his rights were being violated all the time? One of the things that I think is missing from schools is this framing of what we do so that it matters to students, to teachers, and out in the world, and in disciplinary practice.

So this links really well with your research on flow?
Oh, absolutely. As soon as the kids started delving into questions about civil rights, we had things we had to read, things already in the curriculum—*1984* or *Roll of Thunder, Hear My Cry,* and we combined it with some of the Holocaust literature, and the students found nonfiction about immigration, articles on the Internet and in the daily newspaper, and there were things they wanted to talk about from their lives and our community that springboarded from the readings. In essence, we achieved what Applebee calls "curricular coherence" because instead of doing one darn thing after another disconnected darn thing, we combined many things that were really about the same central issues and gave us dif-

ferent perspectives on these issues. So reading *Roll of Thunder* could help the kids read and understand the issues in *Night*. Next we had the kids examining the connections between the civil rights issues in *Roll of Thunder*, in *Night*, in our school, and in some articles we brought in. For example, we read about the Holocaust conference in Iran and asked why anyone would want to deny the Holocaust, so we read texts "against" each other.

The students were operating on the curriculum instead of receiving it; it was up to them to see the themes, the differences, the similarities, what mattered, and how to apply what they had learned in their own lives. At the end of the unit—and of course, this is something we were preparing them for throughout—we had them write an argument about a civil rights issue and how to address it. The writing of arguments is required by the curriculum. Then we had them create a museum exhibit about a civil rights issue we had not studied but that they were interested in. Part of that exhibit had to be a physical artifact like a map or poster set, and it had to have an electronic component to go with it, a PowerPoint presentation or a video documentary, for example; and students gave a speech to introduce their exhibit. As a result, we hit several curricular requirements in one swoop. The kids knew what to argue about and speak about because these things were created in the context of our civil rights study and represented the content that had been learned, as well as demonstrated their ability to argue, speak publicly, and create well-designed multimedia.

Was their documentary a digital story?

Yes, many of them were digital stories; some were interviews with people about a civil rights issue or even a Ken Burns style historical documentary about a civil rights issue using photos, paintings, and primary documents. Again, think of all we achieved in a single unit: we covered several required texts, completed several required assignments, and we did so with true curricular integration and curricular coherence, and did so in a way that engaged and mattered to the kids. Plus, we integrated the use of electronic technologies in our own research, our reading, and of course, in our representation of what we learned to other people. The kids had to write a script for the video documentary; if they made a website, they had to create text for that website. I don't think that traditional kinds of writing are going to go away; I think those things are embedded into electronic technologies.

One of the things that Michael Smith and I found in the boys studies (Editor's note: see *Reading Don't Fix No Chevys*, 2003; *Going with the Flow*, 2006) is that every single boy, even from the poorest inner city school, used electronic technology. The kids from the less affluent schools would go to the library and access, and they were doing stuff that was asynchronous like email. The kids who were from more affluent backgrounds all had their own computers, and they were using iChat and the things that were synchronous, instant messaging and that kind of thing. One of the things that all of the boys were cynical about was how school did not match the literacies that they practiced in their lives and saw other people practicing. They thought school was behind the curve and this made them cynical about the literacies they were asked to practice in school.

How do we do that? How do teachers incorporate new genres such as instant messaging and blogging?

Classroom design is going to have to change, schools are going to have to become wireless, and maybe we'll get desks with computers in them. There will be changes around access—all schools will need to be wireless and students will need ready access to laptops that they can take home. Another challenge is around the instructional use of electronic technologies. Just because you have electronic technologies doesn't mean you are going to have decent instruction. Most often teachers use electronic technology as an electronic worksheet.

A big challenge is using electronic technologies to their full potential. Computer guru Seymour Papert says "the computer is the world's greatest construction kit, but we never use it that way in school." It is the world's greatest research tool, but we rarely use it that way. Teachers really have to get grounded in the inquiry process and how they can use, or get kids to use, the information available on the Internet to do their own research and—I think this is most important—how to use technologies to create new data, analyze data, and represent and share and revise what's been learned. When we reach this point, then we will be using electronic technology as a research tool and a construction kit, and fulfill the special capacities it provides for engagement and learning.

You asked the question about blogs and instant messaging; I've got a couple of teachers who are working on electronic discussion groups. In the classroom, you come in, sit down at your computer, and instead of having a small or large group discussion, there is a question on the class blog or iChat, and then the students enter the classroom and instantly start pursuing the question. There are certain rules: you have to have so many turns, you have to uptake somebody else's comment and extend it, and the teacher can monitor it through TechCommander or whatever monitoring software is available at her own desk, or even just walk around. Then transcripts are printed and the kids can analyze their contributions, so (1) there is a record of accountability, (2) everybody is necessarily involved, unlike a large group discussion, (3) kids develop and apply critical standards about a good discussion, and (4) the teacher can get information immediately from these transcripts about what the kids understood, didn't get, who was contributing in what ways and who wasn't. It is just an example of how a traditional classroom agenda can be pursued more efficiently by using technology.

Technology doesn't supplant traditional notions of talking face to face but, in fact, abets it. I just think that this is one example of how technology can be used to promote the kind of dialogic instruction I think we want and need to have in schools so that kids are involved in constructing dynamic understandings instead of just receiving inert information.

Do writing teachers have to be writers?

I think so. Information-transmission theories leave us open to the charge that "those who can't do, teach." In the sociocultural theory teaching is apprenticeship, so you have to do what you teach. You have to model and mentor and monitor other people doing what you do. At the least, we have to understand what good writers do. I think it is important for teachers to do the assignments they give students or something analogous. I'll always remember one of the boys from our study who told me, "I'm not doing this crap," and I asked, "Why not?" He said, "The teacher wouldn't do this crap." That has become a kind of mantra for me, would I do the work that I'm asking the students to do. Oftentimes, I wouldn't, so I shouldn't ask or expect them to do it.

Later on in that conversation he also said, "The teacher don't even bring her game to school, so I'm not bringing mine." That has become another mantra, am I bringing my game to school? One thing we learned over and over again in the boys study is that kids will only match your passion, your energy, and your commitment, so if you are not excited about a topic or assignment, don't expect it to matter to them. A discouraging finding was that the better students, the ones who are more successful in school, would say, "Don't confuse what I am doing in English with my real reading and writing." They bifurcated it; they saw school and life activities as totally separate.

How do you view the current emphasis on testing?
If you have fifty minutes to write about a topic you don't know anything about and it is a high-stakes test, you are going to make up data. When we have tests that don't fit what real readers and writers do, then we are teaching kids to be dishonest and to make up data. They have no option if they don't know about the topic. George Hillocks pointed out in *The Testing Trap* that we use writing tests that are supposed to test processes but are tests of information. If the kid doesn't know enough about the topic, they can't write on it, so they either lie or it's a test of information, not a test of writing. We also teach kids that this is what writers do, they sit down and write a first draft that's a piece of crap, as fast as they can, and turn it in to someone else for validation. Well, that's not what happens when real writers write. So the tests don't serve the correspondence concept, or the notion that what we learn needs to correspond to what experts know and do. So much of what we do in school doesn't meet the correspondence concept, or what we might call the real writer or real reader test.

One of the discouraging things about No Child Left Behind is that we have these required tests, and the tests are created in such a way as to be cheap and easy to administer. They mostly test information; they don't test deep understanding, they don't test procedures—in other words, they don't correspond to what writers know and do. If you get a dumbed-down test, you'll get a dumbed-down curriculum, and kids are not going to learn what real people do. They are going to be disenfranchised because they are going to know they are just "doing school." A kid will think, at best: let me do it and let me get the heck out of here.

Among my favorite anecdotes from the boys study is one about a boy who said Shakespeare was worthless, nobody was doing it, and I asked, "Why do you have to do it?" and he said, "You just do." I said, "Why?" and I pushed him. He said, "Listen, buddy, every kid in the world has to read Shakespeare; I don't like you sitting here and trying to get me to hold a grudge about it. It is just a bitter pill and you have to swallow it. It's an obstacle and you have to get over it." I said, "Why?" and he said, "The hell if I know…to get to the real stuff." So he saw school as an obstacle to get over to show you are worthy to do the real stuff. School should be the real deal, and that's the challenge for the twenty-first century, to give teachers the authority to create classroom situations that are real-life or simulate it or lead kids towards it.

To make the changes you suggest, a teacher will need to have more control over what they teach. How do you see that happening?
One of the problems with the current movement is that it is based on a mistrust of teachers. If our legislatures and culture are going to mistrust teachers, the necessary changes cannot be made. In our National Demonstration Site for Adolescent Literacy in Maine's Washington County, we had students create portfolios of work, which the students then coded to the state standards. At that time in Maine, we were allowed to use that as an alternative to the state tests. Do you think the kids were psyched up to show that they had already met the state learning standards in their actual accomplishment and therefore not

have to take the state test? They were psyched up and they had actual demonstrable proof that corresponded to real-world activity, that they had met the state standards.

Who should understand the state standards? The kids. They should know the purpose of the learning and what counts as accomplishment. There were kids from Jonesport-Beals High School who were interviewing old lobstermen who had data, records, and memories that had never been put into the scientific record about lobster catches. They made a video documentary, they made data charts, they did a presentation, and they coded it to the Maine Learning Results. All the while they were doing what oceanographers, ethnographers, journalists, and video documentarians do. They could code their work because their state standards actually do make sense when applied in a real context. Then the argument could be made that they don't need to take the state test because they've already proven they have done it. But this process requires trust of students and trust of teachers. I don't think there is a cheap, easy way to demonstrate student learning in ways that make sense if you distrust the classroom teacher.

It sounds like this requires teachers to assert their professionalism.
I think teachers need to step up to the plate, but how can people be trustworthy if they are not trusted? It's the same with kids. If you don't trust them, they can never be trustworthy. If we want more professional teachers, we need to give them more professional authority. According to the standard definition of a profession, teaching is not a profession. Professionalism includes criteria like being self-policing; but people outside the profession police us. It requires that we be self-organizing; but people outside the profession organize us. We must create our own knowledge, such as through teacher research; we let other people from outside the teaching profession create our knowledge. These are responsibilities teachers can fulfill; and if we were given the authority, we would do so, and the kids and their learning would benefit. I don't think doctors or lawyers would put up with the level of interference that teachers get, so that is another challenge for the twenty-first century: to professionalize teaching.

In the meantime, teachers with experience need to assist teachers who might be struggling by implementing and participating in peer mentoring or coaching programs. We can't leave that to the administration or we fail in one of our professional responsibilities to induct others into our profession. Experienced teachers have to say, "Hey, this is an important job and if you are here, we are going to help you." When we see students struggling, we assist them. We need to do the same for our peers. We need peer mentoring programs. We also need to do teacher research, and when policy comes down, we need to say, "Our research shows…" or "The research we did in our classrooms demonstrates…". In other words, we have to create our own knowledge. We have to enter into professional conversations about these issues instead of letting policies be done to us. We need to be proactive instead of reactive. We are the experts and authorities on learning in our classrooms. We need to write op-ed pieces, go to board meetings, become part of the conversation around policy. If we don't, we are not only failing to represent ourselves, we are failing to represent our students, who have no power or voice without us. I think these are political imperatives for the twenty-first-century teacher. If we take up these challenges, then the twenty-first century will be the most exciting and powerful time to teach in perhaps all of human history.

3

Write Before Writing

Donald M. Murray

A Pulitzer prize-winning journalist, Donald Murray was a columnist for The Boston Globe *and professor emeritus of English at the University of New Hampshire. He was a writing coach for several national newspapers, wrote poetry for many journals, including* Poetry, *and authored several books on the craft of writing and teaching writing, including* Learning by Teaching *(Heinemann, 1982),* Expecting the Unexpected *(Heinemann, 1989), and* Crafting a Life in Essay, Story, Poem *(Boynton/Cook, 1996). Don Murray passed away on December 30, 2006. This is one of his very last essays on the writing process.*

One of the many gifts of the writing craft is that our apprenticeship never ends. At eighty-one years old I am still a student to my page. When I first read Chaucer's "The lyf so short, the craft so long to lerne," I believed it was a lament. Now I read it as a celebration. I will never stop learning to write, and I will continue to write what I did not intend. Old in years and young as a writer I am sustained by the certainty that this morning—and the next, and the next—my instructive page will surprise me by revealing what I didn't know I knew. I survive by Shelby Foote's, "Happiness is going to bed knowing you will write in the morning."

During the last thirteen years I cared for my wife who suffered Parkinson's and, eventually, dementia. Even now I miss caring for her. The time this long, last intimacy took increased and yet I kept writing. I didn't know if it was proper for me to disappear into the page when she had no escape. I had no choice. I have lived a double life of reality and imagination. In those years of caring for her I wrote six books, ten new editions of earlier books, 676 weekly columns for *The Boston Globe* as well as articles and poems. Writing was my life raft but I still wonder how I got it done when I had fewer and fewer hours at my desk without interruption.

Playing and replaying the movie of our last years together I recognize again that I, a poor student, do not learn from the external research appropriate in the academy but from ignorance and curiosity. I write my response to my life, and after the first draft is completed I may discover its significance. What has become habit, normal, commonplace will unexpectedly reveal its importance. Looking back at the years of caregiving I find that the most important part of my writing process is the writing I do before writing.

Joyce Carol Oates, probably the most prolific American writer publishing today, explains:

> I always know the ending of stories. I work them out in my head before I write. When you're younger, you might write fifty pages. Of which you'll keep fourteen, but when you get a little older, you can do that early writing in your head. I do a lot of running and walking, and of course I lie in bed in the early morning and am working on my writing, so I just do a whole lot of writing and working things out and throwing things away and trying different things in my head. By the time I get to actually write, I've worked it out pretty clearly, so I can eliminate all those first and second drafts.

If I lie abed in the morning, I fall asleep and I never know the end before I begin and wouldn't want to because it would limit the discovery through writing that is central to my process and the main reason I write, to discover what I didn't know I knew. I do, however, lead the double life of living in the physical world while living in the world of imagination and response.

I lie in ambush waiting to see what grabs my attention: conflict, connection, contradiction, surprise, what isn't and what should be, what is and shouldn't be. Sometimes I will make a note—a word or a fragment of language, a snapshot half developed. I allow my mind to do its work with my interfering. I am most interested in what I don't know, especially about the familiar and commonplace. Grace Paley said, "We write about what we don't know about what we know." This drifty-mind writing is essential to creativity. I am looking for something worthy of exploration.

Circular or invisible writing is difficult to describe. In my life I compare it to my night jump in the paratroops when I tumbled into a starry night and felt I could reach out to touch each star. I tumble through life aware of what is different from what I expect, what small acts have vast significance, how voice reveals meaning, how much thinking is circular not linear.

At first I told myself that circular writing was restricted to brainstorming, which was the title of a book I ghostwrote in 1958 and is out of print, or it was just free writing, the familiar classroom exercise I had so often used in class to help students—and myself—find a topic. Now I realize that writing before writing is far more important than I thought. Circular writing isn't just a technique for "creative writing." It is an underground river that flows before and during all writing. I use this technique when I am writing my novels or my poetry, but I also use it when writing my weekly *Boston Globe* column, textbooks, articles for magazines or academic journals, ghostwriting for CEOs and cabinet officers, memos, letters of sympathy, or a proposal to a publisher for yet another book.

How I Write Before Writing

I live by Horace's counsel written before the birth of Christ, "Nulla dies sine linea," (Never a day without a line)—well, almost every day—but I write in my mind before starting the first page of each day's writing task. Writing before writing is rarely outlining, stating the thesis, drawing a plan, organizing research, drafting titles or leads. It is not formal thinking, using the tools of logic, problem solving, deciding on the emphasis, reading the audience, considering tone, picking out the style, listening for the appropriate voice or style, but a more random form of thinking. When I had a good day despite the demands of caregiving, I went back and studied the conditions and acts that produced my better drafts. Students should be encouraged to do the same thing, building their individual writing processes from the work that went well.

I found that it was not my obsessive time management, not my inherited fluency, not the lottery-like dream of money and fame that made me productive under adverse conditions. It was the kind of drifty non-thinking I did when I sat on Nantasket Beach watching the unachievable girls, the boys who knew what to say to girls that made them laugh; and, of course, wondering if we would win the soccer game while taking note of the streamers of color in the late afternoon sky and how the color changed when it was reflected from the ocean; hoping that we wouldn't have mushy, overcooked spinach for dinner; wondering if I would be a soldier, sailor, or marine in the war that was certain to begin soon; wondering if I could become a writer, why Jimmy Foxx was my favorite Red Sox player, if I'd be able to hold hands at the movie with a girl whose name I cannot remember now.

Of course my teachers were not pleased at my inattention in the classroom, as I traveled through the window and into a past, present, or future world. I have lived my life daydreaming, but I was stupid, lazy, could not concentrate, did not pay attention in class. Now I know that my thinking was not linear but that it was still thinking. I did not and do not want to write out of smartness but out of ignorance, using writing to explore my inner and outer worlds. I didn't know that my drifty kind of thinking would pay my way in the world. I knew I would write; I didn't know I was already writing. In today's jargon I kept out of the box. I learned to keep one part of my brain aware of what my senses delivered. I made connections that surprised my teachers, even contradicted my instructors. They talked about holding me back and forcing me to repeat sixth grade (that was the grade in which I learned more than the other eleven). My elementary principal sought me out on the playground to tell me I was being passed on to junior high because they didn't want me in their school anymore. My classmates thought I was weird. My parents felt I was a stranger in their Baptist home and I was. It took a Pulitzer for my father to take me seriously. A few years ago I read the writer Sandra Cisneros who said, "Write what makes you different." I realized then that when I was failing in school I was developing the skills I would use to write after I escaped school and survived my war.

Goethe speaks up again: "Writing is busy idleness." This productive idleness involves:

Quiet

Turn off the TV, the boom box, the cell phone, the other people in your life, and escape into yourself. Your mind is talking to you, remembering, imagining, observing, connecting, responding to your life, but we live in an empire of noise. We need to escape into ourselves and hear what we are telling ourselves. Perhaps we need to tell our students to stare out the classroom window.

Awareness

Your senses are working, seeing, hearing, touching, smelling, tasting. Pay attention. I sharpen my senses by sitting down, notebook in hand, and listing one hundred specific pieces of information that one sense is telling me. Then I move on to another sense. I believe there is a sixth sense of connection, or hidden significance, that we should exercise. At its simplest I see a woman in my therapist's waiting room. Later I see her house is for sale. Divorce? Commute? New job? What? My seeing is also increased by sketching or taking pictures.

Self-Respect

One of the hardest things for most of us it do is to respect our response to life, especially if it contradicts the opinion of peers. But the best writing comes from contradiction, surprise, uncomfortable insight, a memory that is different from the way you remembered the moment before. Pay attention to your own mind and respect your own response to your life.

Naïveté

The painter Pablo Picasso said, "All children are artists. The problem is how to remain an artist once he grows up." Writers see the world as if it had never been seen before, then we do what a painter does, layering our grown up vision to give depth and significance to what the innocent eye has seen.

Surprise

When your boss says, "I don't want any surprises," leave. In marketing, in science, in research, in scholarship, in the arts, we thrive on surprise. Robert Frost said, "No surprise for the writer, no surprise for the reader." If there is no surprise for me when I am halfway through a column I stop and start anew. I do not calculate surprise but keep writing in my head confident surprise will come in its own way.

Detachment

I am never bored because, although I appear to be gregarious (and I am), I also am a loner. Sometimes I feel as if I lift myself from my chair at the dinner party and watch myself smiling, nodding, chatting with the woman on my right. When playing football, fighting in infantry warfare, experiencing the most intimate moments of a happy marriage, I am also observing myself and the world around me. My teachers kept sending notes home saying, "Donald should concentrate," and my parents told me, "Concentrate!" but I was concentrating, using my double-vision concentration. I am absorbed by the task at hand—I really was listening to the woman on my right—yet at the same time I am detached.

You have been writing in your head all your life—rehearsing a job interview, a plea to borrow your brother's car, a proposal to move in together—but you did not apply it to writing. That was my case. I thought daydreaming and night dreaming were more evidence cut of my stupidity. I did not value my underground river of responses to my life while I was living it. I was also guilty about the uncomfortable observations and ideas that appeared in my underground river of reflection. I certainly did not want my parents, my teachers, my friends to read my uncensored thoughts. One of the great terrors of my Baptist childhood was that God could always tune in to my brain.

Enough talking about what I do. It is time for me to show you how I work. My way may not be your way. I hope it will be helpful to see one professional think by writing before writing. This is not an academic example but a real situation:

The *Boston Globe* expects me to write a "Now and Then" column of five hundred to six hundred words, loosely connected with aging, and I have no topic in mind, nothing I will say that will interest a single reader. I delay starting this column and open the mail. One fan letter. A single three-by-five-inch card. "You're a faker." I fear the unsigned reader may be right but I have a deadline. I start paying attention to what floats through my head:

> Made a bacon sandwich this morning . . . expect the diet police to break in as I eat it . . . it's raining . . . it's raining, it's pouring, your old man is snoring . . . I love it . . . do I have a rain gene from my Scottish ancestors? . . . never met my grandfathers . . . like to meet them and my great-great-great grandfathers . . . can't do time travel . . . retired engineering professor has returned to town . . . why . . . he wrote science fiction on time travel . . . should read *Time Traveler's Wife* . . . I have it . . . do I have to read the books I buy? . . . student asks how I mourned in combat . . . no mourning in combat . . . take weapon, ammunition, morphine from dead or dying and go on . . . time travel . . . it is 1945 in Belgium . . . we didn't live by months, weeks, days, just hours or less . . . took my wife eleven days to sleep her life away . . . I'll get baked potato soup for lunch if they have it . . . I pick up special cheese my wife liked put it back on the shelf . . . hockey game tonight . . .

What do I do now? No grand theories, no profound opinions, just the jumble of common-place that tumbled through my mind. In the beginning I wrote down what has passed through my mind as I have here; but soon I realized that writing down my thoughts slowed and limited the mental tumbling and these days I only write down a word or line that surprised me and I was afraid I would forget. I also may make a note of an image that appeared in the night sky of my mind. While starting this I have seen my wife again and again in her peaceful eleven day sleep.

E. B. White said, "When a mosquito bites me—I scratch. When I write something, I guess I'm trying to get rid of the itchiness inside me." When I look over the fragments of random thought to see what itches, there are a few possibilities:

Bacon sandwich. I could write about what we thought was necessary for health—bread and butter with every meal, gravy, pie, spinach cooked all day, lots of salt—or I could write about cooking "Now and Then" when I was a child, our ideas then of what food made you healthy. The bacon sandwich was something I made as a widower, cooking for himself. The idea of a bacon sandwich came from a British mystery I was reading. I could write about why we read mysteries.

Time travel. I could write about my grandfathers and what I do know. One got fed up with not being able to farm his own land and emigrated to Canada when he was eighty-eight years old. I might write about him or about how I am convinced that most of my responses to the world come from genes developed or modified hundreds, perhaps thousands, of years ago.

Mourning in combat. *Veterans Day*—the title of the novel I am writing—and I could write about my delayed mourning. In combat I thought it funny when I saw a soldier friend sitting against a tree holding his head in his lap. Now I mourn. Why the black humor and why the delayed mourning?

My wife's last eleven days. That's what itches. That and time. My calm adrenalin seconds after my parachute didn't open. Turning into my driveway this afternoon I heard myself repeating, "time fast and slow," an ordinary, meaningless fragment of language that might reveal an unexpected meaning if I followed it across my monitor. Then I decided to follow "time fast and slow" to see where it took me.

The Boston Globe
"Now and Then"
November 1, 2005

Donald M. Murray
Globe Correspondent

As we ripen—I've been on the vine 81 years—time races past us and then stops as if the truck ahead of us suddenly grows larger and we jam on the brakes.

A grandchild becomes a grown-up overnight. I march along the sidewalk of Main Street and remember when a troop train brought me to the University of New Hampshire in 1943. Sixty-two years have raced by me.

I am both here and there like a double exposure on the family Kodak. A boy soldier and an emeritus professor at the same time.

I sit in my chair at the Massachusetts Fields School in Wollaston watching, waiting for the minute hand of the great classroom clock to suddenly lurch forward. Two more minutes until recess. At the same time I rerun again the movie of our 54 year marriage, thinking how quickly the years passed and how much I miss her.

One day I look at my watch as I hurtle out the door of the C-47, but my parachute didn't open, it was streamer that just twisted like a great worm above my head.

I break open my reserve chute but it tangles with the feet of another paratrooper. Adrenalin and training take over. I feel I have all the time in the world to find the knife strapped to my right leg, bring it up and cut myself free so I was no longer a pendulum to the soldier who had been tangled in it.

My streamer partially opens and the ground rises up. I hit and roll with the shock then look at my watch. All this had happened in 47 seconds.

In combat there were no months. No weeks. No days. Just hours or less. We lived in the moment as the Asian philosophers tell us.

I make myself get out of bed each morning, turn off the alarm, and dangle as I am supposed to do so I will not get dizzy and fall.

I turn and look at the other side of the bed where my wife still sleeps. I take her hand as I did for so many of her last days. I wonder how many more years of my unexpected life will be given to me. I glance at the clock. I have dangled for twenty minutes.

I make myself get up, splash water on my face, make myself go over the to do list in my head. Bob, Mimi, Dave, perhaps Dan will be at Young's where I swallow my pills with cranberry juice, eat my fruit cup, drink my black coffee.

I will come home, read the papers, then go to my computer to write this column, my life raft. Later I will plan lunch, think of what the doctor will say, decide if I will return to the condo and microwave dinner or go out to a restaurant where people will chatter all around me. I cannot plan ahead. As in combat I have this hour to live.

I have a sentence that tells me what the next sentence will say, and I am lost in the writing, outside of time, practicing my craft.

How You Can Learn to Write Before Writing

I suggest you take ten minutes, five mornings a week listing what comes to mind when you drive, walk, stare out the window. Read the list and pay attention to:

- What surprises you?
- What connects with another item on the lists?
- What contradicts what you have believed?
- What are you most afraid of?
- What do you see differently from your family or friends?
- What is that shouldn't be?
- What is that should be?
- What answer needs a question?
- What question needs an answer?

Draft five or more quick leads that might begin an article, essay, memoir, short story, screenplay, novel, dissertation, argument, or another genre that might come from this list or from your own response to the list. Sandra Cisneros: "Write about what makes you different."

How Your Students Can Learn to Write Before Writing

I'd suggest you demonstrate what worked for you using my suggestions to you or not. It is important to explain that writing before writing isn't just a method of finding a topic in English Composition. Ask the class to suggest how this approach might help in physics, in history, in marketing, in art, in social studies, and in the jobs they hold while going to school, or in the jobs they work at in the summer.

If writing before writing didn't work for you, don't worry. We are individuals and our minds work in different ways. My way may not be your way—in fact, it might not be my way on another writing project. In seventy-five years of writing, I have not found one single way to do all writing tasks. That's one of the delights of writing. At eighty-one I am still failing in new and interesting ways and then trying new and interesting ways to succeed. Pass out a handout explaining that this technique did not for you, but it does work for many writers and invite them to try it later. If it does work for a student, invite her to give a demonstration or lead the class—yourself included—through an exercise.

And After You Begin a Draft…

If writing before writing becomes your habit, it will change reading of your drafts. The words you have written will not stay on the page. They will connect with that river that runs through your mind as you read what you have written. You will connect with memory, scraps of old information, new observations.

Tom Newkirk brilliantly demonstrates circular, or random, thinking in his *The School Essay Manifesto—Reclaiming the Essay For Students and Teachers* (Discover Writing Press, 2005). In reading it I was impressed by his extended essay, and I found the key to the never completed novel which I have been writing before writing for far too long. I at last commanded myself to begin again today.

I start by reading the first paragraph of the first chapter I abandoned months ago:

Draft one. Ian Blair woke as he had in the war to which he had been apprenticed at 17 and which he still fought every day. Eyes hardly open, breathing slowed, ears scanning the Belgium forest, memory reviewing his craft, not moving, breathing slowly, softly, aware from the quiet and the light reflected upward that night had brought the first snow of the season to northern New Hampshire.

He opened his eyes and focused on his leg brace, standing at attention by the window, paratroop boot still polished as were the two metal braces growing up from the boot, each shiny with wear, the worn leather straps hanging loose at the knee.

As I read it I realize this about the story. It doesn't show but tells. I intrude and instruct too much. I want to reveal Ian's mind responding to his world. I don't like the first person but I'd better try it. While reading this I hear a band rehearsing, wonder how often it snows on November 11, Veteran's Day, see his isolated house moving into town, see him patrolling his woods as if he were still a soldier . . .

Draft two. I wake but do not move, not allowing his helmet to rise above the fox hole's edge. "Fuck."

He touched the soldier skull with

That doesn't work. The skull is real but it is not the place for it to appear. Try again. Listen for the voice that rises from the page. If I am lucky it will, of course, be my voice tuned to the evolving story. In fact, it is the voice that will lead me through the story.

Draft three. I wake in the dark and as always I am not here but there, not now but then. The pale *XXXX* of sunrise reveals a snowy field leading up to dark woods. I can only see the fender edge of my pickup. That's all I need to know I am not in the Ardennes fighting what they now call The Battle of the Bulge but in New Hampshire. Route 133A. Name on the mail box? Blair.

Now I hear a voice that changes with the sentence fragments at the end of the paragraph. Ian becomes tougher, harder-edged than I expected. The *XXXX*s tell me I may need a new word there but don't know what it is and I do not want to slow the flow of the paragraph.

As I drive home from Portsmouth today I find out Ian was not hard-edged.

Draft 4. When Ian retired from the Lakeview Bank and Trust Company, thirteen clients insisted he manage their trusts. In the bank he was nicknamed "the Listener."

He had all the time in the world to hear their stories and their secrets. He kept their secrets. What they didn't know was Ian—patient, congenial, understanding —had a secret of his own. He gave one Tuesday a week at the bank for listening. He no longer wore a blue button shirt and a red stripe tie. No longer a banker's suit but woodman's shirt and red suspenders. Today was Tuesday, and after what he found this morning he had reason to worry about his secret. That morning . . .

This is not what I expected to write but it is Tuesday and Veteran's Day comes on the weekend this year. I don't know what his secret is but I have a hint. That's all I need to keep writing in my head.

4

The Writing Conference

Journeys into Not Knowing

Terry A. Moher

Terry Moher has been a secondary English teacher for twenty-nine years, currently at Exeter High School in New Hampshire, and an instructor for the New Hampshire Literacy Institutes since 1981. She has published several articles on teaching writing.

In one of my favorite short stories, "The Stone Boy" by Gina Beriault, a nine-year-old boy accidentally shoots his sixteen-year-old brother, his idol and hero, while going to pick peas before sunrise. Eugie, the older brother, has agreed to take Arnold duck hunting on the way. When the gun gets caught on the wire fence and goes off, the gunshot kills his brother and, in an act of shock and disbelief, Arnold goes off to pick peas, mechanically following the familiar habit of farm chores, before he returns home. The story follows the community's responses to the apparent cold-heartedness of the young boy in that momentary response to psychological trauma. In one scene, the sheriff interrogates the nine-year-old and asks, "Were you and your brother good friends?"

In the text that follows, Arnold's silent dialogue with himself reveals to the reader how much he loved his brother and how good their relationship was, but because he associates the word *friend* only to others his age, he does not understand the question. The sheriff infers guilt from the silence, Arnold's mute response, and pronounces the boy incorrigible. Had he somehow been privy to the inner thoughts and feelings of the boy, he might have considered asking the question in other ways—or asking other kinds of questions—and gained a different interpretation altogether. His assumption and consequent judgment, instead, impede the possibilities of understanding.

In his chapter titled "Understanding Persons," Zeno Vendler distinguishes between knowing and understanding as disparate processes, a concept which may offer us insight into the complexities of relationships that enhance our abilities to teach. Vendler points out that knowing requires attention to *who*, *what*, and *where*, whereas understanding requires our ability to attend to *how* and *why*. Processes of understanding go beyond what can be explained by information from the observable world. It is "a new dimension" beyond facts and information, involving internal motivation and intention, and the range of human emotions.

After twenty-five years of practicing writing conferences, I hesitate to define what it is I do or what a conference should be. To attempt to do so diminishes the possibilities and capacities we might bring to our students, and they to us, in that paradoxical space between silence and dialogue. Donald Murray addressed the difficult nature of our work as writing instructors in his reflection about teaching writing:

> I considered the writing process as a way of separating the knowing from the not knowing, or, to put it differently, a way of organizing knowing so the writer could be launched into the more important world of not knowing. The process was, after all, a process of learning, exploration, speculation, discovery: the goal was always surprise, the purpose was to write to know. This is the essential challenge of teaching composition: how do we teach not knowing? (Murray 1994, 60)

How do we teach not knowing? The implications of such a question cannot rely upon a codified set of strategies. If what we are teaching engages ourselves and our students in a venture of not knowing, our best practices embrace qualities of uncertainty and ambiguity, qualities that open us to possibilities of learning. Over the years, my own reliance on techniques gradually began to dissipate as I became more comfortable working intuitively with each student and each piece of writing. For years I felt vulnerable (and to some extent I still do) to the administrative demands to identify *exactly what* I am going to teach, what I am going *to do*, and what my students will *know*. The business of schooling presumes precise control.

Years ago a teacher asked me to list for her the questions I use in my writing conferences. As I began, I realized that, like a conversation or dialogue, each conference presented something unique. The amenities of the conference—How's it going? What are you working on? What problems have you encountered?—merely initiate conversation techniques with which to invite students to enter a dialogic space and to reflect on both their written and non-written texts and the promises of both. Relying on a set of techniques means that I may not be open to the responses that may ensue within a conference and that might encourage the student-writer to pursue subtle or obscure paths, ideas not yet clear to him or her, or to me.

Practices, on the other hand, move us beyond mere techniques. A practice is a pursuit which "launches us on a journey in which we do not know what to expect and cannot determine what the outcome should be" (Spohn 2000, 338). Practices, unlike techniques, move us toward other ways of being and offer transformative powers. Furthermore, practices contain an ethics: they are about human relations.

As I attempt to live with Murray's question, "How do we teach not knowing?," I draw on a working definition offered by Harlene Anderson in her work as therapist:

> Knowing—the delusion of understanding or the security of methodology—decreases the possibility of seeing and increases our deafness to the unexpected, the unsaid, and the not-yet-said (Anderson & Goolishian, 1988). If we always see and hear things we are accustomed to, then we will miss, neither see nor hear, that which is different and unique. (Anderson 1997, 134)

The "delusion of understanding" is something of an occupational hazard in our profession; it limits our resources and inhibits our abilities to remain attuned to processes of learning and, thus, to enter into those processes with our students. Composition theorists from the last few decades have echoed a rhetoric of uncertainty, of surprise, of the unexpected, the unknown, the not-yet-known. Anderson describes a professional stance from which we might benefit in writing conferences:

> Not-knowing refers to a therapist's position—an attitude and belief—that a therapist does not have access to privileged information, can never fully understand another person, always needs to be in a state of being informed by the other, and always needs to learn more about what has been said or may not have been said (134).

This definition offers a clear way into what I believe Murray's question compels us to consider—a relationship between teacher and student that is neither unilateral nor initiated by power structures; that is not driven by techniques; that does not presume knowledge; and that, by its nature, may even place us in a somewhat disconcerting position as professionals. In the space of the writing conference, we are compelled to acquire other ways of being with our students—for one, to consider knowledge as something we do not yet have prior to entering this dialogue with our students, and, therefore, we need to develop new ways in which to listen and to ask questions.

Traditionally we tend to consider a teacher-student conference as a unilateral process in which we feel compelled to solve the problems of the writing, and I continue to struggle with that learned tendency. Murray reminds us that, at least initially, "the teacher should not look at the text for the student, not even with the student. The teacher looks at—and listens to—the student watching the text evolve" (Murray 1982, 29). This simple statement offers profound implications for transformation in our teaching. As I work with my students in conferences, my purpose is not to establish my understanding of a writing problem and a set of solutions to the difficulties of the writing assignment; it is, rather, to engage this student in a dialogue in which her own sense of who she is begins to reveal itself.

In the face-to-face conference, our presence and the possibilities of dialogue (i.e., moving back to earlier ideas, listening for the not-yet-written, following our conversational digressions) offer a living dynamic that differs radically from the isolated reading of a finished piece, both in its purposes and in its efficacy for learning. The dialogic space allows me to monitor and mediate, on a conscious level, the student's responses to my questions, suggestions, observations, or directives, as well as to their own writing. If I notice confusion, I can stop and ask what is confusing the student; if there is discomfort, I can gently ease back or directly address the reasons for that discomfort. A hesitation in response to a question might suggest a place where we consider what is happening; and the unspoken is always something for which I must listen. No two conferences can be the same.

Ann had written a five-page piece about the birth of a lamb. She raised and showed sheep, and she had written a small piece earlier in the quarter about it. I collected the writing from this ninth-grade class, took the papers home, and read them all quickly, in about twenty minutes, in preparation for conferences the next day. Reading this way takes the onus off me to read as a judge, to grade, and I enjoy their writing so much more. I'm a far better reader in this mode, as I can focus on their language, the potential it offers, and the implied, as well as explicit, meanings. I noticed in Ann's piece that she led up to the birth, but there was no description or mention of the birth of a lamb. The next day I called her up to the writing table.

"Ann, what's this piece about?"

She looked a little surprised. "You know, the birth of a lamb!"

"Oh." I handed her the paper. "Would you read me that part?"

She suddenly realized what I was doing. "Well, I didn't want to gross people out!" She'd envisioned a graphic description of the birth—the physical, messy details that she feared wouldn't work for her or for an audience. I smiled and suggested she go back to her seat, write for ten minutes, and write the missing details. She returned a short time later and handed me the writing:

> When Nicky sent me up to the house on the hot water run, a twinge of worry settled in, as with the other pile of worries that had already attached themselves to my stomach wall. So many things could go wrong during the gestation; like when our pen door wasn't wide enough and Sophie and Cinmin would both hit the doorway at the same time, squeezing and grunting in an instant, and me yelling and pushing one back, knowing that if they kept trying to go through the door they could damage their lambs inside. Worry, exhaustion; staggering out to the barn to only be met with sleepy eyes. While you know the ewe is in labor, you know the pain she is in, you know, and you can't give her anything only wait and croon softly to her. Having to stand, because you would have to sit in piles of sheep manure if you did. Warming your hands under the heat lamp, because its cold and no matter how much you stuff hay into the door cracks on the floor, you can still feel the draft. When the water bag actually appears, it sweeps away a few worries that so far, everything is going well, a small sigh of relief and another gasp for expectant air. The water bag is in a tissue casing, reddish brown, and if it doesn't burst, a piece of straw or the ewe's weight will make it break. And you wait, hope fills in, because you know that the lamb is soon, because that's what it said in the worn book. And then you see the two hooves, encased in tissue, and hope comes, and then you wait, because if the lamb is in the wrong position the ewe will need help. After Cherrie was born it was like a high, and then you just fill up with such an extreme love for this little existence, and then you help it get warm, and help it stand, and help it get to its mother's now swollen pink udder...

Ann surprises both of us. She punctuates the initial writing with her term *worry* and gradually moves toward *hope* and, finally, to *love*—a structural movement that occurs as she writes. Her details mark her own physical place in the birth: having to push one back away from the door; her crooning; standing in the manure; the cold draft. The physical details she'd been afraid to write had become subtle intimations to the moment of birth: the ewe's water bag "sweeps away a few worries…The water bag is in a tissue casing, reddish brown, and if it doesn't burst, a piece of straw or the ewe's weight will make it break"—the only line necessary of the details she'd wanted to avoid and so hadn't written initially. She brings the reader into the moments of waiting. The rhythm of the piece shifts gradually as she moves from worry and anticipation to relief, a gradually slower breathing rhythm, almost a sigh.

Ann's quick-writing captures what she hadn't anticipated, certainly what I couldn't have known: a weaving of the experience of the birth both emotionally and physically. Ann herself becomes integral to the telling of the birth. Her language conveys the truth of her experience and illustrates the paradox of freewriting as Peter Elbow describes:

> This paradox of increased overall control through letting go a bit seems paradoxical only because our normal way of thinking about control is mistakenly static: it is not developmental or process-oriented because it leaves out the dimension of time. Our static way of thinking makes us feel we must make a single choice as to whether to be a controlled person or an out-

of-control person…but this static model isn't accurate. Most processes engaged in by live organisms are cyclic, developmental processes that run through time and end up different from how they began (Elbow 1973 33).

This delicate balance between controlling and letting go describes the process of quick-writing experiences. Student-writers learn to surrender the control (and, in the process, their anxiety) in favor of possibilities that may (or may not) come to them in the act of quickly capturing their thoughts and feelings. Ann had assumed only one dimension of this writing. What she couldn't anticipate were the ways in which her own emotional and psychic involvement would create a different kind of telling—an internal play of values and language. Such rhythms create one dimension of what we call voice in writing, a quality many of us struggle to teach.

An essential part of my practice relies upon these concepts of freewriting, quick-writing, and digressions that touch upon a non-conscious movement of experience. I began using quick-writing exercises in the early eighties and immediately saw the quality of writing develop. Students who saw themselves as non-writers, who had never liked their own writing or who were afraid to try, dropped their fears in the momentary presence of writing fast and soon discovered that their writing offered, perhaps not the organized, compact essay teachers wanted, but far more varied and often better possibilities of meaning. As long as I valued those possibilities, the potential that even a line could offer, students became more and more comfortable and confident.

After reading aloud the title chapter of *The House on Mango Street* by Sandra Cisneros, I asked students to write quickly about their own house. After a few minutes of writing, Liz, a quiet ninth grader, raised her hand and unabashedly began reading, without introduction:

> I have lived in a household that seldomly has good-byes. My house has a father that if you're lucky calls once a month, but that doesn't fase me. He's like a perfect stranger when he calls. You know the kind that calls just as you sit down for dinner or right as you are slipping away to a good night's rest. When people like that call in our house the usual reply in our house is, "We are not interested," or, "She's not home." My father has made a lot of stupid mistakes in life of my mom, sister, brother and me. It's as almost as if he expects us to forgive him for all the pain he has caused. My father is a blind man when it comes to seeing his many flaws in life. Who knows, maybe someday I'll forgive him for all he has done, maybe someday he will realize his faults in his life and live up to them, and maybe someday when the phone rings I'll say, "Hi, Dad."

She read with a determination and confidence I had not seen in her. The class listened to the voice that emerged, and in the silence that followed we all knew she had arrived at something significant about her own emotional life. And despite her insistence that it "doesn't fase" her, she looks to the possibility of forgiving him "someday." The rhythm of that last sentence, "maybe…maybe…and maybe…" reveals her hopes for the relationship she envisions with her father. For years I have watched students dive into such quick-writing and, more often than not, they have explored the terrain of their own memories, thoughts, experiences, their own preoccupations with life. The boundaries have been pushed aside, and in five or ten or thirty minutes of quick-writing they have been "launched into the more important world of not knowing" (Murray 1994, 60). I can't know my students' experiences or what they know, their versions of my assignments or the places in their worlds where their writing will take them, and I don't want to inhibit these unpredictable processes by judging far

too soon or correcting or responding in ways which tell them it isn't right or good or important enough. I want to encourage this process, their journeys into not knowing.

We might ask what the internal processes of freewriting and quick writing might
look like. In the act of focused concentration in writing, the writer seems able to elude a
self-conscious awareness of what he might have intended or anticipated and acquiesces,
instead, to the unforeseen ways in which writing emerges. For some students this feeling
can be exhilarating if reinforced by my responses and encouragement; but for students who
have followed the confining expectations of "good writing," it may be an uncomfortable,
even risky, proposition. Most of my students would not give themselves permission to
digress, to follow their own words into unpredictable places; in fact, they have usually been
warned not to digress. The advice is meant to keep a final paper focused, but students have
come to believe that they should control the focus from the outset. Veering from their perceived intent or image of what is yet unwritten proves for many of them a necessary process
in the development of their writing; furthermore, easing both of our demands of what is to
occur on the page frees them to explore and divulge the depth of their own thoughts, experiences, memories, and opinions. It is quite an experience to celebrate with each student as
she tentatively tries on this process because it is such an ambiguous, undefined space in
which meaning unfolds, even if in glimpses, for the writer. My practice has been a training
to recognize those glimpses and to teach students how to recognize such insights in their
own thinking and writing.

Eli was a junior in my writing class. She had also been in my sophomore English class
the previous year. She was reserved and shy, rarely speaking in class, and her writing rarely
went beyond a few paragraphs. In the writing class, seniors were working on college essays,
and I asked the juniors to consider them just as seriously. Eli drafted a letter to a prestigious
private school in New Hampshire:

> I would like to attend your postgraduate program so that I can further expand my educa-
> tion. I wish to attend medical school at the University of New York, and I do not feel that I
> have enough educational background to forward myself toward the medical field. I do real-
> ize that medical school is hard to get accepted into, and this is why I would like to attend
> you're school.

My first response was written, meant to encourage her to continue: "How can we get you
to talk more about who you are, Eli? You aren't your transcript—you have a wonderful
presence. What questions might help you write from that strength?" She tried again but the
attempt was not much more effective. My suggestion to "write from that strength" was not
at all clear to her (I'm not sure it would be to me either), and I'm sure she couldn't understand what I meant by "a wonderful presence." Writing such responses usually does little
to help students explore other paths: writers merely add a little to that which they are
already committed, answering questions only simplistically or literally. She had, however,
revealed something new. In conference I admitted I was surprised to learn that she was a
captain of the varsity field hockey team. We talked. I asked what position she played.
"Goalie!" she announced. Again I was surprised to learn that this petite, demure girl was an
athlete, and I saw a passion emerge as she talked with me. I asked if being goalie were different from the other positions, and she let me know immediately that there was indeed a
difference. "Write about what it means to you to be a goalie." I directed her toward her own

passion. I encouraged her to recognize her own expertise and confessed, "I am not an athlete. Don't forget me. I don't know anything about it."

Her next draft came quickly. It is beautifully written, powerful in its expression and voice. Few English teachers I've known have been able to define voice, something we all consider essential to writing. I heard Eli's description of the field hockey player out of a voice I had not before heard from her. Each line and each paragraph moves the piece forward, creating a clear, strong image of the player, and person, she is:

THE FIELD HOCKEY PLAYER

As she walks onto the field, kicking the dirt and grass with her cleats, she plays around with her mouth guard, slaps sticks with a team mate and takes her center position. She looks her opponent in the eye, both eager to play and wanting to taste victory. She takes a deep breath, kicks the mud off her cleats, gives her stick a good luck rub and plays.

"Elegant Violence" best describes a Field Hockey player. Violent in the way that she would do anything to see the ball go in to the net. That includes beating down a Goalie to even beating or running down herself. It doesn't matter what or who she hurts. If the score is tight she can and will do anything. Violent in the way that she loves to see a pile in the front of the opposing net. When the Goalie is down that means players are down and that certainly means action.

Elegant in the way that she looks so agile handling the ball upfield. Her skirt moving with every move she makes. Under the girly uniform lies a tough, rugged woman. All the broken bones, scarred up knees and black eyes only remind her of a game she can never re-play.

As Eli defines the term *goalie,* she also defines a significant aspect of who she is: "Under the girly uniform lies a tough, rugged woman." She is able to articulate "feelings and frustrations" through her identity as a goalie, both physically and emotionally. Eli is able to see herself with "self-esteem and aggressiveness," as a "leader," a good "friend," with the ability to "take pain and hide hurt." This revision is a remarkable expression of her personal identity.

The purpose of the conference is not to praise or to judge the quality of the writing, but rather to encourage students to pursue ideas, feelings, or merely a sense of things which they may not yet have thought out or been able to express, but which may emerge into language between us. I want to assist them in eliciting those issues and help them sustain their venture into that space of not knowing and take on whatever authority they can to resolve those issues. Some students are far more confident at this, though their writing may not necessarily be better. I want to affirm their authority; each decision they make that proves successful in their writing is an experience that will sustain their continued learning.

Jess wrote a poignant, albeit disturbing, personal piece about her experience in a family affected by drug addiction. It was a distressing account of her experience of abuse as a young child for which I was not prepared to respond. She brought me the piece in class and asked me to read it. I read it silently in front of her, appalled, and when I finished I was speechless. We sat for a moment, in silence, and I finally told her that she'd said it all; that she had expressed all there was to say—and well; that this was probably more than most people even wanted to know about such abuse. She seemed satisfied with my response. Then I asked her if she would be willing to try something else, and she nodded. The last line of her paper had drifted between her talking to herself and another, vague audience. I thought the movement toward a more specific, real audience could help her advance both the writing and her understanding. I asked her to consider the fact that people seem to know the technical term, *chemical dependency*, but not its true meaning for people whose lives are impacted by it. "Write its definition with your personal knowledge, something they don't know." She seemed to understand what I asked and left to write a second time. She left the first piece with me and returned the next day with a new piece of writing:

> The words *chemical dependency*, or *drug addiction*, mean something completely different for those people who are struggling with it, or love someone who is trying to overcome its effects.
>
> It means anger, hurt, it is a force that tears apart families, destroys friendships, even alters people's personalities.
>
> I have many memories of the changes in both my parents. Dad was always paranoid, and mom was always searching for a kind of freedom that she couldn't have while married. They weren't even friends after a while. I remember all the violence we had to live with.
>
> There are never reasons for people to start taking drugs. There are only excuses, and maybe factors that led up to the decision to try drugs…
>
> I suppose that the worst part of the whole thing is the one thing that is the basis for the problem.
>
> Lies.
>
> The lies are to cover guilt. The lies cover everything. They end up lying to themselves, the people who care about them, and anyone else who becomes involved in any way with thier lives.
>
> The lies also come in a series of empty promises designed to also handle any left-over guilt…
>
> The unfair thing is what it does to the kids. Those who grow up around parents who are addicts, and are constantly and unendingly getting shafted by the people they should be depending on most.

Revision has been an intriguing concept for me, and a significant one in my practice. Its meaning, to "see again, to perceive an object or subject in new ways," lies at the very heart of teaching writing and one of the purposes of my conferences with students. The possibilities of understanding, of eliciting memory, of creating interpretation, of coming to know new meanings offer significant experiences to their writing lives. Both Jess and I were astounded, and pleased, with the outcome of her revision. The question I'd posed offered to her a significant audience to her life experience. She had intimated in the ending of her first writing a note of warning to others, "what a mistake it can be to yourself and those around you." I asked her to give a new understanding of drug abuse to those of us who can't know what it really means: "It means anger, hurt; it is a force that tears apart families, destroys friendships, even alters people's personalities." What powerful testimony! Her ability to transform this writing from herself as the primary audience to an audience of others developed in part within the relationship we had established in the conference. Had I asked another question, had I responded differently, had she been in a different place psychologically or emotionally, this knowledge may never have revealed itself to her.

Working with adolescents is rarely easy. When my students come to conferences initially, I have to be prepared for the reticence—or even resistance—that has built up within many of them over the course of years to the kinds of criticisms and attitudes of teachers that train them to obey a narrow set of instructions for writing. To begin that aim is to acknowledge the integrity of our students. I learned from conferences with Mark, particularly, about the nature of resistance that many high school students accrue over the years toward school-related learning. They recognize school as an obstacle course of meaningless facts and tests which they must endure in order to reach the goal of getting beyond it all, rather than as an ongoing involvement in meaningful and life-related inquiry. Their (sometimes appropriate) resistance to an authoritarian conception of knowledge expresses itself through the passivity, cynicism, and—perhaps most destructive of all—silences that undermine the purposes of education. That alienation played out in our classrooms is as demoralizing for us, as educators, as it is for our students. Early in my teaching life, I believed these forms of resistance were the faults of the learners or, at least partially, my own incompetence. I had no understanding of the nature and sources of their resistance.

Mark didn't "do assignments," as he put it. This sophomore silently refused to write, yet he had strong, intelligent responses in classroom discussions, opinions that often came across as criticism, but also as unexpected insight. He was a reader, and his voice in this class helped me to reconsider the ways in which I might teach through such resistance. His was one of the first classes in which I encouraged the students to make decisions about their reading and writing, offering selections for readings, choices of writing topics and genres, choices of peers with whom they worked, and various means for evaluation. I replaced the kinds of quizzes and tests that checked to see if they *were* reading with various kinds of journal or response writing—writing in which they could explore their own questions and ideas in their own language and forms. It allowed me, as well, to interact at various points in that process of discovery. If, for example, a student wasn't ready to write a formal essay, other forms evolved: letters, internal monologues, fictional scenarios, lists, questions, each time demanding some thinking that they were not yet ready to do in more formal ways. I found that as they learned to accept the confusion that precedes discovery and to acknowledge the often forbidding and inconstant nature of inquiry, the quality of their writing developed remarkably.

Mark had rejected the written assignments throughout the first months. As a strong reader, he felt competent understanding anything he read and saw no purpose or need in writing down what he felt was already obvious to him: "I don't think I have to do journals for you to know that I'm learning, even though you assign them and I don't do them. Cause I, well, I read the book and I know I understand it, and I don't have to prove it to anyone." He had not before considered writing as a means of thinking or a strategy for thinking out what he did not yet understand—writing to learn. I just gave him some leeway until I could make sense of his resistance and encourage him, rather than stamp him with failure. I tried to focus on what he was doing well and what he was learning, rather than what he refused to do. It was in the conferences that I was able to learn better how to help Mark find purpose and motivation.

In a reading workshop, he chose to read *The Autobiography of Malcolm X* because, he said, a friend had recommended it. He finished it in a matter of days. It wasn't until our conference that he began to respond to the kinds of searching questions I was asking of them. I asked a question he could not answer.

"Is Malcolm X a hero?"

He qualified the question: "Is he a hero? Does that mean is he my hero?"

He was a little perplexed, intrigued by an idea that left him thinking, but careful not to fall into any traps. He returned to his desk to write and to explore his own ideas. It was the first time he had found a reason to write. The conference offered a space in which to acknowledge his ability to think and to challenge that thinking. Without my suggesting it, Mark made a list of pros and cons that helped him think through how he felt about his own question. Then he attempted an answer: "I don't know if Malcolm X is a hero to me. He is sort of a role model because he taught his people that they were men and women that should be treated like humans and not an animal." Mark had created an assignment that made sense to him. He used the list as a means to think more critically about the question, and from that he began to write. He wrestled with definitions of racism, with what he viewed as contradictions inherent within Malcolm X's philosophy, and with his own understanding of *hero*. He then wrote out what he labeled "First Draft":

> Malcolm X was and still is idolized as a hero by millions. Not only blacks, but by all other races. He was one of the most intelligent men in America because he influenced people to do the right thing, and he helped his race to become "men" by the governments standards. He gave his life for his people and he would probably do it again if he had to. He would never give up his pride and his color because he knew that if he did he would have to give up the past and all the wrongs done to his race. He never liked a white man until he saw one that had forgotten his whiteness. He said he looked at things that were done to black people collectively, and not induvidually. I think he should have looked at people induvidually.

Mark had begun by addressing the idea of a hero for "millions," and he questions the "collective" lens through which Malcolm X viewed racism. He doesn't include himself until the second paragraph in which he uses the evasive term, *role model*, not yet ready to address the concept of hero, and again he is critical of the ways in which Malcolm X expressed his philosophy.

> To me Malcolm X is a role model because I like what he had to say about the black race. But I didn't like the way he said it. Every time he spoke he had something bad to say about the white race or white men. But what he did not realize is that if white men had never brought black men to American there would have been less inventions by black men.

By the third paragraph, Mark has tentatively arrived at his conclusive statement:

> Malxolm X is a hero to me because he never quit, he always strived toward his goal and he died for his beleafs and his goal. His goal was to have his race recognize as human beings not as black men or women, negroes, niggers, or afro Americans. He knew his goal could never be accomplished but he still tried as much as he could to succeed. He over came his drug problem.

He arrived at an answer for himself, exploring his own values and criteria by which to define Malcolm X as a hero. When we met about this first draft, I asked Mark to look more critically at some of the statements he had made. I was aware of the risk of losing him at any step in this process. This was the first he had written. He acknowledged that some of the lines, like the reference to inventions, made little sense: "I'm not sure why it's there, anyway." He was willing to look again, to revise, what he had written. He wrote what he labeled the "first draft expansion":

> To me Malcolm X is a hero and a role model because I like what he had to say about the black race but I didn't like the way he said it. Every time he spoke he had something bad to say about the white race. He blamed all the bad things that had happend to his race on white men. He should have recognized his race as a very self-destructive race because he used to

be self-destructive. He was self-destructive because he did cocain, pot, heroin, and down-ers. He also sold drugs and was a pimp. Malcolm is also a hero to me, as well as a role model, because he over came his past to help the future. His goal was to have a peaceful future where people of all colors united and became one large race. He never quit he always strived toward his goal.

Mark then reworked the piece, eliminating what he felt was not important and continuing to write toward a clearer perception of his own attitudes and responses to his reading of the man. His final line read, "He pushed towards a goal he knew could never be accomplished, but he still tried as much as he could to succeed at life and his goals"—his clear definition of a hero. In this writing Mark engages in an inner dialogue about what Malcolm X had to say and how he said it, critically evaluating what he had read. His resistance to rethinking and revising his work dissipated as he sought truth, as he tested out his own ideas and opinions, as inquiry became a personal process.

Mark stopped working for several days after writing his paper, as the class began a writing workshop. Many students were writing fiction. After some attempts at writing something which he wanted to be "different" from the others, Mark asked to be able to read, instead. Reluctantly, I let him. In the next three days he read *If I Die in a Combat Zone* by Tim O'Brien. This time he came voluntarily to the conference, asking what I wanted him to write. I knew I needed to be quick about it. I wasn't sure what we could sustain yet in this tensional space.

"Tell me about his perspective on war."

"What do you mean? I don't understand."

"Try this. You are Tim O'Brien and your brother…"

"He doesn't have a brother."

"OK, your favorite cousin is signed up to go to Vietnam. Write him a letter and tell him what you think."

Silence. "OK, I can do that."

Mark was not yet ready to write on his own, without our conference; however, his willingness to initiate a conference, as well as to pursue ideas in writing, marked changes in his attitude toward his own learning. Our brief dialogues and the questions that arose within them helped him to internalize the questions he would choose that would move him to think further. He returned with the letter:

Jeff,

How are things back home? Over here life is unexplainable. I've heard that you have enlisted, and I regret your desicion, but I'm not going to tell you not to join. It's an experience we will never forget (if you come here). All a man has here is his pride and his courage and his death. Over here there are no laws, no rules, killing is something to be proud about, you can't think about what you do because you'll never figure it out. Have you ever seen a man die? or a man get his legs blown off by a mine? How about seeing the person you just shot still alive watching them die? Over here your just another statistic, or just another victim. The media tells you about the victories, but what about the losses? All you have to do is blink at the wrong time, and your life is gone. I've seen it happen in a mine field. Almost half our platoon dies, men with thier legs blown off, and those were the lucky one's some men have been blown to pieces, there wasn't enough left to put them in a trash bag. I live this now, and will forever. I'll never forget the people that died, and lived it will haunt me forever.

You should see some of the guys here. They love it. I'm not saying I don't try, but I don't go overboard. You can't push it because when you do you usually end up dead.

I'm not trying to disuade you, but I think you should wiegh the options before you make your own desicion, Jeff.

> Sincerly,
> Tim O'Brien
> P.S. Send a picture and write often

A letter writen from Tim O'brien's point of view. I attempted to look at war from his point of view. I think this worked out well because I think I understand him. I have made no revisions (First draft).

The writing helped Mark to explore and express through his own language his understanding of the narrator's experience. His greatest source of resistance, his fear that his writing would not demonstrate the quality of his thinking (a fear we all share as writers), has been largely dispelled, for the moment, anyway, and writing now offers new opportunities for expressing his opinion, and voice. The purpose of this writing is reflective. As Mary O'Reilley suggests, "Reflection is the enemy of authoritarian conditioning" (1998, 7). Mark has resisted the "authoritarian conditioning" to which most students who are successful in school defer, often to the detriment of their self-image, confidence, and learning. His reluctance to write is slowly eroding. He has come to value writing as a means to challenge his own interpretation of reading and of reality, a challenge he felt he had not before been offered.

Earlier in a conversation with him about writing, I had asked him if the questions help him and he had answered, "Yeah. It makes you understand kinda what you think. If you write it down, that's what you think, and no one questions it while you're doing it so you think it's right, you don't know if it's right or wrong and you pass it in." He had already begun to internalize the questions. He had experienced the processes of dialogue that had helped him to generate language and meaning as he continued to carry it back into his writing. Although he continued to be too conscious of a judging audience, the fact that I remained nonjudgmental for this length of time was important for him to be able to write for himself first. Mark, like many others, has learned the patterns necessary to help him do well in an authoritative system. He admitted what he tends to do:

> I'll just write a paper like last year, I was failing English last quarter. I wrote a paper that did-n't even make sense—I got an A plus on it! Like I don't want to swear, but I BS'd my way through the whole thing, the whole entire paper, and I got an A. And that's when I figured out I could lie on anything. I could lie on any paper.

Like many students, Mark tries to make sense of a system that allows and rewards such lying, and because he can't make sense of it, he assumes the fault must be, at least partially, his. He is cynical (for the right reasons) and discouraged about the realities of schooling. In some ways he blames himself for the resistance he feels to what he finds inconsequential, or worse, false. He seems locked in a struggle for truth, for his own expressions of reality. Under such conditions, all that students feel required to do is minimal work, and pushing themselves beyond the edge of the comfortable and familiar seems pointless. As Mark states, "Just because I get a bad grade doesn't mean I don't know what I'm doing...Just because I get an A doesn't mean I have an education."

Works Cited

Anderson, Harlene. 1997. *Conversation, Language, and Possibilities: A Postmodern Approach to Therapy*. New York: Basic Books, A Division of HarperCollins Publishers.

Anderson, Harlene, and Harry Goolishiam. 1988. "Human Systems as Linguistic Systems: Preliminary and Evolving Ideas about the Implications for Clinical Theory." *Family Process* 27: 371–393.

Elbow, Peter. 1973. *Writing Without Teachers*. London: Oxford University Press.

Murray, Donald. 1994. "Knowing Not Knowing." *Taking Stock: The Writing Process Movement in the '90s*. Ed. Lad Tobin and Thomas Newkirk. Portsmouth, NH: Heinemann. 57–65.

———. 1982. *Learning by Teaching: Selected Articles on Writing and Teaching*. Montclair, NJ: Boynton/Cook Publishers, Inc.

O'Reilley, Mary R. 1998. *Radical Presence: Teaching as Contemplative Practice*. Portsmouth, NH: Boynton/Cook Publishers, Heinemann.

Spohn, William. 2000. "The Need for Roots and Wings: Spirituality and Christian Ethics." *Theology Digest* 47(4): 327–340.

Vendler, Zeno. 1984. "Understanding People." *Culture Theory: Essays on Mind, Self, and Emotion*. Ed. Richard A. Shweder and Robert A. LeVine. Cambridge University Press. 200–213.

5

Twenty-First Century Revision

A Novel Approach in Three Acts with Three Points of View

Barry Lane

Barry Lane has been a writer since fourth grade when his teacher, Miss Carolyn Foley, told him he was a writer. Since then he has written short stories, poems, children's books, and created professional books and videos to help improve the teaching of writing at all grade levels. A sought after keynote speaker and consultant, Barry has spoken at literacy conferences and in-service days in all fifty states and presented to teachers in Canada, Romania, France, England, Germany, and South Africa. His books for teachers include After THE END, Reviser's Toolbox, Why We Must Run with Scissors, Discovering the Writer Within, Hooked on Meaning, *and* 51 Wacky We-search Reports. *His website for teachers is www.discoverwriting.com.*

Act 1: English Teachers Behaving Badly

I remember the day I got the call. Her name was Lori, and she was a curriculum director from a local high school. She was a young woman who still had the idealistic glow of the classroom in her soft, earnest voice. She explained how it was her job to design and implement a new language arts curriculum with her staff of eight English teachers from the high school and junior high. She was excited about this new curriculum and organized a big first meeting. To her shock, the English department did not share her enthusiasm. They were, in Lori's words, "more traditional." They didn't think there was anything wrong with the curriculum they had. By the afternoon, when it came time to do the first brainstorming exercise, the entire English department walked out of the meeting led by the Chairman.

"I don't know what to do. They don't want to change a thing," she paused. "Can you help us?"

My first reaction was "OK. Let me get this straight: you want me to transform the attitudes of eight people who don't want to change, who like what they are doing and see no need to do anything differently, into people who embrace change to the point they will rewrite and revise an entire language arts curriculum with little outside help." I thought for a moment. "Sure."

I was very broke.

Since this seemed like an impossible task, I decided to pretend as though I knew what I was doing from the start. That way, when I failed miserably, it would seem like completely their fault.

"OK," I said, with bravado in my voice, "If I'm going to turn this thing around, I'm going to need to know you're on board with me. I need back up."

I'm not sure she understood why I was suddenly talking like John Wayne, but she did agree to my demand that we meet nowhere near the school for our first meeting. I wanted the teachers as far away from their home turf as possible. A weekend trip to the Cayman Islands would have been ideal, but we decided on the reading room of the local public library.

I remember that first meeting like it was yesterday. As the teachers walked into the dark, oak-clad building, they seemed oddly friendly, not the hostile curriculum director-eating clan which was described to me. One of my demands was that Lori not come to the meeting. I wanted them one on one, mano a mano. But now it seemed almost ridiculous. These teachers had names like Bob and Judy and Derek. They were not unreasonable people.

We went around the circle and did introductions. That's when I realized I had failed to plan any activities, or let me put it another way, I had many activities prepared but I was clueless as to which to start with. I decided to do a simple writing lesson that I had never tried before. Recently I had uncovered a box of school papers at my mom's houses. They were from high school and college, and they had all my teachers' comments on them. I read a few of the more cryptic comments to the group. My favorite was from my college freshmen English professor who wrote in the margin next to my misguided definition of Freud's Superego "as a very large ego": a little knowledge is a dangerous thing.

Then I asked the teachers to reflect on paper about all the things that were written on their papers through school. I gave them some paper and ten minutes.

There was a calming silence in the room as the teachers wrote and wrote and wrote. No hostile mob here. Their engagement with the assignment was palpable. After ten minutes they were still going so I let them write longer. After twenty minutes it was time to share.

The first man's name was Tony, and he told of a high school teacher who scribbled what he called nasty notes in the margins of everything he wrote. "Trite." "Huh?" "Ug." Which he didn't realize meant unsubstantiated generalization until years later. He thought he had given teachers indigestion all these years. Then Judy talked about feeling like she was a great writer until she got to college and a professor wrote that her thinking was "shallow." "I was an 'A' student but I was shallow."

We all seem to have had a similar experience. We thought we were OK as writers, and then some teacher came along with a personal agenda and took us down a few notches. My favorite example of this was Nancy who told of an English professor who wrote "F" at the top of the page and "You'll know why in ten years" at the bottom of the page. We all agreed that this might not be cutting edge teaching.

After we shared, it was time for donuts and coffee, but before we took a break I asked them to reflect on what they could do to make their students' experiences with writing instruction better than their own. That's all it took to get them rethinking and reseeing what they needed to do. After my meeting with the teachers, Lori was amazed at their change of attitude and, though I never returned to that school, she called me months later to thank me and to tell me that her teachers had written a first-rate curriculum which was used as a model by the state.

By then I had begun working on a book about teaching revision in writing called *After THE END: Teaching and Learning Creative Revision.* In my travels around the country, I had noticed that students of all grade levels groaned and went limp when asked by well-meaning teachers to revise their words. Teachers complained about stubborn students who changed a word or two just to go through the motions, and others who just refused outright to change a thing. I wondered if what they were talking about had anything to do with writing or was it the same phenomenon recalcitrance that Lori had described about her English department.

These stubborn students saw no reason to change, and because teachers demanded revision, the act became a type of false capitulation to a higher authority. You could even argue that those who revised their writing simply because a teacher told them to, were being more inauthentic than those who flat out refused to change a thing. How could you even begin to teach revision without giving students a valid reason to revise their work? I decided my book would begin with a lesson that showed teachers that revision grew from a desire to say more. There was no reason to revise unless you had a reason. But, can a teacher teach the will to revise? I decided to experiment.

Act 2: Where's Papa Going with that Ax?

You stand in front of the class of ninth graders and say, "Listen, I want to tell you a story and all I want you to do is listen." They lean in with anticipation. Actually, You are lying here, more than half of them don't seem to care and the rest have that glazed over look you see everyday in the first period after lunch. Besides, preludes and introductions mean nothing to high school students. Only the story will convince them it is worthy of their attention. You begin.

"In kindergarten I had a teacher that used to shake kids. Has anyone here been shook?" One young man in the back holds up his hand. "Why did she shake you?" he asks.

"Don't remember." (*Pause.*) "She never stopped."

(*Laughter.*)

"The other thing interesting about this teacher was she never left her desk. We orbited around her desk like electrons fielding one worksheet after another." Some students groan with the memory of worksheets.

"This teacher didn't shake you because you were bad, she shook you because you didn't know the right answer. Back then they had courses for teachers. Answer is in Johnny— he's just holding out. Grab shoulder at point *A* and shake gently. Answer should emerge."

(*Laughter.*)

"I had a friend named Paul. He was shook constantly. He was your basic kinder-gartener without a cause. *(You shake your body like an orangutan.)* But I was Mr. Low Profile. I was going to get through this with as little need as possible for future therapy. *(More laughs.)*

"Then one week I am absent for two days. I miss stuff and she is holding up this flash card asking me what sound is on the card. I freeze. I am still at the age where I think *L M N O* is the letter before *P*. I get the wrong count when we sing the alphabet. *(More laughs.)*

"She says, 'Come up to my desk.' And I hear that firm tone in her voice. This is it, I think, I'm gonna get shook. *(Big laugh.)*

"As I walk to her I hear these voices in my head. One is like a gangster with a Brook-lyn accent. 'I know my rights, lady. I colored inside those lines. You can't do this to me!'

"Another is remembering Rodney who wet his pants when she shook him. Never shook him after that. Rodney had his own special corner. 'Go to your special corner Rod-ney,' and off he would go.

"Another is just curious. 'What's it gonna be like?'

"As I move closer I hear a squeaking sound, my teacher swiveling in her chair, exhibiting her full range of motion. She is orbiting towards me. Then I feel one hand clutch one shoulder and the other clutch the other shoulder, and I start to shake. And I think, 'Where is the answer?' But I don't cry. I just shake for a minute and she says, 'Go back to your seat.' And I go back to my seat, and suddenly it's years later and I am telling my story at your school. What do you want to know about my story?"

There are giggles and good silence, which tells you they were listening. You let it hang there, like the oil heating before the popcorn pops. Then the first curious questions come:

Why did she shake kids?
Were you shook again?
Did you tell your parents?
What did your parents do?

You scribble them on the board one at a time.

You point out to students that questions tend to come in clusters. The follow up question is often stronger than the original. You encourage them to follow up each other's questions. You tell them about inside questions and outside questions. Outside questions are about exteriors: What color was her hair? Inside questions tend to be about interiors or feelings: What did it feel like to be shook?

Then you stop. You thank them and tell them that those questions they asked are gifts to you, because they are evidence of being listened to. In real life there is no evidence when people listen to you. It's quiet.

The other great thing about those questions is that they propel you to a part of a story. Answering them jump-starts you close to a point of tension in the story or an idea about the story. Don't start in the beginning, start in the middle, "in medias res." You call this the potato, the thing that both the writer and the reader want to dig up and find out more about.

You read this lead: "'Where is Papa going with that ax?' asked Fern to her mother as she was setting the table for breakfast." You wait for a student to say, "I know that book. That's the lead to *Charlotte's Web*."

You ask, "Where IS Papa going with that ax?"

"To kill Wilbur," someone says.

"Exactly. Wilbur is both the meat and potato of the story and E. B. White knows it. Why doesn't E. B. White begin *Charlottes Web* with a little intro? For example, 'Nice day today, Mom'?"

"Actually he did. Here is Scott Elledge's biography of E. B. White. It contains the first two drafts of the book. One begins, "A barn can have a horse in it, a barn can have a cow in it." Another begins, "Charlotte was a big gray spider."

E. B. White chose "Where is Papa going with that ax?" Because it was the heart of the story. It was dramatic and it pulled in the reader and the writer."

You read them leads like this one from S. E. Hinton's book *The Taming of the Star Runner* "His boot felt empty without the knife in it." You ask them which questions grow in their minds as readers.

Where is the knife now?

Why did he have a knife in his boot?

You tell them that strong writing raises questions in the reader's mind, questions that readers ponder and the writer tries to answer. That's why crime writer Elmore Leonard says, "Writer's write for the same reason readers read—to find out what's gonna happen" (Lane 1992). Strong leads raise questions but can strong questions can raise leads? Here is a lesson to learn this.

The Magic Flashlight (a group activity)

Writer John McPhee calls leads magic flashlights that shine down through a story, showing the writer what to put in and also what to leave out. One way to think of those questions we have been talking about is that they point your writer's flashlight in different directions. Think of your unwritten story as a dark cellar and your questions as the flashlight. Each points to a different part. Just as your questions about my kindergarten story helped me to find different places to start, you can help each other to find better leads to stories you have already written or new leads to stories you have not yet begun. Here's an activity to learn about this.

1. Form a group of four people and elect a talking stick. This is the stick that gives you the power to talk. The rest of the group must listen.

2. Pass around the stick. Each person has five minutes to either read something they have written or talk about a story they want to write.

3. The rest of the group listens to each story and scribbles curious questions on scraps of paper. Note: Avoid questions that blame the writer or that try to fix the story. Questions like Why didn't you describe him better? These questions are insulting.

4. Don't look at the questions until everyone in the group has a stack in front of them.

5. Next open up the questions and write a lead from your favorite one.

6. Share your leads and discuss your stories.

7. If you liked this activity, try writing questions to yourself and grow leads from them.

What was it like to have questions and not be allowed to look at them? How did you feel when you opened them up?

Someone says, "It was like opening gifts." You say, "Did anyone find the questions pointed them to a part of the story they had not thought about? Next time you are struggling to find a place to begin, write yourself some questions and turn them into leads. Pick the one that pulls at you the most and start in. Questions can help you to revise even before you begin writing, and if you are like most writers, they will not end until your work is published."

Act 3: A Time to Show and a Time to Tell, A Time to Teach and a Time to Write

The English teacher sat at the desk behind the stack of unread papers. She had just scribbled "show don't tell" in the margin again, and she was having an out-of-body experience teachers sometimes get when their commenting pens react before their minds think. She was remembering all the teachers who had written the same words on her papers. She thought of quotes by famous writers. E. B. White said, "Don't write about humanity. Write about a man." Richard Price said, "Don't write about the horrors or war, write about a kid's burnt socks lying in the road" (Fletcher 1993). Great maxims, but were they really true? Sure it was undeniable that student writing improved the more they were capable of writing in concrete physical detail, but wasn't there also a time to turn inward and reflect in abstract ways?

In fact, wasn't thematic insight lacking in her students' work as much as concrete physical detail? "Show, don't tell" was false. The truth was more like Ecclesiastes or the Byrds. There was a time to show and time to tell.

Suddenly, a great wind blew through the open window and the stack of papers scattered around the room, but the teacher just sat there watching the white papers swirl and flutter in the darkness like all those ambitious lesson plans that she had used to teach a new concept but failed to reach the minds of her students. She resolved to stop nagging her students to "show don't tell" and start teaching them to see the difference themselves between the two for themselves. She found a book by Barry Lane called *Reviser's Toolbox* and started teaching one of the lessons.

The next day, she stood before her class. "Who knows what a snapshot is?"

"It's a picture."

"It's a photo."

"Now, what do you think a thoughtshot is?"

"It's a picture in your mind."

"It's what you are feeling."

"Here is a sentence. Tell me if it is a snapshot or a thoughtshot: 'I was scared.'"

"Thoughtshot."

"I am standing on the edge of the diving board."

"Snapshot."

"Simple, right? Well, not really because sometimes they blend together and sometimes it's a little hard to tell. I don't really care. I just want you to know the difference between physical detail and internal thoughts and feelings because it can help you to revise your writing. If you look over your work and see it's all thoughts, 'I was scared. Boy, was I scared. You would be scared too…' you can improve the writing by adding snapshots. 'I stood on the edge of the cliff looking down at the rushing surf.' Likewise if I am stuck in snapshots, 'I ran to first base, I ran to second base, I ran to third base…' I can improve the writing by adding thoughtshots, 'I could almost imagine my body sliding into home plate and bowling over the catcher in one great victory plunge, but my burning leg muscles wouldn't let me.'

"Here is a quick lesson to learn about these two types of detail."

She stood in front of the class and took out her writing notebook from the pocket on her sweater. Though she didn't really feel like writing, she knew this lesson would make more sense to her students if she did it with them. She turned the page with a list of groceries to pick up after school and stared a moment at the blank paper.

Snapshots and Thoughtshots

1. Think of a person you would like to remember, someone from your past—a grandmother, a grandfather, an old friend, a brother, a sister, anybody.

2. Think of where they are physically. In one quick sentence, locate them in a specific time and space. In other words, don't just say, "My dad is at home." Instead say, "My dad sits in the lazy boy recliner in the living room."

3. Now write a quick snapshot of that moment. In other words, describe this one little moment in as much meaningful physical detail as you can. Be careful not to just make a list of details in your paragraph. Rather, just close your eyes and imagine that moment in clear physical detail.

4. Near the end of your snapshot try adding a thoughtshot. It can be just a thought about the moment you are describing, or perhaps even a thought in the mind of the person you are describing.

5. Go back and add snapshots or thoughtshots to your own writing.

She put on some soft classical music and sat there with her students. She could think of nobody to write about, but she thought even if she pretended to write this could be good modeling. Five minutes passed and she saw that most of her students were writing. She went back to her grocery list and added Parmesan cheese, heavy cream, and pesto. She wanted to make pasta in a new way tonight. Somehow it was comforting to think about supper at 11 AM. It gave a sense of forward movement to the day. Then out of the corner of her eye she noticed a small miracle. Dwight was writing. Dwight who often wrote one sentence when it was time to write, Dwight who counted the words in this one sentence as though volume could substitute for the meaning and purpose missing in his words. What could Dwight be writing about?

Her pen moved toward the blank page of her notebook. The words appeared before she had a chance to think them:

> The boy sat at the ceramic desk. His eyes strained to read the words he had written. He gripped the ballpoint pen tightly and with resolute purpose, marking the paper like a dying man scribbling his will in the last moments of his life. He strained to see the image in his mind, then found the words to go with that image. His mind was like a giant typewriter with a new word on each key. It was always hard, but now, for the first time, he could feel the rhythm of his words.

Dad stood in the doorway of the living room. He had the doorknob in one hand and a can of Coors Light in the other. He stumbled, then gripped the doorknob so he wouldn't fall flat on his face. He stood tall in his grease-smeared T-shirt and faded jeans, but not tall enough to make up for all his drinking. Beside him was a green suitcase and it was stuffed with clothes and shaving stuff. A black sock hung out the side like the tongue of a dead cow. "I don't care," he said to her. "I really don't fucking care!"

That was it. That was the last time I saw him.

The timer rang but she continued writing. Many of the students had stopped but she had not noticed. She was no longer their teacher. She was no longer the person who had written the lesson and delivered it so carefully to them. She was not the one who graded paper or assigned homework.

Suddenly the sun emerged from behind a cloud and bathed the whole room with yellow light. "We'll share some of our snapshots and thoughtshots next class," she said in a soft voice, hardly her own. "And remember, if you couldn't think of a person or moment to write about, don't despair. You have an entire lifetime to add snapshots and thoughtshots to your writing. Just remember this lesson, and try it out another time with something that matters to you."

The bell rang and the students began the end of the period shuffle to stuff their learning into their backpacks. As they vanished into the hallway she noticed out of the corner of her eye that one student was still writing. She waited for Dwight to look up in her direction, but his head remained buried in the page and his pen was still moving. She sat back in her seat and found the pink slip: "Please excuse Dwight. He was late for Science because he was finishing a special assignment in English."

As she signed her name to the pink slip and moved toward Dwight's desk, she knew there was nothing in the world she would rather be than an English teacher.

Works Cited

Fletcher, Ralph. 1993. *What a Writer Needs*. Portsmouth, NH: Heinemann.

Lane, Barry. 1992. *After THE END: Teaching and Learning Creative Revision*. Portsmouth, NH: Heinemann.

6

Matthew's Portfolio

Richard Kent

Richard Kent taught high school English, directed the school's writing center, and coached varsity athletics prior to receiving his Ph.D. at Claremont Graduate University. He has written three books about his former teaching practice, including Room 109: The Promise of a Portfolio Classroom, Beyond Room 109: Developing Independent Study Projects, *and* A Guide to Creating Student-Staffed Writing Centers, Grades 6–12. *His writing center book received the* 2006 Book of the Year *award from the International Writing Centers Association, an assembly of the National Council of Teachers of English.*

Six-foot-two-inch Matthew passed around a large plate of chocolate chip cookies to his classmates. Wearing fluffy gray ears and tiny mittens, Matthew gave a three-minute talk about *If You Give a Mouse a Cookie* by Laura Joffe Numeroff, the picture book he had selected to read for English class.

"Look, don't give me any grief," he laughed. "You know my mom's a third-grade teacher."

Matthew really wasn't worried about getting laughed at by his classmates. This book project presentation for the theme of "Age" occurred in mid-January. By then, thanks to portfolios, conversations, and even scrumptious cookies, all of us in Period F had gotten to know one another pretty well.

A self-proclaimed math guy, Matthew churned out four well-crafted portfolios during his junior year in high school. This chapter features Matthew's first quarter portfolio in English class. Through Matthew's work, you will get a glimpse of how I managed up to 120 students and their quarterly portfolios in a theme-based English class. Looking closely at student work provides a lens into a classroom teacher's philosophies, theories, and resulting practices (Blythe, Allen, and Powell 1999, 1–5). Looking at student work also shows us what a student values and what the teacher values.

The Assignment: A Portfolio

First Quarter Portfolio

Formal Papers: Three, highly revised papers, 600–1000 words each

Informal Papers: Two papers, revised once, 600–1000 words each

Journals: Forty-eight, one-page journal entries, first draft, spell-checked only (if word processed), approximately 150 words each

Reading: Five books plus in-class readings

Presentations: Three to five book projects created and presented to class—one book project has to be written using the book project guide

Quarterly Reflection: A written reflection of the class and portfolio, approximately 600–1000 words, is due after portfolios are submitted

When Matthew and his classmates arrive in Room 109 on the first day of school in August, the room is lit with living room lamps, art projects from previous years adorn the walls, and a George Winston CD plays softly on the stereo. We sit knee-to-knee in a circle of chairs with a neatly organized line of portfolios on the floor in front of us. As always, some of the new kids stare at the wooden coffin in the reading corner.

We begin with a class letter (Figure 1) that I have written for them. The central texts of Room 109 English—the pieces we read together—are shorter writings such as class letters, poems, essays, flash fiction (up to 500 words), or songs. These texts are accessible, sometimes with accommodations (for example, a reading buddy), for all of the students in this heterogeneously-grouped, multi-aged classroom. That's right. Over the years, with the support of my school's administration and our extraordinary special education department, I began welcoming all-comers. This one-room schoolhouse approach worked for my students and me because a portfolio pedagogy supports individual learners. In addition, as I've highlighted in my book *A Guide to Creating Student-Staffed Writing Centers, Grades 6–12*, student-editors from our writing center provided the kind of one-on-one assistance that all writers need.

My Dear Students,

Welcome to Room 109. I want you to know that I'm happy to have you here. Together in English class this year we'll make music and write stories, tell jokes and read books. In short, we'll work, play, and learn. There are times when you won't much care for English, Room 109, or me. Things will get hard and hectic, and you'll be stressed out. Don't worry, that's normal. Sometimes learning is difficult; it's a struggle. Sometimes learning is like slow dancing and takes no effort at all. My advice? Let it happen.

Now, about our room. Stop reading this letter for a second and look around. I put stuff up on the walls because it makes me feel at home—it makes me feel comfortable. I hope it does the same for you. If you have something you'd like to put up, go for it.

Figure 1   Class Welcome Letter

Behind my desk are photographs of family and friends. Feel free to go over and take a look. You'll see pictures of my teams, too. Above the door is one of the State of Maine soccer teams I took to England. We had a blast. Just to the right of my desk is a poster of the first championship team in any sport at Mountain Valley High School: the 1989 MVC Soccer Champs. They were the best people. Also behind my desk is a collection of pictures of students who graduated over the past few years. Oh yeah, and the Red Sox T-shirt up on the curtain rod? That's Jamie Ippolito's. We both love the Sox!

Room 109 has history. This is the place where Craig Dickson put his hand through the window. The place where the lacrosse team held its first practice. Here, too, is where Janet Hoyle stood up one day and said, "I'd like to sing the class a song that I wrote." Room 109 is where *The Book of Cult* was composed. Borrow it and have some laughs. It's also where Duncan MacIsaac gave me a special gift (don't ask), Jenn Nisbet conducted my funeral, and Mike Gawtry body slammed me because I was being a "royal jerk." And finally, in this very room Amy Welch and Dave Kasregis read ALOUD the letters of James Joyce—you'd have to read the letters to understand just how *incredible* that is!

English is a funny subject. As far as I'm concerned, English is everything. Some days we sing or build; others days we paint or hike. Every day we're reading, writing, and talking. You might get a bit concerned when you read the letters from former students in a moment. Don't worry, you'll do fine.

Now me. A warning: You will discover in time that I am not perfect. In fact, you may have already discovered that. Like you, I have good days and bad days. I work hard at trying to be fair and treating everyone well. I never succeed. Never. I always end up hurting someone somehow. I'm sorry for whatever stupid, insensitive thing I might do. But please know that I'm trying the best I can. If you do the same, we'll have a whizbang of a year together.

Over the years in Room 109 we have studied a bit of everything, including English literature and quantum physics, poetry and infinity, commas and history, fiction and projectile vomiting, black holes and teaching, music, diversity, men, women, art, Tolstoy, Stevensian Thought, Frost, and drooling. We do everything and anything because English is just that: reading, writing, speaking, listening, performing, observing, cooking, and a whole lot more.

This year's theme in Room 109 is balance. We need balance to stand, to talk with others, and to laugh at ourselves. We need balance for poetry, novels, movies, sentences, and paragraphs. Balance plays a vital role in sports, in relationships, in classrooms, in families, in eating, and in swimming. Heck, without balance you wouldn't be able to sit where you're sitting or read what you're reading. So, it's important stuff.

This year you'll be writing your own book. It's called a portfolio. Look closely, for no matter what you've heard, *portfolio* is not a four-letter word. Really. Also, you need to know that most of the time in here you are in charge. That's weird, but you'll get used to it. Trust yourselves, for very soon you will be out in that big, wide, screamer of a world doing life on your own. Looking at it that way, English class ain't nothing.

My phone number is 364–2953. You may call me if you have a question, problem, or if you just want to chat. Please don't call after nine in the evening. I'm old and I need my "handsome sleep." No wise comments.

(Continues)

Figure 1 Class Welcome Letter (*continued*)

So, that's it. Now I'll pass around letters from former students. Enjoy. Their ghosts are sitting beside you. Listen, ghosts or not, you should know they all survived.

Welcome. I'm glad you're here.

Your Loving English Teacher,
Rich Kent

P.S. For next class write a first-draft, five-page, double-spaced-12-font-Roman-spell-checked autobiographical sketch (life story). This is a first draft freewrite, so don't worry about grammar stuff right now. Just write with reckless abandon! Also for next class you will need one large three-ring binder and a journal book. And finally, your class, F/Blue, is responsible for reading and responding to portfolios at the end of second quarter in mid-January. Make plans now to spend either a Saturday or Sunday morning here at school. Your keeper (parent or guardian) is invited to come in to read and respond, too! The more the merrier.

Figure 1 Class Welcome Letter (*continued*)

Once the students finish reading my welcome letter, I pass out a collection of welcome letters from former students. Some of these letters instruct, others provide motivation...and then there's Brian's:

Dear Student,

If you take English and get Mr. Kent, don't worry. It's the easiest class you'll ever have. He doesn't give any homework. You don't have to read any books. It's great! He let's you fool around as much as you want, and he's a real nice guy. If you haven't had a lot of work before, don't worry because you certainly won't here. If you are fortunate enough to get Kent's class, I will leave you with a 2-word thought...JUST KIDDIN'!

Sincerely,
Brian T.

Next, each student receives a model portfolio to look at. I hand Matthew, a gifted soccer player, a portfolio by a senior teammate that Matthew admires. None of these portfolio models are perfect. Instead, I've picked doable examples, not mindblowers. The common features: each portfolio is complete and each author is someone I'd call a good kid. Yes, it's kind of a set-up.

For the next ten or fifteen minutes there's quiet in Room 109, save George Winston's piano, turning pages, and whispers.

As you've read in the welcome letter, the yearlong theme is balance. Sub-themes over the year include topics such as humor, diversity, and boredom (we live in small town Maine); these topics last from one to nine weeks. Our first quarter's theme, "The Self," lasts all nine weeks of the quarter. Beginning our studies with "The Self" grounds most of my students' writing in the "the expressive" (that is, writing closest to talk), a meaning-making tool for young writers (see, for example, Pradl 1982; Britton, Burgess, Martin, McLeod, and Rosen 1975; Martin 1983; Rosenblatt 1978).

This first quarter theme is about coming to know one another, about sharing, about building that learning community we've all heard a lot about as teachers. There are as many ways to build community as there are teachers. For me, I want each student in each class to know that they're an essential part of what we've built together. Yale's James Comer says, "The reason we learn has a lot to do…with our relationships with important others. We are motivated to learn out of relationships" (Young and Rubicam Foundation 1991, 77).

That first day of class I field lots of nitty-gritty questions and make very clear the Friday, end-of-the-school-day deadline of the life story. By now you'd think there would be griping about how much writing and reading has been assigned (five books, five papers, forty-eight journal entries…), but most of the kids learned the previous June who they had landed for English class and had heard about the portfolio. Most of us who have taught for a long time in the same place live on our reputations—the tricky part each year is living up to them.

Next, I ask students to select a book. Our in-class library of three thousand volumes—novels, biographies, autobiographies, magazines, essays, videos, graphic novels, audio books, comic books, how-tos—isn't the result of an exorbitant budget (my average classroom allowance from the school over a ten-year period was about $350). Over several years we developed this library by

- writing to parent-caregivers to ask if they have books to donate;
- offering extra credit to students who donate books—any books;
- dropping by yard sales—boxes of books often cost next to nothing;
- visiting the local library—ten-cent used book sales happen every day;
- connecting with secondhand bookstores in search of bargains;
- checking out the bargain tables at big box bookstores;
- asking friends, family, and colleagues to donate books;
- having a student write a letter to the editor soliciting books;
- having the local paper reporter write an article on reading, highlighting the need for books.

Kids hover around the bookshelves. Those who have been in Room 109 in previous years feel comfortable enough to offer recommendations. Matthew chooses *Into the Wild* by Jon Krakauer after paging through *Succulent Wild Women* by Sark. His girlfriend is in our class, so Matthew measures his book choice with care.

The quarter begins.

Matthew's Writing

His first quarter portfolio includes the required five papers, each ranging between eight hundred and one thousand words. During the first quarter, the genre of most of these papers remains the student's choice. Allowing student choice helps me get to know my new students as writers and as people.

About half of my students took me up on summer work for extra credit that year. It's a simple requirement: I send out eight class letters over the course of the summertime; students are asked to write eight letters to me. I respond to their first letter with a postcard. Matthew wrote six summer letters, mostly about his American Legion baseball team.

Life Stories and Building Community

Matthew and every last one of my 117 students submit five-page, first draft autobiographical sketches by Friday afternoon. For the next three days, the Labor Day weekend, I hunker down and write letter responses to each life story (Kent 1997, 14–18). When I first began writing back, I managed one to two paragraphs to each student. After a few years of practice, I began cranking out four-, five-, and six-paragraph letters. Here's the opening paragraph of my six-paragraph letter:

> Welcome to Room 109, Matt. I know together we will have a year of adventure and discovery. I also know you'll be challenged by yourself; this is truly the focus of the class. The thought of Matthew K. challenging Matthew K. is hair-raising and interesting, wild and fascinating. I look forward to watching as Matt Kellogg reinvents himself throughout the course of this school year. Hold On!

My letter also attempts to focus on technical aspects of a student's writing. Since I had read six summer letters by Matthew as well as his life story, I had enough information to offer the following:

> You use commas like I used to eat M&M's, tossing them into a paper recklessly and with abandon. This, we will help you with.

> At times you write full paragraphs of noun-verb-complement sentences with no variety. These sentences tend to drag and drone. We will help you bring life to your paragraphs as well!

While reading the students' life stories, I highlight one sentence from each essay to use in a collection, or what I call a synthesis (Kent 1997, 21–23). After returning the students' life stories with my responses, I then pass out a class letter with the collection of quotations. Here's a small sample that I titled "The People of Room 109":

> I am a junior. I should be a senior, but like I said, I've learned the hard way.

> My hundred mile hike was incredible and I'm glad I made time for it.

> I'm not sure I know what I want to do with my life. I find that my interests change frequently, and I worry that I will never be able to be content with one career.

> My father and mother are in New York working construction.

> Reading is my life.

> I was brought up in an alcoholic family.

> My mother cried when she read my autobiography.

> I would like to become a neurologist.

> I've never met my biological father.

> It's important to be a good person.

As you might imagine, these teenagers love these collections of quotations. I include writing from all six of my classes, so the synthesis ends up being ten or more pages long. There's laughter and giggling and whispered "look at this one"; there are also moments of stilled silence as they read themselves and their classmates.

The final piece of this activity: kids write letters back to me. This "unit" is time-consuming and exhausting for me. But the benefit of connecting personally with my students sets the tone for the year.

Portfolio Papers

By the end of the quarter, all five of Matthew's papers have been thoroughly revised, an option open to all students that usually results in a higher assessment. As required, he includes each copy of the revisions in his portfolio. He worked with a different editor for each draft of each paper, as did most of my students. Because that process doesn't mirror how most writers work—we usually work with one editor to begin with—I asked students to use the same editor through the first three revisions. In the end, some did and some did not (Kent 2004, 47–51).

When studying with James Britton and Dixie Goswami at Bread Loaf a half dozen years earlier, I learned about and experienced the three modes of writing (transactional, expressive, and poetic—see Figure 2). In time, I came to understand the central place of expressive writing in an effective writing classroom. The principal text for our summer studies, *The Word for Teaching is Learning: Essays for James Britton* (Lightfoot and Martin 1988), influences my classroom work and thinking to this day.

The following offers a glimpse at Matthew's five papers. Included are the paper titles, the descriptions Matthew wrote on his portfolio cover sheets, the central mode(s) of writing each paper represented, the number of revisions included in the portfolio, and one selected paragraph.

Autobiography—Life Story
Title: "Life of a Country Boy"
Matthew's Description: "In this paper I reflected on the first 16 years of my life.
I looked at why I am who I am today."
Mode(s) of Writing: expressive
Revisions included: 6

Then came the middle school. I played three varsity sports throughout the three years and attended many dances. Some might think that this would put a shy country boy right over the edge, but St. John's [elementary school] and the role my parents took in my life kept me modest and out of trouble…While all my friends were making out for the first time underneath the bleachers, I was still amazed that some girl wanted to wear my hat or hold my hand. Never did kiss a girl throughout my middle school days. Oh well, I won states in skiing when I was in the 8th grade.

Values Paper
Title: "Values"
Matthew's Description: "I told of my morals and beliefs, showing how they affect me today."
Mode(s) of Writing: expressive, transactional
Revisions included: 7

The educational system that this country gives to us is sometimes taken for granted. Even though my enjoyment of school is not always at its maximum, I do appreciate the opportunities it presents. School is a possibility to learn about the world and how we interact with other people. Along with education, it gives us a chance to spend time with friends, meet new

Transactional:

1. Informative/Functional: to convey information or to explain ideas, facts, or processes
   Description, biography or profile, procedures or processes, information report, research report, brochures, business reports, case studies, charts, graphs, career plans, directions, guidelines, histories, how-to manuals, minutes, newsletters, overviews, pamphlets, posters, resumes, regulations, rules, summaries, surveys, tables . . .

2. Argumentative/Persuasive: to influence or convince another of one's ideas or judgments
   Literary analysis, problem/solution, controversial issue, evaluation, speculation, advertisements, awards, tributes, commercials, complaints, cover letters, editorials, eulogies, evaluations (others), feature articles, job applications, marketing memos, petitions, proposals, rebuttals, requests, reviews (all types), self-assessments, warnings, web pages . . .

Poetic: to give shape to an idea, experience, or observation

1. Narratives
   Adventures, mysteries, fables or tall tales, fantasy or science fiction, historical accounts, realistic stories . . .

2. Poetry
   Ballads, songs; concrete, visual; formula verse; free verse; rhyme formats

3. Scripts
   Dialogues, monologues, radio plays, digital story scripts, video skits, hypermedia . . .

4. Practical texts
   Journals, logs, letters (all types), newspaper stories, interviews, obituaries, profiles, parodies, satires, speeches . . .

Expressive: to discover, identify, or clarify ideas or experiences for self or for others

Literacy autobiography, life story, autobiographical incident, personal reflection, multi-genre essay, memoir, lists, sketches, diagrams, journal or learning log entries, notes from reading or interviews, email exchanges; letters of advice, affection, apology, complaint, congratulations, invitation, protest, self-disclosure, sympathy, thanks; responses to literature . . .

Adapted from the works of Britton 1973, 1983; Claggett 1996; Lightfoot & Martin 1988; Martin 1983; Moffett 1983; Strong 2001, 2005.

Figure 2   Three Modes of Writing

people, and perform a variety of extracurricular activities. Being an active member of our school, I feel I am using this opportunity to its fullest potential.

Life Work—Life Passion Paper
Title: "Hopes for the Future"
Matthew's Description: "I told of my hopes of becoming a psychologist and why I think I would make a good one."
Mode(s) of Writing: expressive
Revisions included: 6

Many children fantasize about growing up to be a Major League Baseball player or an astronaut. I also grew up having these dreams. There comes a time, however, when we distinguish the difference between our fantasies and reality. We realize that the probability of landing on the moon or playing third base for the Red Sox is inconceivable. Sometimes it's difficult to see these goals realistically, but doing so will help us grow as people and broaden our choices for the future. After understanding this, we begin to look at our talents and ask ourselves questions about what may make us content and successful in our occupation.

Credo
Title: "Credo"
Matthew's Description: "More thoughts, ideas, and values that I believe in."
Mode(s) of Writing: expressive, poetic, and transactional
Revisions included: 5
There is no question in my mind [that] we are all formed into the people we are by our surroundings. Males and females, growing up in the city or the country, having one parent or two, the events and occurrences of our life shape us into who we are…Taking the time to understand other people's ideals, as well as our own, can shape us into mature, intelligent people…We all have our morals, values, and beliefs. Here is a list of mine:

> Admit when you're wrong, you'll feel better.
> Unfortunately, parents are usually right. We should listen to them more often.
> It's OK to admit you like mushy-gushy movies.
> Don't wear jeans every day.
> Life was easier when we had phonics books and girls had cooties.
> Late to bed; early to rise.
> Dive. You just might catch it.
> Don't worry about it.
> Pray.

Free Choice Paper
Title: "Team '96"
Matthew's Description: "Telling the stories and thoughts of my freshman year in soccer."
Mode(s) of Writing: expressive, transactional
Revisions included: 5

Walking into my first high school tryout, I was both confident and scared out of my mind…I walked past the horseshoe pits to our practice field by myself. I wasn't nervous about meeting people, as I knew many of the freshmen and sophomores from the previous seasons. What I didn't realize was there were so many juniors and seniors. I knew them only from watching high school games in the years before. To my surprise, however, many of them greeted me with

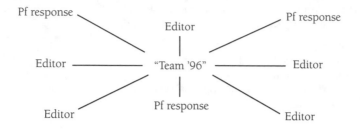

Figure 3   Responses to Matthew's Free Choice Paper (Pf=Portfolio)

a handshake and "Welcome to the team." I would later find out that Coach Kent put them up to it, but it was comforting at the time.

Matthew worked with a total of eleven different editors on these five papers, including his two parents, three adult family friends, and six student-editors from our school's student-staffed writing center. Figure 3 illustrates the feedback scheme for one of Matthew's formal papers. (I've included "Pf Response." Those are the letters written to Matthew at the end of the quarter about his portfolio. More on that later.) Clearly, Matthew's work was subjected to a broad and diverse lens, in keeping with Sally Thomas' assertion that "narrow lenses don't help us see the richness of our students' strengths" (Classroom conversation, Claremont Graduate University 2000).

What's stunning to me throughout Matthew's revisions—and throughout other students' drafts—is the amount of commentary written by editors. All of these editors showed different levels of competency. Some editors focused on the technical side of writing; others paid more attention to content and suggested places for further development or trimming. All of the editors wrote personal comments to Matthew.

Editors' Feedback

Throughout the many drafts of Matthew's five papers, his editors wrote 142 comments ranging in length between four and seventy-five words. Of these comments, eighty-seven focused on conventions (e.g., "Is there a way to use substitutes for 'it'? Maybe not.") and fifty-five spoke about Matthew the person (e.g., "Good decision [not to smoke or drink], even when it seems like you are the only one").

Altogether, editors wrote Matthew nearly two thousand words of commentary—ten double-spaced pages—in response to his writing during the first quarter. Further, the editors suggested 254 corrections (e.g., verb-tense agreement, punctuation, and word choice) throughout the drafts of the five papers. The rich dialog between Matthew and his editors calls to mind Wiggins' assertion that "[a]ssessment done properly should *begin* conversations about performance…" (1993, 13). The comments provided Matthew with detailed information about his writing performance; in addition, their words helped this young man think about the person he is becoming.

While examining the editors' comments, I found incorrect and conflicting advice. What did Matthew do to resolve the contradictions and make decisions about his manuscript? He did what writers do: he conferred with a more knowledgeable writer/editor (for conventions, that was his mother) or reviewed the editorial suggestions and made up his own mind about correctness.

Journal

Matthew's journal is handwritten and kept in a black, hardcover book. These classy-looking journals always seem to be on sale at some bookstore somewhere for $5.95. Each class period we devote the opening eight to ten minutes to writing journal entries. Sometimes I assign the topic, often about the theme we're studying; other times students just write. Daily journals—expressive writing—give students practice and establish an every day ritual that helps the class start off (usually) in a quiet, reflective way. That first day of class I passed out a two-page handout with a dozen prompts focused on the self such as these:

> "One life; a little gleam of time between two eternities; no second chance for us forever more."
> —Carlyle

> "In life, I have but one simple desire: To tear down the sky."
> —Alberto Tomba (ski racer)

> "To a worm in horseradish, the whole world is horseradish."
> —An old Yiddish saying

> "In every crowd are certain persons who seem just like the rest, yet they bear amazing messages."
> —Antoine de St. Exupery

> "If a man does not keep pace with his companions perhaps it is because he hears a different drummer. Let him step to the music which he hears, however measured or far away."
> —Henry David Thoreau

I have thousands of journal prompts, but in the spirit of less is more I only hand out a few at a time. Here's the opening and closing few lines of one of Matthew's first quarter journal entries:

> When we were little, the world was ours. There were no limitations on anything we could do. Singing, dancing, drawing, anything. Over the years, however, we become embarrassed and afraid to do some of these things in front of others. Why? you ask. It's because of other people. The people who make you feel uncomfortable. When you try to be yourself and have fun, there's always someone with a bad attitude that will want to take it away from you. In the perfect world, we would all be like kindergarteners. We would all laugh and sing and not be afraid to do anything. It probably went wrong somewhere around the third or fourth grade...Then there's the people who I really admire. The people who just don't care what others think of them. They'll sing anywhere, dance anywhere, and they're not afraid to go against the norm. I guess sometimes I'm like this, but like everybody else, there are certain people and certain times where it's easier to just go with the flow.

Book Projects

> *For Love of the Game* by Michael Shaara
> *Letters to my Son: Reflections on Becoming a Man* by Kent Nerburn
> *Einstein's Dreams* by Alan Lightman
> *Into the Wild* by Jon Krakauer
> *Room 109* by Richard Kent

Matthew read these five books for first quarter and created three projects. He produced two artsy book projects: the first, a pen and ink drawing of a man for *Letters to My Son* and the second, a handcrafted, eighteen-inch-high wooden door with frame, decked out with a brass doorknob and hinges. Labeled "Room 109," the door opened to reveal a series of quotations from my book, *Room 109*. I still have this project.

Each quarter, one of the book projects has to be written. I supply over twenty prompts to serve as guides and students may select any of them (or create their own). They're asked to write for about ninety minutes-first draft, spell-checked only. Matthew wrote five pages on *For the Love of the Game* by Michael Shaara. He used the following ten guiding questions or prompts:

- In a paragraph or two, tell the story of this book.
- Why should someone read this book? What lessons can we learn by reading and thinking about this book?
- What character do you most relate to? Why? Would she or he be a friend of yours? What characteristics of this person do you admire? What makes this person stand out above others in this book?
- If you liked this book, what three factors made you like it? List them and explain them. What other good books have you read that had similar qualities?
- How did you happen to pick this book out of all the books available? Did someone recommend it to you? If so, why did you take their recommendation?
- In the great scheme of things, why is this book one that everyone should read? If it is not one of those books, why not?
- How did the setting affect the characters? How was the setting important to the book?
- Talk about the various secondary characters. How are they important to the book and to the main characters?
- If this was one of those books that you couldn't put down, what other similar books have you read? What makes them good?
- Assuming you liked your book, what would you say if someone said, "That was the worst book I have ever read"?

The following is one paragraph from Matthew's written book project:

For Love of the Game by Michael Shaara is a book about baseball and a love story all comprised in one. What better two topics to have written about? It takes place in the present day Major Leagues where Billy Chapel seems to be past his prime as a big league pitcher. After spending seventeen seasons with Atlanta, and surely headed for the Hall of Fame, the organization wants to trade away the best pitcher in baseball history. Billy Chapel is now left with the decision whether to end his baseball career on a high note with the team he loves or prolong his career with a city that wants to squeeze a few more years out of him.

"Write what you know" is perhaps the most common precept in the teaching of writing. These expressive responses to books they've read enable my students, as James Atwater writes,

to make sense for themselves of what they have seen or read or done or talked about by composing it for themselves In their own words. Thus expressive writing is fundamental to learning —in any subject matter—because it enables children to internalize knowledge, to make it
part of themselves, by putting it together in their own terms. (Lightfoot and Martin 1983, 109)

Writing Center Editor Experience

Matthew served as an editor for many of his schoolmates. The value of the editing experience is well-articulated in a portion of his quarter-end reflection:

> Reading other people's papers has also helped my own writing. Both extremes can help your
> writing, whether the paper is horrendous or brilliant. Correct[ing] the poorly written papers
> can give you an opportunity to recognize where mistakes are being made. This can be trans-
> ferred into your own papers by recognizing when you make the same mistakes. By reading the
> well-written papers, you can get an idea of what good writing is all about.

Virtually all community colleges, colleges, and universities have student-staffed writing
centers on campus. If you're preparing your students for that next level of post-secondary
study, having a writing center at your school could be an important consideration.

Feedback, Assessment, and Evaluation

Matthew received letter responses about his finished portfolio from a student colleague
(Kristi M), his mother, and me. Normally two students respond to each portfolio during a
portfolio-reading weekend, but for some reason Matthew's portfolio didn't receive the second student commentary. It's important to note that all students were required to spend
one Saturday or Sunday morning—about three hours—in school during the academic year
to read and respond to portfolios. They had the option to come in more often for extra
credit; Matthew took advantage of that opportunity.

I'm including one paragraph from each portfolio response letter to Matthew:

Kristi's Response:

Awesome introduction to "Hopes for the Future"! After reading about 20 billion Life Work
papers, I bet Mr. Kent loves when people write stuff like you did. Wooo, psychology! That's
what my Work paper is all about too. You know, in a way that paper kind of ties in with your
other two. Did you plan that?! Your first two papers describe tons of things about you that
would be really impressive qualities for a psychologist. It's especially cool that you are involved
in so many things. I always thought a well-rounded person would make a better psychologist
simply because they'd have more background for understanding their patients. I mean, the
more you experience during your own life, the more you can help people understand what's
going on in their own. Nice choice, and good luck!!

Teacher's Response

It has been a pleasure to have you as a classmate here in Room 109. What you've shown me
in these past eight weeks is the attitude and the work of a scholar. I do not say this lightly. In
class discussions, you add your thinking without being domineering. You listen well to others; you enjoy a good laugh; and you know when someone is struggling. You're a sensitive

member of our class. You give us balance and you provide, through modeling, a quiet kind of leadership. Any college will be fortunate to have a person of your caliber on campus.

Mom's Response

What an incredible journey! Thank you for allowing us to visit so many facets of who you are and what you stand for. I remember walking the Martin Road before you were born wondering who you were and what kind of person you'd become some day. Then you arrived and it was so easy to see and hear your likes and dislikes…[A]s I sit and read this portfolio this evening, I am filled with so much emotion. You're ready to fly. You've touched my heart with your words, Matt.

Portfolio response letters help students hear the story of their writing and of themselves as people. Breaking away from the single teacher response is critical if we hope to provide our students with authentic feedback. A few years before Matthew entered Room 109, several of my students and I were asked to present at a college of education not so far from our hometown. Kathy, a senior, summed up her portfolio experience by holding up two artifacts:

This is my rank card. It tells you with numbers how a teacher thought I did with their work. This is my portfolio. It shows you with words and ideas what I think and what other people think of me and my work.

Add to Kathy's words those of Peter Elbow, and we begin to see how a portfolio pedagogy can inspire student work and thereby learning:

Portfolio assessment helps the learning climate because it reinforces continuing effort and improvement: it encourages students to try to revise and improve poor work rather than to feel punished or to give up because of the poor work they started with. It gets away from a "putting time in" model for learning and instead makes for a more forward-pointing dynamic of "building toward your best" (1986, 167).

Let me highlight the various components to the feedback, assessment, and evaluation features of this classroom. First, and most important, feedback to Matthew and his colleagues was ongoing. Editorial comments on papers, oral and written feedback for book project presentations, in-class discussions on class themes, portfolio response letters, one-on-one teacher conferences, portfolio assessment sheets (Figure 4), and student reflections all combine to give the portfolio author an emerging picture of his work (Figure 5).

When you review Matthew's assessment sheets (Figure 4), you'll need to know that he received five additional points for writing letters in the summer, volunteering to respond to portfolios on a Saturday morning, working as a student-editor, and revising all of his papers thoroughly.

Matthew's Reflection

In his five-page, end-of-quarter written reflection, Matthew constructs himself as a writer:

Throughout the past eight weeks, my writing process has changed immensely. First, I feel I am a much better writer now. I owe this to working harder and to the people who edit my papers. Compared to papers I have written in the past, I feel I spend a great deal more time writing. I now look at each sentence and see how I can improve the wording so it sounds more professional. My word choice has also improved greatly because of my vocabulary and the use of a thesaurus. My editors have refined my writing by giving me a standard of the

---

109 Portfolio Assessment

Name ___Matt___
Date ___First___
Class Period ___F1___

Year in School ___Junior___
Assessment

95 *High honors. Congratulations*

Books Read:

Difficulty:	Very Strong	(Strong)	OK	Weak
Amount:	Very Strong	(Strong)	OK	Weak
Variety:	(Very Strong)	Strong	OK	Weak

Projects:

Interesting:	Very Strong	(Strong)	OK	Weak
Artistic:	(Very Strong)	Strong	OK	Weak
Original:	(Very Strong	Strong)	OK	Weak

Journals:

Interesting:	Very Strong	(Strong)	OK	Weak
Diverse:	(Very Strong)	Strong	OK	Weak
Amount:	Very Strong	(Strong)	OK	Weak

Paper Assessment:

Topic Development:	(Very Strong)	Strong	OK	Weak
Organization:	Very Strong	(Strong)	OK	Weak
Details:	Very Strong	(Strong)	OK	Weak
Sentences:	Very Strong	(Strong)	OK	Weak
Wording:	Very Strong	(Strong)	OK	Weak
Revision:	(Very Strong)	Strong	OK	Weak
Mechanics:	(Very Strong)	Strong	OK	Weak
Appearance:	(Very Strong)	Strong	OK	Weak

Figure 4 Assessment Sheets: Front

rights and wrongs of English. From my first paper to my last, I believe you can see a big difference between first drafts. I'm not continuing to make the same mistakes as the portfolio progresses. Instead, I try to solve some of my problems from the previous papers.

Throughout his reflection Matthew's tone is upbeat. He feels successful and knows pretty much what needs to be done as he moves on to the next academic quarter and his next portfolio. He feels in charge of his learning and, in fact, he is. But he's not alone.

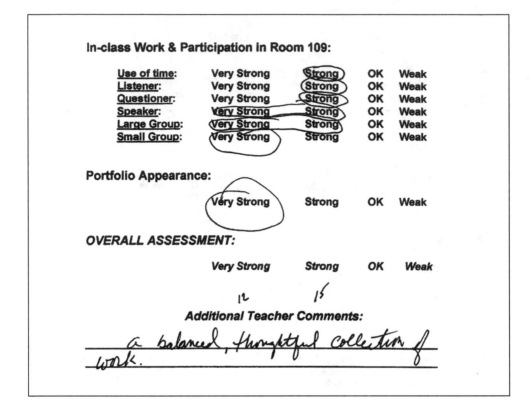

In-class Work & Participation in Room 109:

Use of time:	Very Strong	Strong	OK	Weak
Listener:	Very Strong	Strong	OK	Weak
Questioner:	Very Strong	Strong	OK	Weak
Speaker:	Very Strong	Strong	OK	Weak
Large Group:	Very Strong	Strong	OK	Weak
Small Group:	Very Strong	Strong	OK	Weak

Portfolio Appearance:

Very Strong   Strong   OK   Weak

OVERALL ASSESSMENT:

Very Strong   Strong   OK   Weak

12   15

Additional Teacher Comments:

a balanced, thoughtful collection of work.

Figure 4 Assessment Sheets: Back (Continued)

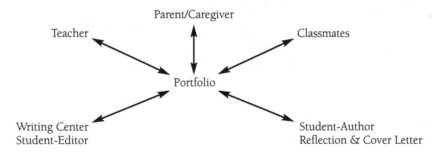

Figure 5 Room 109 Portfolio Response System

Suggested Reading

Allen, David. 1998. *Assessing Student Learning: From Grading to Understanding*. New York: Teachers College Press.

Works Cited

Blythe, Tina, David Allen, and Barbara S. Powell. 1999. *Looking Together at Students' Work: A Companion Guide to Assessing Student Learning*. New York: Teachers College Press.

Britton, James. 1970. *Language and Learning*. Harmondsworth, UK: Penguin.

Britton, James, T. Burgess, N. Martin, A. McLeod, and H. Rosen. 1975. *The Development of Writing Abilities Ages 11–18*. London: Macmillan.

Claggett, Fran. 1996. *A Measure of Success: From Assignment to Assessment in English Language Arts*. Portsmouth, NH: Heinemann-Boynton/Cook.

Elbow, Peter. 1986. *Embracing Contraries: Explorations in Learning and Teaching*. New York: Oxford University Press.

Kent, Richard. 2000. *Beyond Room 109: Developing Independent Study Projects*. Portsmouth, NH: Heinemann.

———. 2006. *A Guide to Creating Student-Staffed Writing Centers, Grades 6–12*. New York: Peter Lang Publishing.

———. 2004. "Revision: Different Editors for Different Drafts?" *New England Reading Journal*. 40: 47–51.

———. 1997. *Room 109: The Promise of a Portfolio Classroom*. Portsmouth, NH: Heinemann.

Lightfoot, Martin, and Nancy Martin, eds. 1983. *The Word for Teaching is Learning: Essays for James Britton*. Portsmouth, NH: Heinemann.

Martin, Nancy. 1983. *Mostly About Writing*. Portsmouth, NH: Heinemann-Boynton/Cook.

Moffett, James. 1983. *Teaching the Universe of Discourse*. Portsmouth, NH: Heinemann.

Pradl, Gordon, ed. 1982. *Prospect and Retrospect: Selected Essays of James Britton*. Portsmouth, NH: Heinemann.

Rosenblatt, Louise. 1978. *The Reader the Text the Poem: The Transactional Theory of the Literary*. Carbondale IL: Southern Illinois University Press.

Strong, William. 2001. *Coaching Writing: The Power of Guided Practice*. Portsmouth, NH: Heinemann-Boynton/Cook.

———. 2005. *Write for Insight: Empowering Content Learning, Grades 6–12*. Boston: Allyn & Bacon.

Wiggins, G. 1993. *Assessing Student Performance: Exploring the Purpose and Limits of Testing*. San Francisco: Jossey-Bass.

Young and Rubicam Foundation. 1991. *The One Place: A New Role for American Schools*. New York: St. Martin's Press.

7

FAQ on Grading and Assessment

Thomas Newkirk and Richard Kent

There are any number of publishers, software designers, and high-priced educational consultants who market evaluation systems for writing assessment—they promise to lift the burden of grading from our shoulders; they offer to remove any taint of subjectivity and uncertainty, to ease the workload, to help us arrive at some golden, indisputable number that can be assigned to a piece of writing. In some cases they have programmed computers to look for stylistic features correlated with good writing, so the human element can be eliminated altogether.

We, however, believe that anxiety goes with the territory. Show us a teacher fully at ease with a grading system, one who is sure that his 85 is reliably lower than his 86, and we will show you a fraud or at least someone mildly delusional. In this section we will do our best to deal with the nagging questions any writing teacher must face—all the while realizing that that there is an inescapable, subjective element to grading.

Should I grade everything a student writes?

No. If everything is focused on the grade, students will read your comments as justifications for the grade, and you will begin to write those comments as justifications. Revision may turn into a kind of unpleasant bargaining—"If I change this paragraph will my grade go up to a B+?" We suggest that grading be deferred until the student has produced a body of work that can be assessed. In this way, teacher comments can focus on what is going well in the writing and improvements that can be made through revision.

We also feel that there should be a strand of writing—journal writing and in-class writing—that can be read and quickly assessed with a check for a satisfactory effort. Students might select their most effective pieces of informal writing to be included in their portfolio for a grade.

What should a grade be based on—quality of writing, effort, improvement?
This is the most important question a teacher must ask. It might seem logical and fair to base grades solely on writing quality—but then a good writer who makes no progress would be evaluated more highly than a less proficient writer who makes great progress. On the other hand, a system that gives top grades for effort and diligence may offer the student a false picture of his or her abilities. The key, it seems to us, is to reward students for diligence *and* for the quality of writing they produce. Here is one way this might be done.

There can be a set of performance goals which might include expectations for types of writing to be attempted, for revision, for participation in response groups, for meeting deadlines, and for self-assessment. A student who meets these performance goals will receive a grade no lower than a B. Higher grades will be awarded to students who, in addition to meeting performance goals, produce writing that is distinguished in some way (particularly effective use of detail, voice, complexity of thinking, quality of research). Students will fall below the B level if they fail to meet performance goals.

Such a system provides a strong reward for the hardworking student who may, at least at the beginning of the course, be behind some of his or her peers. And it recognizes that top grades must be earned both by meeting performance goals and by producing distinguished writing.

What are rubrics?
Rubrics have long been used in large-scale assessment, and increasingly they have been used in writing classrooms. Typically they specify the criteria (and sometimes the weighting of the criteria) that will be used in evaluating a piece of writing. One of the first rubrics, the Diederich Scale, was developed by the Educational Testing Service in the 1960s to get reliable evaluations of writing. The scale looks like this:

General Merit

	Low		Middle		High	
Ideas	2	4	6	8	10	
Organization	2	4	6	8	10	
Wording	1	2	3	4	5	
Style, Flavor	1	2	3	4	5	

_____

Mechanics

	Low		Middle		High
Usage	1	2	3	4	5
Punctuation	1	2	3	4	5
Spelling	1	2	3	4	5
Presentation	1	2	3	4	5

_____

Total   _____

The Diederich Scale would be considered an analytic scale because it evaluates various components of writing. State assessments tend to use holistic scales, with papers given a single score on a scale that may run from 1–6. For each number on the continuum there is a description of the proficiency level, often referring to the same kinds of traits that are used in the analytic scale.

The Diederich Scale is a generic rubric that is designed for use with a variety of types of writing. Other rubrics can be tailored to the kind of writing being evaluated. For example, a rubric for persuasive writing might focus on claims and evidence, while one on narrative writing might focus on descriptive detail.

Many of the currently popular rubrics for evaluating writing are variations on the Diederich scale. For example, the widely used 6+1 Trait® Writing focuses on the following criteria:

- Ideas, the heart of the message;
- Organization, the internal structure of the piece;
- Voice, the personal tone and flavor of the author's message;
- Word Choice, the vocabulary a writer chooses to convey meaning;
- Sentence Fluency, the rhythm and flow of the language;
- Conventions, the mechanical correctness; and
- Presentation, how the writing actually looks on the page.

How useful are rubrics for assessing writing in the classroom?
This, of course, depends on how they are used. Rubrics, when used in the discussion of student writing, help provide a critical language for discussing writing quality. These rubrics may have even more credibility in the classroom if students generate them inductively following their own discussion of the merits of various pieces of student writing. To the extent rubrics facilitate a discussion of writing quality, they are clearly useful.

But we have also seen rubrics used as a quasi-mathematical shortcut to assessment. Students may receive a paper back with scores for ideas, organization, etc. leading to a total score. It looks so official and objective. But what does it mean to get a six out of ten on organization? What does that tell the writer? What confusion did the writer's organization cause? We believe that writers need to know how human beings read their work, and ultimately they need to create an inner reader that can anticipate the response of actual readers. Simply being given a number for a criterion is no substitute for a real reader's response.

Finally, we both know of teachers who use programs such as 6+1 Trait® Writing as a week-by-week, month-by-month curriculum: "This week we'll focus on ideas and next week we'll hit organization." As writers, we know this approach is doomed because this is not the way writers work.

How should we prepare students for state assessments?
Timed writing assessments are unavoidable—and will remain so. We believe that this form of writing should be treated as a genre that students need practice mastering. We reject the idea, however, that a writing program should focus exclusively or primarily on test preparation. Students in strong writing programs—where they attempt a range of genres, get feedback, revise and edit—usually do very well on these types of assessments.

It is also clear that teaching students rigidly formulaic, predictable writing (the five-paragraph model) may prevent them from scoring in the lower range, but it will also probably keep them out of the higher range as well—where evaluators will expect a distinctive writing voice, complexity of thought, or the ability to think against conventional wisdom.

Here are some prudent steps to prepare students for this kind of writing assessment:

- Share previously released prompts with students, and have them use the state rubric to score some of the released papers.
- Attempt one or two of the released prompts under test-like conditions and use the rubric on their own papers.
- In preparation to writing, stress the importance of reading the prompt carefully, taking time to plot out an essay response, and to writing it in paragraphs. Answers written without any indication of paragraphing almost automatically get lower marks.
- Many prompts for the secondary level ask for some form of argument. Stress the importance of claims and evidence.
- Students should be willing to take a contrarian or unpopular viewpoint. The SAT test prompts are notorious for asking students to choose between two positions. Here, for example, is one of the prompts posted by the College Board:

  Are people more likely to be productive and successful when they ignore the opinions of others? Plan and write an essay in which you develop your point of view on this issue. Support your position with reasoning and examples taken from your reading, studies, experience, or observations.

  The obvious approach would be to take a side, where a more complex—and probably successful—essay will work against this choosing of sides to complicate the issue (though that's not easy to do in twenty minutes).

What is portfolio assessment?

It is useful to make a distinction between portfolio assessment and portfolio pedagogy. In portfolio assessment, the student is often asked to select pieces of writing done over a term that represent his or her best work. This writing has typically been revised and edited (hopefully). Often the student writes a cover letter in which there is a self-evaluation of the writing enclosed. Using portfolios in this way may ease the burden on the teacher to be constantly giving grades during a term.

Portfolio pedagogy is best described in Rich's book, *Room 109: The Promise of a Portfolio Classroom* (Kent 1997). The portfolio in his classroom is more than a collection of assigned writing as you can see from "Matthew's Portfolio" (Chapter 6). Rather, Rich gave broad guidelines about the kinds of work that needed to go into the portfolio—responses to reading, journal entries, longer written projects, descriptions of projects—and students are given considerable freedom to make decisions about the focus and pace of the writing. Rich also builds into the process extensive levels of commentary and feedback—from parents, from classmates and student-editors in the school's student-staffed writing center, and from the writer. The class curriculum is based on a series of themes (for example, humor, balance, diversity) and students are asked to represent these themes in their portfolio writing, projects (artwork, for instance), and class presentations.

Because of the choice involved in the Room 109 portfolios, students are encouraged to consider these themes—perhaps a dominant interest in their lives—that can hold the collection together. The end result is a book that the student creates.

One issue that any form of portfolio use creates is providing ongoing information to students (and parents) about student progress. Some teachers give in-process estimates or provisional grades along the way. This pressure for frequent grades is likely to increase as schools make grades accessible to parents through the Internet.

How can I respond usefully to writing, given the heavy teaching load I have?

This is a perennial problem for English teachers. Any system of response and evaluation must be workable. There are, to be sure, those teachers who write as much on a student's paper as the student, who spend hours, days, weekends—their lives—writing responses. We admire these teachers, but we wouldn't like to be like them. The first requirement for any system of response grading is that it be sustainable. An exhaustive marking system is, well, exhausting. It leads to burnout and limiting the amount of writing students attempt. And, in the end, the number of trials—the repeated attempts at various kinds of writing—may be more valuable than infrequent writing with extensive teacher commentary.

The goal, then, is to maintain the flow of student writing and to use your time judiciously in giving response. So here are some ideas:

- As we noted earlier, some informal or in-class writing can be read quickly and given a check to indicate it is satisfactory. You might indicate with a star or check sections that are particularly effective—but not give any additional response.
- When you do write comments, focus on one or two primary concerns. For inexperienced writers, the major issues usually have to do with focus (what is the most important thing you are saying) and elaboration (where do you need to say more).
- Don't underestimate the power of "intelligent liking." Don Murray, Pulitzer Prize winner and writing guru, has always stressed the importance of building on strengths, rather than focusing on problems. This provides emotional support for the writer, but it also provides useful feedback on what is working.
- Not every writing problem must be—or can be—solved on a particular piece of writing. Remember that you can go a long distance by taking small steps if you take enough of them.

Can peer evaluation help in assessment?

Peer evaluation can be useful if there is specific guidance. If students are just asked to respond, they typically offer vague comments like "I can relate to this" and then begin talking about what happened last weekend. It is often useful to ask them to prepare a response in writing before they meet with the writer. We are including below a set of questions that can be used for personal essay writing:

Response Sheet—paper and author _____

1. List three details, word choices, or other parts of this paper that you find effective.
   1.
   2.
   3.

2. State in one sentence what you see as the major point or intention of the paper.

3. Does the writer provide detail and support to help convey the main impression or point of the paper?

4. Is there any place in the paper where the writer could have provided more information? Where is that place?

5. What other suggestions do you have for the writer to revise the paper? For example, are there more and better ways to make the point of the paper?

   Writer's response to these comments. Based on this response, and your own reading of the paper, what changes would improve the paper in a revision?

Another very simple but useful strategy is to have the writer mark his or her paper in the margins: a single line for a section they are not satisfied with and a double line alongside a section that they thought effective.

We find it easier to respond to a piece of writing if this self and peer evaluation has gone on first. We often end up agreeing or elaborating on an observation made by the writer.

You haven't mentioned correcting mechanical errors. Are you suggesting those are not important?
Of course, they are important, but we don't think they should be a primary concern with beginning writers. We are convinced that correcting all mechanical errors is unproductive and time-consuming work. We also believe that gaining mastery over the conventions of writing comes primarily from extensive writing and reading—more than any error correction we do. But there are clearly things we can do as teachers.

- Often students could correct certain problems, if they saw them. But they don't proofread, or they do it so quickly they don't see anything. So when students hand in their writing, we can set aside the last five or so minutes of class for them to slowly proofread and correct anything they see on the draft. They often catch quite a lot.
- I also draw sentence editing/correcting exercises from the students' own work. We edit together maybe five sentences a class.

- We can assign groups in the class to teach a particular punctuation mark, particularly ones that students tend to avoid: the dash, parentheses, colon, semi-colon. Many students are so unsure of punctuating dialogue that they fail to include it in their writing. In other words, the problem is not so much that students make errors as they don't use the resources that are available.

- If a student makes serious mechanical errors, I find that the only solution is to sit down with him or her and review a section of a paper. Usually the students is making the same kind of error over and over again. I try to identify what that error is, show how it can be corrected on that one section of the paper, and ask that the student see if he or she can find any more examples on the rest of the paper.

What is NCTE's position on assessment?

NCTE Beliefs about the Teaching of Writing
Writing Study Group of the NCTE Executive Committee
November 2004

#11. "Assessment of writing involves complex, informed, human judgment."

Assessment of writing occurs for different purposes. Sometimes, a teacher assesses in order to decide what the student has achieved and what he or she still needs to learn. Sometimes, an entity beyond the classroom assesses a student's level of achievement in order to say whether they can go on to some new educational level that requires the writer to be able to do certain things. At other times, school authorities require a writing test in order to pressure teachers to teach writing. Still other times, as in a history exam, the assessment of writing itself is not the point, but the quality of the writing is evaluated almost in passing. In any of these assessments of writing, complex judgments are formed. Such judgments should be made by human beings, not machines. Furthermore, they should be made by professionals who are informed about writing, development, and the field of literacy education.

What does this mean for teaching?
Instructors of composition should know about various methods of assessment of student writing. Instructors must recognize the difference between formative and summative evaluation and be prepared to evaluate students' writing from both perspectives. By formative evaluation here, we mean provisional, ongoing, in-process judgments about what students know and what to teach next. By summative evaluation, we mean final judgments about the quality of student work. Teachers of writing must also be able to recognize the developmental aspects of writing ability and devise appropriate lessons for students at all levels of expertise.

Teachers need to understand at least the following in order to be excellent at writing assessment:

- How to find out what student writers can do, informally, on an ongoing basis.
- How to use that assessment in order to decide what and how to teach next.
- How to assess occasionally, less frequently than above, in order to form judgments about the quality of student writing and learning.
- How to assess ability and knowledge across multiple different writing engagements
- What the features of good writing are, appropriate to the context and purposes of the teaching and learning.
- What the elements of a constructive process of writing are, appropriate to the context and purposes of the teaching and learning.
- What growth in writing looks like, the developmental aspects of writing ability.
- Ways of assessing student metacognitive process of the reading/writing connection.
- How to recognize in student writing (both in their texts and in their actions) the nascent potential for excellence at the features and processes desired.
- How to deliver useful feedback, appropriate for the writer and the situation.
- How to analyze writing situations for their most essential elements, so that assessment is not of everything about writing all at once, but rather is targeted to objectives.
- How to analyze and interpret both qualitative and quantitative writing assessments.
- How to evaluate electronic texts.
- How to use portfolios to assist writers in their development.
- How self-assessment and reflection contribute to a writer's development and ability to move among genres, media, and rhetorical situations.

Any last comments?

There is still a huge subjective factor in grading. For example, we can't put out of our mind the effect a grade will have on the student. Some students will accept a B+, others (along with their parents) will think that their future is ruined. Do we practice conflict avoidance, even subconsciously? We are very close to some students—and others remind us of the students we intensely disliked in high school. We may know that one student was tending to his terminally ill grandmother while he was completing his final research essay. Can we factor all of this out and be objective?

Probably not. It's a very human business. We stumble along trying to be as fair as we can.

Suggested Reading

Diederich, Paul. 1974. *Measuring Growth in English*. Urbana, Illinois: National Council of Teachers of English.

Elbow, Peter. February 1993. "Ranking, Evaluating, and Liking: Sorting Out Three Forms of Judgment." *College English.* 187–206.

Hillocks, George. 2002. *The Testing Trap.* New York: Teachers College Press.

Kent, Richard. 1997. *Room 109: The Promise of the Portfolio Classroom.* Portsmouth, NH: Heinemann.

Kirby, Dan, Dawn Latta Kirby, and Tom Liner. 2004. *Inside Out: Strategies for Teaching Writing*, 3rd ed. Portsmouth, NH: Heinemann. See especially Chapter 14, "Grading and Evaluating."

Spandel, Vicki, 2004. *Creating Writers Through 6-Trait Instruction.* (Fourth Edition). Upper Saddle River, NJ: Allyn and Bacon.

Tobin, Lad. 1991. *Writing Relationships: What Really Happens in a Composition Class.* Portsmouth, NH: Heinemann. See especially Chapter 4, "Responding to Student Writing II: What We Really Think About When We Think About Grades."

White, Edward. 2006. *Assigning, Responding, Evaluating: A Writing Teacher's Guide.* Boston: St. Martins Press.

8

The School Essay

Tracking Movement of the Mind

Gretchen Bernabei

Gretchen Bernabei has taught grades four through eleven in San Antonio's public schools for nearly twenty years. She spent nine months "working backstage" at the Texas Education Agency's Division of Student Assessment, where she participated in the thoughtful test-building process. Her first book, Why We Must Run With Scissors: Voice Lessons in Persuasive Writing, *co-authored with Barry Lane, shares her philosophy and many of her favorite lessons. Her other books include* Reviving the Essay: How to Teach Structure without Formula *and* Lightening in a Bottle: Visual Prompts for Insights.

Why the Five-Paragraph School Essay Has Enjoyed a Long (if Tortured) Life

Say the word *essay* to students and you will probably hear a groan. Ask a teacher, "Would you like to read fifteen of my best student essays?" and you'll hear worse than that. The word *essay* even sounds like a hiss. You could try masking the essay assignment with different language, calling it a paper, a composition, or an expository piece, and the resulting dread would be the same. School essays don't have a very inviting reputation.

Essays in their natural habitats are a different kind of writing, however. People listen to them on the radio; they purchase magazines that feature absorbing essays; they email compelling essays to their friends along with "you-have-to-read-this" messages.

What are the differences between the dreaded school essay and the celebrated real-world essay? Traditionally, school essays are comprised of five paragraphs, featuring a thesis statement in the introduction. Real-world essays range in length and structure, and few treat you to a summary in the opening paragraph. Not many students look forward to writing school essays, and not many teachers would voluntarily read them. School essays are boring to write and boring to read. Essays in the real world are completely different.

Why, then, does the five-paragraph essay persist? The answer lies in a classroom of thirty-four students, each with blank paper and an assignment. You can hear it: "Miss…what do I say?" Without some kind of guided structure, many struggling students would be unable to produce writing at all. They need help. So to help students, we give them some kind of scaffold, some organizational help to develop their thoughts on paper. We guide them through the simplest, most accessible thing we know how to teach, and students try their hardest to give us exactly what we ask for. When it comes to essays, we just don't ask for much. Even when students' essays have sparkling introductions, include zippy, memorable language, and make profound points—even when they are A+ papers—150 of them sound remarkably similar. In his NCTE (National Council of Teachers of English) monograph, recently reprinted by Discover Writing Press, Thomas Newkirk explains, "I suspect that many teachers teach the form—or variants of it—because they see no teachable alternative" (2005, 40).

A Few Teachable Alternatives

In order to find alternatives, we have to consider what essays are. What's the purpose of an essay? Michel de Montaigne originated the form hundreds of years ago so that his family and friends would know him better, or so he said in the foreword of his essay collection (1957, 2). That means essays are the equivalent of verbal scrapbooking, surprisingly enough. Thomas Newkirk sets out the philosophical and structural differences between these essays and the traditional fleshless school essays:

> At the beginning of the *Phaedrus*, Socrates meets young Phaedrus and asks him, "Where have you been, and where are you going?" It is, I believe, more than just a casual question—it is the question that we need to ask students. If writing is to be a "unique mode of thinking," we should ask how writing can foster and track movement of the mind (2005, 28).

The purpose of the essay is *to track movement of the mind*. Our minds do continually move. And essays must be relatively short—shorter, say, than a novel or a full-length movie script. So, essays could comfortably track movement of no more than a glimpse into a person's thinking.

Therefore, one way to write an essay would be to model after Socrates' questions. Look at the questions below, and find a pair that you could answer in just a few pages:

- What is one thing you know, and how do you know it?
- What have you done, and what has that shown you?
- What have you seen, and what do you think about it?
- Where are you now, and how did you get there?
- What is one thing you think, and what has led you to think that?
- What is one thing you believe, and how did that belief evolve?

All of these questions are identical in the way that they help pinpoint one aspect of the relationship between these two factors:

In tracking the movement of our mind, why would we need both experience and thoughts? Writing about what we know without adding any experience would produce something philosophical (perhaps) or intellectual (perhaps) or opinionated (undoubtedly) without any interesting how-do-you-know evidence. Writing about what we've experienced without divulging what we think about it is like writing a diary that involves only the writer, and the reader's just not invited in. Adding the thought to it makes the experiences belong to everyone. In the words of teacher Shelly Bell, adding the thought "transfers the story from you to everyone. It isn't just about you anymore; your life lesson applies to all of us. It makes it universal."

Some writers would be able to take off with these questions and no further assistance. Other writers (including most of the writers in my classes) appreciate a step-by-step process, at least until they become confident and inventive. Breaking down a complex process into concrete steps is the craft, the fun of teaching. For essay writing, these steps can work:

1. Decide what to say. If the content centers on what we know and what we've experienced, then either of those would be a suitable entry point.

2. Design a structure. For this step we'll throw out the standard five-paragraph essay for now and try out some other text structures, using kernel essays. These will enable the writer to check the logic, flow, and effect on a reader in order to decide if the kernel is worth expanding into a full essay.

3. Flesh it out. Every writing teacher carries an arsenal of ways to take a sentence and elaborate, or deepen, or say more, or explain.

Decide What to Say

An essay could begin with a memory, a life lesson, or a topic. To begin with a memory, have students write a "quicklist" and guide them to list moments in their memories in different categories.

The instruction would go like this:

"Students, number your papers down the side, one through twelve. [Pause and let them do this.] Let's talk about the difference between a moment and an era. How long does an era last?" [Solicit answers.] "How long does a moment last? [Point out how many students clicked their fingers to answer.] So now we're going to think of moments from your life. We'll make a list. It's a Quicklist.

"For numbers one, two, and three, write down words or phrases which remind you of moments in your life when you were proud of someone.

"For numbers four, five, and six, write down moments in your life when you had to struggle in some way.

"For seven, eight, and nine, list memories in addition to the first six, memories you'd like to keep if robots were erasing your memory tomorrow.

"For number ten, write a memory involving an animal, either someone's pet or a wild animal, any animal memory.

"For number eleven, write a memory involving a gift you gave someone else.

"For number twelve, write down a time someone put money into your hands, any money. A nickel, a dollar, a check, any memory about money."

Now students have a beginning topics bank which might look like Eric's below.

Eric's Quicklist

1. the time my brother learned a song on the guitar
2. my dad's promotion
3. when my mom decided to go to beauty school
4. trying to get into the school for the arts
5. when my brother was throwing a fit in the restaurant and I had to take care of him
6. when I was picked on in elementary school
7. when Christian was born
8. when I got into the school for the arts
9. the time I learned to play guitar
10. when the dog bit me when I was 10
11. the bead animal I made for my grandpa
12. my uncle's handshake and the $20 bill

In order to turn one of these memories into an essay, ask the students to choose a memory then write a two-minute version of it. During these two minutes, they will deeply revisit that moment as they write. Now they will have what they experienced, and all they'll need is what they think to turn this memory into an essay. You can ask them to cover their two-minute writing with their hand and listen to your voice. "Of all the millions of moments you've experienced in your life," you will tell them, "this one bubbled up to the top for reasons of your own. It's valuable to you not just because of the memory itself, but also because it came to you loaded with life lessons. After this moment in your life, there were some things you understood differently than you had understood them before. Think of one of those life lessons and begin one more sentence with 'I've learned that sometimes…' and finish that sentence."

Here's what Eric's looks like:

> I was at a family gathering, and I was getting ready to leave. I was saying good-bye to everyone and I went to say good-bye to my uncle. I shook his hand and pulled away. He had put a $20-bill in my hand. It wasn't the $20-dollar bill that made me happy; it was the fact that the family gave it to me for nothing. (I've learned that.) Sometimes the gift of family is a lot better than any gift that can be given.

In this case, we started with memories, or what we experienced, and added the life lesson, or what we think. The sense of play in this writing happens when the writer discovers a life lesson that his experience leads him to, or earned insights. Eric did not sit down to write about "the gift of family," nor did the teacher ask him to write on that topic. Eric might choose to expand this into a full essay.

Or the essay could begin with the thought. One way to stockpile thoughts is to do a great quotations search, to copy and keep quotations that students find compelling or true. Another way is to build lists of life lessons, or truisms, that they've learned along the way, like this list written by students looking at photos.

> You can find adventures anywhere in life. —Jake
>
> You are never alone in this world. —Maria
>
> There is only so much that your body can take. —Jeff
>
> Siblings often fight and argue. —Pat
>
> Kids like to take risks. —Abdalla
>
> The army is always looking to recruit young people. —Chris
>
> Kids don't realize that as they grow up they will drift away from each other. —Melissa
>
> Helping friends makes the day much better. —Samantha
>
> You can trust only your family. — Rudy
>
> Don't take your brothers and sisters for granted; you never know what might happen. —Sharon
>
> Big sisters or brothers set the example for younger brothers and sisters. —Perla
>
> Disobeying your parents can turn out to be fun but can get you into trouble. —Heather
>
> Enemies will hurt you, but friends will always be there when you are in need. —Jih Hye
>
> Friends have bonds. —Brian
>
> People should help one another in times of struggle. —Stephen
>
> All the good you do always comes back in a great way. —Ryan
>
> Young people are active. —Adam
>
> People will drop what they are doing to help someone else out. —Sarah

Another way to create a bank of thoughts is to find life lessons in songs, in literature, in movies, or in conversation to copy and keep.

In addition to using a memory or a thought, an essay could start simply with a topic. If you look at the table of contents in Montaigne's collection of essays, you will see titles like "Of drunkenness," "Of conscience," "Of smells," "Of sleep," "Of a monstrous child". After asking students to list four or five random subjects they could talk about for a while, you can compile a handy list of interesting subjects, not altogether unlike Montaigne's (Figure 1).

Design a structure

For structure, students learn first to borrow from the teacher; second to notice, capture, and imitate structures from literature or mentor texts; and ultimately to invent their own. The question that needs to be answered by the structure choice is "How do I know this?" Students think about how their mind has moved around this thought, and choose whichever structure would serve them best. The teacher models how to work a thought

the trauma of the emergency room
the heartbreak of breaking up
the drama of high school
the fun of playing volleyball
the stupidity of teenagers
the distrust of flying piranhas
the heartbreak of losing someone
the irony of toothpicks
the throes of passion
the trauma of cows
the feeling of outrage
the heat of light
the delay of the inevitable
the end of reason
the state of being
the feeling of air
the hurt of loss
the passion of love
the emotional breakdown of death
the excitement of friends
the smiling of a happy friend
the fury of hatred
the mystery of life
the instinct of survival
the feeling of winning a game
the drama of flowers
the loneliness of being away
the heartbreak of paradise
the disregard of the public
the excitement of winning
the heartbreak of hurt
the smell of an old book
the joy of love
the drama of girls' lives
the pleasure of fun
the sadness of death
the belating of laughter
the glory of Earth

the love of bubblegum
the joy of writing
the thrill of flying
the confusion of life
the excitement of new experiences
the trauma of dance
the heartbreak of games
the trauma of being lost
the sorrow of war
the horror of darkness
the tragedy of time
the love of football
the excitement of victory
the loss of innocence
the killing of souls
the adrenaline rush of playing a show
the heartbreak of first love
the shame of eating alone
the sense of fear
the warmth of a midsummer's day
the false sense of security
the drama of friendship
the excitement of summer
the insanity of stress
the happiness of life
the trauma of kitty litter
the joy of a roller coaster
the melancholy of secrets
the fear of truth
the loneliness of heartbreak
the heat of the night
the stupidity of adults
the inquisitiveness of speech
the love of war
the love of peace
the beauty of man
the sickness of school
sadness of a baby
the boulevard of broken hearts
fear of war in Iraq

clothes hanging on the line
suds in the bucket
flower pens
bottle rockets
yellow custard
whiskey
redneck women
Taco Cabana
busses
Frisbees
redneck women
lowriders
doorknobs
key chains
pina coladas
soccer balls
dead men
chocolate labs
blue eyes
license plates
white T-shirts
muddy tires
Joshua trees
burnt CDs
coffeemaker
braided bracelets
ballpoint pens
cowboy hats
Superman
toilet paper
raging bull
whipping boy
another planet
red balloons
baby carrots
hospital beds
Barbie dolls
white crustacean
legal documents
diving board
jack of hearts
tears in your eyes
diaries
flip-flops
lollipops
crocodile
hospital sheets
money
hairballs
hometown
ice cream
houses
horses

home
paintball
guitar strings
rocking chairs
trains
tortillas
paper
cheese
graves
phones
church
waffles
boxes
beaches
folders
trashcans
diamonds
books
saddles
monkeys
golf club
clothespins
cruise ships
hairspray
sponge
tractors
windows
cake pans
confetti
lying
tongues
parties
smile
eyes
aces
rice
ducks
feet
eggs
road
stairs
flag
hair
dogs
stars
boys
trees
guns
pens
VCRs
fire
cars
wax
pie

Figure 1

through the structure and demonstrates, using any handy thought or life lesson like the first one in the list above by Jake: "You can find adventures anywhere in life."

The Story of My Thinking

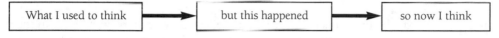

I used to think that you have to be a special personality type, like a pirate or a trick rider, to have adventures.
But then our family spent some time on my grandfather's farm.
And now I think that real adventure can be in all kinds of backyards, ready for everyone.

Comparing Notes (Mine and Others)

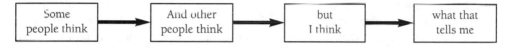

Some people think that adventures happen only at special times like holidays. Other people think that adventures have to include travel.
I think that you can find adventures anywhere in life.
That tells me that people decide how much adventure to have in their lives.

Evolution of a Term (word or phrase in the prompt)

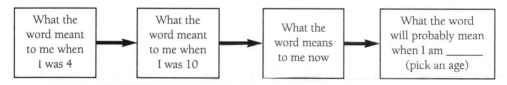

When I was four, adventure was a herd of tricycles in the driveway.
When I was ten, adventure sounded like hoofbeats on my grandfather's farm.
Now, adventure means being an activist for a better world.
When I'm old, adventure will be vicarious: the thrill will be in hearing about my children's adventures.

Tevye's Debate

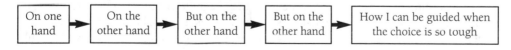

On one hand, adventure is what makes us alive.
On the other hand, adventure can kill you.
On the other hand, if you're careful, you can have adventures that leave you healthy.
On the other hand, if there's no element of danger, how can there be excitement?
I guess I'll figure out my priorities on a per-adventure basis, safety versus thrill.

To try out a text structure students write a kernel essay: they begin by writing down their thought at the top of the paper, copy their choice of text structure boxes below the thought, then write one sentence per box, as modeled, to see if that structure will work for them.

After writing kernel essays, students read the kernel essays to a partner or group, and they will know whether they have a cohesive thought process.

I've heard Harry Noden explain one of the most wonderful pieces of teaching advice: when you're giving students something really complex to do, oversimplify the directions. It would be asking too much to have students invent their own structures before they know what the structures do. So when students use text structures for the first few times, it helps to give them several to choose from. Once they've become familiar with these, it's only natural that someone will raise her hand: "I need another box in mine…could I put one more?" or "Could I combine two of the boxes from this structure with two from that structure?" The best answer is "Try it…let's see how it works." When it does work, we add the new structure to our class collection and let the innovative student name it.

Students voice appreciation for kernel essay writing because it's truthful, it's short, and it yields fast results. It respects students' time and need not to be given drudge work, in that they don't have to write two or three pages to see how their ideas work out. They can see it in two or three sentences. Furthermore, there are no more writing conferences about the next step: "I've finished my introduction…what do I do now?" or "I'm not really sure where to go from here…"

Every student has a roadmap of their beginning, middle, and end and the choices for expanding which parts and how much.

Cris Tovani, teacher and author of *I Read It But I Don't Get It,* said to an audience one time that "school should not be a place where the young ones go to watch the old ones work." When we give students essay assignments that include a form, a required number of paragraphs, suggested outlines, we're doing all of the creating. We're tracking the movement of some hypothetical mind and asking students to match up their thought processes to ours. It's no wonder they need help getting onto our wavelength with each sentence they write; what they're doing is completely unnatural, and it's more about the teacher than the student. Conversely, when they choose a structure and begin with trying out a kernel essay, the creative and analytical processes begin with little assistance beyond encouragement.

Once students play with text structures, they begin to see them in their reading. My students read Dr. King's "I have a dream" speech the week after we began working with text structures. "If Dr. King had been working from text structure boxes like ours, what would his have looked like?" I asked my students. One student contributed this:

"I have a dream" speech by Dr. Martin Luther King, Jr.

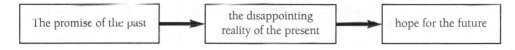

Another student decoded the structure of Dr. King's speech like this:

"I have a dream" speech by Dr. Martin Luther King, Jr.

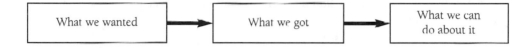

I would like to have enough time in class to ask students to use Dr. King's structure and find a topic or thought that would be an honest fit, just to see what all of their essays would look like.

Soon students are noticing structure in all kinds of texts, and these found structures become part of the bank of their choices for their own writing. We post them on the wall; we laminate small versions and put them on the text-shopping area in the classroom. In the appendix of her book, *What You Know by Heart*, Katie Wood Ray treats teachers to a wonderful sampling of what she calls "structural possibilities," or patterns to model using mentor texts (2002, 157).

Finally you can ask students to create original text structures. Ask them to list five or ten important things they know, then choose one. When they think about how they know that, they can try their hand at drawing it up into boxes. If you put the teacher-written samples on the overhead, the students might use them as a reference. It's exhilarating to see teenage thought processes, captured on paper, sparkling in their young outlook. Here is the first one produced in one of my classes, by Alyssa.

Discovering a Lie (Alyssa Flores)

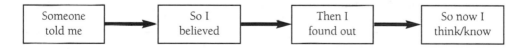

When I first looked at this structure, I thought Alyssa had in mind some disappointment or cynical thought. Then I read her kernel sentences, as she tried out her structure:

> When I was little, my parents told me about the Easter bunny.
> So I believed that every Easter he came along and hid eggs and presents for me.
> Then one year I saw my father hiding the eggs.
> Now I realize that my parents wanted me to have a good childhood.

I was surprised to discover that the movement of Alyssa's mind involved not cynicism or disappointment, but an innocence and appreciation not obvious in her text structure's name or boxes. As her structure is used by other students tracking other "lies uncovered," the tone will most likely vary, but most telling to me was my own predicting what Alyssa's kernel essay would say, almost composing it myself when I looked at her text structure. Given the permission, students really do prefer to do their own thinking. And given the tools, they prefer to do their own composing too. It's really humbling to remember this, and in our wish to help, we teachers sometimes do just too much thinking and composing for our students.

As soon as other students saw Alyssa's text structure and listened to her kernel essay, they got started creating their own structures and trying them out. The structures that worked well went onto the wall and other students used the collection for the rest of the year. Here are some of the favorites:

Cause and Effect (Celeste Ramirez)

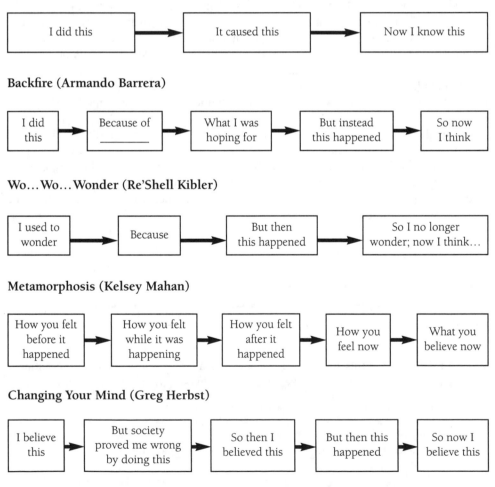

| I did this | → | It caused this | → | Now I know this |

Backfire (Armando Barrera)

| I did this | → | Because of _____ | → | What I was hoping for | → | But instead this happened | → | So now I think |

Wo…Wo…Wonder (Re'Shell Kibler)

| I used to wonder | → | Because | → | But then this happened | → | So I no longer wonder; now I think… |

Metamorphosis (Kelsey Mahan)

| How you felt before it happened | → | How you felt while it was happening | → | How you felt after it happened | → | How you feel now | → | What you believe now |

Changing Your Mind (Greg Herbst)

| I believe this | → | But society proved me wrong by doing this | → | So then I believed this | → | But then this happened | → | So now I believe this |

With This In Mind (Ashley Brzostowski)

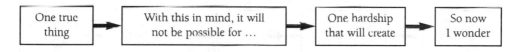

Find the Truth Through Experience (Nathan Hay)

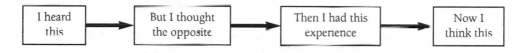

Confusing Testimony (Jessie Tubbs)

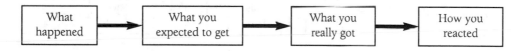

The Real Deal (Amber Wojtek)

A Box of Chocolates (Marco Vidaurri)

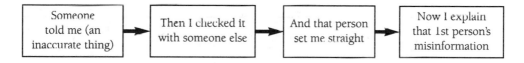

True Friends (Dash Dalrymple)

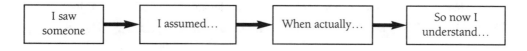

Change of Heart (Anissa Castañeda)

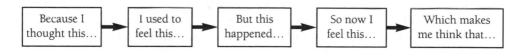

Hindsight Reflections (Amanda Grosch)

The Right Choice (Rebecca Dschuden)

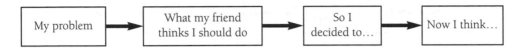

Wishful Thinking (Gisela Navarro)

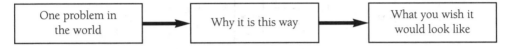

Gisela tried out her structure:
Religion is something peaceful and spiritual, but people have been fighting over it for years.
People cannot hear or accept the ideas of other people.
I wish that everyone could be open-minded and understand each other. We'd have world peace.

Crossing the River Again (Clayton Graham)

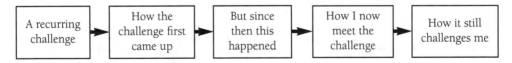

Clayton worked out his kernel essay:
In my life, a recurring challenge is whether or not I should do my homework.
When I started middle school, it was go hang out with my friends or do my homework.
But I soon realized I got bad grades because I didn't do my homework.
So I started to do my homework.
Now I'm still faced with the same challenge, but I still make the right decision.

Fleshing it out

After students have written three to five kernel essays, they're able to choose their favorite to work on, expanding it into a full essay. It's clear that given more time and resources, most of the kernels could be grown into a novel-length memoir or a full-length movie script, so expanding them into a few pages is hardly daunting. But still there will be struggling writers who need help, tools for expanding or elaborating. Here is a list of surefire tools which can answer the question, "How can I say more here?"

- Snapshots (Lane 1993, *After THE END: Teaching and Learning Creative Revision*)
  Students freeze the action, imagine a snapshot of the scene, and describe it in detail.
- Thoughtshots (Lane 1993, *After THE END: Teaching and Learning Creative Revision*)
  Students freeze the action, zoom in on a character's thoughts, and write them in detail.
- Jerktalk, or the "doubting chorus" (Lane and Bernabei 2001, *Why We Must Run with Scissors: Voice Lessons in Persuasive Writing*)
  Students imagine someone doubting the things they say and prove themselves as they write.
- Ba-da-bing sentences (Bernabei 2005, *Reviving the Essay: How to Teach Structure without Formula*)
  Students use the three-part sentence pattern to enable a reader to climb into the skin of the writer.
- Brushstrokes (Noden 1999, *Image Grammar: Using Grammatical Structures to Teach Writing*)
  Students use grammatical structures to add variety and depth while sharpening the visual images in their writing.
- Elaboration Twister (Lane and Bernabei 2001, *Why We Must Run with Scissors: Voice Lessons in Persuasive Writing*)
  Students ask, "How do you know?" and spin a spinner onto icons of elaboration stationery, and use the icon as a cue for their evidence source.
- Depth charging (Carroll 2002, *Dr. JAC's Guide to Writing with Depth*)
  Students learn a guided technique to deepen their writing, beginning with one of their words.
- 3-D memory (Linda Stubbs, forthcoming)
  Students use a layered target to check to see that they've included at least one memory, details, feelings, and a life lesson.
- 3-Questions technique (Lane 1993, *After THE END: Teaching and Learning Creative Revision*)
  A listener hears the piece, then writes down and gives the writer three questions.

Clearly, we've only just begun to explore alternatives to the five-paragraph essay. But just as clearly, students embrace how much they get to do, and the resulting essays make startling reading. Glimpsing into the movement of our students' minds is not a task for the faint-hearted. If we really do want them to tell us what they think and why they think it, then we'd better brace ourselves some. The payoff is worth it. Pieces of writing that answer these questions do make fascinating reading. They are unique. Their endings are different from their beginnings. And every once in a while, along comes one with five paragraphs.

Works Cited

Bernabei, Gretchen. 2005. *Reviving the Essay: How to Teach Structure without Formula.* Shoreham, VT: Discover Writing Press.

Carroll, Joyce Armstrong. 2002. *Dr. JAC's Guide to Writing with Depth.* Spring, TX: Absey & Co.

Lane, Barry. 1993. *After THE END: Teaching and Learning Creative Revision.* Portsmouth, NH: Heinemann.

Lane, Barry, and Gretchen Bernabei. 2001. *Why We Must Run with Scissors: Voice Lessons in Persuasive Writing.* Shoreham, VT: Discover Writing Press.

Montaigne, Michel de. 1957. *The Complete Essays of Montaigne.* Trans. Donald Frame. Stanford: Stanford University Press.

Newkirk, Thomas. 2005. *The School Essay Manifesto.* Shoreham, VT: Discover Writing Press.

Noden, Harry. 1999. *Image Grammar: Using Grammatical Structures to Teach Writing.* Portsmouth, NH: Heinemann.

Ray, Katie Wood. 2002. *What You Know by Heart.* Portsmouth, NH: Heinemann.

Tovani, Cris. 2000. *I Read It, But I Don't Get It.* Portland, ME: Stenhouse.

9

The Many Ways of Multigenre

Tom Romano

Tom Romano teaches writing and English methods in the Department of Teacher Education at Miami University in Oxford, Ohio. Upon retirement, the late Ken Brewer, poet laureate of Utah, wrote a poem that ended with these lines: "It's not the teaching I will miss;/it's the being taught." That stance-learning from students-coupled with his own passion for writing has fueled Tom's teaching for more than thirty years. In summers, he teaches at the University of New Hampshire in the New Hampshire Literacy Institute. Tom's most recent book is Crafting Authentic Voice *(2004).*

What may be the sweetest piece of *Up the Down Staircase* is the clear, crisp voice of the students. As an English teacher I can't help but love hearing the voice of students.

—Melissa Hill, College Senior

First, a story from deep in my teaching life:

Mid-May, 1988. Not much school left. Not many more written words by 150 teenagers. It's evening. My daughter, home from track practice, has commandeered the family room. She eats leftover broccoli-and-cheese casserole, talks on the telephone, keeps an eye on a television sitcom, and, somewhere amid all that, does homework.

One room away I sit at my desk, a glass of red wine within reach, a stack of research papers near. I am undaunted. These papers are the fruition of a new research assignment I've tried with high school seniors. Instead of producing one long expository paper, students are writing about their topics in many genres. Although each piece is self-contained, making a point of its own, taken together, all the writing creates a unified whole. I call the assignment a multigenre research paper.

I reach for the first one. Brian's. What a great kid. School plays, musicals, chorus—a delightful young man who combines intellect, wit, and irresistible charm. Students from every clique in school like Brian. Teachers, too, from the chemistry lab to the art room. Brian has written his multigenre research paper about John Lennon, his musical-social-political hero who was killed in 1980, when Brian was nine-years-old. He's titled the paper "The Long and Wonderful Odyssey of the Walrus—A Heart Play."

I turn to the first piece of writing:

Unfinished Music #1—John

He hit the pavement
ass-first
Yoko raised
his
head.
He wanted to embrace her
but a hundred people
were
standing on
his arms.
     Oh, God, Yoko, I've been shot (Romano 1995, 122)

I stop sipping wine. I hear neither the sitcom's laugh track nor my daughter's occasional outbursts of personality. I am rapt, immersed in a world of fact and imagination, surprises of language, information, and creativity—all this woven together by a high school kid. I am a progressive English teacher with sixteen years of experience, a master's degree in English Education, and an active professional life in the Ohio Writing Project. Still, during these weeks in May when students show me what can be done with multigenre, I sense my teaching of writing, my very career, changing forever.

What's Wrong With Exposition (Well-Written, Pointed, Voiceful Exposition, Of Course)?

Nothing. But expository writing is not the only genre in town. My department's webpage has links to thumbnail biographies and photographs of faculty and staff. At the end of my biography, I listed two non-negotiables of my teaching: 1) "He reads a poem at the beginning of every class" and 2) "His students write in different genres, not merely expository essays."

A colleague objected to my use of *merely*. It demeaned expository writing, he said. My colleague works hard to get students to write well-argued, fully supported exposition. I think he is right about my choice of adverb. *Merely* disses expository writing. I know, however, where my subconscious disdain comes from: the predominance of expository writing in education. As students move through school, they write fewer and fewer poems, metaphors, images, stories, and narratives. Exposition becomes their sole writing diet: reports of various kinds, summaries, essay exams, traditional research papers.

I oppose such exclusivity. Writing is a big world mural, not a snapshot. Writing is book reviews, email messages, poems, journal entries, news stories, love notes, editorials, technical instructions, so many genres and subgenres that assembling a comprehensive list of them is impossible. Although I remain steadfast in my opposition to genre monopoly, my expository colleague will be glad to know that I changed *merely* to *only*.

I don't want students to become Johnny-One-Genres, which is what I was until I got to college. In Milton White's fiction writing courses, I started paying attention to the craft of writing. Later as a young teacher, I read Daniel Fader's *Hooked on Books*, and the territory of writing opened further: I began to keep a journal along with my students, became, in fact, crazed about that daily, contemplative writing. Finally, at twenty-nine-years-old, after reading Marge Piercy's poetry on the recommendation of a former student, I wrote my first free verse poem-in my journal. Oh, yes, I'm for multiple genres. I'm for teachers pushing students into genre promiscuity.

I shudder at how bereft my world of writing was for so long. I won't let similar narrowness happen to those I teach. My students are primarily college juniors preparing to be English teachers. I want them to carry my bias for genre inclusiveness into their own classrooms and affect countless teenagers. I want writers in high school, college, and beyond to contribute to the big world mural of writing, to experiment audaciously in many different genres, not ~~merely~~ only exposition.

Narrative Thinking

Multigenre writing calls for students to use the power of narrative thinking (Elbow 1990, 191), thinking that renders experience, thinking that reveals rather than explains. It isn't that discursiveness, formal analysis, and logic are bad. On the contrary, that kind of critical thinking is vital for students to develop. I do not, however, want a world in which people don't learn through and express themselves in narrative thinking, through stories, metaphors, images, and poetry. These forms have the capacity to reach readers' minds and emotions. Whitman ([1855] 1981) gives us this to think about:

> Logic and sermons never convince,
> The damp of the night drives deeper into my soul (52).

We could debate "never convince." There is plenty of logic and analysis out there that is both rationally convincing and emotionally moving—the summation of Atticus Finch in *To Kill A Mockingbird*, for example. Still, I understand the spirit of Whitman's lines. Many teachers, in fact, have gone even further in getting students to embrace other ways of knowing and communicating. They encourage, and even require, students to go beyond words altogether and include in their multigenre projects drawings, photographs, paintings, and other visual elements. Some of my students have transformed their multigenre papers into multimedia projects that included computer graphic technology, digital images, and recorded voices and music.

While expository forms like clear explanations, succinct position statements, and tight little arguments surely have a place in multigenre papers, often genres of narrative thinking can make a point vividly and powerfully and be pleasurable to read. For example, Carrie, one of my recent students, investigated art intelligence. She wondered if artistic thinking might help teenagers write better, even understand literature better. She wanted to know why some students continued to grow as artists and other students stopped making art altogether. This poem was part of her multigenre paper:

Grey Area

As a little girl, I studied my mom
while she wrote the weekly grocery list.
I mimicked her hand gestures,
the way her arm moved
back and forth, around,
then a dot here,
a slash somewhere up there,
then begin to flow once again.
When I was certain I had made the same gestures
using my hand-me-down Crayola Crayons,
I ran to my mom
eager for her to praise me
for learning to write at such a young age.
"No," she said, "those are not words,
but that is a beautiful picture.
Here, let me hang that on the fridge."

Carrie's poem requires heightened meaning-making. I must visualize, examine character behavior, infer, and judge. Her title is playful and meaningful, hinting of the grey matter of the brain, intellectual grey areas, and the mixed messages we sometimes send and receive. The child is striving to demonstrate how she's learned to write. Mom makes it clear that her daughter has not produced writing, yet rewards the work by placing it on the refrigerator. Now that could lead to a child's bumfuzzlement!

Carrie gives readers room to think. Her poem is emphatically implicit. And while that expression might seem oxymoronic, I stand by it. Emphatic implicitness is what artists strive for—to be clear and meaningful without being heavy-handed. Emphatic implicitness is what Milton White wanted fledgling fiction writers to achieve.

Carrie renders experience. She doesn't explain it. She doesn't analyze it. She narrates a seminal event through a free verse poem and expects readers to make meaning. I want students to have opportunities to write that way as part of their school experience, right along with opportunities to explain and analyze. Multigenre writing demands narrative thinking. It's risky. Readers might not get the writer's intentions. That's the way I want it. Students grapple with the same dilemma that poets, playwrights, and fiction writers do.

Multigenre Papers

I've been teaching for thirty-two years—high school students for seventeen years, college students for fifteen. I've learned things about multigenre writing that would have helped my high school students. For one thing, I don't always require students to write multigenre research papers. Sometimes my students write multigenre papers from the "countryside of the soul." The research is inward. Students have written about friends, relatives, relationships, experiences, and places—subject matter they knew well but had never examined with the rigorous thinking that writing requires. Invariably, writing from the countryside of the soul leads writers to explore psychological terrain they hadn't intended.

In most cases, however, I ask students to conduct research that requires them to gather information and insights beyond their experience. Brian's inquiry into John Lennon was an example of that. Sometimes students combine inward and outward searching. My English methods students, for example, write multigenre papers about one of their field experiences. Students build on concepts of learning and ideas for teaching and classroom management gained from academic courses, but their primary material comes out of their ethnographic lives as they observe and participate in the culture of a language arts classroom.

Countryside of the soul…research…a blending of both. You'll have to decide how multigenre papers can best serve your students' growth and development. Regardless of the territory they explore with a multigenre mind-set, their trip will be invigorating.

Interview with a Skeptic

Let's slow down. Where did multigenre come from?
For me, the spark was *The Collected Works of Billy the Kid* by Michael Ondaatje. Many writers have experimented with genre, though. In the 1920s and 1930s, John Dos Passos wrote novels that included stylized narrative techniques, his own drawings of characters and scenes, and even thumbnail biographies of real people that interrupt the fiction. In the mid-nineteenth century Herman Melville experimented with narrative in *Moby Dick*. Fifty years before that William Blake created poems he cradled in his own illustrations (Phillips 1997, 26).

This blending of genres probably goes back even further.
It does. But in my reading experience no one has broken so radically from traditional storytelling as Ondaatje does in *The Collected Works of Billy the Kid.*

How so?
Ondaatje had researched Billy the Kid, but he didn't write a straight biography or even a historical novel. Instead, he rendered events through poems, narratives, dialog exchanges, fragmented scenes, a song, a newspaper interview…

Multiple genres.
Multiple voices, too. Sometimes you aren't sure which character is speaking or who is being written about.

Postmodern, huh?
Or maddening. The intriguing thing Ondaatje does, though, is to use imagination.

Imagination?
For example, late in the book you encounter a poem that occurs while Billy the Kid is dying.

What's wrong with that? Sounds in keeping with multigenre.
The poem is written from Billy's first person point of view.

Now I've got a problem. Billy the Kid was real, not invented. Ondaatje can't know what he was thinking as he died. No one can.
An omniscient author can. Billy's thoughts can be imagined.

Imagination in a book that comes out of research?
Ondaatje uses imagination to make characters breathe and settings palpable. He melds research information with his sensitivity to human experience to render what might have been true.

Might?
Flannery O'Conner said that imagination is a form of knowledge (qtd. in Murray 1990, 110).

She was a fiction writer.
Albert Einstein wasn't.

So?
Einstein was the quintessential person of science and mathematics, and he understood imagination's powerful role in knowing and learning. "Imagination," noted Einstein, "is more important than knowledge" (Moncur, 2006).

I don't know. I've got some cognitive dissonance here, but go ahead.

The Multigenre Assignment

I hope you are on board at this point, happily acknowledging a place for narrative thinking and creativity, excited about the possibility of multigenre, ready to make room for it in your curriculum. That's what I did as a high school teacher and continue to do as a college teacher preparing twenty-year-olds to teach English in secondary schools. To guide them through their multigenre research project, I provide students with a handout they can read, annotate, and refer to. It's part guideline, part caution, part pep talk:

The bulleted requirements give students something to check their progress against. You'll note that my students must create a prose poem and flash fiction-flash fiction is a memorable, fictional rendering of compressed life, usually under 750 words (Thomas and Shapard 2006, 12). These subgenres require students to be precise with language, vivid with imagery, and implicit with meaning. Their brevity, power, and mystery make them perfect for multigenre papers. But why prose poems and flash fiction as requirements?

MULTIGENRE RESEARCH PROJECT

This is a chance to pursue a passion, a chance to answer a question about a topic of consuming interest to you and to communicate your learning through a multigenre research project, where you explore the emotional as well as the factual. This is a time to be expansive, a time to try the untried.

Choose a person, idea, trend, era, movement, cultural phenomenon, thing, place, etc. and become a mad researcher, a wigged out, immersed learner, pursuing information vital to satisfying an insatiable curiosity and achieving peace of mind.

Required Research Sources Of Your Inquiry:

- At least one book (or two or three-read fast, become an expert).
- Articles
- Primary material: interviews, testimony, observations
- Internet sources*

*The Internet contains the good, the bad, and the ugly. It is democratic, but there is no screening for quality. Gauge the depth, accuracy, and quality of what you find in cyberspace. Even if it is first-rate, I definitely don't want you to simply paste material from a website into your paper.

I want to see an original mgp from you, one grounded in a thorough research understanding of your topic. I want you to expand and deepen your knowledge, maybe even develop wisdom. I want you to refine your writing skills and increase your powers of communication. When I read your paper, I want to be informed, but even more, I want to be *moved*.

Genres or pieces your multigenre project must contain:

- Brief expository piece, 250–350 words. Make this vivid and informational. Explain, explore, argue. This piece can appear as a mini-essay, or you can drop the exposition into a form that fits your mgp.
- Preface/Introduction/Dear Reader
- Prose poem
- Flash fiction
- Poetry in contemporary free verse style
- A visual element
- Bibliography
- Note page
- Unifying elements

These nine bullets are required, but to create a fully realized mgp, you'll need to write more pieces than these. Range as widely as you want. Go for this.

Students can, I'm quite sure, live happy, literate, productive lives without experiencing them. Prose poems and flash fiction are requirements in my multigenre scheme because I am interested in reading and writing them. What passions in your literate life will you require in a multigenre assignment?

Research Design

To launch students into their multigenre work and to thwart that blackguard, procrastination, my students write a research design. This initial foray into their inquiry is good for them as writers and me as teacher. They get untracked; I begin involvement with their work. Both of us become invested.

RESEARCH DESIGN

A research design jump-starts your inquiry. By putting words on paper, you'll come to think things you would not have thought had you only mused about your topic. I want you on the Internet and in the library early to learn what information and resources are available.

The research design must be typed. Make margins wide enough so that I can write comments, ask questions, and make suggestions.

Parts of your Multigenre Research Design

1. Name your topic.
2. Describe what you know about your topic (Without consulting anything, go to the keyboard and list what you already know. Let it sit a day or so, then come back to edit for redundancies and refine for specificity). Do this as bulleted entries if you like.
3. Tell what you want to learn about your topic. (Remember Curious George? You be Curious Miami Student.)
4. Describe the origins of your research. What sparked your interest? Why do you want to know more about the topic? (This is me being Curious Tom.)
5. List a dozen questions you have about your topic (or twenty or fifty).
6. Describe your plan for collecting information.
7. Provide a preliminary bibliography. (Don't bail out here. Be expansive. Get a sense of the territory ahead.)

To show students what I am expecting in terms of length and quality, I include with these instructions a research design by a former student. These designs usually run two or three single-spaced pages. You can look at research designs by my college students at www.users.muohio.edu/romanots/. Also available on that website are several full-length multigenre papers, writing prompts your students can try, and an annotated bibliography of every article and book about multigenre writing my graduate assistants could locate. You can find multigenre work by high school students in Melinda Putz's *A Teacher's Guide to the Multigenre Research Project* and accompanying CD-ROM (2006). Camille Allen shows the work of fifth graders in *The Multigenre Research Paper* (2001). My *Blending Genre, Altering Style: Writing Multigenre Papers* features the work of college students, teachers, two high school students, and a seventh grader (Romano 2000). Google *multigenre* and you will find a multitude of websites that contain the multigenre work of students of all ages. And after you have done a multigenre project with your students, you'll have numerous examples to use, ones that you feel even more invested in

Supporting Students All the Way

I don't disappear once students begin their inquiry. I'm right there working to support and nudge and push. I confer with students individually. I organize time for them to meet in peer groups to talk about their progress and discoveries. I establish weekly checkpoints for students to turn in pieces, which keeps them accountable and me informed. I teach genres and prompt writing from students to launch pieces they otherwise would not try. By doing all this, I seek to generate a creative current in the classroom.

Early on, I lead students in brainstorming activities to examine categories that might lead to interesting writing:

- indelible moments (Dracula rising from his coffin at sunset)
- important things (garlic, crucifix, wooden stake)
- meaningful places (Castle Dracula, Transylvania, Renfield's mad mind)
- crucial characters (Harker, Mina, van Helsing)
- central acts (Dracula sucking blood) (Romano 2000, 123–130).

The information that surfaces during this brainstorming can spark ideas for writing throughout the project. College sophomore Megan Solon wrote a multigenre research paper titled "Growing Up Spanglish." Megan created characters to dramatize issues involved with Hispanic populations in the United States. Her main character is fifteen-year-old Marisa Vasquez, daughter of a Cuban-born mother and New York City-born father of Puerto Rican parents. Some important "things" in Megan's topic were stereotypes, cultural misconceptions, and identity. In response to a prompt asking students to write a dream a character might have, Megan wrote a monologue complete with literary allusions that gives full voice to Marisa's frustrations:

> You want to tell me about your dream. The "American Dream," the "I have a dream." Well let me tell you, baby, that mine is "A Dream Deferred"; yeah, I said it. Go ahead and snicker. But it's there, each day, shriveling up like the proverbial raisin from all the hatred flying from your eyes. Like the boat you see me come to work in everyday, to you, I'm no more American than that purse you wear on your arm. I scream foreign. I exude different. And I see you shudder as my tongue flutters with the trills of my Spanish "rrrrrrrrrrrrr." For I will not give it up. You want me to be American, speak American, look American, talk eat sleep dream feel buy make sigh American. All I can say is I do, I am, I will, I'm trying. But, for one day, can you stop asking

whether we're better in your "melting pot" or your "tossed salad," and start seeing us as people, not ingredients? Because I'm tired of being the pepper in this salt-saturated slab of land some like to call America. I'm not here to spice up your life; I'm here to live mine.

I want students to know that their multigenre writing occupies a front burner, even if we are engaged with other activities, too, during their work. The assignment isn't merely due on a particular date. Multigenre writing must be part of our classroom work. I respond to checkpoint pieces, I introduce students to genres and styles, I write memos to students if I see problems developing. I know that immersion in multigenre will be synergistic. The reading, talking, researching, and writing will lead to further reading, talking, researching, and writing.

However long you ask your students to work at their multigenre project-five intense weeks or an entire semester-it is imperative to lead students into writing, into producing first draft words on paper they can interact with and bring "the second genius" to (Stafford 2003, 36). Multigenre writing is generative, not terminal. The more students write, the more they discover to write. Many of the requirements of your curriculum will fit naturally into multigenre. Perhaps you will teach students to write dialog or to experiment with different points of view or to write vivid description or succinct exposition. Teach students this content and guide them to turn the writing that comes out of it to their topics. Multigenre encompasses so much that we value in teaching literacy skills that it should fit seamlessly into your curriculum. Students' papers will grow right along with their knowledge of writing, reading, speaking, and listening.

A Sample Lesson

Last year one of my students introduced me to *The Book of Qualities* by J. Ruth Gendler (1984). Gendler personifies ninety-nine qualities or emotions like Beauty, Terror, Wisdom, Blame, and Ambivalence. She makes the quality a character and writes a mini-sketch about its actions, thoughts, preferences, and relationships with other qualities. The results are prose poems or flash fictions that are short, subtle, and insightful. Gendler accompanies many of the pieces with her exquisite line drawings.

I knew I wanted students to try including a piece like Gendler's in their multigenre papers. Such writing would nudge students to analyze their topics and add flesh and blood to abstractions. It would give them practice in characterization, writing in present tense, creating personification, considering comparisons and contrasts, working with implication and inference, and writing incisively. It would also, I figured, be fun. Without telling students what I was up to, I asked them to list qualities or emotions that were involved with their research topics. Next we examined some of Gendler's examples. I showed them experiments I had written about Regret and Procrastination. Students then revisited the qualities they had listed, chose one, talked about it with a partner, then wrote.

In his research of the Marine Corps, one student thought of two qualities that were inextricably related:

History loves Tradition but gets sick of Tradition following him around all the time. History is wise beyond his years and everyone always looks to him for answers. He constantly reminds people of what was and what is to come. Tradition, on the other hand, finds what he thinks are the best traits of History and mimics them—forever. Tradition is a wonderful thing, for he keeps History fresh in the minds of everyone lest his wonderful vault of knowledge he forgotten. Unfortunately, Tradition is loyal to History to a fault. "So what if your newfangled idea makes sense," Tradition says, "we've been doing it like this for two hundred years."

"That's exactly the point," Change pipes in. "The old way is more than outdated This way is faster, cleaner, easier, and cheaper."

"I'll have none of it," Tradition replies.

History sits by quietly for he knows that Change is inevitable. He also knows that Tradition is nearly impossible to reason with.

John Casey, College Junior

The multigenre process is protean. Students plan, write, plan anew, write more. My writing prompts urge along intellectual curiosity, discovery, and work. Students—even type A ones—usually love it. The levels of engagement and accomplishment that students achieve often lead them to tell me that the multigenre project is the most fulfilling writing assignment they've ever done.

Prime Spots

There are two areas of multigenre writing I wish I had realized the importance of the first time I taught it to high school students. Their papers would have been even more satisfying.

Beginnings

Milton White, my college writing teacher thirty-seven years ago, stood before us, holding one of our short stories. "This," he said, "is what you want an editor to do." With that, he turned the page.

When readers encounter a new piece of writing, those first words are all that matter. That goes doubly for multigenre. One of my students wrote, "I just love that once my mind matches the rhythm of the multigenre it feels just as smooth and full as any narrative." Many readers, though, are thrown by the unconventionality of a multigenre paper and will stop reading before their mind matches that multigenre rhythm. Those opening words must pique readers' curiosity so they have no choice but to read on.

I require students to write introductions, prefaces, forewords, or "dear reader" pieces in which they take readers by the hand and tell them what they need to know in order to read the paper with purpose. Since introductions have the potential to be insufferably boring, the challenge for the writer is to be engaging, informative, and brief.

The introductory piece carries a heavy responsibility. It is the writer's chance to establish an appealing voice— one skilled in storytelling—that delivers pertinent information, sharp perceptions, and delightful surprises, sometimes with a bit of humor (Romano 2004, 24) Here is an introduction that made me want to turn the page. It's from "What's in a Name?" by Sara Dominguez, a college freshman:

> It's really of no consequence that I have taken five years of Spanish. I really only took it because it was required in high school, and I figured if I got that far I might as well keep going. In every Spanish class I've ever taken, when the professor scanned the attendance sheet on the first day

of class it was always the same scene. They would call my name, I would dutifully raise my hand, and their eyebrows rose at my definite lack of Hispanic semblance, yet each time they felt obligated to pursue the matter. «¡Sara Dominguez, hola! ¿Qué tal?» It never failed. I suppose it could be considered ironic that I am really, truly awful at speaking in Spanish. So then, what's with my name?

I could begin with my claim to fame regarding my surname. There is a street in Mexico that was named after one of my ancestors. He had been a revolutionary and got his tongue cut out. However, the story of my blood that I prefer to tell is a much more recent and unembellished one than that of revolutionaries and war. It's a love story: a story of wealth and prosperity, and of anguish and tragedy. This is the story of my grandparents in stark black and white. This is the story of Alberta and Carlos, and the path I took to find out about them. Please watch your step.

Lately, I've encouraged students to experiment with how they begin. One student recently showed me that the introduction does not actually have to come first. Andrew, a college senior, wrote a multigenre research paper about the October 17, 1961, massacre in Paris of French-born citizens of Algerian heritage. Victims were handcuffed and dumped alive into the Seine to be drowned. After the title page, the first writing the reader encounters is this poem:

> There's a river in Paris
> that in young romantics' dreams
> runs a clear blue.
> It reflects moonlight
> as brightly as sunlight
> and each ripple casts light
> and tells a story of twirled up skirts
> and hard-soled shoes
> that dance on the quays until dawn.
> There's a river in Paris
> that in young Algerians' dreams
> runs a thick black.
> It reflects nothing
> and keeps at its mud-bottom
> the faces and forms
> of those who disappeared.
> And each ripple tells the story
> of one more who was lost.

The contrast that Andrew's words highlight, the images of light and dark, the alternate romantic and ghastly scenes, the simplicity of the language all hook me. On the next page Andrew followed the poem with a double-spaced page of expository writing in which he introduces the topic and his stance in writing about it.

The Return of the Birthmark: Unifying Multigenre Papers

After students have started their multigenre work, I show them an excerpt from the Marx Brothers' *Animal Crackers* (1930). One character in the movie is a pompous art collector. Chico has a hunch the man is a fraud and finally remembers his identity: Abe Kabibble, not an art collector at all, but a former fish peddler from Czechoslovakia. He can prove his hunch by locating Kabibble's prominent birthmark. Chico and Harpo wrestle the man to the floor and find the silver dollar-sized birthmark on his forearm. Kabibble offers Chico and Harpo a bribe to keep quiet. They want the bribe increased. After hilarious banter, slapstick, and unsuccessful negotiation, Kabibble huffs off. Chico reveals that amid the mayhem he has stolen the man's necktie. "Whadda you got?" he asks Harpo. Harpo pulls back his sleeve—the birthmark!

Students' laughter is spontaneous. They had forgotten the birthmark and were delighted at its reappearance. The comedic scene sticks with the students and dramatically illustrates the essence of unity in multigenre papers: repetition and surprise.

- Repeat images, details, or language in a number of genres throughout the paper. (In a portrait of her deceased grandmother, Andrea repeats in different pieces the image of a garish Christmas sweatshirt her grandmother often wore.)
- Render a fragment of a scene containing an essential detail, then repeat the detail later as part of a fully developed scene.
- Repeat a pattern of significant quotations, pictures, or titles. (In writing about Marilyn Monroe, a high school girl titled each piece with a Monroe movie and ended each piece with a Monroe quotation.)
- Use a genre later to answer an earlier genre. (I once wrote a poem about my father then followed it with a letter about him written by my mother. Together the two views reveal a more complex character than either does alone. Some students have answered genres by rendering the same event from two different first person points of view.)
- Break long narratives into parts and spread them among other genres. (This prevents an exceedingly long piece from breaking the rhythm of the multigenre paper, and it also provides readers with the pleasure of picking up a familiar story line as they read along.)
- Repeat a genre or form of writing. (In a paper about campus rape, one student wrote six prose poems in the style of *The Book of Qualities*: Shock, Denial, Blame, Pain, Anger, and Acceptance.)

Such conscious unifying not only increases the satisfaction and fulfillment of readers, it also lets writers experience the shaping and crafting of writing.

What Multigenre Does for Students

I began teaching multigenre writing because it seemed to hold such promise for students' learning, expression, and creativity. That promise has born out. But multigenre does even more:

1. Students meet benchmarks and standards in writing, research, reading, and vocabulary development. (In *A Teacher's Guide to the Multigenre Research Project*, Melinda Putz devotes a chapter to this topic.)

2. Students experience how creativity and imagination are crucial components of interesting, thought provoking research.

3. Students practice skills of grammar, usage, punctuation, and spelling.

4. Students practice skills of analysis and synthesis.

5. Students exercise multiple intelligences.

6. Students experience the exhilaration of conducting inquiry that is driven by a personal need to know and the opportunity to communicate in multiple genres.

7. Students learn to be expansive in their writing.

8. Students experience the synergy of sharing ideas and accomplishment with community members with similar goals.

9. Students experience agency as they shape and structure their papers and show what they know beyond teachers' expectations.

This list was compiled with the help of the teachers enrolled in ENG 6991: Multigenre Writing, offered June 2005 through The Ohio Writing Project at Miami University.

Conclusion

From: Laura Lavallee
To: Tom Romano
Subject: Multigenre Success!!!
Date: Fri, 13 Jan 2006 11:17:04-0500

Hi, Tom:

I just wanted to send you a quick note about the successes of the multigenre paper in my senior critical analysis class this semester. I think it's one of the best things I've done as a teacher. I couldn't believe the quality of work I got from these students.

First quarter, they wrote a multigenre paper on their fiction reading book. We just presented today multigenre paper's from "the countryside of the soul." Wow! is all I can say. The topics ranged from Star Wars to the death of a parent. I actually had a student come up to me after class and thank me for assigning this, saying that she now understands her classmates much better. A student who hasn't done any work all semester not only did the paper, but told me that "it was actually fun." I am blown away right now. It's almost surreal. I shared with them my multigenre paper on my parents' marriage throughout the process. I felt awkward at times, giving them such a personal glimpse into my life, but I felt it brought me closer to all of them and allowed them to write about personal things as well. So I'm thanking you for passing this all on.

Take Care,

Laura LaVallee

Laura's astonishment and pedagogical joy are not uncommon for teachers who dive into multigenre. As with most ideas we try, this one takes trust. It was nearly two years after reading *The Collected Works of Billy the Kid* before I tried multigenre with one group of high school students. You can be fiercer of heart than I. You can be more like Laura. After experiencing multigenre writing herself one summer at the University of New Hampshire, she launched into the project quickly once school began.

Multigenre appeals to me because of my literary tastes, writerly passions, and sense of responsibility as a writing teacher. Like my former student Melissa, I, too, "can't help but love hearing the voice of students." Immersion in a big topic of personal importance is invigorating. That emotion combined with the opportunity to write in multiple genres awakens a boldness of expression in students. They contribute to that big world mural of writing. They are not Johnny-One-Genres. Their confidence rises with their accomplishment.

"I am large," wrote Walt Whitman. "I contain multitudes" (78). Through multigenre your students can enter the same intellectually creative territory that Whitman inhabited. Students' subjective experience with this melding of research and creativity can positively affect their attitude toward writing. I'm betting it will positively affect your attitude toward teaching.

Notes

1. Many forget how Melville altered traditional narrative style in *Moby Dick*. After the table of contents, readers encounter the "Etymology," which explains the origin of *whale* and how it is spelled and pronounced in thirteen languages. Following this are twelve pages of quotations about whales from literature and the Bible, one quote after another with no words by a narrator linking them or providing context. Some chapter titles are followed by parentheses containing stage directions for scene and character. Chapter 40 is even set up like a modern movie script with the name of a character centered on the page and under it the lines that he speaks.

Works Cited

Allen, Camille. 2001. *The Multigenre Research Paper: Voice, Passion, and Discovery in Grades 4–6*. Portsmouth, NH: Heinemann.

Animal Crackers. 1930. Directed by Victor Heerman. Paramount Pictures.

Elbow, Peter. 1990. *What Is English?* Urbana, IL: National Council of Teachers of English.

Fader, Daniel N., and Elton B. McNeil. 1966. *Hooked on Books: Program and Proof*. New York: Berkley Medallion.

Gendler, Ruth. 1984. *The Book of Qualities*. Berkeley, CA: Turquoise Mountain Publications.

Melville, Herman. [1851] 1964. *Moby Dick*. New York: Holt, Rinehart and Winston.

Moncur, Michael, ed. *The Quotations Page*. www.quotationspage.com/quotes/Albert_Einstein/

Murray, Donald M. 1990. *Shoptalk: Learning to Write with Writers*. Portsmouth, NH: Heinemann.

Ondaatje, Michael. [1970] 1996. *The Collected Works of Billy the Kid*. New York: Vintage Books.

Phillips, Rodney. 1997. *The Hand of the Poet*. New York: Rizzoli International Publications.

Putz, Melinda. 2006. *A Teacher's Guide to the Multigenre Research Project: Everything You Need to Get Started*. Portsmouth, NH: Heinemann.

Romano, Tom. 2000. *Blending Genre, Altering Style: Writing Multigenre Papers*. Portsmouth, NH: Heinemann.

———. 2004. *Crafting Authentic Voice*. Portsmouth, NH: Heinemann.

———. 2006. *Multigenre Writing*. www.users.muohio.edu/romanots/.

———. 1995. *Writing With Passion*. Portsmouth, NH: Heinemann.

Stafford, Kim. 2003. *The Muses Among Us: Eloquent Listening and Other Pleasures of the Writer's Craft*. Athens, GA: University of Georgia Press.

Thomas, James, and Robert Shapard. 2006. *Flash Fiction Forward: 80 Very Short Stories*. New York: W. W. Norton & Company.

Whitman, Walt. [1855] 1981. *Leaves of Grass*. Franklin Center, PA: The Franklin Library.

10
Poetry Arrives

Maureen Barbieri

Maureen Barbieri has taught middle school in New Hampshire, New York, and Ohio, and high school in South Carolina. She now teaches English education and literacy courses in the Department of Teaching and Learning at New York University's Steinhardt School of Education. She is also a member of the faculty at the University of New Hampshire's Summer Literacy Institutes. Her first book, Sounds from the Heart: Learning to Listen to Girls *(1995), received the James N. Britton Award for Inquiry with the English Language Arts from the National Council of Teachers of English as well as the International Educator's Award from the Delta Kappa Gamma Society. Her most recent book is* Change My Life Forever: Giving Voice to English Language Learners.

I believe the world is beautiful and that poetry, like bread, is for everyone...
—Roque Dalton

Crab apple trees blaze fuchsia. French tulips stand proud, ruby red, purple, and creamy ivory. Daffodils bloom—thousands of them, a gift after September 11, 2001, from the people of Holland—along with grape hyacinth, blue gentians, and bold-faced pansies. Music fills Washington Square Park—banjo, saxophone, bass, guitar, drums—as painters set up easels, and cocker spaniels strain their leashes. Wide-eyed babies in strollers wear sun bonnets now instead of snowsuits. Tourists snap photos of ancient gnarled trees or wrought iron fences, and old men bend over chess boards. Schoolkids dart about on razor scooters or roller blades. And the chatter at the sidewalk café tables is a cacophony of language: German, Spanish, South Shore Long Island. At New York University's Skirball Center for the Performing Arts a new festival opens, and we are treated to Hip Hop Unbound, two whole weeks of music, dance, conversations, and spoken word poetry. Spring has come to the city.

April in New York, when the weight of winter dissipates almost overnight and neighbors, aloof all year, offer tentative smiles on the way to work. Spring. More sunshine. Lighter burdens. A hint of optimism in spite of the morning's paper. But what really seems more compelling is the poetry. April is National Poetry Month, a time for poems to appear daily on computer screens, for new collections and classic anthologies to fill bookstore windows, and for students and teachers across the city to immerse themselves in language.

With the testing mania mandated by No Child Left Behind; the proliferation of cell phones, BlackBerries, iPods, text messages, and video games; the obesity epidemic resulting from our addiction to fast food and our aversion to physical exercise; our ever-increasing American acquisitiveness and sense of entitlement; and the inane political spin on cable television, poetry tends to get short shrift. Teachers struggle mightily to meet standards and defend themselves against a public's apparent lack of trust in their effectiveness.

Why Poetry?

Sharon Olds says:

> Language shapes us. We read poems through the brain, but poetry is about our deepest feelings. The feelings endure, and the craft of poetry helps us figure things out. The thing you feel is precious. When we're in need, when someone dies, at all our most important moments—falling in love, the birth of a child, any crisis—this is when our species seems to require a more formal language, a beat. Within each life, people go to poetry, to express our strongest feelings (Panel discussion, "How Poetry Saved My Life" April, 2006)

If we know anything about adolescents, we know that they live in the world of their emotions. Depression in young people is on the rise, and so are eating disorders, cutting, drug abuse, promiscuous sex, teenage pregnancy, and even suicide. We as a society appear to be failing our kids at every turn. The things they feel are indeed "precious," intense, and urgent, but where and how do we make room for this in our classrooms?

One year after September 11, at the Geraldine Dodge Poetry Festival in New Jersey, Naomi Shihab Nye called the tragedy "a failure of language," a complete breakdown in communication, in our willingness as citizens of the world to listen to and understand one another (September, 2006). In an effort to put her faith once again in the possibilities of language, she published a collection of her own poems about the Middle East called *19 Varieties of Gazelle*. In her introduction she writes about the tragedy:

> Poetry slows us down, cherishes small details. A large disaster erases those details. We need poetry for nourishment and for noticing, for the way language and imagery reach comfortably into experience, holding and connecting it more successfully than any news channel ever could (Nye 2002, xvi–xvii).

What is it we really seek to do in our work as English language arts teachers? What is it that matters to us? And what is it that we believe matters to our students? What are the experiences we want to share with them and enable them to have long after they have left our care? Certainly, being able to live in this world with empathy, to look carefully and critically at ourselves and at unfolding events, and to remain determined to forge human connections has to be somewhere in the mix of what we hope for. Certainly, helping students come to realize the inherent value and power in their own thinking, their own voices, their own efficacy must be central to our work. Our students must know that they have the capacity to imagine a world beyond the one we experience in this moment and to dare to shape what happens next, each in his or her own way.

Being lovers of language—the power of words to generate thought and to discover meaning in experience, and then to communicate meaning to others (Murray 1986, 3)— we have put our faith in the teaching of literature and the teaching of writing. Readers and writers, we are convinced, stand a better chance of enduring this precarious life. (Of course, there are no guarantees.) And poetry seems essential. Poetry, this most intimate of all genres, offers hope for developing empathy, for expressing outrage, and for discovering small moments of solace.

Our challenge, of course, is to seduce students into poetry in ways that appeal to them and don't alienate them. Billy Collins, former poet laureate and contemporary poet extraordinaire, in addition to his own seven books of delightful poetry, has given us two collections of other writers' poems that are enticing to teachers and students alike. In *Poetry 180: A Turning Back to Poetry and 180 More*, he offers a wide range of poems and urges us to read one a day in our classrooms or over the school's public address system. (These poems are also available on the website www.loc.gov/poetry/180, one for each day of the school calendar.) The poems address a panoply of human experience and emotion and appeal to most students because of their pertinent subject matter, surprising imagery, and welcoming language.

Finding Time for Poems

"We don't do that kind of fluff in here," one teacher told his intern in a city high school, when she asked if she could read some poems with students and then encourage them to write their own. Other student teachers, excited and eager to explore poetry with adolescents, sometimes meet similar resistance from cooperating teachers who prefer to teach novels or vocabulary or topic sentences, also worthy endeavors. But time is short, as we know; so, in class after class, I make the case for poetry, reminding my grad students, future teachers, and teachers that poetry is like oxygen. We all need it every day, in big gulps and in quiet breaths. And the secondary school students we teach need it too. How else will we learn to savor the moments we have here on earth? How else will we honor the wonder and beauty and decency around us? How else will we hold onto sanity?

In some schools, where teachers must build their literacy lessons around prepackaged curricula, poetry may not happen in any depth at all until April. So, while we would much prefer a whole year of poetry (see Nancie Atwell's book, *Naming the World*) my students and I celebrate April because this is when windows fly open, skies seem a little bluer, and the tenor of the conversation changes. April is sunnier, more curious, more open to possibility. In April, poetry arrives.

There are poetry readings in the city all year, of course—poetry lives and thrives here—but now in all the dry cleaners, bodegas, and coffee shops, fliers announce nearly nightly readings in every neighborhood from Lincoln Center to the Nuyorican Café. Sharon Olds, Mary Karr, and Terrance Hayes at Barnes and Noble in Union Square read their own poems and other poems that have touched them in a presentation entitled "How Poetry Saved My Life." Uptown at the 92nd Street Y, Mary Oliver reminds us that poetry is all about paying attention, learning to love this world by noticing what's around us. "Tell me, what else should I have done?" she asks in "A Summer Day." "Tell

me, what is it you plan to do with your one wild and precious life?" (Oliver 1992, 94)
A relevant question for each of us and for each of our students. "Pay attention," she
insists, and we want to. Oh, how we want to.

Ways to Pay Attention

Jenn Abrams, a former student turned eighth-grade English teacher, is helping her kids
learn how to pay attention. She launches her poetry study by bringing in old photographs
of herself as an eighth grader and tells her students not only what's happening in the picture, but also the story that led up to this moment, the backstory. In one photo Jenn is
wearing a shiny party dress, leaning against a car. There's a boy wearing a suit in the background. Of course, the kids ask, "Was he your date?" But Jenn tells them about the dress
and what it took for her mom to buy it, all the sacrifices she had to make, and then how
her grandmother tailored the dress, and we begin to understand what kind of a family Jenn
comes from. Next she asks students to bring in their own photos from home, either of
themselves or of people or places that have mattered to them, and to freewrite stories
behind these pictures.

Inspired by Nancie Atwell's work with poetry, Jenn compiles packets of dozens of
poems, mostly contemporary, in a variety of forms and on a wide range of subjects. She
reads aloud Ron Wallace's "You Can't Write A Poem About McDonald's" and Billy Collins'
"Introduction to Poetry" and leads discussions of what poems can be about. She then asks
her students to choose a poem from the packet each night and to share their reactions in
class. "What do you love about your poem?" she asks. Then, "Is there something in your
poem you don't care for?" and, "Is there something in your poem that confuses you?" Thus
students see how wide poetry is, how there are lots of ways to react to poems, and how we
are all moved by different things. They understand that we use many lenses to view this
world and that poetry usually helps us see ordinary objects, experiences, and situations in
new ways. They are learning to pay attention.

Jenn teaches a lesson on "falling in love with words." She is a runner and explains
that, for her, the dictionary definition of *running* is just not adequate. So she makes her
own definition:

> **running** *v.* 1: when the sun rises and my day begins 2: a place for me to think, or not 3: free-
> dom 4: wind, rain, heat, cold 5: an hour with my students in my mind, wondering about yes-
> terday or the day before 6: something I love and need 7: something I make my own

Face glowing, she talks about her love of running and also her passion for words. There are
certain words that give her goose bumps, and she knows there are words the kids love too.
She asks them to look through their writers' notebooks at freewriting they have done and
to circle words that jump out at them for any reason. What are some words they might
examine just as she has examined *running*?

Sonia considers the word *plunk*, relying on her impressions of rainy days in the city,
and learns to love words just as much as Jenn does. Her poem reflects the sense of playful-
ness that we wish all students could experience when they fool around with words. There
is whimsy in the poem and a real awareness of what rain can be.

plunk

Tip-tap
Pitter-patter
Patter-pitter
The wind rustles.
Whispering-whispers
Howling past my ears.
Sleak curtains

FALL

Plunking into deep puddles.

Slapping against windows.

Squishing-squelshing

In my boots
As I walk
Through the rain.

Throughout the month-long poetry immersion, Jenn continues to read poems with her students and asks them to look to Mary Oliver's, Billy Collins', and Naomi Shihab Nye's poems as mentor texts. They might be inspired by the subject matter in these poems, or they might borrow a line or imitate a particular technique. The important thing is to look very closely at each poem and emulate it in some way. (This approach is demonstrated eloquently in Nick Flynn and Shirley McPhillips' *A Note Slipped Under the Door: Teaching from Poems We Love* [2000].)

Jenn gives her students disposable cameras, and together they set off to explore the neighborhood. They snap building facades in Chelsea, red pears on fruit stands, even cracks in the pavement, as well as the late afternoon sun on the Hudson River.

Osamu writes about what he notices in the neighborhood, using the pantoum form he has just learned about from Jenn.

Who Was He?

Who was he?
A homeless man sitting on the street,
Wearing a dirty assortment of clothes,
Looking at me.

A homeless man sitting on the street,
With a small coffee cup half filled with cash,
Looking at me,
And I wondered.

With a small coffee cup half filled with cash,
I look at him,
And I wondered,
Is he staring at me with resentment or sorrow?

Jenn and Brenna Sevano, her New York University intern, share poems from Betsy Hearne's *Polaroid* and Cynthia Rylant's *Something Permanent*; and students learn about the strong connections between visual imagery and language crafted into poetry. Finally Jenn's students each compile a personal poetry anthology consisting of eight poems, reflecting how their observation work and their mentor texts have inspired them, as well as what they have learned about extended metaphor and other poetic devices.

One of their favorite places to visit turns out to be their own school roof. Mary writes:

Roof

like an old paper,
skid across the dusty tiles
or a soccer ball
because we're on the roof.
the roof is loud,
and you know that's good
kicked at such an angle,
days when we went outside
for different reasons.
the roof is quiet,
carried across the ground
by the wind.
to make it swirl,
the roof is so dry
the sun is always bright enough.
the roof is so wet…
the roof is dusty…
the air is always warm enough.
the roof is…

Jason Zanitsch is a ninth-grade teacher at a school in Brooklyn that focuses on community service. He has designed his curriculum around themes of social justice, which he describes by drawing concentric circles. First, his class studies what it means to be a high school student, exploring all the skills this requires; next they look at skills involved in being a teenager today; next what it takes to be a citizen of New York; and finally, a citizen of the world. Students are required to complete fifty hours of community service each year, but many do even more, Jason explains.

Poetry is intricately woven into Jason's class. He starts by reading them "I wanna hear a poem," written by Steve Colman, the 1998 Slam Champion, which begins:

I wanna hear a poem
I wanna learn something
I didn't know
I wanna say "yes" at the end,
because I'm sick of saying "so?" (page 1)

"Every urban kid loves this poem," Jason says. "And rural kids I've worked with get the passion in it too." Next he asks students to find specific examples of poems that use alliteration, sensory imagery, similes, metaphors, repetition, and other poetic devices from among the many poetry collections in his classroom. He is a fan of Billy Collins' *Poetry 180* and *180 More*, and one of his students' favorites from the latter collection is Carol Ann Duffy's "Valentine" because it's filled with surprising metaphors: "I give you an onion./It is a moon wrapped in brown paper./It promises light…" (Duffy 2005, 141)

After the scavenger hunts that lead to discussions of what makes poetry work, Jason asks his students to freewrite about whatever is on their minds, with an eye towards composing poems of their own. They write to find their topics first and then craft poems using some of the techniques they have learned from all their reading and listening to professional poets. Why does this teacher make room for poetry throughout the year, no matter what else they are studying? "For me it's all about youth voice," he says. "It's why I wanted to be a teacher."

They go out into their neighborhoods and compose photo essays and poetry about what they see. Urging his students not to flinch, but to tell instead the raw truth, Jason asks, "What are some issues here?" and, "What needs to be changed?" Later, as they move to the largest circle in the curriculum and begin to examine more global issues, he will ask them to think about culture, create art, and write poems that will make their voices heard. Jannelle's anguish is clear:

God's Back Hand

God's Back Hand is where I live
God's Back Hand is where we moved to…
It's like the further you walk in
The further you get lost
Only darker and dingier as your
Slumber becomes deeper and deeper as time passes by…

Those vulgar names we use today.
Luscious, D-lite, CoCo, Peaches, Pepa, and how can I forget Vanilla,
Cherry and Chocolate?
What are we, the new mix of flavors for Coca-Cola and Pepsi?
All we just do is put a little extra of ghetto fabulous in it.
You don't hear the white smart lady named Sally putting that on
Her child's birth certificate or calling her that for a nickname,
Do you?
No, that's exactly what I thought.

Young men, life isn't about baggin' which shorty with the big ass
And the voluptuous round firm breasts.
That's how you plan on finishing school and getting a job?
Nope.
That's how y'all plan on getting to the NBA?
Nope.
Think man.
That's why God gave you your precious brains.
I hate to see you waste something that precious to be caught up in the game.
The Hustle, the Money, and the Drugs.
Fellas! Fellas! I don't hear y'all…

When I look at y'all today, I see DISGUST.
This is what has been made into God's Back Hand.
He should take that same hand and slap
Y'all for a
Damn reality check…

You the Hispanic.
You the Grenadian, Jamaican, Trinidadian, Barbadian, and all
Those who have West Indian ancestry running through those
Very veins.
This is God's Back Hand…

God's Back Hand is where I now call home.
Only for now I accept this hellhole as my neighborhood,
To be the home sweet home that I used to call Crown Heights.
But this is where I live
God's Back Hand.

—by Jannelle

At the end of the first marking period, Jason asks his students what they want to learn next, and their responses are uncannily similar. "We want to write more poetry" is the overwhelming choice. Jason hypothesizes that the reason for this is that the culture is "saturated with music" and that poetry is the most personal, most subjective, way to express themselves. "More than any other genre, more than journals or diaries or letters or stories, poetry lets them be themselves."

Jason's students write poetry all the time now, whether or not it's assigned, and they are constantly asking for his reaction. He is delighted but not surprised. He is a fan of spoken word poetry for its accessible subject matter, it style, and its images. "It's all about the clever turns," he explains, "not about the big idea." Of course, spoken word poetry can also be a bridge to other forms of poetry, and he makes sure that his kids receive a good variety, including more traditional poems like "Annabel Lee" by Edgar Allen Poe and contemporary poems like "Tony Steinberg: Brave Seventh Grade Viking Warrior" by Taylor Mali. Jason's advice for teachers reluctant to bring poetry into the classroom? "Don't be afraid of it. You have to find poetry that you like, that you really like, and then you can start by sharing that with your kids. It's a beginning. They'll know if you mean it, and they'll take it from there."

Poetry Builds Community

Like Jenn and Jason, other New York teachers have myriad ways of bringing poetry to life, from looking closely at the classics to asking kids to bring in favorite song lyrics. In Eric Viets' ninth-grade classes, students listen to "Mullet," a spoken word poem by Sage Francis, and talk about what the composer is trying to say. What they appreciate is the language play, the different perspective the poem articulates, and the intensity of the mood, all elements in other poetry as well. Eric likes to fill them in on the history of this art form, the roots in the Harlem Renaissance, the thirty year evolution of the hip-hop movement. The theme for his poetry study is "Creating Order from Chaos," and so they study form, looking at poems across the years from Shakespeare to Tupac Shakur. Students peruse dozens of collections and choose poems that appeal to them and then stand up in front of the class and perform these. Eric talks about poetic devices like rhythm, repetition, enjambment, and imagery and invites students to take turns presenting poetry lessons of their own, choosing a particular focus. The poems they write, Eric says, reflect the chaos that is often their lives. They write every day for four and a half weeks, sharing their drafts, getting supportive feedback from their classmates, and compiling their favorites into personal anthologies.

I AM

I am a strong young woman
I wonder, why?
I hear all the drama,
I see the fighting…

I am a strong young woman.
I pretend it doesn't bother me.
I feel, like someday, everything will be okay.
I touch the hearts of other young women and
I worry about their pain too.
I cry to let all these worries out, but
I am a strong young woman.

I understand, I have to get far in life.
I say everything happens for a reason.
I dream of a world filled with happiness.
I try to do my best.
I hope my best is enough.
I AM a strong young woman
                                           —by Johanys

Pain in the ass,
bossy
mother.
Irresponsible,
Stubborn
Daughter.
One retarded dog.
Hardly a complete
family,
but content,
despite its flaws.
Of course they have problems,
lies,
secrets,
between them,
but they're content,
despite their skeletons.

One day they will expose themselves,
the fire,

the anger,
will burn down their home,
and the "family" will never be the same…

The content-ness
will turn into suspicion
mistrust,
shame,
and though the love will remain,
the trust will take time to
regain.

—by Anah

In the Introduction to her poetry collection, Anah writes:

Poetry is not just love and butterflies…Poetry is about who YOU are…It's about what you fear, what you desire, what's possible or impossible. It's about pain, happiness, or even expressions you can't quite place…It's courage, being able to pour out your heart, reveal every inch of your soul for all to see, experience how it is to be YOU, for just a moment…It's LIFE.

Eric understands this. Studying poetry, he insists, is something he'll continue to make a priority in his teaching. "I'd do this again in a heartbeat," he insists. "Even more than the poetry itself, what's great is the community that has developed. We got to know each other through all this writing. I saw another side to them and they saw that too. The kids have been really supportive of one another. That's the best thing to come out of this."

Poetry Connections in Grade 12

Taneka Nugent begins her poetry study by asking twelfth-grade students what their experiences have been with it so far:

It is so universal and I think it is a part of everyday life. You can think of poetry by just waking up and seeing the Sun.

I really hate it because it makes me think too much and things that I don't want to remember. I really hate that seeing or knowing the truth.

I hate writing poetry. I find it hard to write. I get writers block. I find it worse having to read poetry. I think it's sort a hard to understand.

Determined to help her students have more positive experiences with poetry, Taneka distributes copies of Rosalie Morales' "I Am What I Am" and George Ella Lyons' "Where I'm From." After reading these together, students freewrite for a few minutes in their notebooks and later shape poems, using the published poems as models or mentor texts.

Where I'm From

I am from the yellow skin, dark eyes, and black hair,
from the Great Wall and Yellow River

from the 5 yellow stars in a red flag
I am from the tragedy of Tiananmen Square,
from the great leader of Mao
I am from the stereotypes of "Asians are smart"
from the mathematical brain.
I am from the Yanj tree
whose branches have grown into a crowd
I am from the beautiful village
where the lazy pigs are always sleeping and
the hungry children looking for food. Also
the wild flowers blooming the whole summer
I am from the Chinese genes
We eat rice as always.
I am from the country of China.

—by Mei Yui

I am a

Lone leader
With all the answers…
A silent layer, with an internal bang…
I am the door that should not be opened
I am a weapon
I am a solution to your problems
All you have to do is ask.

—by Ricky

After writing this poem, Ricky turns his paper upside down and quickly writes another one in much smaller handwriting and with many words crossed out and rearranged. Taneka finds both poems intriguing, two examples of Ricky's emerging voice and evolving sense of identity.

To be honest, I don't know who I am
My life doesn't have a road…No matter how far you travel or how fast you are.
Once you're in my world there is no way out
I agree that I am different but I guarantee you that there is no one like me
People don't notice that I'm different
because I am wearing a mask, a disguise to fool them
People see me as a big guy, who can care for you, make you laugh, and whatever, but
inside I'm something more.

—by Ricky

It's All About the Hip-Hop

Taneka shares Tupac Shakur's *The Rose That Grew from Concrete* with her class and gives them copies of "Untitled."

"Of course, they were that much more interested because it was Tupac," Taneka explains. After reading the poem, she asks them to jot down their thoughts on what spoken word poetry is and a lengthy whole class discussion ensues. "They give examples. They debate. They ponder." Next she asks them to think of expressions they've heard people use in their daily lives or in music or in film, and again they share their responses. She plays "Mother" by Two Tongues from *The Spoken Word Revolution: Slam, Hip Hop, and the Poetry of a New Generation* edited by Mark Eleveld, Marc Kelly Smith, and Billy Collins. They list the lines, images, and expressions that catch their attention. "They have great material there," Taneka says. They choose one line as inspiration and write three-line poems of their own. For homework students are to eavesdrop on the conversations and sounds of the city as further sources of poetry (Flynn and McPhillips 2000, 35)

"Hip-hop is huge in this city," Taneka says. "We can't really talk about poetry without it." The spoken word poets have deep roots in the African American literary tradition and believe that reading traditional poets is essential to their own work as they speak out against racism, oppression of working people, and other geopolitical injustices.

"It's difficult to define what spoken word poetry is," writes Zoe Anglesey in *Listen Up: Spoken Word Poetry* (1999, xvii).

> On one end, traditional mainstream poetry tends to fit nicely on either the page or the stage, often with a great deal of decorum. When read before the public, contemporary poetry needs few props other than an expressive voice. On the opposite end, the performance arts may combine many elements, including voices, dance, music, and visual and media arts, as well as poems or texts that transmute into monologues or fully developed scripts. Hip-hop or rap, as a predominantly African American popular and commercial art form, stands between spoken word and the performance arts. Both spoken word and hip-hop derive from the oral tradition, and both forms appeal to overlapping demographics.

Young teachers know this is true—this universal appeal—and attribute it in part to the fact that kids' lives are so filled with music.

Stanley Kunitz says, "If we want to understand what was happening at any given time in the history of the race, it is to poetry we must turn" (1995, 11). Right now, and for the past thirty years, our history has included hip-hop. When I confess my discomfort with modern rap lyrics, my student John Banks reminds me that poetry has always pushed the boundaries, always made us a little uneasy. That's part of why it matters so much. "Think of Pope," he says. "Think of Neruda and Walt Whitman writing about the human body. Don't you think they made people uncomfortable?"

Of course. John reminds me, too, that his students—all our students—have complicated lives and that the violence and sexuality in the rap songs are not news to them. Holding a spotlight to racial injustice and other oppression is a huge part of this music, which started on the streets and in the parks long before it ever hit the airwaves. Poetry of the people. Poetry of our time. With its roots in African and Caribbean music and the poetry of the Harlem Renaissance, this music resonates with today's young people. Bringing their issues, their anger, and their voices into the classroom, John knows, is not only respectful and appropriate, but necessary, vital.

Poet Nikki Giovanni is impressed with young hip-hop artists, although she acknowledges that her radio is not always tuned to their stations. She explains:

It's not for us older folks. It's for the young people. I've learned not to judge what I'm hearing about rap—the lyrics that offend—because I remember my mother didn't like Ray Charles, and my grandmother didn't like Billy Epstein. Every generation dislikes the music of the next generation. (New York Arts Festival, New York, NY: Channel 13, May 2006)

Emphasizing the close connections between poetry and music, she explains that she writes her own poems to gospel music or soul or jazz.

But for some veteran teachers hip-hop still presents problems. We may feel we don't know enough of the history, the roots, or the complexity of this particular cultural phenomenon. "Not all rap lyrics are misogynistic or violent," John tells me. Here's our chance to invite the kids to take the lead. We can ask them to share their expertise, to teach us what it is they find so appealing, is it the rhythms, the beat, the repetition, the lyrics, the imagery? Here's a chance for legitimate dialogue. Rap music, like all poetry, is about sound and about surprise. What does this artist do that sticks in your memory? What will you take away with you once you've heard this rap? Showing respect for our students' knowledge seems imperative. April is a time for new conversations, after all.

Song Lyrics—Poetry Arrives

Lauren Suprenant's twelfth graders have studied the transcendentalists for several months, and she decides to move into poetry as a natural extension of their work. First she asks them to bring in song lyrics that express some of the ideas and values they have looked at in transcendentalism. They choose John Lennon's "Imagine" and songs by Simon and Garfunkel and Bob Marley, among others. Lauren asks them how they make meaning of music, the soundtrack of their lives. Why do you like it so much? she wonders. They like the rhythm and the lyrics, the room each song leaves for personal interpretation. While they balk a bit at the thought of studying poetry ("I don't get all the deep meanings, so I just give up," they told her) Lauren is able to persuade them that what they feel about music is also true of poetry.

She then passes out copies of six poems, including Mary Oliver's "Wild Geese," Marge Piercy's "The Art of Blessing the Day," and Frank O'Hara's "Ave Maria," and students quickly see connections between these poems and the work of the transcendentalists. She asks her students to get into groups to read and discuss the poems and then to present each one in a way that makes it accessible to the class. "I want them to convey meaning through their performances," she explains.

Some students are more adroit than others, so Lauren adds another dimension to her planning. She plays a recording of Lucille Clifton's "Homage to My Hips," and this has a huge impact on the class. "If you were going to perform this, how do you think Clifton would like to hear it?" she asks. So two students, a boy and a girl, volunteer to perform the poem. It is as Judith Michaels has written, a perfect example of how physical a poem can be, how closely our bodies can align themselves with language (Michaels 1999). When they finish, the class gives them a standing ovation. Hearing Lucille Clifton and then their classmates presenting "Homage to My Hips" motivates everyone, and the succeeding poetry presentations help create meaning of the various poets' words.

For Frank O'Hara's "Ave Maria," for example, one boy reads the poem while others in his group create a colorful paper collage behind him. Another girl does an interpretive dance as her classmates perform a choral reading of "Wild Geese" by Mary Oliver.

Lauren's students would like to read and write poetry throughout the year, not just in April, and some of them find ways to do this, even without teacher direction. "Whatever the assignment is," says Belinda, "if it can be at all creative, I write poetry. I just like creating images. My poems are a mix—a little bit of hip-hop, some spoken word, music, my neighborhood, everything around me gets into it. I read a lot of Nikki Giovanni and Maya Angelou, and they also influence me." When the class reads *The Great Gatsby*, Lauren asks them to do some research on the time period and find their own ways of sharing what they discover. Belinda chooses the Harlem Renaissance, making sure to focus sound and rhyme in true hip-hop spirit. She's proud to read her poem aloud with gusto, and the music in it is impossible to miss:

The Harlem Renaissance Lives On

Back then our freedom of expression
Caused our progression in American society
Though you may think the Renaissance is long gone
It still lives on inside of me
You see, black people made it through the pain and strife
Now all we wanted was a piece of life
Before, our hearts were empty
We had no identity
America robbed us of what we were meant to be
Through the arts we expressed
What was on our chests
To show that our culture can not and will not be second guessed…

Poems by Langston Hughes, inspiring blacks
Josephine Baker performing an act
The visual arts of James Van Der Zee
Or the intellectual thoughts of Marcus Garvey
All of the leaders in this Renaissance were the wind beneath our wings
And allowed us to fly
The Renaissance is still alive, through my own eyes
Our freedom of expression
Caused our progression in American society
Though you may think the Renaissance is long gone
It still lives inside of me.

—by Belinda

Belinda and her classmate Andre, another avid poet, like their poems to have a beat, and when they read their words aloud the effect is striking. "The rhymes come easily enough, but what's more important is the meaning, what the words sound like and what they convey," Andre says. Both students feel that being given lots of freedom to choose their own subjects in poetry is essential. Andre is influenced by his Zen Buddhist beliefs and his martial arts experience, as well as by hip-hop. "Poetry has to come from yourself," Andre explains. "Writing it helps you understand your emotions better. It's like playing an instrument or like painting a picture. The medium is voice."

Because poetry is meant to be spoken and heard, Lauren's students offer renditions of their own poems on the stage for an audience of other classes. Their voices, their posture, their facial expressions and body language all work together to create a dramatic impact on the listeners, who appreciate the poets' efforts.

Poetry All the Time

When we think about the experience of writing, certainly we want it to be one of change. How has writing poetry changed these teachers and these students? They are learning how to pay closer attention to the world, how to harness the power of words to give voice to their anguish, their hope, and their pride. They are learning that they are part of a long history of human beings who have endeavored to make something from nothing and to use what they know to create metaphors of resistance or protest, metaphors of praise or hope, metaphors for what it means to be human. Such experience should not be limited to a unit in April. No. Poetry belongs at the heart of every secondary English curriculum, if what we really seek is bigger change, change in perspective, change in faith, change in behavior. Poetry can heal, yes, and it is sustenance in times of catastrophe; but poetry can also be a call to imagine what might be possible in the twenty-first century. Certainly, our students have the capacity to envision a world more compassionate, more meaningful, more just than the one we are handing over to them. We want them to have bits of poems and whole poems, whole bodies of poets' work available to them as they navigate their lives because "it can help to say words" (Keillor 2005, xvii). We want them to know that their own words can also shed light, revealing meaning in experience, shaking listeners to the core, and making a difference in this broken world.

Works Cited

Anglesey, Zoe, ed.1999. *Listen Up! Spoken Word Poetry*. New York: One World/Ballantine Publishing.

Atwell, Nancie. 2006. *Naming the World: A Year of Poems and Lessons*. Portsmouth, NH: Heinemann.

Clifton, Lucille. 1980. "Homage to My Hips," in *Two-Headed Woman*. Amherst: University of Massachusetts Press.

Collins, Billy, ed. 2005. *180 More*. New York: Random House Trade Paperbacks.

————. 2003. *180 Poems: A Turning Back to Poetry*. New York: Random House Trade Paperbacks.

Colman, Stephen. 2003 "I Wanna Hear a Poem." *Burning Down the House: Selected Poems from the Nuyorican Poets Café's National Poetry Slams Champions*. Eds. Roger Bonair-Agard, Stephen Colman, Guy Lecharles Gnozalez, Alix Olson, and Lynne Procope. New York: Soft Shell Press.

Dalton, Roque. 1994. "Like You." *Poetry Like Bread: Poets of the Political Imagination*. Ed. Martin Espada. Willimantic, CT: Curbstone Press.

Duffy, Carol. 2005. "Valentine." *180 More*. Ed. Billy Collins. New York: Random House Trade Paperbacks

Eleveld, Mark, Marc Kelly Smith, and Billy Collins, eds. 2004. *The Spoken Word Revolution (slam, hip hop & the poetry of a new generation)*. Naperville, IL: Sourcebooks MediaFusion.

Flynn, Nick, and Shirley McPhillips. 2000. *A Note Slipped Under the Door: Teaching from Poems We Love*. Portland, ME: Stenhouse.

Giovanni, Nikki. 2006 Comments on the role of poetry. New York Arts Festival. New York, NY: Channel 13.

Hearne, Betsy. 1991. *Polaroid and Other Poems of View*. New York: Margaret K. McElderry Books.

Keillor, Garrison, ed. 2005. *Good Poems for Hard Times*. New York: Viking.

Kunitz, Stanley. 1995. "Speaking of Poetry," in *Passing Through: The Later Poems, New and Selected*. New York: W. W. Norton.

Lyon, George Ella. 2006. "Where I'm From." *Naming the World: A Year of Poems and Lessons* by Nancie Atwell. Portsmouth, NH: Heinemann.

Mali, Taylor. 2003. Conviction. "Tony Steinberg: Brave Seventh Grade Viking Warrior." Track 20. Words Worth, Ink & Wordsworth Press, CD-ROM.

Michaels, Judith Rowe. 1999. *Risking Intensity: Reading and Writing Poetry with High School Students*. Urbana, IL: National Council of Teachers of English.

Murray, Donald M. 1986. *A Writer Teaches Writing*. 2nd ed. Boston: Houghton Mifflin.

Nye, Naomi Shihab. 2002. *19 Varieties of Gazelle: Poems of the Middle East*. New York: Greenwillow Books.

O'Hara, Frank. 1995. "Ave Maria," in *The Collected Poems of Frank O'Hara*. Los Angeles: University of California Press.

Olds, Sharon. 2006. "How Poetry Saved My Life." Panel discussion. Barnes and Noble Booksellers. New York City.

Oliver, Mary. 1992. "A Summer Day," in *New and Selected Poems*. Cambridge, MA: Beacon Press.

———. 1992. "Wild Geese," in *New and Selected Poems*. Cambridge, MA: Beacon Press.

Piercy, Marge. 2000. "The Art of Blessing the Day." *The Art of Blessing the Day: Poems with a Jewish Theme*. New York: Knopf.

Poe, Edgar Allan. 2006. "Annabel Lee." *The Oxford Book of American Poetry*. New York: Oxford University Press.

Rylant, Cynthia. 1994. *Something Permanent*. New York: Harcourt Brace & Co.

Wallace, Ron. 2006. "You Can't Write a Poem About McDonald's." *Naming the World: A Year of Poems and Lessons* ed. Nancie Atwell. Portsmouth, NH: Heinemann.

11

Learning from Goldilocks

A Primer on Story Structure

Monica Wood

Monica Wood is the author of four novels, including the American Booksellers Association bestseller Any Bitter Thing. *Her widely anthologized short stories have been featured on public radio, including the NPR program* Selected Shorts. *She also writes books for writers and teachers, including* The Pocket Muse: Ideas and Inspirations for Writing *and* The Pocket Muse Endless Inspiration: More Ideas for Writing. *She has written three teaching guides:* Short Takes: 15 Contemporary Stories; 12 Multicultural Novels: Reading and Teaching Strategies; *and* Critical Reading Activities for the Works of S. E. Hinton. *She maintains an active website at* www.monicawood.com.

"I don't know what to say beyond 'it's good' or 'it isn't,'" says a teacher friend of mine. Armed with writing prompts, sample stories, and a peer-reviewer schedule, she shoulders into her creative-writing unit with all due determination and a vague but unquenchable dread. As a fiction writer, I want to reassure my friend, and any other teacher facing similar qualms, that you don't have to be F. Scott Fitzgerald to be a good writing teacher. In fact, Fitzgerald would have made a *terrible* writing teacher—he didn't have a tenth of your patience and equanimity. You don't need literary genius to teach creative writing; the good teaching skills you already possess will suffice, as long as you supplement them with a basic working knowledge of fiction-writing technique.

That's where I come in. Having taught fiction-writing workshops for about twenty years to students of all ages, I've learned to separate what is teachable from what is not. You can't teach students to love fiction, or to love writing, or to love revising (especially that!); you can't teach talent or persistence or inspiration. But you can teach, say, the difference between the first person and the third; or how to alter sentence structure to create suspense; or how to manage dialogue to recreate the gist and spirit of a conversation without resorting to a tedious blow by blow.

The great bonus of teaching the craft of fiction is that it often leads students to the very things that are unteachable. What we call talent is often nothing more mysterious than the intersection of knowledge and determination. *Love* might be too strong a word, but I have borne witness to more than a handful of students who grew to love writing after they discovered new ways to do it. At the very least, learning new writing techniques will enhance your students' appreciation of the difficulty of making good fiction—and of writing well in general—and give them a new sense of power over their own work.

There are many hundreds of books and articles about the many hundreds of aspects of the fiction-writing craft. For the single most improving tool in the kit, however, my vote goes to story structure if your goal is to help students put together coherent, readable, interesting stories. And once students learn what structure is, how it works, and how to apply it, many other story elements begin to fall into place more seamlessly. Best of all, a good working knowledge of structure almost completely eliminates that all-too-common cry from the abyss: "I wrote the beginning—now what?"

Short Story, Genre Fiction, and Literary Fiction

Before we begin our primer on story structure, let's make sure we're speaking the same language. You have, no doubt, already noticed that students, influenced by television and the movies, have wildly varying notions of what a teacher means by *short story* or even *fiction*. You can save yourself a lot of grief by defining your terms from the get-go. Your terms and standards may differ from mine—I have the luxury of being persnickety, to say the least, on the subject of literature, because I don't have to face a classroom of fourteen-year-olds five times a week—so you will probably want to modify my suggestions to meet the unique exigencies of your classroom. But, just so you know, here are my definitions, which serve as ground rules for every workshop and course I teach regardless of the students' ages:

1. A short story is a work of prose fiction, anywhere from a couple of paragraphs (a short-short) to fifty pages in length, with most magazine-length stories running ten to twenty-five double-spaced manuscript pages;
2. a short story has a beginning, a middle, and an end;
3. a short story is about characters in trouble or distress.

And, as a preemptive strike against common beginners' missteps, it helps to say also what a short story is *not*:

1. A short story is not a memoir in which the events being recounted really happened;
2. a short story is not a parable, philosophy, or manifesto in which the point of the story is the concluding moral;
3. a short story is not an anecdote in which an incident is recounted verbatim without applying story technique.

It also helps to educate your students at the outset on the difference between literary fiction and genre fiction. Genre fiction (murder mystery, romance, fantasy, spy thriller, science fiction, horror) follows a strict formula honed to meet reader expectations: the sleuth follows a series of clues to discover the murderer's identity; the woman bests her rival or overcomes a misunderstanding to marry the man of her dreams; the evil force from Planet Zok threatens life as we know it unless the struggling hero marshals his secret powers; the State Department pencil pusher discovers a government plot that can be thwarted only by cracking a computer code. These stories, while immensely entertaining—and in many cases well-written and thought provoking—nevertheless plug interchangeable, often stereotyped characters into preordained plots.

Literary fiction, on the other hand, aspires to art. It attempts to illuminate the human condition and uncover universal truths. It applies itself to questions rather than answers. It attends to complexity of character and employs evocative language to uncover layers of story. *The plot develops from the characters, and not the other way around.*

Genre fiction (with a few exceptions) aims only to entertain; literary fiction aims to enlighten, provoke, connect, *and* entertain. Ask the students to compare *To Kill a Mockingbird* or *Ethan Frome* or *Roll of Thunder, Hear My Cry* to any entry in the Babysitters' Club or Goosebumps series, and they'll get the picture. The Harry Potter series is a good example of genre fiction (fantasy) that aspires to something more. Whether or not it succeeds might make for a fruitful classroom discussion.

At the risk of sounding like Sister Ernest, my fourth-grade teacher at St. Theresa's, I suggest for this lesson that you place strict limitations on the kind of stories your students write. Give them free rein during other lessons or in their journals, but demand literary fiction for anything to be discussed or evaluated by you or their peers. Be clear and don't apologize—there are few enough defenders of artistic merit these days! Ergo: no hack-and-slash, no romantic melodrama, no monsters, no murders, no wizard wannabes, no sitcoms. By limiting your students to literary fare, you are asking for their sincerest effort at creative expression and making it almost impossible for them to imitate something they've already read—or, worse, watched on TV.

After the predictable squawks of protest, announce that you're about to make their task much easier by showing, in three stages, how good, strong, literary stories are made. And, if they can't come up with an idea that doesn't involve a serial killer in a hockey mask or a boy at wizard school, ask them to begin simply, with an ordinary person in an ordinary place who encounters a perplexing problem, an unexpected event, or another character who is upset over something.

Stage One: Basic Story Structure

A basic, classical story structure contains six elements:

1. *The setup.* This is the given of the story, the basic state of affairs as the story opens. Often the setup consists of a character, a place, and a time.
2. *The complication.* This is the person or event that upsets the status quo. The complication alters the given of the setup.

3. *The rising action.* These are the events that result from the complication. Usually, rising action builds in intensity.

4. *The meanwhile:* This is either a parallel plotline, a subplot, or background information, and it can take can take several forms: a flashback that shows a past event; background information on the character that explains or intensifies his present circumstances; a scene taking place in another location or happening to another character.

5. *The climax.* This is the final, resolving event, the scene to which all the other scenes have been heading toward.

6. *The denouement.* This is a fancy word—French for *outcome* or *conclusion*—that refers to the ending. In contemporary fiction, the denouement usually consists of a line or paragraph composed in such a way as to leave a final image, or impression, of the story.

To show how this basic story structure works in practice, let's apply the six main elements to something all students can recognize. A humble fairy tale usually offers a solid, straightforward example. Here are the six elements applied to "Goldilocks and the Three Bears":

Setup: Three bears go for a walk to gather berries while their porridge cools.

Complication: Blonde perpetrator breaks in.

Rising Action: Perp chows down, breaks a chair, gets some shut-eye.

Meanwhile: Bears get home and survey the wreckage.

Climax: Discovered in Baby Bear's bed, perp screams and flees.

Denouement: "And they all lived happily ever after."

In contemporary fiction, the meanwhile can get really complicated. An enhanced meanwhile here would have Papa Bear contemplating his past while he gathers berries. He might remember his service in the Hundred Bears' War and how the war trauma prevented him from successfully providing for the first Mrs. Bear, who left him in despair after he refused to move to her family's territory in Meanwhile Forest, where the war started in the first place. He felt like a failure but eventually met the second Mrs. Bear, had Baby Bear, and felt good and complete for the first time in his life. But then, horror of horrors, he gets back from berry-picking and realizes that he has not been safe from mayhem after all, for here is his dear little home, burglarized and vandalized by some unknown creature! Could this mean war—again?

In contemporary stories, the meanwhile usually weaves in and out of the central plotline of the story, adding drama and depth to the character and events.

A Reinforcing Exercise for Stage One

Once you've presented the six elements of a basic story structure, break students into groups of eight and have them write an eight-line story. One student writes the first line, which is the setup; the next writes a one-line complication; the next three students write one line each of action resulting from the complication; the next writes a one-line climax;

and the last student writes a last line, even if it is simply "They all lived happily ever after." The idea here is not to make great literature—in fact, the stories will be funny and silly— but it reinforces for the students that well-structured stories, even stories of eight lines, have a recognizable architecture.

Stage Two: The Triangle

Students will respond to the seeming simplicity of the six-element structure diagram, and that may be enough for your purposes. The six-element structure is most useful for working out a basic plot, and it can also be used to help analyze any story you might be reading or assigning for class. But if you want your students, especially older ones, to write (and read) fiction in a more sophisticated way, you can present the triangle model as well. In this model, the three points of the triangle—plot, story, and design—compose a structure that accounts for lots of layers and subtleties.

Most people use the terms *plot* and *story* interchangeably, but for our purpose in discussing structure they are actually two very different entities. *Plot* is the "what happens next," the series of events that keep readers reading. *Story* is the underlayer, the subtext, the emotional content that makes the tale worth reading—and rereading.

Let's start with plot. There are two basic plots out there, done in many millions of ways:

Plot one: A stranger comes to town.

Plot two: Somebody goes on a trip.

"Goldilocks and the Three Bears" employs both, to comic effect. To demonstrate the difference between plot and story, have the students sketch out a basic "what happens next":

1. Sam arrives at a birthday party.
2. Sam spies a toy airplane and hides it inside his shirt.
3. The birthday girl gets angry when she catches Sam taking the toy, engages him in a fight, and her mother steps in to settle the matter.
4. Sam thinks of his life at home and decides he must have this toy, no matter what the consequences.
5. The toy airplane gets broken when Sam tries to hold on, and Sam is asked to leave.
6. Sam heads for home, defeated and ashamed.

There you have it: a bare-bones plot. And only plot. (Notice that it follows the six-element structure as well.) There is no story here yet, because story is what happens between the lines. Story resides in how the story is told, not the "what happens." It comes from the ironies and subtleties of motivation and character that get conveyed through carefully crafted language.

For example, Sam's tale takes on one color if we open with something like:

Sam rang the doorbell with a single, jaunty ding, his undernourished face glowing with anticipation

—and quite another if it opens with:

Sam pressed and pressed the doorbell with the heel of his hand, annoyed at the breeze rear-ranging his well-cut hair.

The plot is exactly the same, either way: a kid named Sam arrives at a birthday party. The language, however, changes everything, suggesting the boy's innocence and humility in the first instance (Good Sam), and the boy's arrogance and condescension in the second (Bad Sam). What a monumental difference in the way the reader perceives the story! Will it be about an innocent, possibly impoverished boy who can't resist the dazzle of a brand-new toy, or about a spoiled brat who takes anything he wants out of long habit?

Let's skip to another part of the story. When the mother tells Sam to give the toy back, she could say:

"Your people never taught you any better. I suppose it's not your fault."

Or, she could say:

"You arrogant little pipsqueak, I'm sick of you and your phony parents!"

Same plot: Mom steps in. But entirely different story.

The ending, depending on language, could devastate the reader, who feels Good Sam's humiliation and pain, or it could give the reader a satisfied harrumph as Bad Sam finally gets his comeuppance. One ending for Good Sam:

Sam left the grand house, his clothes too thin against a sudden wind that stung him on the long and dreaded walk home.

A different ending for Bad Sam:

Sam left the house in a fury and waited for his driver just down the block, in a spot where the other kids wouldn't see him.

Again, same plot: a kid named Sam, who has stolen a toy and gotten caught, leaves the birthday party because the mother insists. But the story for each could not be more different.

By reinforcing the distinction between story and plot, you can open the way for your students to begin writing—and reading—with more attention and appreciation. Ask them to consider some classics of the reading list—*Ethan Frome*, *Of Mice and Men*, *To Kill a Mockingbird*: such seemingly simple plots that explore great, many-layered stories of lost innocence, ambiguous moral choices, the redemptive power of love, the frail and sometimes ruinous connections between human beings. In any supplemental readings, ask students to summarize the plot first, then fill in the story.

To have a plot *and* story is to have a great head start, but those key ingredients need a thoughtful design in order to work their full magic. Design is the key to completing a structure that feels cohesive, finished, and rendered in such a way that no other possibility feels right—a story, in other words, that holds.

Design is the sum of the writer's technical decisions. Is the story told by a first-person narrator or in third-person objective narration? Are events recounted in chronological order, or rendered as a back-and-forth cut between past and present, using flashbacks? Does the story unfold in present tense or past tense? Does it consist of one long stream-of-consciousness, a series of short vignettes, or a traditional scene-follows-scene? Does it feature lots of dialogue or lots of narrative, or a little of both? Does the writer use irreverent, rollicking wordplay, or quiet, straightforward prose?

The effect of these technical choices can't be overestimated. Inexperienced writers can't anticipate the havoc that often ensues after a seemingly small design change. (Try changing every *she* to *I* in a given story, or every *is* to *was*, and watch the story lose its focus, its magic, its sense.) Writerly frustration is a predictable outcome of that domino effect, but only if the writer is unprepared for it. Forewarned really is forearmed.

We can design Bad Sam's story as a first-person narrative, write it in present tense, and get a more immediate sense of unfolding experience, which might help us turn Bad Sam into Can't-Help-It Sam. Or, we could design Good Sam's story in the birthday girl's point of view, which might help us turn Good Sam into Whiny-and-Annoying Sam.

The triangle approach to structure, though more sophisticated than the six-element model, can also be translated into a simple formula that students can remember, rely on, and learn from:

PLOT + STORY + DESIGN = STRUCTURE

A Reinforcing Exercise for Stage Two

To illustrate the importance of design as the completing element in a good structure, have the students take turns changing a single design element of "Goldilocks and the Three Bears," and begin to tell that familiar tale to the class. Some sample design changes:

Mama Bear as first-person narrator

Goldilocks as first-person narrator

Third person, Baby Bear's point of view

All dialogue

Present tense

Objective narrator, cutting back and forth between Goldilocks in the house and the bears out on their walk

This simple exercise is both entertaining and instructive. As soon as a student tries out the story from Mama Bear's point of view and begins, "I made the porridge this morning but, as usual, Baby thought it was too hot, and Papa thought it was too cold. There is absolutely no pleasing these two, and they treat me like the maid…" you realize that by changing one design element, the student has to tell an entirely different story. A writer might have in mind a certain plot, one that will reveal a certain story, but without the proper supporting design, the thing will collapse as surely as a badly designed building.

Stage Three: Mending Structural Breakdowns

Students might complain that even after following the guidelines for story structure, they still can't get beyond the beginning of the story. Here's where stage three kicks in: troubleshooting. Try asking the following five questions, either as a general teaching tool for story writers or as a spot-check for stories in progress. You can also turn to this list as backup if you find yourself saying, "I don't know what to say beyond 'It's good' or 'It isn't.'" You will note that all of these questions relate directly to story structure.

1. Where Is the Trouble in the Story?

Remember, stories are about trouble:

> trouble getting in;
> trouble getting out;
> trouble with people or animals;
> trouble with machines or institutions;
> trouble finding something;
> trouble with the thing found.

The list goes on. Stories don't really begin until the first sign of trouble. Remind your students that nobody cares to read about Mr. and Mrs. Fabulous living in their wonderful house in Perfectland—unless a platoon of termites is about to declare war on the final supporting beam.

2. How Does the Trouble Occur?

Trouble can come into a story in many guises:
It can be *obvious* or *overt*:

> —a boy breaks a toy at a birthday party
> —a girl breaks into the home of three bears

It can be *unexplained* or *mysterious*:

> —an unknown vandal sprays a message on a character's door
> —the grandfather comes to visit wearing a trashcan lid as a hat

It can be *disguised as good fortune*:

> —a sixth-grader wins a writing prize (and invites the jealousy of her rivals)
> —the older brother brings home a new dog (who turns out to upset up the family)

If there is no discernible trouble in any of these guises, then the story has not yet really begun.

3. When Does the Trouble Occur?

The trouble should occur sooner rather than later. If everything is still just dandy on page four of a six-page story, then the structure is out of balance. The story spends too much time on the setup, leaving no time for a story to develop through rising action. This is a common beginners' problem. I call it "the long front porch." The reader is left waiting too long on the porch before the writer opens the door.

4. Is the Complication Missing?

This problem is one you'll see over and over: the student mistakes a good setup for a setup-plus-complication, when, in fact, it's all setup, setup, and more setup. Lack of a bona fide complication is the most common reason for stories to end up going nowhere.

Remember: the setup is the given of the story, the status quo, the general circumstances, the state of affairs that the reader finds in place as the story opens. It is the first element in the six-element story-structure model.

The complication is the second element in the six-element story model. The complication is the person, event, or thing that upsets the setup; it alters the status quo; it changes the general circumstances; it imposes itself on the general state of affairs. You have to train students to recognize a good complication. Start here:

A Setup	A Complication
sets up the status quo, the given	imposes change upon status quo
suggests what the character wants	gets in the way of what the character wants or alters what the character wants
provides a point of interest	provides a point of departure
provides occasion for reflection	forces action

To explain, go back to a plot they know:

Setup: A boy named Sam goes to a birthday party; he's having a good time (Good Sam) or having a lousy time (Bad Sam); there are balloons, clowns, cake, other kids, decorations; he feels like an outsider and wants to belong (Good Sam) or he feels superior and bored (Bad Sam). This is the given of the story: a kid at a party.

Complication: The boy steals a toy. Instantly the situation described by the setup changes. Suddenly it's not just a nice birthday party, it's a crime scene, an occasion for stress and repercussions. Pressure has been placed on the boy, who has been caught and now must do something—deny, insist, fight back, run away. This is called a point of departure. The story must now go someplace. Will the boy be punished? Will he make a scene? Will he apologize? Will he give the toy back? Will he break it? Will the other children make fun of him? Will he be asked to leave?

Inexperienced writers often fail to recognize that even a good, interesting, busy setup is not enough to launch a story. The story could go on for pages and pages with singing clowns, presents being opened, songs being sung, dogs running through the rooms, rain and snow and heat and gloom of night, but the basic situation doesn't change at all until a true complication—an ominous announcement, a stranger at the door, a stolen toy—is imposed upon the status quo.

5. If the Trouble Is Abstract, Does It Also Have a Concrete Form?

Some students (teenagers especially) are prone to introducing complications that are too abstract to function properly. One story I see a lot is one I call "The Depressed Person." In this story, the setup is a happy place where all should be well, and the alleged complication is that the character is depressed and either wants to kill himself or wants to stay in bed ruminating on his existential angst. "The whole point of the story is that nothing happens," the author will say, to which you must respond, without apology, and with a full commitment to preserving the integrity of artistic standards: "The very least that readers expect of a story—the barest minimum requirement—is that *something must happen.*"

Referring to guideline #4 above should help the students recognize that a crucial story element is missing. A depressed person crying in bed is not a complication; it is a setup. Something must happen to upset the status quo of the depressed person, something that forces him to act. The phone must ring with an emergency that requires action; a neighbor must stop by with a lost dog; a crack in the ceiling must begin writing messages. In other words, the writer must reconfigure the alleged complication so that it forces action or provides a point of departure or alters the status quo. Otherwise, she can call it writing but she cannot call it a short story.

One way around this common problem is to ask students to give their abstract (inner) complication a concrete (outer) form. This can be taken on as a class project—a group brainstorming that can give the beleaguered writer moral support and tons of great ideas. Here are some examples of abstract concepts translated into concrete story-forming actions:

Abstract Complication	Concrete Form
Lucy secretly hates her boyfriend	Lucy buys an ugly dress to wear to the prom
Milton is a depressed poet	Milton goes to the library and loudly recites poetry in the quiet room
Al is friendless and dying	Al places an ad for paid funeral-goers
Sam feels unloved and unwanted	Sam steals a toy at a birthday party

All in the Service of Art!

So there you have it: a basket of tricks and techniques for helping your students gain more knowledge and intention. All writers, of course, hope for the perfect form to arrive by intuition, and sometimes—hallelujah!—it does. But you can't make a body of work out of happy accidents. Sooner or later you have to burrow deep into craft and tunnel through the mud just like every exhausted scribe who ever preceded you. Craft is power, and I hope you and your students will feel the full force of that power. Good fiction-writing technique, though hard to master, can be attempted by anyone armed with the right tools. Intense scrutiny of form forces you and your students to read and write with more focus, more joy, more appreciation. It occasions so many moments of glimmering, gratifying accomplishment. I wish many of those moments on you and your students. Happy writing!

12

Writing and Reading from the Inside Out

Nancie Atwell

Nancie Atwell teaches seventh- and eighth-grade writing, reading, and history at the Center for Teaching and Learning, a K-8 demonstration school she founded in Edgecomb, Maine, in 1990. When she wrote this chapter, she was teaching middle school English at Boothbay Region Elementary School in Boothbay Harbor, Maine. Nancie was the first classroom teacher to receive the National Council of Teachers of English David H. Russell Award as well as the Modern Language Association's Mina P. Shaughnessy Prize for distinguished research in the teaching of English.

We are pleased to reprint Nancie Atwell's classic essay, "Writing and Reading from the Inside Out." Originally an electrifying talk she delivered in Lebanon, NH in 1983, it lays out a vision of literacy instruction that she developed in the first edition of *In the Middle: Writing and Reading with Adolescents*. She has added an Afterword to this essay in which she outlines ways in which her teaching practice has evolved.

I'm an English teacher, certified to teach grades seven through twelve and currently teaching grade eight. I go to a party. I'm introduced to a stranger. He says, "What do you do?" I say, "I'm an English teacher." He says, "Oh. Then I guess I'd better watch my grammar."

This conversation occurs often enough—even at faculty parties—for me to realize I'm a stereotype. Like all stereotypes, I'm one I don't like a whole lot. Fueled by red ink, I'm the self-appointed guardian of your language—somebody so obsessed and narrow it's not outside the realm of possibility that I'd critique your sentence structure at a cocktail party.

I'm the doorman at what Frank Smith (1983) calls "the club." And there's no access to anyone who can't name and define the parts of speech; who doesn't know George Eliot's real name; who won't appreciate the stories and poetry in some publisher's latest version of a literature anthology; who can't name the Roman equivalents of the Greek deities; whose paragraphs don't conform to Warriner's models.

It's like Ken Kesey said: you're either on the bus, or you're off the bus. For a long time, I was virtually alone inside the bus. Other adults—including most of my elementary school colleagues—were on the outside. They were generalists; I was the expert. English was my field. I read literature and subscribed to *The New York Review of Books*.

My students were outsiders too—although every year I'd let a few aboard. The gifted ones, right? Whom I'd recognize and elevate, loaning them my own books and responding to their independent writing in private meetings after school.

I reinforced the stereotype. I taught English as a body of knowledge a few would get. The rest would never get it. (These were the ones I'd intimidate at cocktail parties.)

But sometime over the last three years, when I wasn't watching, the bus filled to its limits and the walls dissolved. The metaphor became irrelevant because suddenly everyone was inside the bus—inside written language. I was there; my colleagues and principal were there; all my students were there.

Let me illustrate.

One afternoon last September five things happened within one fifteen-minute period that put a serious crimp in my cocktail party stereotype.

Bob Dyer, the principal at my school, put a novel in my mailbox with the note, "I think you and your kids might enjoy this."

Underneath Lord's book was my copy of Francine Du Plessix-Gray's *Lovers and Tyrants*. The resource room teacher had returned it with the note, "God, can she write. Thank you for this."

Under Francine was a message from Nancy Tindal, a kindergarten teacher: "Do you have time some afternoon this week to respond to my Open House speech?"

When I went back to my classroom, I found a note on the chalkboard from a former student who'd borrowed a novel the week before: "Hi. I was here but you weren't. I love *Portrait of Jenny*. Who is Robert Nathan? Your favorite freshperson, Amanda."

And finally, Andy, another freshperson, came by with a copy of an interview with author Douglas Adams that he'd promised me over the summer.

It was only because these things happened one on top of another that I noticed and considered what was going on. These teachers and students and I are in on something together. I'm going to call what I have around me, what we have together, a literate environment. By *literate* environment I mean a place where people read, write, and talk about reading and writing; where everybody can be student and teacher; where everybody can come inside.

This chapter is about how we teachers can shape our classrooms and schools as literate environments—how we can help everyone approach written language from the perspective of insider. I'm grateful to Tom Newkirk for his article "Young Writers as Critical Readers" (1988) and the notion of bringing students inside written language as critics, as enthusiasts, as participants.

It's as participants in the processes of writing and reading that students—and teachers—become insiders. We become participants when we open up our classrooms and establish workshops where students and teachers write, read, and talk about our writing and reading. I'm going to separate writing and reading for a while and talk about them one at a time, so I can more effectively talk about them together later on. And I'll start with writing, because that's where I started in my own classroom and school, my own literate environment.

Writing Workshop

I teach writing and reading as two separate courses each day to three heterogeneous groups of eighth graders. These groups include special education students. All my students write every day. And every day, almost everybody is doing something different. These are some of the things you'd see them doing if you visited writing workshop.

As insiders, these writers have intentions: things they decide they want to use written language to do. They find their own topics and purposes for writing.

Using insiders' jargon, they call their writing a draft. When drafting they try to get down on the page what they know and think, to see what they know and think.

They read drafts of their writing—to themselves and aloud to each other and me—in conferences. We listeners tell writers what we hear and don't hear. We ask questions to help writers think about what's on the page. Sometimes we offer, from our own experiences as writers, alternative approaches or solutions. But we can only offer. Writers who are insiders may reject our advice.

As fellow insiders, we applaud when writers find ways to accomplish what they hoped to accomplish—as they shape the content of their writing and make graceful meanings. Sometimes we suffer all the heartaches and headaches of insiders along the way.

All this thinking, writing, and talking takes time. Writers in a workshop take all the time they need to make the writing good. And I haven't even touched on the most time-consuming and least visible insiders' activity: all the writing that happens in the heads of people who write. Donald Graves calls this planning "offstage rehearsal": "I wrote this poem in my head, lying in bed this morning" or "On our way home, I knew I wanted to write about what had just happened."

Finally, with pieces that are going public, writers clean up. They put their writing in the forms and formats their readers will need. They edit. Their teachers help, talking with them about new skills and rules, always in one context: how to get this piece to read as the writer wants it to. With their own intentions at stake, insiders take rules seriously. They use the rules and conventions; the rules and conventions don't use them. These writers will never be intimidated by English teachers at cocktail parties.

It sounds nice, doesn't it? Well, getting it to happen is one of the hardest things I've ever done.

Up until three years ago, nobody wrote much of anything at my school. Nobody wrote because nobody taught writing. Nobody taught writing because nobody was trained to teach writing.

Then, with the help of Dixie Goswami of Middlebury's Bread Loaf School of English, fifteen teachers at Boothbay Elementary School established our own, homegrown, in-service program. Its goal was a K-8 writing curriculum. To get there, we *together* got inside writing. We became writers and researchers and started looking at how people write, why, and the conditions in which people get good at writing (Atwell 1982). The Atkinson Academy reports of Donald Graves, Lucy Calkins, and Susan Sowers (1978–81) were our research models as we looked at ourselves and our students as writers.

In the end, the writing program we sought to develop was bigger than a program. It became a way of life. Writing workshop is perpetual—day in, year out—like breathing, but sometimes much, much harder. We're continuously gathering ideas for writing, planning, writing, conferring, and seeing our writing get things done for us in our real worlds.

Mary Ellen Giacobbe provides a helpful summary of the multitude of qualities characterizing a writing workshop. She brings it down to three: time, conferences, and responsibility.

Writers need time—to think, write, confer, write, read, write, change our minds, and write some more. Writers need regular time that we can count on, so that even when we aren't writing we're anticipating the time we will be. And we need lots of time—to grow, to see what we think, to shape what we know, to get help where and when we need it.

This help comes during conferences. In conferences we share what we've written. Others read or listen to our voices, tell us what they perceive, and help us reflect on our information, style, and intentions.

Discovering our intentions is what responsibility is all about: As a writer, what do I want to do, need to do? Does this piece of writing, as it stands, do what I want it to? If not, how might I change it?

As young writers work with these questions, other writers work with them, some of them teachers. We teachers respect a writer's final say but, along the way, describe the options we've gleaned from our own experiences as writers collaborating with other writers. Mary Ellen Giacobbe calls this "nudging." We nudge by sharing what we know; we acknowledge the writer's ultimate responsibility by accepting it when a suggestion isn't pursued. But next time around, we nudge again.

When we allow time, conferences, and responsibility, we create contexts in which writers write and get good at writing. We expect students to participate in written language as writers do. And their efforts exceed our expectations as they make written language their business. At our school over ninety percent of K–8 students specifically identify themselves as writers.

I know these same principles of writing are at work in many schools and classrooms. Occasionally I'll become naive and complacent and imagine that we're on the cutting edge of a trend sweeping the nation, that the U.S.A. is one, big, happy busful of insiders. And just as soon as I start feeling smug, something comes along to take the stars out of my eyes. More often than not, the something is a realization about my own teaching. My most recent encounter with reality concerns the teaching of reading.

Reading Workshop

At my level, junior high, there seem to be two ways a reading course can go: either a skills/drills/strategies approach—essentially an extension of elementary programs—or a watered-down literary criticism approach of the type found in many high school English classes. Until two years ago my approach to reading was the latter: pass out the anthologies, introduce the vocabulary, lecture about genre or theme, assign the selection, give a quiz on comprehension and vocabulary, conduct a whole-class discussion postmortem, and some-times assign an essay. Students also had two periods each week of sustained silent reading.

A little over two years ago, I began to be aware of the contradictions between my beliefs about writing and my instruction in reading. I confronted a situation Tom Newkirk called "the writing ghetto"—the one period each day when my students climbed aboard the written language bus, sat behind the wheel, and drove. What they and I did as writers in our writing workshop, and what they and I do as readers in our real lives, bore little resem-blance to what went on in my reading classes.

A personal digression: what I do as a reader.

As a reader, I usually decide what I'll read. But I get help—recommendations—from my husband and friends, with whom I talk a lot about books, and from reviews. I also draw on my prior experiences as a reader. I like Margaret Atwood's novels, so chances are I'm going to like her new one. And I go back to books I've read, reentering and reconsidering writing I love.

Sometimes I engage in activities that involve reading when I can't decide what I'll read. For example, the text is required for the course; the application has to be correctly filled out; I want to serve an interesting, edible dinner. But nobody had better do anything so outright silly as give me a vocabulary quiz, a comprehension test, or a chance to respond that's limited to the kinds of questions found in teachers' guides or high school essay tests.

I read a lot, at least a couple of books a week. And I have routines, times I know I'll read and count on reading—before I go to sleep at night; in the morning when Toby, my husband, is in the bath; at the breakfast table on weekend mornings. Some of my reading happens away from books. I think about characters, plot twists, and turns of phrase. I play back lines of poetry. I suddenly see, in something that happens in my real world, what an author was getting at.

Do you see what I'm getting at?

The elements that characterize writing workshop characterize my behavior as a reader. I exercise responsibility, deciding what and why—or at the very least, how—I'll read. I spend regular, frequent time reading and thinking about others' writing. I confer with other readers, talking about books naturally as an extension of my life as a reader.

And much of this talk takes place between Toby and me at our dining room table, talk about novels, poems, articles, and editorials, plus general literary gossip. That dining room table is a literate environment where we analyze, criticize, interpret, compare, link books with our own knowledge and experiences, and go inside written language.

I'm dwelling on my dining room table because it's become the metaphor I use when-ever I think or talk about what I want my reading classes to be. As my teaching of writing was transformed by my getting inside writing, so my teaching of reading changes as my stu-dents and I get inside others' writing; in short, as we *read writing* just as we *write reading*.

To get my dining room table into my classroom, I started with the issue of time, expanding independent reading to four class periods per week. In addition to having lots of regular time for reading, kids decide what books they'll read and at what pace they'll read them: again, issues of responsibility. They mostly read books that tell stories—fiction, memoirs, autobiographies, and biographies—and poetry. I added many titles to the class-room paperback library, then included collections of my students' writing as we published magazines through the school year.

Last year's eighth graders, including eight special education students, read an average of thirty-five full-length works, from Blume to Brontë to Verne to Vonnegut to Irving—Washington and John.

The remaining issue, of reading conferences, is one I had to work with. I teach reading to seventy students. I needed a practical way to initiate and sustain good, rich, dining room table talk with each of them. So, in September every eighth grader received a folder with a sheaf of notebook paper clipped inside and a letter from me that included these instructions:

> This folder is a place for you and me to talk about books, reading, authors, and writing. You're to write letters to me, and I'll write letters back to you.
>
> In your letters talk with me about what you've read. Tell me what you thought and felt and why. Tell me what you liked and didn't like and why. Tell me what these books meant to you and said to you. Ask me questions or for help. And write back to me about my ideas, feelings, and questions.

The use of correspondence was inspired by the dialogue journals kept by sixth-grade teacher Leslee Reed and her students (Staton 1980). I reasoned, why not use writing to extend kids' thinking about books—to go inside others' written language in conversations that are written down? My hunch was that, since writing allows for a kind of reflection not generally possible with speech, our written talk about books would be more sustained and contemplative than oral conferences. Another consideration was the possible connections students might make between what they read and wrote. As a researcher, I wondered if their own writing and the writing they read would intersect.

My students and I write back and forth almost three thousand pages of letters each year. For the remainder of this chapter, I'll take you inside two of these sets of correspondence and show how two eighth graders got thoroughly inside reading and writing by participating with me and their peers as readers and writers. And, most remarkable to me, I chose these students because I thought they were ordinary. As I looked closer, as often happens with teacher-research, I discovered how extraordinary they are.

Daniel

I'll start with Daniel. You probably already know him. He always wears this outfit: jeans, duck boots, and a flannel shirt over a T-shirt. He owns a dirt bike, a .22, and twenty lobster traps. Daniel wants to be a lobsterman full-time when he finishes school.

At the beginning of grade eight, students answered questions about themselves as readers and writers. Daniel estimated, "I've read maybe one or two whole novels in my whole life." He'd never bought a book or borrowed one from the town library, and he'd read one magazine, *Dirt Bike*. He could name one book he enjoyed reading, Beverly Cleary's *Runaway Ralph,* and he said his ideal novel would be about motorcycles and races. In answer to the question, "Are you a writer?" Daniel was one of the ten percent of kids who said no. He also said, "I don't like what I write. I never like it."

The first week of school I gave Daniel a new novel and told him I hadn't read it yet but knew that the author, Susan Beth Pfeffer, wrote well for kids. I invited Daniel inside. He took *About David,* read it, and at the end of September told me what he thought.

9/30

Dear Miss Atwell,

About David.

I liked it because it made me feil it happened to me. it was one of the first books I read that I enjoyed. Because I don't read much. I liked it when they talked about David and the feilings his friend and family (or lyns parents) felt.

10/1

Dear Daniel,

Do you think you'd read more if you could find more really good books? Your note about *About David* made me sad. It seems like you haven't found many books you've enjoyed. There are so many novelists who describe people's feelings as well as Pfeffer does.

For example, I think you'd like *Tex,* by S. E. Hinton. Have you read it?

Write back.

Ms. Atwell

Dear Miss Atwell,

I don't think I would read more because I am too bissee. did you ever read *About David?* no, I have never read this book.

When I got around to reading *About David,* I wrote to Daniel about Pfeffer's intentions:

10/25

Dear Daniel,

I read *About David* on Wednesday. You're right: it's definitely a book about feelings. I couldn't imagine where Pfeffer could possibly go after opening her novel with a suicide/double murder. But the way she slowly develops the aftermath—focusing on the effects of David's actions on the people who are left—just knocked me out. Thanks for recommending it.

Ms. Atwell

Our correspondence continued. Then, at the end of October, I panicked about grades—about how to evaluate independent reading—and placed myself squarely between Daniel and books. I set a minimum number of novels to be read each grading period. Daniel, who had finished three novels by this time, revolted.

Dear Ms. Atwell,

Why should people get bad grades because they don't like to read or are slow?! In my case I can't find books I like. All the books I've tried to read I don't like but the 3 I read. I am just saying it's not fair!

Daniel

11/3

Dear Daniel,

You're right. I won't give bad grades to people who read slowly. If you put in the time and use it well, you'll get a good grade.

I also won't give bad grades to people who don't like to read. It depresses me that people sometimes feel that way, but I won't give someone a bad grade for an opinion different from mine.

I do give bad grades to people who don't read or don't use reading time well. In this class, which is called reading, I'm expecting my students will read.

I know hundreds of good books, as good as the ones you've read this year and liked. Mrs. Fossett does, too. Talk to us, and listen to us. Okay?

Ms. A

Daniel responded: "Thanks for explaining the situation. I will see Mrs. Fossett. And find more books. I'm going to the town library with some friends on Friday, and I'll look for some books."

I received a quick note the following Monday: "I did not have good luck at the library, and I will have to go out of town to find a good set of books."

That Daniel and his friends were going to the town library as a social occasion was one of many first signs that a literate environment was emerging among eighth graders. In fact, through the rest of the school year, Daniel referred to David, Lance, Amanda, Jenny, and other kids in the class and conversations they'd had about particular novels and authors. Another small sign was Daniel's plan to look for books to buy, to own.

Other signs appeared. In the spring Daniel started taking books home to read. I asked why. He responded, "I took it home because it was getting interesting and I just simply liked it."

In December I gave Daniel a copy of *Tex*, and he discovered S. E. Hinton. For the remainder of the school year, he was independent as a reader. With a few exceptions we spent the rest of the year talking about books Daniel discovered. The motivation to find writers he wanted to read was inside him.

12/22

Ms. A.,

I found *That Was Then, This Is Now* and it is a very good book. I put *E.T.* back. I'll try it after I finish this one. Or I will find one more of S. E. Hinton's books like *The Outsiders*.

Capt. Daniel Alley

Daniel finished *That Was Then, This Is Now* on January 6 and wanted more Hinton.

Ms. A.,

Now I won't have to get that book and read it. Thanks. Do you know any other good books that are by S. E. Hinton? *That Was Then, This Is Now* was a real good book, but I wish it could have ended a lot more happy than it did. It was so sad because you could see Bryen loosing his brother or best friend and it changed his whole life from good to bad.

Daniel

Daniel was one of a number of readers who began to suggest revisions in books they read. For example: "I wish Paula Danziger had made the father less like a cartoon character." "This book got good as I got into it, but I think the author should have tried a different lead." "Parts of this novel make no sense and the author should change them."

I think this kind of criticism reflects what students were doing as writers in writing workshop at the same time they were reading stories. In writing workshop they analyzed what they wrote for strengths and weaknesses. They went after effects, playing with the sound of their writing. They worked on providing sufficient detail, on recreating reality for their readers. They experimented with techniques—different kinds of leads, ways of using dialogue. They shifted focus by deleting and expanding content. And they talked with me and other writers about what they were doing. I think printed texts stopped seeming sacred to these authors: everybody's writing became fair game.

Daniel started the year by writing a series of one or two paragraph business letters—to the Honda Motorcycle Company, Hubba Bubba Bubble Gum Company (he'd found a piece of strawberry in his pack of raspberry), and actresses Loni Anderson and Valerie Bertinelli, among others. He churned these out. I worried that none of this writing meant much to him. I suggested topics and other modes—I nudged. And I waited.

Then, in December, Daniel started a series of long narratives describing the nonfiction adventures of Daniel and his friends Tyler and Gary and their boats, motorcycles, and bicycles. It's my theory that these emerging topics reflected the writing Daniel was reading: stories about boys on their own without adults, loyal to each other, told with humor and occasional lyricism. In December, Daniel was reading S. E. Hinton and trying to write S. E. Hinton. He published all of these stories as photocopies for Tyler and Gary.

This is an excerpt from "Camping," a five-pager and the first memoir in the Daniel-Tyler-Gary series, which he completed the first week in January.

> We were on a ledge, so we put the tent so it was half on the rock and half on the dirt. We sat back and looked off. We could see out over the harbor about four miles. "I'm hungry. Let's eat," Tyler demanded.
>
> "Not yet. We only have a little food," I said, taking charge.
>
> "I'll starve!" he said sarcastically.
>
> "Let's do something before dark," Gary said.
>
> "Like what?" I said, like there was nothing to do. We sat thinking for a while.
>
> "Let's go for a ride," Tyler suggested.
>
> "Yeah, to Alfred's store to get some cigars!" We grabbed our helmets and took off down the trail. The lady working at Alfred's knew their parents, so I had to go in!
>
> "Let's not bother with cigars," I pleaded.
>
> 'Don't worry about it; it's going to be easy," Tyler said casually.
>
> "Easy for you to say. You're not going in!"
>
> 'Don't be a pup! Just go," Gary laughed.
>
> "I'm goin'! I'm goin'! Don't rush me!" I said, as they rushed me. I had on a baseball cap, down touching my sunglasses to hide my face. I also had my collar turned up and stood on tiptoe so

I looked bigger. I walked in with a piece of paper, like a shopping list. I looked around like I'd never been in before. I asked for William Penn Braves, like I did not know what they were.

"How many?" the lady asked.

"Five please."

When I got outside, I sighed with relief. (I did not tell them, but I was kind of scared.)

In the spring, Daniel started reading a new genre, survival-in-the-wilderness novels. He started with Arthur Roth's *Two for Survival*, about two boys trying to make it out of the woods to civilization after their plane crashes in a snowstorm. At the same time, Daniel started "Trapped," his own first piece of fiction, about two boys trying to make it out of the woods to civilization after their motorcycle fails in a snowstorm. As Daniel put it, "*Two for Survival* is getting to sound like my story in parts."

Daniel worked on "Trapped" for five weeks, writing it in two parts. He wrote one draft and made only minor revisions on the page. Most of the exploring for this piece went on in Daniel's head. He spent time sitting and thinking before almost every word he wrote. He talked a lot about this story with other writers. He worried about the credibility of Mike, his narrator and main character. He wondered whether he had enough detail "so readers could see it happening," something he'd observed twice in his letters to me about Hinton's writing. Daniel also consulted a Boy Scout manual to find out about frostbite symptoms and treatment.

I'll share just the conclusion of "Trapped." In the story so far, Chris and Mike, out motorcycling on a springlike day in February, get caught in a snowstorm and pitch camp. When the temperature drops quickly, Chris suffers frostbite, which Mike treats. Mike makes various attempts to get them both rescued. His plan to tie Chris on the motorcycle and bull their way through the snow has just failed:

> I felt the cold again as if I were coming out of an invisible shell. What could I do? Darkness had begun, and I felt like falling into a deep sleep. I was so tired I didn't feel the cold, and I felt weak and limp. I untied Chris, which wasn't easy in my condition. I knew now the snow was too deep to travel in. I grabbed his shoulders and slid him off the seat. His foot got caught on the foot peg. I pulled and the bike came flying over and we went down, too. I felt my back hit the snow, and I lay there silently. How long could this last? It was then I remembered my grandfather telling me all those stories about storms that had lasted for five or ten days. This brought the little hope I'd held down to almost nothing.

> Suddenly I heard a low, muffled rumble. I sat up and strained to listen. I heard nothing but the rustle of the trees in the wind. After about five minutes, I heard it again, and it hit me like a bolt of lightning: it was the plow truck doing the road!

> I stood up and mindlessly ran toward the faint sound. I only made it a few feet before I collapsed in the knee-deep snow. I again frantically tried to run, but felt dead. I looked toward the sound and saw a yellow, flashing tint through the black, frozen night.

> It came closer; I could hardly think. I was warmed by the thought of being saved as the headlights came into sight. With my last remaining strength I stumbled toward Chris. I stood towering above him and screamed, "We're saved! We're saved!" There was no reaction.

> "Get up, Chris! Someone is here to pick us up." Still he didn't move. I panicked, not knowing what to do. I was really scared now, that the truck would go by and we'd be lost forever. I blindly wobbled about fifty feet in front of the truck…and it stopped.

Daniel loved "Trapped." His letters to me consistently included his opinions on how authors were concluding their novels; he loved his conclusion. He said, "I wanted to give the feeling of being trapped and then, at the end, just spring the trap and stop the story there, like, you're free."

At the end of the eighth grade Daniel wrote, "I have said all along that to write well you have to like it. Well, I like it. Yes, I am a writer. I learned to write by gradually writing and getting better…I used to say I wasn't a writer. But I didn't know that even if I'm writing in school, I am still a writer. My best pieces are the ones that sound like a professional writer wrote it."

Over his eighth grade year, Daniel read twelve novels and wrote me thirty-five letters. He used this year to get inside professional writers' prose and to write reading. And he did this because he had time to read and write his own choices of books and topics, as well as chances to talk with other readers and writers about good writing.

Tara

The gains students like Daniel made thrilled me. This pleasure was compounded by the equally impressive growth of other students, some of them already dedicated readers at the beginning of eighth grade. Tara, Daniel's classmate, falls into this category.

In September Tara said, "I love to read because I love to travel, and good books make me feel like I'm living in the story." She regularly bought books and could name half a dozen novels she'd read over the summer. Tara named her favorite books by listing their authors—Judy Blume, Lois Lowry, and Laura Ingalls Wilder. Books she didn't enjoy reading were textbook anthologies: "…books like *Thrust* and *To Turn a Stone* because the stories are boring and because I didn't like the questions after."

During her eighth-grade year, Tara continued to love books. She read fifty-one novels, September to June. And, like Daniel, at the start of the school year Tara provided information about herself as a writer. She, like Daniel, said, "No—I'm not a writer. A good writer needs a good imagination. That's not me."

Tara did not connect the writing she read and the writing she wrote. Although, unlike Daniel, she loved to read, the stories she read were someone else's domain—someone, somewhere, graced with a good imagination. Staying on the outside of written language, Tara read *reading*. And in writing class I fought with her for months as she accomplished little of her own, convinced she had no imagination and nothing to say. The little she wrote she didn't like: a long, unfocused piece about the first day of school that she abandoned; a couple of letters to the principal about school policies; a report for science class; a narrative about a babysitting experience that consumed pages, came to no point, and was eventually abandoned, too. I lost sleep over Tara.

But in reading class, Tara wrote—pages and pages and pages of letters. She was fascinated with what she did as a reader and how it compared with what I did when I read.

9/27

When I read, it's a special time for me to be alone. I sit on my bed with a pillow leaning against the wall and another one on my lap so I don't have to hold my arms up. I get completely relaxed. Also, after I finish reading, I just sit for a while thinking about the book. So by the time I see anyone, the feeling is gone. The only thing that bothers me is when I get a phone call or if it's time for dinner and I'm right in the middle of a good book. I try to get the interruption over with so I can get back to reading. How about you?

When you read, do you do it to take your mind off your problems and to go into a different world, or just for pleasure, or both? I think I do it for both.

Also, if you have your mind on a problem and then try to read, do you have to concentrate a little bit in the beginning to set your mind on the book? I'm just wondering because this happens to me.

Someday I'll write about students' reading processes as they describe them. For example, Tara articulates nicely how she plans ("Now I have about six books lined up to read, but I think I'll read *A Wrinkle in Time* next") and how she revises: how she re-seeks meaning ("I finished *Waiting Games*…I had to reread the ending a few times before I understood it" and "The ending of The Outsiders works so well I feel like starting over and reading it again").

Tara also wrote and talked a lot about how what she read made her feel. She cried when Paul died in *P.S., I Love You;* when a boy character behaved badly in another novel she wrote, "I don't know any boys like Danny, but if I did I'd want someone to dump him, just to show him how it feels"; she said, "*A Ring of Endless Light* gave me this wonderful feeling inside I just can't explain."

At the end of December Tara and I started talking about what authors were doing to give her feelings, as in this exchange about L'Engle's *Ring of Endless Light*.

> …I think this book is a good example of describing your surroundings and your thoughts and feelings. What I mean is: I can think back to parts of the story and see pictures of what it looked like. It's great to be able to do that! I really *love* this book! It's one of the *best* I've ever read!
>
> Tara

> 12/20
>
> Dear Tara,
>
> I know exactly what you mean. And the feeling you carry with you is a warm one, a contented one, right? I just reread the novel *The French Lieutenant's Woman*, and I'm carrying its "feeling" with me today. I suspect I'll go home tonight and re-read its first ending (it has two) as a way to extend the feeling. What is it about good writing that allows us to do this? What makes good books have this effect?
>
> NA

> 12/20
>
> You're right about my feeling—that's what it's like. I sometimes re-read parts of books just like you might do. I think it is because the authors include so many thoughts, feelings, and descriptions that we can "lose" ourselves in the books, in the writing.
>
> Tara

From January on, Tara wrote letters about authors as people making decisions—choosing how they'll present information; controlling tone, voice, and style; doing specific things to give her reading feelings. Her new vocabulary and perspective came from two sources: the way I talked with her about books and the way students and I talked about their writing in writing workshop. For example, she wrote:

> I like *My Darling, My Hamburger*. I like the technique of the letters. I also like the way the boy's feelings are told—in most novels boys are only objects that talk…In *And You Give Me a Pain, Elaine*, I like the way the author brings everything together. The small episodes are so different—it's almost like the author wrote many short stories and put them together. Yet they all fit. Like a puzzle!

And of *Where the Red Fern Grows*, Tara wrote:

> I love the descriptive words, the detail, and the way everything ties in…This book shows a new way to begin a story—going back in time through thoughts…About *Red Fern*: I pictured the boy as Daniel. I don't know why. Maybe because he's that type.

Like Daniel, Tara's major literary influence in eighth grade was S. E. Hinton, who drafted her first published novel, *The Outsiders*, at her dining room table when she was fifteen. Tara, too, started modeling her writing on Hinton's. This excerpt is from March.

> I loved *The Outsiders*! I can't believe Hinton was only 15! It's really interesting the way she asked her friends for help…My latest poem ("Sleep") I thought of on the way to Sugarloaf. I planned out just what I wanted to say. In the part where I repeat myself I did that because of *The Outsiders*. The only reason I thought of doing it this way was because of this book.

I asked Tara if she were noticing herself reading differently, coming at others' writing as someone who's a writer herself. She replied:

> What you said about reading like a writer—I never used to do that. Last year I wouldn't have known what you meant. I guess I really do read books differently now. It's interesting because lots of times I don't realize it when I learn things, but this is something I'm aware of.

Once Tara named it, she knew it. From this point on, she refined her theory:

> I just realized I'm starting to like books with points: books that make me think, that have meaning…One of the best things you've done for me is you've opened books up, almost like dissecting something in science. I think I enjoy them more now that I can understand and appreciate what the authors have done.

> For me, writing and reading are starting to combine. The other night my dad and I were talking about me and why I *love* to read but don't enjoy writing. "I think it's because I can't write the kinds of things I like to read." This was the night before I wrote "Beautiful Mountains."

"Beautiful Mountains," a vignette written at the end of March, was the first piece Tara wrote that she thought was good. It was a breakthrough for her as a writer.

Beautiful Mountains

"This is so fun, and it's beautiful!" was all I could think as Justine and I skied down Lower Winter's Way. We were at Sugarloaf, and this was our first run down. Justine was a little ways ahead of me, but I was too involved in making sure I didn't fall to watch her. This entire slope was covered with moguls, so I had to pay attention. Every so often we would stop to look around.

It really was beautiful! There were mountains all around, and the trees were so weighted down with snow most were bent over. The mountains were bluish with lots of white patches. There were clouds covering the peaks. I had never seen anything that looked like this, so as we skied down, my mind was filled with beautiful pictures.

All of a sudden, Justine's voice interrupted my thoughts. "Tara!" she yelled in a horrified voice. "Look!" My eyes focused on where she was pointing. Two ski patrolmen were dragging a rescue sled about fifteen feet away from us. The only part of the person that we could see was the face. It was a woman; she reminded me of a mannequin. Her eyes were closed, and even though I've never seen a dead person, that is what I think one would look like. She had fair skin, but underneath it was very dark. She looked so cold. She also looked like she was in pain—tensed up, I guess…dead; that's the best word to describe how she looked.

The sled passed by in a matter of seconds, but it was long enough to get a picture of her fixed in my mind. I looked again at the once-beautiful mountains. All I could see was her. I'll never know if she was dead, but beautiful mountains will never look the same.

Tara's comments about "Beautiful Mountains," her writing, and her reading were the germs of a report she wrote in May. I gave her a nudge, asking if she'd be interested in studying and describing what happened to her as a reader and writer. She was interested. In her lead, Tara lays claim to the title she had refused before: writer.

> My Thoughts About Reading and Writing
> (How They Help Each Other to Help Me)
>
> By Tara
>
> I, as a writer, learned to write by reading, writing, listening to other people's writing, and discussing my writing.
>
> The way reading helps me is when I "open up" a book I've read. To do this I sort out the parts I like and don't like and decide why. I notice how the author started, ended, and tied the middle together. Then, I look for good describing words and the way thoughts and feelings are used.
>
> I try to decide whether or not the book is "good." For me a "good" book is one that I enjoy, one that fully takes me into another world, one that is believable, one that I get so caught up in I want to finish it, and one that I can picture in my mind
>
> When I finish a book, if I can go back and picture different parts, I know the author added many details and descriptions. This is something I try to do with my own writing.
>
> Madeleine L'Engle's books (*A Wrinkle in Time* and *A Ring of Endless Light*), *Where the Red Fern Grows* by Wilson Rawls, and *Find a Stranger, Say Goodbye* by Lois Lowry are all good examples of this kind of vivid writing.
>
> Learning to write well also takes a lot of practice. In the two years I've been writing, I've only written one piece I would consider "good." But I've learned from all the mistakes in my other pieces.
>
> I also learn from other people's work. My one "good" piece ("Beautiful Mountains") was written the way it was because of a few, very good stories by other authors.

I kept "Beautiful Mountains" in my head (without much conversation) because of a story I really liked by my friend Justine Dymond, entitled "A Night in the Life." I made a point with my piece because of *The Outsiders* by S. E. Hinton. I added and took out certain details because of other students' stories I've heard that have too many, not enough, or the wrong details.

Also, when I finish a good book I like to sit and think about it for a few minutes. When I read "Beautiful Mountains" to my class, there was a few-second silence at the end. I could tell people were thinking about it. This is the kind of response I wanted, and it made me feel good about my story.

Reading letters have also been a big help. Talking (writing) has helped me to understand reading and writing much more than I used to.

All these factors, combined as one, have helped me in gaining knowledge about reading and writing. I read and write differently now and, I would say, better.

Conclusion

All these factors are combined as one in one place: the literate environment of a writing and reading workshop.

I've called upon metaphor to characterize this environment. It's Frank Smith's reading and writing club. It's the Merry Pranksters' bus that holds everyone. It's a dining room table with seventy chairs around it.

A literate environment is not a program—for example, a monolithic writing process featuring prewriting, writing, and revising, or some other combination of locksteps. Neither is it teachers and students corresponding about books. In schools, a literate environment takes shape wherever written language is the natural domain of the children and adults who work and play there.

I've described my own attempts at establishing a literate environment, my own particular methods. But it's beyond specific teaching methodologies that Daniel and Tara point me. They—and all the other eighth grade readers and writers—leave me with a fellow feeling I haven't known before as a teacher. Now that I'm off my English teacher pedestal, I want to deepen and extend this feeling the rest of my years in the classroom.

I think my students and I will find our way together. We're partners in this enterprise, all of us moving together *inside* writing and reading.

Afterword: Nancie's Final Tweaks

Twenty-five years after Daniel and Tara, I'm still teaching seventh and eighth grade English and still trying to perfect the literate environment of my classroom. I'm not discouraged by either "still."

I love young adolescents—I know I'll laugh hard, be surprised in a good way, mostly, and learn something every day I get to be their teacher. And I like the challenge of figuring out methods that will offer my kids sense, skills, and satisfaction as writers and readers. Crafting pedagogy—determining how students can best learn to write and read literature—remains my favorite act of authoring, as well as the satisfying, intellectual challenge that keeps me in the classroom.

Looking back on Daniel, Tara, and workshop teaching in the early 1980s, I can recognize the same conditions that underpin my methods today. My seventh and eighth graders continue to write and read in a workshop because this is still the closest a classroom can get to a context that supports the real work of writers and readers. Students have time in class to write and read. They choose their topics for writing and books for reading. And they confer with me and one another about their emerging drafts and about the published writing that they're reading. Time, responsibility, and response are bedrock. The significant difference between then and now? It's my role as the teacher.

In 1981, when I transformed my English classes into writing and reading workshops, I didn't yet realize what was possible for my students as writers and readers. I invented the rules as we went along, based on my observations of their experiences. I understand now that this was a necessary step in my professional evolution—to begin with what a classroom looks, sounds, and feels like when kids are functioning as writers and readers, versus doing an English curriculum—before naming the new classroom ground rules. For me, at this juncture, it was more sensible and productive to emphasize *context*—to focus on how the variables of time, choice, and response can comprise a literate environment—because I didn't yet know how or what to teach. In Daniel and Tara's workshop, there were no mini-lessons and minimal teacher expectations. I couldn't see myself as an authority figure because I was learning almost as much as my kids.

Today, in addition to sponsoring the conditions for writing and reading, I teach my students how to act as writers and readers. To extend the metaphors of the 1980s, I drive the bus; I set the table; I founded a literacy club and I'm its honorary president. Through mini-lessons about topics, genres, conventions, and techniques of craft, as well as an individualized spelling program (Atwell, 2002); daily poetry discussions (Atwell, 2006); and specific, grounded expectations and guidelines for writing and reading workshops (Atwell, 1998; Atwell, 2007), I demonstrate to seventh and eighth graders how to write well across genres, how to read with fluency and engagement, and how to become critics of literature. I learned to tip the balance: while my students still have big voices, I have a big voice, too, as a literate grown-up.

I know some things about writing now—about efficient, productive ways to plan, draft, revise, and edit; about where ideas for writing come from; about principles of crafting texts so they read as literature; about the qualities of effective writing in many genres; and about the conventions a reader's eyes and mind expect. In mini-lessons I teach the approaches that can make a difference and try to leave little to chance. I no longer hope a writer like Daniel will intuit his way into writing effective narratives, by way of the stories he reads; instead I demonstrate to my students the knowledge I've gleaned along the way as a reader, writer, and teacher of memoir and short fiction.

Likewise, in writing conferences, I stopped merely reflecting back the drafts—or lack of same—of a student like Tara, hoping she might invent solutions to her problems as a writer. Now I level with kids, as an experienced grown-up working with less-experienced kids. I listen, but I also make suggestions, give advice, identify problems, and demonstrate solutions. Conferences have become occasions for teaching my students about what else they can try as writers. Between my lessons to the whole group, conversations with writers, and kids' own experiments and discoveries as writers, individuals develop a repertoire of strategies that help them change their writing for the better on purpose. They become more productive, more literary, and more satisfied—convinced that their writing matters, both to the people they are today and the people they might become.

Raising the stakes made a difference, too. Over time I moved from a handful of guidelines about what writers should do in writing workshop to—as figures one and two illustrate—lists of expectations and rules so specific I can barely squeeze them on a page. But as I learned more about good writing—about the experiments, habits, and intentions that make a difference—I learned to ask more of my student writers. In turn, I raised my own stakes: it's my responsibility to teach students *how* to meet high expectations for planning, writing, organization, work in genres, quantity, and quality. Again, twenty-five years ago I didn't know what to expect of Daniel and Tara, and I had few specifics to teach them. Now I understand: my job is to create a literate environment *and* expect a lot, teach a lot, and continue to develop my own knowledge of demonstrations, approaches, and model texts that will invite excellence and show kids the way.

In revisiting Daniel, Tara, and the beginnings of my writing and reading workshops, I recognize and celebrate the power of real writing and reading. But because I didn't yet have specific methods to help them, students spent a fair amount of time spinning their wheels before they got hooked—Tara as a writer and Daniel as both. Over time they did engage, and they did come inside. I think this is a tribute to the sheer power of time, choice, and response—of books and topics freely chosen and opportunities to chat with a teacher and peers about one's writing and reading.

So, if Daniel and Tara showed up in my classroom come September, I would continue to trust in the power of stories and self-expression to entice their engagement. But I'd also be more active about easing the way—with booktalks about great titles in our classroom library; with daily check-ins to make sure that every reader is happy and engaged; with topic mini-lessons that invite a writer like Tara to realize how much she has to say and a writer like Daniel to begin the school year with writing that matters to him; with lessons about genres and principles of craft that give writers the models, advice, and inspiration they're looking for; with individualized spelling instruction that targets each student's confusions and uncertainties; and with the expectation of *quantity*—of numbers of pages read and drafted—because productivity is the foundation of anyone's skill as a reader or writer.

The gains that Daniel and Tara made still thrill me: in this early incarnation of writing and reading workshop, they and their classmates became writers and readers. Together we learned how a teacher and her students could write and read from the inside. Today, the knowledge I gain as I continue to write, read, and teach takes me even deeper. Conveying my knowledge to my students—showing, telling, and expecting—affords them more pleasure and more power. Teaching from the inside makes it that much more likely that writing and reading will change kids, sustain them, and make *inside* feel like a worthwhile place to spend a lifetime.

Find topics and purposes for your writing that matter to you, your life, who you are now, and who you might become.

Create and maintain plans of your territories as a writer: the ideas, topics, purposes, genres, and poetic forms you'd like to experience and explore.

Make your own decisions about what's working and what needs more work in pieces of your writing. Be the first responder to your writing, and learn to read yourself with a critical, literary eye and ear.

Listen to, ask questions about, and comment on others' writing in ways that help them move their writing forward toward literature.

Take notes and create a handbook of information presented in writing mini-lessons, recorded chronologically, with a table of contents (Rief 1992).

Produce **at least 3–5 pages of rough draft each week** (Rief 1992). Recognize that good writers build quality upon a foundation of quantity.

Work on your writing for at least an hour every weekend.

During this academic year, produce finished writing in each of the following genres:

- 3–5 poems
- a memoir
- a short story
- a review
- a profile
- an essay

Attempt professional publication.

Recognize that readers' eyes and minds need your writing to be conventional in format, spelling, punctuation, and usage. Work toward conventionality and legibility.

When you're stuck or uncertain, use the resources available to you in this room, including your writing-reading handbook and your lists of writing territories. And experiment with the techniques I've shown you in mini-lessons and conferences.

Take care of the writing materials, resources, equipment, and computers I've provided for you.

Each trimester, establish and work toward significant, relevant goals for yourself as a writer.

In every writing workshop, take a *deliberate stance* (Harwayne 1992) toward writing well. Try to make your writing literature, and use what you've been shown in conferences and mini-lessons to help you get there.

Work as hard in writing workshop as I do. Recreate happy times, work through sad times, discover what you know about a subject and learn more, convey information and request it, parody, petition, play, explore, argue, apologize, advise, sympathize, imagine, look and look again, express love, show gratitude, and make money.

Figure 1 Expectations for Writing Workshop, 2006–2007

1. Save everything: it's all part of the history of a piece of writing and your history as a writer, plus you never know what you might want to come back to later and use. On the computer, either label and save each of the multiple versions of a piece on your hard drive, or print a copy of each draft and file it.

2. Date and label everything you write to help you keep track of what you've done (e.g., *plans*, *draft #1*, or *title brainstorm*). On the computer, label multiple versions as D.1, D.2, etc., and type your name and the date on everything before you print it.

3. Write on one side of the paper only. Always skip lines, and always print double-spaced. Both will make revision, polishing, and editing easier, more productive, *possible*. Professional writers always double space until the final copy. You may wish to draft single-spaced on the computer, so you can see more text at a time, but shift to double-space when you print, revise, and edit.

4. Draft your prose writing in sentences and paragraphs. Draft your poems in lines and stanzas. Don't go back into a mess of text and try to create form. Format as you go: real writers do this, too.

5. Get into the habit of punctuating and spelling as conventionally as you can *while* you're composing: this is something else real writers do.

6. When composing on the computer, **print a double-spaced version at least every two days.** Then, away from the computer, read the text with a pen in your hand. Consider and work with the whole text as a piece of literature rather than a part-at-a-time on the screen.

7. When composing on the computer, spell-check only at the very end, when you formally edit, and record any misspellings (*vs.* typos) on your personal spelling list at this time.

8. Understand that writing is thinking. Do nothing to distract me or other writers. Don't put your words into their brains as they're struggling to find their own. Instead, find your own small room, close the door, and listen to your voice.

9. When you confer with me, use as soft a voice as I use when I talk to you: *whisper*.

10. Confer with peers when you have a reason to. Use a conference area, and record responses on a peer conference form, so the writer can leave the conference with a plan and a reminder of what happened. Limit peer conferences to occasions when you have a specific problem that could benefit from a specific friend's response.

11. Maintain and update an individual proofreading list. Refer to it when you edit your writing.

12. Self-edit as completely as you can. Use a red pen, and complete an editing check-sheet to show what you know about conventions of writing.

13. When a piece of writing is finished, clip or staple everything together, including plans, drafts, editing checksheet, and peer conference form, and file it in your permanent writing folder, with the final copy on top. Remember to record every finished piece of writing on the form inside your permanent folder. Collect data about yourself as a writer, look for patterns, and take satisfaction in your accomplishments over time.

14. Write as well and as much as you can: work hard and make literature.

Figure 2 Rules for Writing Workshop

Works Cited

Atwell, Nancie. 1982. "Class-Based Writing Research: Teachers Learn from Students." *English Journal*. 70: 84–87.

———. 1998. *In the Middle: New Understandings About Writing, Reading, and Learning*. Portsmouth, NH: Heinemann.

———. 2002. *Lessons That Change Writers*. Portsmouth, NH: *first*hand / Heinemann.

———. 2006. *Naming the World: A Year of Poems and Lessons*. Portsmouth, NH: *first*hand / Heinemann.

———. 2007. *The Reading Zone: How to Help Kids Become Skilled, Passionate, Habitual, Critical Readers*. New York: Scholastic.

Giacobbe, Mary Ellen. July, 1983. Classroom Presentation at Northeastern University Writing Workshop. Martha's Vineyard, MA.

Graves, Donald, Lucy Calkins, and Susan Sowers. 1978–81. "Papers and articles initiated at the Writing Process Laboratory". University of New Hampshire, Durham, N. H.

Harwayne, Shelley. 1992. *Lasting Impressions: Weaving Literature into the Writing Workshop*. Portsmouth, NH: Heinemann.

Newkirk, Thomas. 1988. "Young Writers as Critical Readers." *Understanding Writing*. 2d ed. Ed. T. Newkirk and N. Atwell. Portsmouth, NH: Heinemann.

Rief, Linda. 1992. *Seeking Diversity: Language Arts with Adolescents*. Portsmouth, NH: Heinemann.

Smith, Frank. October 1983. "Reading and Writing Club." Maine Reading Association Conference. Bangor, Maine.

Staton, Jana. 1980. "Writing and Counseling: Using a Dialogue Journal." *Language Arts* 57: 514–18.

13

Plugging in to Twenty-First Century Writers

Sara Kajder

Sara Kajder is an assistant professor at Virginia Polytechnic Institute and State University (Virginia Tech). A recipient of the Conference on English Education National Technology Leadership fellowship and a former fellow through the Center for Technology and Teacher Education at the University of Virginia, her research focuses on uses of emergent technologies in developing readers at the middle and secondary levels, as well as methods that are useful in leading teachers to effectively integrate technology into their pedagogy and curricula. Prior to her work in teacher education at the University of Louisville and the University of Virginia, Kajder taught middle and high school English language arts in Montgomery County, Maryland, and in Pittsburgh, Pennsylvania. Amongst over forty national and international conference presentations and twelve published articles, she is a nationally known speaker and the author of Bringing the Outside In *(2006) and* The Tech Savvy English Classroom *(2003).*

Introduction

Walking into sixth period language arts, I was met by thirty-five tenth-grade students who each read and wrote at thirty-five different levels. The bookshelves along the rear wall held less than thirty bedraggled copies of the core texts we'd be reading together and sixteen copies of *Elements of Literature* anthologies stacked on the shelves along the walls. There was one computer (a barely functioning Apple Classic IIE) in the rear corner of the room. It took no time to survey the tools at hand. It took significantly longer to dig into the literate lives of the students who made up our community of learners (to use the district's latest buzzword).

On-level English in this school meant that this was a class of students who hadn't scored highly enough on the previous year's assessments to be placed into standard or honors or advanced placement level classes. To be honest, I was surprised, a little dismayed, and genuinely frustrated by how strongly these students resisted when I spoke to them as readers and writers. They wanted—no, they pleaded—for worksheets. The English classroom they knew was about writing on the line, selecting from the word bank, and waiting for the next bell. They didn't want to be seen.

As I grew to know them, I was overwhelmed by who they were as readers and writers outside of our classroom walls. EunSui maintained a weblog detailing his experiences as an ESL student that was widely read and received more hits in a day than our school site did in a month. Gerald, Ashley, and Amber were amazing photographers. Leah was compiling a family digital video to be shared when her older brother left to serve in the Gulf that November. Brit and Sam played PS2 games every afternoon, playing one another but also tapping into a global network, interacting with players in an international field. Every student in the class had some interest that was anchored in authentic reading and writing; it was just something that lived well outside of our classroom, and something that hadn't yet led them to see themselves as uniquely and richly literate.

One week into the school year, I asked students in this class to help me generate a list of the tools that they use as writers. Sahar, a boisterous student with boundless energy, worked as our scribe, listing her ideas alongside the occasional idea offered up by the crowd. The class list included the standards—pen, pencil, paper, typewriters, computers. Not a shining moment in my teaching, it had taken us close to six minutes to just get those words on the board. And then Sahar added the word *weblog*.

Sam called out from the rear of the classroom, "I'm not down with that," leading several of his peers to look at the new content of our list.

I pushed Sam, "Tell me more."

"That's not writing. You asked us for tools we use as writers. That means stuff from in here. That can't be on the list."

Sahar defended herself, "If this is brainstorming, I can keep this up here. I write more in my blog than I EVER do in school. It stays."

After what felt like an awkward, charged pause, Ted offered, "Well then, put down iMovie." Before I knew it, the list had grown to include video games ("Because I get to make up the story as I make decisions—that's writing"), highlighters, sticky notes ("If it lives on a page and I write on it, it's a tool"), notepads, Wikipedia, stencils, podcasts ("My speaking is like writing aloud"), digital cameras, cell phones ("We text message notes from classes, so isn't that writing?"), and spreadsheets ("I like to make lists").

I offered, "Let's go back to what Sam had to say. Tell me about what from this list is 'in here.' Or, in other words, tell me about the tools and spaces that we use in school or in class."

We made a chart using a transparency (which was quickly added to the list), creating two columns: school tools and out-of-school tools. School tools included no surprises: pens, pencils, pens, typewriters, notepads, stencils, computers (with the note: when we're in the lab), highlighters, and sticky notes (with the note: when we have supplies). Everything else (Wikipedia, cell phones, podcasts, video games, computers [with the note: because we never get into the lab]) went onto the out-of-school side.

As we talked about the division between these two columns, some really big ideas began to emerge. Those literacies and tools that these students valued the most were the ones that lived almost completely outside of our classroom. To kids, this wasn't a question of resources as much as it was a question of content. As Gus explained, "This is what I'm wired to do. You'll never see it here because school is about print. It isn't about what's next." Or, as Ted added, "Writing in school is about telling answers, but writing online or with these things is about what I see, what I know, and how that interacts with the people who are reading my work." Or, as Sahar shared:

> When we use technology in school, it's to produce. We type a paper. We make a PowerPoint. When I write with technology outside of school, it's because I have something to say and someone is actually listening.

Teaching English with Technology

Teaching with technology amplifies instructional practice. Sometimes this means calling out those moments where planning, curriculum, and tools come together to move students in new, powerful directions. In others, for all of us, it reveals holes in planning, misreading of content, instability in resources or the network, and, most critically, those moments where we allowed the technology to come ahead of our instructional goals and students' needs.

Thinking in a really general, global way, integrating technology into the English classroom affords us with unique opportunities to teach actively, build classroom community, build interpretive community, and lead students to read and to write for real, authentic purposes. Teaching is an interactive process that begins and ends with seeing our students. As a teacher, I am continually surprised by how much more complicated this kind of responsive teaching is than it seems, as it is ongoing and never completely finished. Put in another way, bringing technology into the English classroom provides us with multiple ways of seeing students' strengths as readers and writers.

One of the biggest lessons that I've learned in working with students and twenty-first-century writing spaces is that new technologies now allow us to work with multimodal composition in ways that transcend the paper-string-glue-and-tape projects that I formerly used. Multimodal texts offer layers of meaning and open up what counts as communication within the English classroom. Or, in other words, opening up assignments so that my students can compose as filmmakers (e.g., using iMovie or Windows Movie Maker) or as graphic artists (e.g., using Photoshop or flickr.com) allows me to engage more students, to welcome more of them into a rich community of readers and writers, and to give them a reason to really value what we do in English class.

What this requires is emergent technology use not the urgent technology use that has typified much of what we've done in the past fifteen or so years since computers have arrived in our teaching spaces. We've urgently hurried to wire classrooms, loaded them with new equipment, and required teachers to spend instructional time using tools that were largely unfamiliar or that didn't solve our instructional problems. Urgent technology use has resulted in students averaging less than fifteen minutes of access a week within secondary classrooms (Norris, Sullivan, and Soloway 2003, 22). Emergent technology use is different. It requires time spent deeply considering the instructional value added by new tools, and time spent crafting instruction that puts content and instructional goals ahead of teaching the technology.

This doesn't require that we become technology experts. It requires that we continue to work as readers and writers, and that means paying close attention to the important changes that are happening to the ways we read and write within a twenty-first-century, "flat-world" culture. It means valuing an expanded definition of what it means to be literate. It means having a willingness to see students and to learn together. It means asking hard questions—of our curriculum, of our teaching, of our learning, and of our students. As much as I advocate learning from students, I disagree strongly with those who argue that our students are digital natives. Kids are digital immigrants, too, when it comes to purposeful and powerful uses of emergent technologies as readers and writers. If anything, teachers are more important than ever.

The vignettes ahead won't teach you how to use those software tools, but they will lead you to think with them like an English teacher. There are two guiding questions essential to the work ahead:

1. What are the unique capacities of this tool? (i.e., what can I do with it that I can't do with anything else?)
2. What does it allow me to do that is better (instructionally) than what I could do without it?

The tools that we have available for this type of writing, composing, and meaning-making are going to change—easily within the life of this book, and absolutely within the life of our teaching careers. However, those two essential questions will remain the same and will remain valuable tools to help keep your thinking focused on teaching and how to move students. In critically considering the multiple modes, mediums, and means at our disposal in relation to our students' needs and skills as readers and writers, we create enormous possibilities for where our classrooms can lead.

Stepping into Classrooms

Emergent technologies provide opportunities for users to do more than just access information or content. This read-write Web changes our roles from readers (and writers if you were developing your own website) to readers, writers, editors and collaborators. The new techie terms to know include: weblogs, wikis, RSS feeds, podcasts, screencasts, aggregators, social bookmarking, digital storytelling. The ability to now easily communicate in new modes and with new audiences for new purposes has big implications for how we use these tools in the English classroom—and raises some big questions. How does reading and writing in these online spaces impact our understanding of what it means to be literate? How do we best use these tools to engage student readers and writers to purposefully and effectively use these tools?

Each of the narratives that follow will walk us into a different English classroom where teachers and students are working with emergent technologies as readers, writers, thinkers, speakers, viewers, directors, editors, collaborators, and listeners. We'll explore the unique capacities of each of the tools but will spend more time looking at the potential instructional value that each brings to our work with student writers.

Reinventing Literature Circle Discussions Through Podcasting

Students in Room 7B have several tools at their disposal when it comes to selecting books for independent reading and, eventually, use in peer literature circles. Shelves of books grouped by topic and genre line the classroom. Posters hanging on the wall depict cover art or student constructed ads for particularly compelling titles. A binder holds the monthly newsletters developed and distributed by the local teen outpost library. An entire wall in the rear of the class is filled with student written sticky notes, which share reactions, responses, and suggestions related to past and present readings. In this classroom, the most used resource sits at the rear of the classroom where a single computer houses the class library of podcasted literature circle discussions. To listen, students select and play a five- to seven-minute clip compiled and broadcasted by their peers.

Owen sits at the computer, selects the folder of discussions on Lois Lowry's *The Giver* and selects a file labeled "why this book." After double clicking on the file, he hears a musical intro, which is immediately followed by the voices of his classmates:

> "Hello, and welcome to our fifth and last podcasted discussion of *The Giver*. Amidst other topics, we talked a lot this afternoon about why this is a really important—no, a really cool read. So, listen up . . ."

What is a podcast?   Deemed the 2005 Word of the Year by the New Oxford American Dictionary, podcasting has the potential to become a transformative teaching technology. In the simplest possible terms, podcasting, especially in the classroom, is the creation and distribution of amateur radio (Richardson 2006). Though the term emerged linked to Apple's iPod, podcasting is the online broadcasting of audio content, which a listener subscribes to using free podcatching software like iTunes, iPodder, or HappyFish. Once a user has subscribed, podcasts are downloaded onto a computer (or MP3 player if you want to go portable) and are available for on-demand listening.

To create a podcast, the only tools you need are a digital audio recorder (or, in most of the classrooms in which I work, a computer with a microphone), access to a server on which you store the file, and a means of publishing (ranging from a web page to an RSS feed) the content that you create. In all honesty, the ease with which these can be created and made available makes it much more important that we focus on the content and having something to say rather than where to point and click. More sophisticated podcasts (called *enhanced podcasts*) can include video that includes text, images, and other multimedia, but to keep the entry point low and the emphasis on the task (as opposed to the technology), I focus on using purely audio podcasts.

Though there has been a relative explosion of class podcasts available through iTunes, several can be located by going to class or school system websites. The likely content of what you'll find? Some teachers podcast lectures or classroom content for students to access outside of class. You will find lots of examples at http://epnweb.org. Others challenge students to create podcasts, which synthesize material learned like those at Radio WillowWeb at Willowdale Elementary School in Omaha, Nebraska). Social studies and humanities teachers are podcasting oral histories. Science teachers are asking students to broadcast experiments as a play-by-play, and math students are narrating the steps taken as they solve problems and work with complex functions. The key is having something important enough to say that others are using and learning from the content. Podcasting is about knowledge creation and communication, not where you click.

Into the classroom   Literature circles, or book clubs, provide classroom spaces in which student readers do the work that proficient, engaged readers do. We read self-selected, interesting books and seek opportunities for rich, authentic discussion. Literature circles crashed miserably in my early attempts as I continued to violate the cardinal rule—let the students choose from an assortment of texts. I felt locked-in to my assigned curriculum and would try to run literature circles around *The Scarlet Letter* or *The Great Gatsby* as a means of engaging student interest and generating meaningful discussion. I would go home exhausted from days of running around from group to group, feeling as if I needed to be wholly present in each circle in order to keep the discussion moving, focused, reflective, and useful. Furthermore, I required students to complete inauthentic essay assignments at the close of each discussion.

After working with colleagues, reading everything I could find by Nancy Steinecke and Smokey Daniels, and sitting in on sessions at NCTE, I made some instrumental changes. Instead of locking-in to a set text, I started creating thematic units that allowed for student choice of rich, compelling texts that weren't necessarily on the required list but that were rigorous and linked to the themes the required texts pointed toward.

My role changed. Instead of sitting in on the literature circle, I circled the classroom, listening, observing, and facilitating. One part of this change had to do with changes in how I documented what was happening. I now use two varying kinds of culminating reports: "noticings" about group process (Steineke 2002) student group podcasts of their discussion work. As Daniels (2003) writes:

> the book projects that follow literature circles are not natural, relevant, or energizing activities. Instead, they are something we teachers assign just to evoke a tangible product, something that can be graded" (90).

Through podcasting, the relevance of students' work is ratcheted up as the audience is no longer just the members of the circle or me in the moments I grab in each circle. Podcasts allow students, and anyone with access to the class website, to be both a producer and a consumer of content.

What does that mean for what happens in the English classroom? Each group discussion is recorded using either a laptop from the school wireless cart or a digital voice recorder (very often a student's iPod, removed from the locker or backpack where it's typically required to be kept and plugged into a small microphone called an iTalk). Only student voices are present in the discussion, as they've already been through training earlier in the semester—all of which allows for them to completely own the discussion. This is their space to think, to play, and to push. At times, students are asked to upload, or podcast, the entire discussion. More regularly, however, I ask students to mix their file (using a free audio tool like GarageBand on a Mac or Audacity—a cross-platform tool available online) so that they extract specific parts of the discussion. On the classroom wall, I hang the following list of prompts that they use to focus their work:

1. What questions were left unresolved?
2. Which moments of the discussion were the most compelling?
3. What parts of the discussion might help convince a peer to read it?
4. Where did the discussion fall apart or fail?
5. What are the key ideas emerging in your conversation of this text?

Students' podcasts sound like polished radio shows, often beginning with self-recorded or self-mixed audio introductions with echoes of NPR and the punch of an adolescents' chosen beat. More importantly, students will also add their own framing audio to the podcast, either setting up what we're about to hear or synthesizing or commenting on the content throughout the file. In doing so, podcasting invites these students to naturally evaluate their own work and set goals for subsequent discussions. Evaluation has become less about students seeking out my feedback and more about their own responses to the dialogue, work and products of the circle.

This work has become as much about writing as it has reading and listening. Students write in order to record their reactions to the reading; to plan their contributions to the discussion; to note what happens within the group; to capture questions that emerge; and to evaluate their processes, contributions, and work. Much of this is unprompted, emerging as students seek to produce strong podcasts. As Eliot wrote in his reflective journal, "I no longer know how to read without a pen and paper nearby—I write to think. I write to speak. I write to bring it back to the book. It just makes sense." Because these are real kids, there are great discussions and ones that go absolutely nowhere. However, as Darik explained, "If I write, at least I've got something to work with."

Once we became more comfortable with podcasting, I took things one step further by broadening the community of participants in our class literature circles. Using Skype (www.skype.com), a free online Internet telephone service, and a laptop linked to the Internet, we were able to invite other students, experts, authors, community members, and teachers to participate in our discussions. Skype allows up to five participants to share the same conference call and includes a tool that allows for recording. Sometimes we'll invite an author through email to call in and discuss a text with the class. More regularly, we contact scholars or experts to add a layer of authenticity to our work and communicate that reading and writing means something outside of the classroom as well as inside our shared space. Or, we'll engage with other students who are working on shared or similar projects and texts. As Seth explained in class, "Our discussions are global...People all over are talking with us about what we read and what we think, and then we all get to listen again."

In the listening, students are also finding power in the work. To keep things secure, we publicize the URL that houses our podcasts only to the class community and those who participate in the conversations. These pages get more hits than the district website in a school system that serves over 125,000 students each year. Students are downloading their work and the work of their peers. Some of this is prompted by students' desire to revisit the conversation. As Corey offered, "I learn from hearing what I said. But, bigger, like, sometimes I get stuck on one thought—and I'm blocked there. If I re-listen, I discover things I didn't hear." Others use the discussions to prompt their reading, to dig more deeply into a complex text (as Shelley shared, "If I'm reading something that makes no sense, I like seeing how another group went at it"), or to improve their own discussion skills. Warner put it plainly, "I listen to really hear what others said, but I do so to figure out how to do it better...to read, to share, to question, to make this matter."

Collaborative Writing with a Wiki

Leading reluctant readers to engage with literary texts can pose a significant instructional challenge. For Mrs. Jackson, a third year, tenth-grade English teacher working with a new curriculum, this was compounded by a robust reading list that began with Hossenin's *The Kite Runner*. In thinking through her instructional goals, Mrs. Jackson ticked through many objectives but centered on three: to engage students in reading for an authentic purpose, to develop the beginnings of an interpretive class community, and to begin exploration of the course's essential understanding that literature is a mirror of human experience.

In order to foster collaboration and "provide students with a real group of readers to talk with," she uses the Global School Network (www.globalschoolnet.org/index.html) and ePals(www.epals.com) to locate a class in a multileveled, international school in London who are also reading this same text. Working with the teacher of that classroom through email, she decides that while reading this novel her students will work in small groups with the paired class to write a shared/collaborative essay on a topic connecting their experiences in reading the novel and the issues that it raised.

Using a wiki (www.pbwiki.com) as the online writing space, student groups were able to log in and add their writing to the essay, leaving one another notes, suggestions, and edits. With the bank of three computers in her classroom, she plans to cycle student groups through the computers, each receiving one day per week for the duration of the six-week unit. Students will also be welcome to use the class computers before and after school and during break periods and lunch.

Where students spend a majority of class time reading and discussing the novel (using multiple graphic organizers and instructional scaffolds to work their way through what is a challenging read), Mrs. Jackson notes that not only are her typically reluctant students contributing to class, but the level of their discussion surprises her almost daily. She explains:

> It usually takes me months to get students to trust me enough to be willing to read and to feel strong enough to read...and I think that this has everything to do with the ways in which they are writing while they read. Several students talk about this as real writing, not because it's just their words on the page, but because the writing reflects a discussion and a reason for reading that goes beyond what we typically have happening in the classroom. I don't teach them how to use the wiki—that part is transparent enough that it wasn't needed. Instead, I'm teaching them how to develop ideas, how to read closely, and all kinds of collaborative skills.

What is a wiki?   A wiki is a collaborative website where anyone can add content and anyone can edit content that has already been published. An immediate caution: this doesn't have to be as open as it sounds, and the classroom reality demands a tighter use. I use a variety of free wiki websites (e.g., www.pbwiki.com) in schools, each of which allows us to easily password-protect the site, create unique log-ins for each user, and follow the changes as they are made to the content of the pages. The content of the wiki is viewable to anyone who knows the URL. However, to contribute, edit, change, or comment on content, a user would have to have both a log-in and a password.

When it comes to the unique capacities of a wiki, the first thing to consider is the origin of the name. In Hawaiian, *wiki-wiki* means "fast." Publishing occurs quickly on the wiki, which is an effective motivator for student writers. Adding content or making changes to the page is as simple as it is quick. Every page in a wiki had a link that reads "edit page." By clicking on that link, users are brought to a page that presents the text within an editable area in which to change, delete, revise, and add new content. It is no more complicated than the text box used for entering the content of an email. Finally, each wiki page also has a page history used to follow the changes made and the identity of the writer who made that change. So, if need be (and we know that can happen when working with kids), you can use the history page to revert back to a previous version.

Wikis present an opportunity for editorial responsibility and ownership that, in our experience up to this point, has led students to value and protect the site. Student writers respond not only to the "anywhere, anytime" nature of the wiki, but also the ability to use it to connect with writers outside of the classroom.

In the classroom   Students in Mrs. Jackson's class developed several different essays with their collaborative partners, each responding to a different prompt developed by the student writers. For example, one group took a quote from the novel that they struggled with, asking, "America had no ghosts, no memories and no sins. How does this statement hold meaning for Amir? How does it mean for us as readers?" Another pondered a favorite story shared by Amir and Hassan, asking, "How does it mean different things for each character—and what are the implications of those different meanings? Yet another group tackled the course's essential understanding, asking, "If literature is a mirror of the human experience, what is being mirrored here?" In each instance, students wrote questions that pushed them to think about and write about areas of the text that were authentically problematic, challenging, and curious to them as readers.

Students reflected on the use of the wiki in their class journals and spoke openly throughout the work. The most difficult issues the work surfaced had little to do with the technology and much to do with the task. Students felt that writing a collaborative essay in response to literature didn't leave room for contradictory positions because they wanted the essay to have some unity and coherence. As Dee explained, "Writing here was about being a group more than fitting in what I thought. I'm present—not, like, in just my words, but in the ways that I led and contributed to the words of the group." Mrs. Jackson found that students were turning, without prompting, to their writer's journals to develop their own ideas and responses before testing them out with the larger group. In doing so, Ben explained "I get to play with my thinking, make sure that it's somewhere that's permanent, and lift something out to the group when it helps us. My thinking gets to be present in both places."

An unanticipated result of this work emerged in the ways that students valued the audience of readers and writers working on the wiki. Stanley, a student who started coming to school forty-five minutes early each morning just to have access to a computer, explained, "My writing means something. This is like a conversation where I get pushed—and I get to do some pushing." The blurring between the role of reader and writer emerged as students engaged both with words as they appeared on the screen and their own emergent contributions. As Thakhai offered, "I read because someone was listening to me." In other assignments, Sahar would typically submit half-finished work, if anything. Here, she was a regular contributor, explaining, "I didn't have the pressure of it just being my words on the page."

Where in my own teaching I felt that I struggled with students to lead them to value revision, it happened naturally and without prompting as students wrote collaboratively within the wiki. Not only were students brought into collaborative construction of knowledge through their writing, but they returned to the wiki for five months following the class project. Gus explained:

> I liked seeing how the thing grew. We started with so many questions—and clicking on the changes allowed me to see us actually figuring things out. I don't get that when I write. I write what I think and then I'm done. Here, I don't get done. This writing isn't like school-writing. This writing matters.

Writing Online Fan Fiction

It wasn't until reading Rosa's end of the semester portfolio letter that I came to really know her as a writer. She was one in a class of thirty-seven eighth grade, on-level English students who had quite honestly kept me on my toes since our first day together. It wasn't that they weren't bright or immensely talented. It was simply that they were resistant—to school, to the tasks that we worked on together, to even those ideas that I thought were bursting with the most energy and potential. And there were a lot of bodies in that classroom. That said, Rosa was a good student who did just enough to not appear on my radar screen.

Her letter, like the stack before it and under it, offered her reflections on the assignments she'd included in her portfolio and set some goals for her work in ninth grade. However, on the last page, she included the following paragraph:

> I know that this is a class in how to be a better reader and writer, but I think that I can do most of that without being here. I know what I like to read, and I know what I like to write. I never really read before I found Harry Potter, but now I read and reread, not just those books but others like them. Bigger than that, I write. I write Harry Potter fan fiction and share it within Sugar Quill and some other websites. I spend hours on this because it's writing that matters. I write for an audience that writes back. And, through that feedback, I've learned about adverbs and prepositions and ways to make my writing lively. I've learned about character development and ways to develop a narrative. I don't have anything in common with the kids in this class, and I do what I need to get points. I write to get it done in school. I write to share what I think online.

What is fan fiction?   The first group of students that I worked with as a student teacher introduced me to the idea of fan fiction, only here we were writing well ahead of the invention of the Internet and technology only played a role through the actual tools we used to generate the writing. Very simply defined, students would write stories based upon the characters, themes, ideas, and settings of other published works or series. Where most based their work on movies or television shows, some worked from books or even cartoons. This wasn't writing that was done for points or grades. It was done completely outside of the classroom and was shared within a community of student writers who were all invested in the same work or series. I quickly found that I had students who fought me tooth and nail to submit a reflection when reading *The Red Badge of Courage* who had written full novels built from characters and themes from the Star Wars series.

There are a host of websites, which provide writers with a place to post their work and receive feedback from a community of readers (e.g., FanFiction.net, or sugarquill.net—a site dedicated solely to publishing fan fiction related to the Harry Potter series). Some invite ongoing submissions, chapters of a work that continues to be developed and built upon—sometimes in response to the community—and some require that the work be posted as a finished piece. The popularity of these sites is enormous, with FanFiction.net hosting millions of stories in dozens of languages. When I talk with students about the appeal, the first response is readership. As Rebecca, a tenth grader with a range of contributions to a variety of fan fiction websites explained:

> If I write here, I'm guaranteed someone is reading it. I don't even feel that when I turn something in for class. Really, I'm choosing what to write, following the rules as they're set by the original and the community I'm writing for, and then reading what someone had to say—usually within a couple of hours. Isn't that why we write? I only wish my teachers got that.

The feedback that writers receive in these online spaces can range, just as it regrettably ranged in my classroom as I learned how to structure peer review so it moved writers forward. That said, at the highest end of the continuum, many sites, like the Sugar Quill, offer a beta-reading where new writers undergo a peer-review process that goes through multiple drafts before a piece is accepted for publication. Within sites like FanFiction.net, feedback runs the range of constructive criticism from invested writers who are part of the system's review board to pat-on-the-back comments from random readers. It's important to note that some websites do not moderate comments and are not a smart choice for classroom use as flames (aptly named) and spam don't contribute in any useful way to the development of a young writer.

I do use teaching with fan fiction as an opportunity to discuss copyright. Most students articulate that if something is online, it's free or open for their own consumption, viewing, and use. I strongly recommend that teachers take the opportunity to discuss copyright and, here, copyright of a derivative work. What's important is that the creator of the derivative work must identify and credit the preexisting work. So, if I'm writing a fan fiction using the characters from the Harry Potter series, I need to be crediting the original work of J. K. Rowling. Some online fan fiction websites require a disclaimer that is posted at the top of the page, explaining that the author does not own in part or full any aspect of the original, takes original credit only for original aspects in the fan fiction, and is publishing for the enjoyment of fans and not for any profit. Others go so far as requiring that the writer receive permission from the original author or owner of the work. The critical part is for teachers and students to closely read the guidelines and disclaimers for any online site in which they are posting work, and to understand how the law protects original and derivative works.

In the classroom As much as students are hungry for the response that publishing to a fan fiction community garners, they are equally hungry for opportunities to follow their own interests as writers. Yes, writing on demand is a necessary skill. But, in providing student with opportunities to write in response to their interests, questions, and models which they find intriguing, we give student writers authority over the texts they are producing.

I want student writers to be active, engaged, fluid, and flexible. I want them to take risks, both in what they are saying and the ways in which they use language to communicate their thinking. That kind of writing is happening for a lot of student writers in these online spaces, provided in part by a community that simply won't accept a piece that doesn't move the collective thinking ahead or that doesn't contribute new thinking, new energy, or new responses. At the very least, knowing about how my student writers are working outside of class to engage in these spaces is important to the ways in which I can move them forward when writing inside of class. And, perhaps in those moments where I can carve out a space in our instructional time together, I can open my teaching just enough to allow students to work in these communities, as writers, as respondents, as readers.

Perhaps the most intriguing aspect of this work for me as a classroom teacher is that as students post comments and discuss their writing with readers, writers are developing a vocabulary for talking about writing, strategies for revision, strategies for handling and incorporating feedback, and ways to develop their writing into more robust pieces. Do we do this in class? Absolutely. However, in providing students with additional venues and places to practice the art of writing alongside the work of critically developing one's work, we're taking a step toward answering the question why do I have to learn this? by demonstrating how writers work and how communities respond. And what matters about the technology isn't where to point and click, but the ways in which teaching can be about openings as opposed to the boundaries often in place through the walls of our classrooms or the confines of content.

The lessons here for me as a teacher aren't about how to move a community such as this into the classroom as much as they are about seeing student writers in and outside of the classroom; the ways in which our students respond and hunger for choice; the ways in which they grow from invested, timely feedback; and the possibilities for ways that communities can move writers who are working at a variety of different levels and stages. Different from the other examples that we've discussed at this point in the chapter, this isn't an example of doing something new with a new tool. Instead, we're simply posting to an Internet site and collaborating, a tool and capacity that has been in place for some time. What is new is seeing my students' writing within the context of a global, responsive community. What is new, for me, is thinking about the ways in which students are using online writing spaces as a pen, paper and printing press all in one while networking with one another across boundaries, and the ways in which their uses of writing outside of school put new and important pressures on the ways in which we use them inside of school. Bottom line: no matter the tool, no matter the space, students are still looking to us to teach them how to do it well.

Conclusion

Our work as English teachers is rooted in leading students to engage with (read), produce (write), and talk about texts. Surrounding that root is a range of tools or technologies or change agents that are continually challenging our understanding of what a text or a reader or a writer is or does. As soon as I begin to list the new or powerful technologies for constructing and expressing meaning, I'm immediately behind and no longer current. Apart from the technologies themselves, the wikis and blogs and podcasts, is the reality that our students are using new modes, mediums, and means for communication—and this is being done in places that take us well outside the walls of our classrooms. This isn't about doing familiar things in pretty much the same familiar ways, like moving an essay to PowerPoint. Instead, it's about doing new things with new tools alongside our students—and valuing the multimodal knowledge that they already are bringing into our classroom.

Each new technology adds to the set of texts, tools, and change agents in place in our curricula. That said, technology is not the goal. Student writers and readers are at the center of our instruction. And, we as mindful teachers, critically and deliberately prepare our students for success outside of our classrooms by engaging with the most powerful cultural tools available. We do so through the smart, effective use of the unique capacities of multimodal tools and emergent online tools like those discussed in these pages. The goal has been to provide you with models and voices that lead you to see your students and classroom in what's discussed here, and to provide tools that lead you and your students to engage more deeply and more closely in your work together. Ultimately, it is an invitation to examine, play, invent, reinvent, and join in the conversation.

Works Cited

Daniels, H. 2003. *Literature Circles: Voices and Choice in Book Clubs and Reading Groups.* 2nd ed. Portland, ME: Stenhouse.

Norris, C., T. Sullivan, J. Poirot, and E. Soloway. 2003. "No Access, No Use, No Impact: Snapshot Surveys of Educational Technology in K-12." *Journal of Research on Technology in Education* 36 (1): 15–27.

Richardson, W. 2006. *Blogs, Wikis, Podcasts and Other Powerful Web Tools for the Classroom.* Thousand Oaks, CA: Sage.

Steineke, N. 2002. *Reading & Writing Together: Collaborative Literacy in Action.* Portsmouth, NH: Heinemann.

14

Inside the Digital Classroom

Dave Boardman

Dave Boardman teaches English at Messalonskee High School in Oakland, Maine, and works with the Maine Writing Project on literacy initiatives. Named an Instruction Technology Educator of the Year in 2006 by the Association of Computer Technology Educators of Maine, he is the founder of LiteracySparks, *a non-profit working on technology and literacy issues for rural adolescents. For more information visit his website, www.literacysparks.org.*

The telltale burst of computer startup music punctuates the room as we begin our ninety-minute English class at a rural Maine high school. Some students have arrived early, midway through lunch, to browse online before their surfing range is focused for our work; and others straggle in just after the bell, grab the last laptop from the cart, and wait for the wireless connection to recover from the surge of twenty-five new entrants to our ramp onto the digital highway. In different ways, my students experience the sense of accomplishment that comes with their transformation into probing writers and insightful, critical readers. They use computers, MP3 recorders, digital cameras, video, and music to investigate themselves, the world around them, and the ways that things fit together, or sometimes don't. It's never perfect, often messy, and periodically snarled with glitches. But learning and creating happens in many ways.

- Maine students trade life stories on a daily basis with kids in California.
- Students and their teacher share revision ideas through a private online forum.
- Book reviews, self-help tips, abuse prevention resources, and resiliency strategies highlight a student-produced calendar to help stem a local suicide epidemic.
- Teens write about something they have learned or a place that holds a special meaning to them, and then combine images, writing, narration, and music to create a digital story.

- Novice journalists print the news they gather in an online newspaper, then convince the computer lab director to make their work the homepage of every computer in the lab.
- We share digital photos of our world on Flickr, and then write about the images we select.

As new students arrive in my classroom every semester, our use of technology changes as well. The work of my students takes a new shape as they develop their own connections to books, find writing topics that inspire multimedia responses, and explore links with other teachers and different classrooms. Technology and the promise it holds to motivate and empower my students remains a constant part of my classroom.

The Debut

As I make the last-minute adjustments to an LCD projector, Jake, an eighteen-year old senior who will barely graduate if he holds out for the next two months, paces in front of the chattering crowd of 350 teenagers. He isn't a guy who shows chinks in his self-esteem, and if anyone were to call him a writer, he would have quickly fired back a standard, "Yeah, right."

Today was different. We were screening *Crosswalk Terror*, a three-minute public service announcement that Jake and his team had completed just hours before. The video is predictable: an aging Chevy careens up the school driveway, hard rock blaring from the speakers, just in time for the local football star to amble unwittingly through the crosswalk. No mystery, just suspense and hysterical, slow-motion, multi-angle stunt flips surrounding a clear message: drive safely. I had seen the film a dozen times, and taking advantage of a school-wide assembly, I coaxed the boys into showing off their work.

Jake, Bruce, Frank and Jerry did not usually have their work showcased. Their school identity came through their pushed-back ball caps, Carhartt jackets, and the rumble of their trucks tearing out of the parking lot. Standing at the front of the auditorium as the crowd quieted, the boys looked as though they were about to issue a public apology.

I remember Jake in the moments before we killed the lights. "But Mr. Boardman, it's not real good."

"Trust me," I told him. "They're gonna love it."

The raucous crowd didn't let us down, and my team of four filmmakers, guys who'd seen more time in detention than any other students I'd known, were blushing stars. Steady laughs and clapping baffled the four kids. They had instantly gained reputations as writers and creators. "Yeah," I heard Jake say as they packed up, "it's not like you just point the camera around, man. You gotta know what you're doing. You gotta write it."

Two years earlier, asking any of these guys to write was agonizing; they just wouldn't put the words down. Conscious of their struggle to succeed as writers, they often gave up, refusing to take on the status of incompetent. Their rebellion came in what was their most powerful response, an outright refusal to be seen as unsuccessful. They went down with an F or scraped through with a D, maybe not so much feeling the sting of failure, but the satisfaction that comes from knowing you've protected your dignity.

Three weeks into our senior English class, Jerry followed the script he helped write as he sped his rusting Impala toward the fateful crosswalk while Jake and the rest of the crew filmed from different angles. As I watched from a hallway window, a colleague shook his head. "You trust those guys with that equipment?"

Beyond the entertainment value and even multimedia possibilities of teaching writing with technology, my students are willing to dig deep as writers when they are empowered with tools to make the work genuine. That sense of validity, of respect, and the willingness to work at crafting words doubles when students see my respect by ensuring their access to the technology they need to get the job done well, even when it has meant providing them with some of my own gear. When I think back at my colleague's question, I remember that we were talking about guys who found little of value in school for them and were rarely offered much that would make a difference in their lives. In return for my show of respect, I usually found the same returned.

The Power to Publish

The digital classroom isn't necessarily one with racks of video gear in the corner or carts of laptops. Technology motivates students in part by enabling them to present their voices to the real world. We've all given those writing assignments, assigned a grade, written a few kind words and some practical suggestions, just to watch the writing discarded. Did the sentiments ever matter, either theirs or ours? Giving students a portal to the outside world seemed to change that idea that writing doesn't matter.

The benefits of infusing my classroom with technology became clear as a journalism class I developed evolved from a traditional to digital mode. Because they wrote for a public audience, my journalism students often took extra care with their writing. But for many students, the process from story idea to publication was one that was devoid of power and responsibility. Typos or convoluted sentences didn't seem to matter so much in an article for *The Mango*, our print newspaper that was circulated through school and the community. Writers knew the editors would catch their error, editors knew I'd catch their blunders, and I'd hear offhandedly about the ones that saw print. Even our online edition of *The Mango* failed to develop that sense of ownership that I was hoping would prompt my students to write their best. Their writing had not only to get through the editors and me, but now would be held up from publication until the school system's webmaster updated the pages. The system was designed as a series of checks and balances, but also worked as a hierarchy of power and privilege, and when writers do not retain ownership of their words, their sense of commitment and responsibility dwindles as well.

In 2005 my students started "RamblerBlog" at Blogger.com, and student writers in my journalism program had direct access to their readers through a weblog, an easily updateable website that gives its members the power to electronically publish. Students became the authors of the weblog, and I set few guidelines. Nearly any topic was fair game. We reviewed the federal laws surrounding Internet use and schools; and we talked about Internet predation, identity theft, and all the reasons why we couldn't use full names, and why I had disabled the ability of readers to contact writers directly. I told them that real-world access came with a responsibility, both on their part and mine. They would have direct access to post their writing without prior approval by me or our administration. We set up an editing system, but writers retained final control over their published work. My dozen or so students and I talked daily about what they were writing, and collectively we brainstormed ideas and solutions. Our ninety-minute class ran as a nonstop writer's conference, and the conversations about writing and life have never been richer. And when students decided their story was ready, they hit the Publish button, and their work was online and on the screens of readers.

Here's a glimpse at some of the first year's headlines:

- "Where Are You Going?" – The annual narrative of graduates and their destinations.
- "What's in Your Wallet?" – Get ten people to show the contents of their wallet. You never know what's coming.
- "PDA" – Not the technology, but the trouble with Public Displays of Affection.
- "Commitment" – One student strives for a martial arts black belt.
- "I'm the Master of Low Expectations" – A review of malapropisms posted on a teacher's door.
- "The Boy Called Skinny" – A profile of an amiable, slender senior.

The topics were self-selected, though weekly brainstorming sessions usually generated far more potential stories than we could cover. We weren't looking to be the definitive voice of news and opinion for the Winthrop community, but rather a collection of voices. Looking back over the site, that's just what came of the project. Students got a chance to try out their own voices, and after a supportive technology lab director surreptitiously set every computer's homepage to "RamblerBlog," the feedback was fast and steady.

Students wrote with the understanding that I was no longer their audience—I was just one small part of a readership that might pass their entry by altogether or linger over every word. That idea made our constant conversations on writing more meaningful to some of my students. Turning it in wasn't good enough anymore. Their work was going out with their name, and that matters for most teenagers.

Not every writer, however, was ready for publication. The class blended special education students with seniors who would graduate at the top of their class. I had trained several proficient bloggers as writing coaches—part diplomat and ego booster, part grammarian and sentence constructor—and their help was freely offered and usually gladly accepted. With the bulk of my students working so independently, I was free to pull up a chair and spend twenty minutes by the side of a struggling writer, time all too often missing from a day at school.

Giving my students control of their own public voice as writers does not come without risks. Anyone who has walked through the corridors of a public high school is cognizant of the fact that not every word from a teenager's mouth or keystroke is a gentle one. But students understood that the same rules of polite behavior and appropriate language that I enforced in my classroom were active on our portals to the world as well. Part of the solution comes in creating the kind of classroom atmosphere that values respect, honesty, and trust. And as a backup, I scanned for the latest postings before school started, at lunch, and sometimes as I graded papers in the evening. Just in case.

Publications don't just happen in the traditional sense of magazines and newspapers. Students in one traditional English class came up with an idea to use the young adult novels they were reading as the basis for a calendar focusing on teen issues. After several suicides over the course of a year traumatized our student community, one of my sophomore classes lobbied for several grants and created a calendar on teen issues that they distributed throughout our town. The project transformed the classroom from a teacher- and curriculum-centered model to one that centered on writing and communicating through a service-learning project. Students mixed a focus on curriculum, a laudable goal of trying to assist peers in trouble, and a heavy use of technology. The calendar, "Help Teens Survive," drew involvement from local counselors, police, state agencies, and community leaders and left students with the feeling they had accomplished something meaningful in English class. That reminder stayed with them as they turned the pages over the course of the year.

California Dreaming

Weblogs provide a means for students to write for a genuine audience and receive something any writer treasures: response. They provide a space for students to use the Web at its next level, as contributors, rather than merely users of information. The Maine Learning Technology Initiative has put computers in the hands of every seventh and eighth grader since 2002, but many of my students had just used the machines as tools for information retrieval rather than creation. A pilot weblog project between fifty of my students and thirty juniors at San Francisco's Galileo Academy of Science and Technology helped students become creators of conversations as we brought the writing out of our classrooms, and into a digital hallway that linked diverse cultures and gave a purpose to the word crafting we did in school.

Sponsored by the National Writing Project, The Maine to California Connection offered a secure, password-protected space where my classroom connected to that of Joel Arquillos, then a social studies teacher at Galileo. Our students inhabited an Internet zone where the conversations that took place in my own hallways developed with teens my students would never meet. Few of my students, who hail from a state that has ninety-six percent Caucasian residents, have met an immigrant to the United States. Nearly all of my students speak only English, and many of them live in typical middle-class homes. The Maine to California Connection gave them the chance to write with students from diverse ethnic backgrounds who described the challenges and excitement of city life, everything from crossing paths with drug dealers to the latest Giants game. They wrote with teens like Ken, who described the Golden Gate City at night:

> I saw a nice, beautiful, full, round moon that flashed the bay. When I turn my head left, I saw the beautiful buildings in downtown. Those buildings are bright and beautiful. San Francisco at nighttime is beautiful when there's no fog around the sky. When you look up at the sky, you could actually see the stars.

This was a new world for my students and these California youth, many first generation Americans, who were mystified by my students' days off because of a sudden snowstorm, or by stories about the deer that narrowly escaped opening day of hunting season. In one of my handouts to students as we started the blog, I gave them my underlying reason for moving what had typically been a notebook journaling requirement into the weblog forum:

> Why this Blog?
>
> The blog started, in a way, out of a frustration; many of you were writing incredible journal entries, yet had no format for sharing those thoughts, whether you wanted to, or thought about that, or not. I'm not talking about the personal stuff. I'm talking about what you think when you walk through the forest, when a friend dies, when a friend goes off to war, when you face one of those decisions you so often face. Or the happy stuff that we need more of—the birth of a foal, the marriage of a sibling, the grade you thought you'd never get but somehow pulled off. How frustrating to see all this writing purely in the isolation of marble-covered journals.

My students knew I respected their words—they saw it in my steady responses to their writing. And as I sought to move their writing to a more open forum, I wondered whether they would revolt. My fears were instantly put aside, though. The project in its first year was a huge success, and my students, mostly sophomores through seniors, posted through the school year, trading stories of major life experiences or thoughts on the latest Napoleon Dynamite look-alike. They shared the news of the weird, like Rosie's post about the New Hampshire boy charged with digging up a corpse.

> So creepy and wrong!
>
> Okay, I was listening to the radio yesterday at like 5:30 AM. And they were doing their little news bit. Not like actual news but news that's weird or funny. But this time it kind of made me want to puke. A seventeen-year-old boy from New Hampshire dug up someone's grave and stole the skull! How sick is that??! And guess why he did this? This is the sickest part…He wanted to make a BONG! Out of a HUMAN SKULL! There is something wrong with this kid.

Often the writing was the loose, free chat of teenagers. But sometimes the issues became serious. Carla, a senior who needed only my class to graduate, left our town to escape an abusive relationship and moved to her mother's small coastal town. She joined our conversation, reconnected with friends, and earned her English credit, all through her coastal town library's Internet connection and our weblog. Her post, "Important Decision…and I need help," set off my teaching alarm bells, and immediately had her surrounded by concerned weblogging friends from our classroom and caring adults. Her question was the kind that reminds me of the weight teenagers sometimes bear: "Do I tell my brother that our father is dying?"

Derek, my teen-angst poet, made the weblog his homepage, and wrote steadily, letting loose bursts of poetry rich with the imagery of 50 Cent and Eminem, but without the vulgarity, one of the few rules I enforced on the blog. But as students began posting in greater number, I privately questioned the validity of my students' writing in this semipublic forum and issued a new directive to my students: lose the slang, the IM-speak, the email-ese. Clean up the language.

The weblog was just one component of the writing my students undertook; formal papers, letters, and research components in multigenre formats rounded out our work. But what concerned me was the apparent lackadaisical approach many students took toward what they posted. Derek's thoughts on love might have contained a dozen typos and at times other used the instant message slang that many used with great fluidity, a bridge sometimes between their language and my own. Many of my students saw no need to change.

Derek's rap, "Super Saucy Saucyy" was one of those pieces that left me wondering what I had started when I first began the weblog.

> Come with me an' start a new life
> Possibly be my wife, who's to know, if we take it slow, how far we'll go.
> But if ya ever want to know, give it a chance, let's dance
> To the beat, we be rockin' the heat, neva take a seat

So I acted. I issued the "proper English" rule: the slang had to stop, the writing needed to be as refined as any other formal English we wrote in school. I wasn't expecting King's English, but the casualness of my students' writing had to end. But I had momentarily forgotten that Derek was one of those boys who traditionally had not written for English class, but wrote prolifically on his own. Was it fear that my colleagues would see my students' writing as inappropriate? Probably. Chalk it up to uncertainty of that ongoing argument over whether technology was helping my students write better, or sanctioning their slide into a flaunting of grammatical rules and a degradation of the English language. What I was soon to realize was that it didn't matter. My students had been writing.

The new dictate I issued changed that. Suddenly it was as if Derek had gone on strike; immediately, his writing ground to a halt, and I had little idea why. But I noticed something had grown seriously wrong in our budding community of writers when I read Brandon's reply to Mayra's poem, a piece that loosely experimented with creative spelling like "realli" for "really" and playfully changed zeroes for the letter o to create a visual, as well as meaningful, statement about a broken relationship. It seemed as if he never noticed the sense of loss the writer exhibited, the mental anguish of a lost love, or the hope at a new start.

> Hey, Mayra A nice poem…I am tempted to say that the coolest thing about that poem was the fact that you used "i"s instead of "y"s. But they say we have to write all formal and non-email talk.

Struck by the potential harshness of his response, I immediately waived the proper English rule, and my student writers actively began posting again. Later on, Derek told me why he valued writing on the weblog when he often disliked writing traditional school assignments:

> You don't have your teacher telling you that this is the correct punctuation or this is the right way your sentence structure needs to be. It's written as you feel it should be written. If you want to use slang or something, you put it in there. I mean, you can't tell somebody how to write. They write the way they do, and on the blog, you can do that. You write the way you do.

I still wonder at Derek's thought, that "you can't tell somebody how to write." Many writing teachers would disagree, and at times, I do as well. But Derek wasn't talking about the formal writing that develops a first impression with a new employer, or persuades an opponent to cross sides in an argument. His highly revised, formal writing produced a serious, reflective college essay, as well as an A grade in my course. The weblog, though, was often the place where he put his thoughts together and tried out his ideas, a space where he wrote the way he wanted to. And finally he wanted to write.

Weblogs offer possibilities for links like our cross-country project. But other possibilities make starting easier. The free program Moodle (http://moodle.org) provides weblog software suitable for fully online classes or the traditional class with an occasional interactive component. Its security features keep students safe, and hosting the software on a school computer makes it part of the school's infrastructure, easing parental concern over Internet postings. Edublogs (http://edublogs.org) provides free, fast blogspace for educators, and its branch, LearnerBlogs (http://learnerblogs.org) offers the same for students.

Consider some of the possibilities:

- Students share writing in progress, and peers respond with suggestions for revision.
- Book conversations develop an online component with links to author websites, connections to related topics, or questions for extending thinking.
- A weblog becomes a digital portfolio and students have the opportunity to view their peers' blogs through shared postings.
- Class weblogs host student-generated audio files, video clips, and still photos as writing responses.
- Guest writers—authors, politicians, business leaders, sports figures—are recruited to join the classroom conversation through a weblog.
- Texts are shared beyond classrooms; students in Cambodia and Maine share thoughts on a survivor's story of the Khmer Rouge genocide; teens in urban New Jersey and rural Maine trade perspectives on a novel.
- Parents view a teacher weblog to view homework assignments, or students out of school for a day download the material distributed in class.

The Maine to California Connection lasted a second year and expanded slightly, then faded as the teachers involved changed jobs, took on other projects, and lost those moments of collaborative conversation needed to manage a project like this. Future exchanges will continue to emerge for my Maine students, and as I consider the possibilities, I always remember Derek's words of enthusiasm for his writing in the digital forum of our weblog. "It's like, 'Wow. Somebody else actually out there is feeling the same way I am. I'm not the only person on this planet that is feeling this way.'"

Telling Our Stories

It's an early spring morning, and my class of twenty-three freshmen at Messalonskee High School in Oakland, Maine, is in chaos. A third of the students have an arm raised, and periodically someone moans, "Mr. Boardman...I don't know what to do..." I suggest they try their help menus and ask each other for the technical answers. The hands drop for the moment. At least one student stares at her screen with a look of horror, as though her laptop just froze and she forgot to save. I toss out another friendly, "Make sure you're saving your work" admonition, and wince for the girl who just mutters, "Yeah, no kidding." Down the hall, one girl sits in the English department's cramped book closet, reading her essay into my MP3 recorder. Two others are in another wing—a teacher friend has offered her room as a recording studio. A boy is scribbling his latest revision into his notebook and already has my iPod to record his narration. It's chaos, but students are creating digital stories and writing with an intensity that they've never had before.

Just as students find my classroom a place where they have the power to present their own words to the world around them, they also discover that a multimedia approach to writing can be far more engaging, and much more demanding, than traditional essay writing. The concept: students write about one of two topics, describing either a place that holds special meaning for them or something they have learned, and explore how that has changed them. They then scour family albums, magazines, or even several royalty-free photographic websites for images that relate, either explicitly or symbolically. After revising their writing until the piece flows, they record their own narration and use Microsoft's Movie Maker and Photo Story 3 to piece together a coordinated montage of voice, background music, and images.

With a cart of twenty-five laptops in my classroom, high-speed wireless, and a skilled technology integration team ready to help, the project seemed an easily manageable one, something that I knew my students would latch onto. But when I started, I wasn't certain how blending pictures, music, and narration would help writers. My students made the answers clear.

Brenda, a fifteen-year-old freshman in a class for struggling readers, wrote her digital story on the first time her dad took her on his tow truck to help a stranded motorist. After revising her piece, "The Call," four times, she began reading her narrative aloud, only to discover the words she was glossing over as a silent reader now stumbled her as a speaker. Like other students, Brenda quickly discovered the reason behind revision, something I had tried to show students for months. As I coached Brenda on several initial drafts, I sensed her resistance to suggested changes starting to grow. My ideas as a writer and editor were beginning to impinge on her ownership of her own work. In any other project, the revision would have ended and we'd move on to another assignment. But when my suggestions for revising ended and Brenda began to feel and hear her own halting reading of the story, she went back to her drafts, smoothed the rough spots or the areas where the meaning seemed convoluted, and tried again. It was just the kind of independent revision I'd been seeking from students with little success.

The technology seemed daunting at first—scanners, digital cameras, audio equipment, laptops, and several different programs at once—multiplied by twenty-plus students. But I always found several students in each class who knew their way around the basics, and resources through a National Writing Project grant connected us with technical support. Establishing a set of guidelines also helped keep students from rushing through the process. A few of the ones I relied on included:

- Starting off with a long, 800–1000 word essay that was revised several times, then trimmed back to the 350-word digital story narrative. Students wound up with narratives that were tightly focused and already well-revised.
- Banning right-clicking of Internet images, except from royalty-free websites that offered free photo downloads.
- Encouraging students to use magazine photos, notes, symbolic images, and self-produced music to for their projects.
- Providing several inexpensive digital cameras as loaners so all students had access to equipment.
- Helping students develop a genuine venue to showcase their finished work. A district technology night gave them a perfect chance to demonstrate their skills.

Between help menus, student experts, and support staff glad to see technology in use, the problems that halt any technology project were easily overcome. Models for students to view before the project starts are easily available on the Internet, and some, especially from online sites like the BBC's "Capture Wales Digital Storytelling" project in Wales, provide approachable and hugely entertaining examples that hone students' critical visual literacy skills as well. Just use your favorite search engine to identify sites. Overall, most students spent close to twenty hours on their digital stories in addition to outside writing time, but the commitment was worth the investment.

"I learned a lot about making voices flow with words and how to really crack down and revise a piece of writing that I've written," one student wrote in his reflection on the project.

> In revising the piece after reading it aloud, I learned that in order to avoid stumbling while recording, I had to change the wording of certain things…I finally figured out that even in reading in order for it to sound right the paper needed dramatic pauses and rhythm.

The realization of my students was widespread and just what I was hoping for.

The digital classroom offers unlimited, transformational possibilities. Students explore another culture by writing to peers across the country or around the world; they visit an online writing center and check their sentence-crafting skills; or they devise a way to save a life. They share thoughts about an author's intentions by collaborating in an online forum, and they talk in the digital hallways while I linger on the edge, sometimes eavesdropping on the learning, other times guiding the conversation. There's a lot going on, and from year to year, something else offers a glimmer of promise, one more tactic in helping one more writer. Technology adds volume to our conversations, and our digital classroom is helping students discover a more resonant voice on their way to becoming proficient, independent learners.

15

Space to Imagine

Digital Storytelling

Lisa C. Miller

Lisa C. Miller is an associate professor at the University of New Hampshire, where she teaches journalism and digital storytelling. She won a 2005 Teaching Excellence Award from the university. She is the author of Power Journalism: Computer-Assisted Reporting *and has published articles and poems in* Quill, Conscience, *and elsewhere.*

First we hear a soft piano melody. On the screen in front of us we see the word *Nana* superimposed on handwritten letters sent from New Guinea and Manila. Then the voice of the storyteller grabs our attention: "As I look through old photo albums, I find a picture of a young girl, full of life, passion and dreams, always smiling and taking life by the horns. What were her dreams when she was my age? I wonder, since I never got to ask her when I was six…There is so much I wish she could tell me of her adventures." As we listen, rapt, photographs of this young woman riding her bicycle, at a cookout with her family, and in uniform as a member of the Women's Army Corps appear on the screen, then fade into other pictures.

We're not in a dark movie theatre watching the latest blockbuster romance (though we are eating movie popcorn, courtesy of my students). We're in a writing classroom, sharing the stories my graduate students—who are also public school English teachers—have created using text, music, their voices, photographs, and computers. We're sharing digital stories.

Storytelling is how we live. Telling stories, we reveal ourselves to others, making friends and creating communities. We try to better understand things that happen to us; to solve problems and get help when we need it; to preserve family traditions; to offer others the information they need and want.

As teachers, we tell stories to help students understand ideas, experiences, processes, and issues. A narrative helps them follow a new idea and better visualize and remember it. We teach students to tell stories effectively so they can succeed in school, but also so they can understand each other's lives and ideas and make their voices heard in the world.

We think of stories in terms of words, written and spoken. But in this computer age storytellers can include more. Digital stories start with text but then marry the words to images—video and still—and voice-over narration and music. Some call this multimedia storytelling, while others say it's filmmaking. None of the labels captures the magic of a speaker talking, as the poetry of the words and the power of photographs come together in a moving, shared experience. The computer makes it possible, even easy, for anyone to put these components together to make movies that matter. And whatever you call it, our students need and want to learn how to tell stories this way.

The Writing Process

When we take our students through the writing process to create a report or essay, they practice the different types of thinking and preparing and revising that go into a strong piece of writing. They learn that great writing doesn't appear by magic and that they can get better at different parts of the process. They learn the power of their own experiences and voices.

With digital storytelling, words and the writing process matter as much as ever. We still must take students through that process, from coming up with an idea to collecting information to focusing and organizing to drafting to revising.

The process isn't a completely different animal when applied to digital storytelling. We just have to stretch it, open it up some to include multimedia. For example, when students are figuring out what to tell a story about, they may consider not only the written brainstorming and mapping they do, but also what images (photographs, artwork, video) might make for a story that matters. When they are collecting information, whether for a memoir or research paper, they will also collect images, sounds, and music.

But the writing, the script for a digital story, is paramount. If students don't take time to write the stories they want to tell with the computer, they won't get below the surface of their ideas. They may create beautiful slide shows, but they will not tell stories that matter. As Bernajean Porter, author of "DigiTales—The Art of Telling Digital Stories, says, " A story should be remembered for its soul, not the bells and whistles." Teaching digital storytelling is still teaching writing.

Why Go Digital?

There are pragmatic reasons. Computers aren't going away. More jobs are going to require the ability to use video-editing, image-editing, and sound-editing software as more content is put onto the World Wide Web. Advertising, public relations, journalism, teaching, technology jobs—all are going to require strong computer skills.

Also, many schools now have students create digital portfolios. Digital storytelling is a way for students to create original content for such portfolios, rather than only scanning into a computer reports they have written.

Students will really engage with this kind of work; it's active and visual and fun.

But the most weighty reason of all is this: We can't afford not to teach this kind of writing. Our students live in world of digital storytelling. They see interviews, concerts, news presentations, advertising, and history-in-the-making online. They need to be visually literate, understanding the power of photographs and film, so that they can look at a photograph that has a strong visceral kick and consider whether that photo tells the whole story or only one side of the story. They need to be able to sort through the visuals and voices and text on the World Wide Web to find the stories they need and to determine what is true.

Moreover, if they're going to be active citizens of the world, they need to be able to tell their own stories using writing, visuals, and technology.

Many websites, some created by teachers and schools, offer terrific examples of digital storytelling. You'll find personal stories, such as "Practice Makes Perfect" by a fourth grader about preparing for his first piano recital, or "My Potato Story" by a high school student about her struggles to fit in when her family moved to this country from South Korea. But you'll also see projects dealing with literature, math, history, music, art, and social studies, such as one middle school project called "Grass Born to be Stepped on: Women's Rights in China." Some schools have turned digital storytelling projects into community projects, with students gathering oral histories from local residents and putting together websites about where they live, or helping residents create their own digital stories and post them online.

Effective digital stories, like strong research or personal essays, do more than deliver information. They take the audience on a journey. As your students create their stories, you'll want to them to consider what dramatic questions their stories will answer or what puzzles they will lay out and perhaps solve.

Ask teachers who use digital storytelling in their classrooms, and you'll hear stories about students, reluctant writers, who for the first time immersed themselves in the world of words and images for these projects. The technology and use of visuals appeal to many such students, and students who struggle with writing but are really good at computers (or art) come to the project knowing they have some expertise—maybe even more than the teacher. This power can give them confidence that can carry through the writing.

What will you do for the world? That's the question eighth grade teacher Patricia Emerson wanted to pose to her students when she began her project in my digital storytelling class at the University of New Hampshire. She also hoped her story would serve as a model for ones they would create. Patricia worked first to keep her script brief, about five hundred words, while still getting her message across. She asked peers in her workshop whether the brief bits she included—a conversation between her and her son about changing the world, another about an essay contest about citizenship at her school, a letter from a former student—would be clear to an audience that didn't know her or her school. She worried that she didn't have the right images to tell her story, and she searched the Web for pictures of Gandhi and of South Africa, where she'd traveled in 2004. And she wasn't sure she wanted to record the narration herself, wasn't sure her voice was right for the piece. In the end, she used a mix of photographs, including historical ones of peace marches, the U.S. Capitol and the Lincoln Memorial, along with others of her students working on a research project about AIDS and South Africa and raising money to fund after-school programs for adolescents in Cape Town's poorest townships. The pride and joy in her voice came through in the digital story when she read from a student's letter: "In all my life, even what I can imagine in my future, I don't know if I'll do something as important as what we did this year with South Africa."

Where to Start

Digital storytelling involves learning in two main areas: the writing or creation of effective stories and the software or other technology you and your students will use. Remember that the stories are the central focus of these projects; the computer and software are merely tools for telling these stories.

Creating a digital story will probably take between sixteen and twenty-four hours for each student. The amount of time it takes will, of course, also vary depending on how many computers your class has access to and whether you can have students do some of the work at home.

Get your students to work on short pieces, maybe three minutes long with a script of five hundred words or so, especially the first time you do this. Longer projects take more time, of course, but they can also lose steam as they go on and will take up more space on a computer hard drive. Several of my students were dismayed when I gave them this limit because they had longer stories to create (and some of the stories ended up being seven or eight minutes long). I suggested they try to tell only part of their story this time. A tight focus makes digital stories meaningful and powerful.

For a three-minute story a student will probably need twenty to twenty-five different images, though that's not a hard-and-fast rule; I've seen interesting stories created with only four or five. In general, though, you'll want an image up on the screen for only four or five seconds before you move to another one.

Fear of Technology

The truth is my students, and their students, probably understand how to do more on the computer and the Web than I ever will want to know; it's certainly true that when I demonstrate something in class, I usually have a student who knows how to do it more quickly or easily and, when something doesn't work, a student who can figure out why. I'm at peace with this. I think this is a good thing, as I said earlier, since it gives tech-savvy students some power and standing in the class they didn't have before, and may make them more invested in the class. But we still have so much to teach—how do you use the computer to learn about X? and how do you use the computer to demonstrate what you've learned? The students can do many technologically sophisticated things, but they don't always know why or even how best to use these tools for research, learning, relating, and storytelling. And that, along with whatever subject matter we specialize in, is what we teach them.

I guarantee that sometime during the process of working on digital stories, a computer or software program will crash. It's just the nature of this beast, and when you're using a program such as Movie Maker 2, you're asking the computer to do the most it can do at its highest level—which will occasionally prove to be too much. Have your students save their projects early and often. Make them repeat this phrase together as a mantra: save early and often.

If a program or website or computer command doesn't work, I don't worry (too much). I've learned to admit it when I don't know something, since bluffing through it never worked. Students are usually patient and helpful, and we solve problems together. So don't be daunted by the software or equipment, or afraid of glitches; plunge in with your students.

There are websites (again, many created by teachers) that offer information about software and hardware as well as tutorials and tips. Try doing a Google search using the word *tutorial* and the name of your software program such as iMovie or Movie Maker.

The Software and Hardware

You can create digital stories in your classroom with limited resources or go all out with complicated software and sound equipment. All you absolutely need is a computer, a digital camera, and a microphone you can use with the computer (and many computers come with a built-in mic). These days, if you work on a PC, the program Windows Movie Maker came with it, free. If you work on a Apple, you'll have iMovie. You can even use PowerPoint to create a story.

You and your students can also use PowerPoint to revise photographs and create some special effects. If your school has Adobe Photoshop or a similar program, students can manipulate images with that. Software exists for creating artwork, original music, and storyboards. And you might want to use a program such as Final Cut Express HD or Adobe Premiere to put your movie together; these days, such programs may allow students to try more sophisticated moviemaking techniques than do the free programs. (They are also more complicated programs to teach.) A program such as Flash will allow students to create animated films.

You'll also find other free software on the World Wide Web that allows you to edit the sound or narration you want to use for your digital story. If you have access to a scanner, you can scan into your computer photographs and other artwork for your movie. If your students are going to incorporate video, you'll need to have a camcorder they can use.

Some of the most effective stories online, though, aren't particularly flashy in terms of video or special effects; and that's one aspect of digital storytelling you'll want to talk to students about when you look at examples of stories. What is most effective? What adds or detracts from a story?

Last year I did a digital storytelling project with second graders, and I taught a course in digital storytelling for graduate students, most of whom were K–12 teachers. The kids wrote fiction; they had to come up with characters, then figure out what those characters wanted or needed, what obstacles stood in the way of getting what they wanted or needed, and how to overcome them. The students wrote and illustrated the stories, and each one was between five and six pages long.

I took pictures of all of the pages of the books, using my digital camera, and then downloaded those into my computer. I used a handheld digital voice recorder to record each student reading his or her story, and I downloaded those sound files into the computer. Then I put the pictures and narration into PowerPoint, creating a PowerPoint show for each student.

In my graduate class, students downloaded digital photographs into the computers as well as using a scanner to scan some in. We even took digital photographs of photographs to download. They used microphones or the digital recorder to record their narration. Then they used Movie Maker 2 and another free Microsoft program, Photo Story 3, to put together still photographs, narration, and music.

The basics of the hardware and software are not hard to get down. Before you try a story in class, you may want to create one of your own, just to see what works and what doesn't. But don't be intimidated, and remember there is a lot of technical help on the Web and elsewhere.

Back to the Process

While we usually talk about the writing process for an essay as though it were linear—idea, collection of information, focus, organize, draft, revise—we know it's recursive and looks more like a tangled ball of yarn than a straight line. For a digital story, that ball is even more tangled, which is one of the exciting parts of teaching and working on a digital story. If students find writing boring, or if they refuse to revise, or think revision is a less-than-important part of the process, digital storytelling can change that thinking. It's such an active process, involving not just writing, but thinking about how to tell a story with pictures and sound and music too. And as each element is added to the scripted story, the writer must revise, perhaps in a way he or she has never done before.

Just as I believe that students should sit with pen and paper to take notes in class or write a draft because that physical act makes a pathway in the brain, the writing and planning and revising of a digital story is a physical as well as a mental act. After completing their own digital stories, teachers in my summer class said digital storytelling would help their students see the process of revision in new ways, allowing them to actually see and hear the way revision can work.

When they are creating digital stories, students must pull together and examine and move around the photographs or other art they want to use. They must use software on the computer or drawings or sticky notes on a piece of posterboard to plan out the story, putting the words and story together, adding art, eliminating art, adding words, changing words. They are writing a poem, a tone poem with art, and one of the most important parts of the process is making sure the words and art work together. When in the story can art alone tell what the writer wants readers to know? When in the story do we need words? How many?

In the eighth edition of *Write to Learn*, Donald M. Murray sets out these steps for the writing process: Write Before Writing, Research Before Writing, Begin Writing, Keep Writing, Finish Writing. Here's how they work with digital storytelling.

Write Before Writing

This is the brainstorming, mapping, peer workshopping, and anything else students do to figure out what they want do write about, and the part of the process is no different for a digital story than for a regular story, except that students might begin thinking here about photographs they might use, in addition to the words they want to tell their story with.

Many of the stories you can read on the Web are personal ones, about obstacles overcome, achievements, important people in someone's life, memorials, stories about work or hobbies or collections. There are also stories about processes, to teach someone something, or about historical events. There are stories about events in the news and the ways they affect people. The most important element is that it should be an idea that really resonates with the writer, an idea that matters to him or her.

In the summer class I taught at The University of New Hampshire, I told the teachers before they came that they must have some idea about what they wanted to write about, but that it didn't have to be set in concrete. I suggested, since some of them would be coming from far away and wouldn't be able to get back home to pick up photographs, that they bring photos or other artwork or mementos they thought they'd want.

So as students are working toward an idea and a script, they are already thinking about what they might want to show, visually, as part of the story.

One of my students said she thinks she won't show her students any digital stories until after they've written a script, because she wants them to understand that the writing is paramount. I can see the usefulness of this, but I think it might make sense to show them a couple just to emphasize how short they must be, how concise, how tight, like a poem.

At this beginning you may want to show students examples of the World Wide Web, or you may want to wait until they've started writing, so that they concentrate on that piece of the work first, rather than the visuals.

Research Before Writing

Now students collect details and information from their own lives, if they are writing personal stories, or from other resources. For a digital story the writer must also collect photographs or other art, sounds, and music. Here's where the process starts to bend in on itself. You write, you find photographs that seem to go with the writing, but then you find a photo you truly want to use, and then you rewrite to match that. You find there are parts of the story you have no photos for and you go looking. You try out different music, thinking about the pacing of your story, and you do all of this as you're trying to refine your script.

For a word person like me, a former print journalist, this writing and creating is an exciting challenge. I'm not used to thinking about partnering words with pictures. It's this magic, the pulling together of all the pieces, that makes this such a wonderful process. It's also what makes this such a useful process for students. The youngsters coming into first grade today have never lived in a world without computers or an Internet, or twenty-four-hour news TV, for that matter. As they get older and begin to work on the World Wide Web, they are bombarded with flashing ads, wild graphics, photos, and videos, and websites with links to links to links, etc. And as TV watchers, they also have waves of talk and sound and motion crashing over their heads every day. How do they make sense of this? How do they pick out what's important? When is there a real, meaningful message in something, and when is it just flash and bang? You can get at these issues in the classroom, having students analyze digital stories for content, talking about audience and the writer's intent and whether the story works or does not. And as you talk about this, you can get them thinking about the messages of their own stories and how they can best get them across—with their words, their art, their voices.

Where Do They Get the Stuff?

If students can take their own photographs, create their own art work, film their own videos, even compose and play their own music, their stories will be truly theirs—and they will avoid issues of copyright. If they're going to use items they find on the Web or in a book or magazine, the same fair use guidelines apply as for any other work. Most importantly, stress to your students that they must credit everything they use. Too often my students pull things off websites without noting where they got them or who created them in the first place. Make sure your students keep good records of this and include the credits in their digital stories.

Students can download music from a CD to use, but copyright guidelines apply here too. One way to use a small piece of music is to loop it so that the same piece plays again and again, for as long as is needed. This meets copyright guidelines because you're actually using only a few seconds of a song.

Keeping Track of the Stuff

Keeping elements—images, text, sounds, and music—organized is an important part of the digital storytelling process. When you start, have each student create a folder to keep his or her materials in; then have each create subfolders within that folder for the other elements of the story. This way, they'll always be able to find what they need. And, these days, programs such as iMovie and Movie Maker don't actually copy these files into the movies you create with them. The original files aren't copied into the program; they remain in their original location on the hard drive of your computer. The programs then point to those files wherever they're located on the computer and display what's in the files as part of your movie. For example, if I make a movie on my computer at school using a photograph of my nephew John, I can't copy that movie and show it on my home computer unless I also copy the photo onto the home computer so that Movie Maker can find it and display it as part of my movie. If students have all the elements of their digital stories in a folder, it will be easy to copy those, along with their completed movies, to CDs or flash drives.

Begin Writing

Here students will begin drafts of their scripts, using information they've collected and any prewriting they've done. You may want them to workshop scripts with their fellow students. They can ask themselves and their peers questions: What is the point I want to make with my story? Why am I telling this story? What dramatic question will it answer? Why does this event or process or story matter? What's my role in the story and the telling?

You'll want to talk about audience too. Who are the stories aimed at? Fellow students? Family members? Friends? If the stories are going to be put up on a webpage, will an audience who doesn't know your students understand these stories? The Web is a new outlet for publishing, and students must consider how they want to present themselves to a global audience.

Once they've completed a script and recorded the narration, students will return to this part of the process to begin writing or creating their story. Whatever software program they're going to use, they'll import into it all the elements of their story and begin matching the script or narration to the images. They'll want to consider again the questions they answered for themselves as they worked on their scripts.

DIGITAL STORYTELLING ON THE WORLD WIDE WEB

Use your favorite World Wide Web search tool to find sites mentioned in this chapter. Search for "Digital Storytelling in the Scott County Schools" or "KQED Education Network My Potato Story" or "Grass Born to be Stepped on: Women's Rights in China."

You can find more resources, examples, and links if you search for these sites:

The Center for Digital Storytelling

Tech Head Stories

Educational Uses of Digital Storytelling

DigiTales

Search for "The Educator's Guide to Copyright and Fair Use" and "Education World" and you'll find clear guidelines for use of digital material. There are also websites where students can find royalty-free or copyright friendly images, sounds and music; some are free while others are available for a small fee. Some are created by teachers especially for school projects. Search for "Soundzabound—Royalty Free Music Library for the Schools" or "Pics4Learning." The sites listed above include links to other such resources.

Storyboarding is a important part of the digital storytelling process. Basically, this means laying out visually what images will be used, in what order, and connecting them with the text or narration. Students can do this using software programs designed especially for this or with pieces of paper or, as my students did, with huge sheets of newsprint and sticky notes. They can draw pictures to represent photographs or art they will use, or simply label sticky notes with something that represents an image. They map out what words are going to go with what images, what images may stand alone, and in what order the images should be displayed. The sticky notes allow quick changes as the writer develops the story. It's an active form of planning that will grab students and help them see how their stories will come together.

May 25, 2006. I'm at the Center for Digital Storytelling in Berkeley, California. Since I am going to teach a digital storytelling class in July at the University of New Hampshire, I've come to learn first-hand how to do this. I've carried with me a bunch of photos of my family, not sure what story I'd actually try to tell. But as I try brainstorming and writing some leads, I realize there is one issue that I'd been trying to come to terms with. I have three siblings and eight nieces and nephews I love madly. But at the age of forty-eight, I'm not married and never had children—and I've reached the age where I've had to admit to myself that I'm never going to do so. So in a family that sees raising kids as the most important job in the world, what's my role? I want to answer this question in my story.

My script begins with a description of a family dinner at my grandmother's when I was a kid. "Those days, in my family, the men sat in one room talking of baseball or changing the oil in their cars, or of when it would be time to take down the storm windows, put up the screens. The women cooked and set table and talked about ironing shirts, washing babies, and what it was like to be happy, and sometimes just to get by, though the words they used were not these." I can use pictures of my family members to illustrate much of my story, but not this part. Pictures of my grandmother and my mother won't have the impact I want the line to have. They will put a face on this idea, and I don't want that—I want it to stand as something many of us do and feel. I go out on the Web and troll for pictures until I find one, on a copyright-right free site, that I think will work: the image of shirts blowing in the wind on a clothesline, shot from below so that the backdrop is bright blue sky. I think this symbolizes women's work, work that has to be done, that often goes unnoticed. Work often done with love, but also sometimes just because it has to be done, because doing it keeps the family running smoothly. It's a beautiful picture, but it gives people space to imagine what they want when I get to that part of my story. That's what I want.

Keep Writing/Finish Writing

Here, as students work on scripts, they'll continue to make their focus clear, work on organization, discuss their writing with peers, and revise until their scripts are done. This process will continue until the whole digital story is done, because students have to figure out how their words will go together with their images before their scripts are finished.

If more than one student is going to work on a story at a time, get earphones for the computers! Students will have to listen to their narration over and over as they work to match it to their images, and without earphones they will drive you and everyone else crazy.

Each software program works a little differently from another, but the basics remain the same. You'll open your moviemaking program and import the pictures, video, voice-over, and music from elsewhere on your hard drive or from a CD or portable drive. You'll see icons for each file on your computer screen and be able to view or listen to them. Then you'll create your movie, matching visual elements to sound, by clicking and dragging your files to a storyboard or timeline box displayed on your screen.

The software will allow students to display one image for as long as they want, with or without voice-over; to make all sorts of visual transitions between images; to move in close or out from one part of a photograph; to play with special effects on photos and different colors and fonts for text; to add slides with text in between photographs. They'll be able to add music and control the volume of the music too, so they can bring it up in one place and down in another. Through this, then, they'll be thinking about pacing, about the impact of the art, about how a viewer will hear the words and put them together with the art. One intriguing aspect of the art is when a storyteller wants to use a photograph, say, that is a literal showing of what's being discussed in the movie, and when he or she wants a photograph to act as metaphor, to stand for an abstract idea.

Talking these issues through and going through the process of creating digital stories will give you a way into discussing them when students work on other writing projects. How and when does metaphor work? How can you make a reader "see" something when you write about it? How quickly can you and should you get to your main point?

Talk to teachers who've tried digital storytelling and you'll hear stories of reluctant writers drawn in by the technology, the active role they must play and the choices they can make.

The Economy of Poetry

Earlier I mentioned it's good to keep stories short, about three minutes long. To do this, students actually create poems when they create their scripts, in the sense that they've got to tell a whole story quickly, making every word count. Much revision of scripts will probably involve cutting out material that isn't necessary and, again, thinking about where a picture and brief text, or only a picture, can do some of the work of telling the story, rather than several sentences. With the most successful digital stories, students are pushed to get to the heart of what they want to say and to use concrete language to say it.

Graduate student and high school teacher Jennifer wants to tell a story about the difficult year she and her husband lived through and how they've come out of it stronger and closer. In her first draft of a script, she writes, "Lately our lives had been like a fast-moving class five river. Turbulent. Testing, Unsure of the direction ahead, many times we were just holding on, nervous about tomorrow." The draft is prose, about six hundred words long. But she has a vision of her story as a piece of poetry. She reviews all the photos she's gathered of their trip to Montana, choosing ones she thinks can stand alone without words. As she puts together her storyboard, adding and deleting photos, she focuses and reworks her script until the final draft is seventeen lines of poetry that begin, "Do you remember letting down the reins so your horse could drink from the stream? The branches tickling our arms as we swung them to clear a path?" Photographs appear on the screen of herself and her husband on horseback; of the gorgeous mountains and river; of wildflowers red, yellow and purple; of their wedding. Soft dulcimer music plays. Some of the photos are matched to text, but many move the story along without words. The poem ends this way: "The Montana Valleys bring us back to who we are...Like the western fires, our skin has been charred, but now little flowers dance among our feet." The photo that accompanies these words is of a burned-out part of the forest, where blackened tree trunks stand but wildflowers grow.

The Power of Voice

Of course every digital story isn't exactly the same. Some are photographs and text only or photographs and music only. But I and my students have found that stories with a voice-over narration have the most impact.

I grew up in the age of television, but my parents were radio babies first, and I remember my grandfather listening to Red Sox games on the radio. I love listening to the old radio shows, "The Shadow" and "The Green Hornet," making up in my head the pictures to go with the voices and sounds. Garrison Keillor and his "A Prairie Home Companion" radio show weekly gives listeners around the country a chance to create mental pictures of the doings of the residents of Lake Wobegon.

In my journalism classes, when I talk to students about quoting people in their stories, I say that the power here is that the sources get to talk directly to readers and that we love to hear people talking.

In a lot of great storytelling, we let the characters speak directly. Imagine if the story of the big bad wolf were told this way:

Then the wolf angrily told the pig to open up. The pig cheekily refused. Then the wolf threatened to blow the pig's house down.

instead of this way:

"Little pig, little pig, let me in," said the wolf.
"Not by the hair on my chinny, chin chin," said the pig.
"Then I'll huff and I'll puff and I'll blow your house in," cried the wolf.

When we hear how a character (or a storyteller) says something, this moves the story along; it gives us some insight into the person speaking and the reasons he or she is saying something; it gives us a sense of immediacy, of being there; it makes concrete and real what is happening.

The voice of a written read piece can be very personal, very particular to the content of the story, or more that of a neutral observer, as it's supposed to be with news coverage. What matters is that someone is telling the story. One of the best parts of my work with the second graders and their digital stories was seeing the grins appear on their faces as I played back what I'd recorded. Many of them had never heard their own voices that way before.

A digital story doesn't have to include voice-over narration; students can use written text between photographs or superimpose text on top of artwork. But often stories done this way lack the punch of those with a narrator talking to the audience.

One Computer, Two Computers, Three Computers, Four

If you have access to a computer for every student in your class, plus a tech person to work with you, you're all set. If you don't, you'll have to find ways to make sure each student gets the time he or she needs on a computer to finish a story.

You might have students work in twos, with pairs switching off on the computer work. You could set up different workstations for recording the narration, for finding images and music, and for putting the movie together. Then you could have students move through these workstations so everyone gets a chance to do the computer work. Get students to do as much planning as possible, including storyboarding, before they begin creating their stories on the computers.

For technical help, you might find parent volunteers who are computer-savvy and could help. This would be a great project for getting older students to work with younger students too; bring some high school students in to help middle or elementary school kids complete the digital work.

Working on these projects should be fun, not agony. Try not to let computer glitches drive everyone nuts; break the work down into steps and don't work on any one step for too long. As you go on, some students will master some steps more quickly than others and can answer questions others have about the software or hardware.

The Last Parts of the Process

Once students complete their projects, the stories can be burned onto CDs, saved on flash drives, and uploaded to webpages.

The big finish should be sharing the movies with peers. Even if students have been workshopping the pieces as they go along, I guarantee they'll be amazed by the final projects when they can see everything put together.

You'll find many rubrics online for assessing digital stories. You may want to work with your students to come up with criteria for assessing the projects before they begin.

A Final Word

Media literacy, visual literacy, technology literacy, information literacy—we use these terms to encompass skills and understanding students must have to succeed in this century. Digital storytelling can help students develop the thinking and skills they need. Consider some of the questions you and your students might explore as they work on digital stories: What makes photographs or art powerful? How are these used in ways to persuade people to a certain point of view in advertising or public relations or editorial presentations online or even in what is supposed to be objective journalism? What role does music play in making us feel a certain way as we listen to it? How do words and text and music work together? What's the best way to help someone understand and remember information—through text or diagrams or both together? How can you figure out what the creator of a digital story—or a documentary or a feature film—intends? Do films based on books rework authors' messages? What are ways to determine if sources of information online (which students may use to gather information and images for their digital projects and other work) are reliable and balanced?

There's no end to the possibilities—or to the amazing stories students can tell.

Pamela is a high school teacher who teaches film as well as literature courses. Her digital story is about her sisters and a memory of their childhood together. We watch and listen as images of a country store, bright-colored bottles of soda, racks of candy bars, the butcher, the butcher's handsome teenage son show up on the screen. And we remember. Pam tells us in her digital story, "On hot afternoons, my sisters and I walk to Zych's corner grocery store. We cross Elm Street to get to the store where tall hollyhocks, heavy with pink blossoms, frame the front door. We climb the two stairs and open the screen door, letting it slam behind us as the spring pulls it shut…Sometimes we go to Zych's store to see the oldest son, Tony." Here, everyone laughs, for Pam didn't have a picture of the real Tony so she used one of the young Mel Gibson. "He is so handsome and my sister and I blush deep red each time we see him. He touches my hand, giving me change, and I swear I won't wash it for at least a whole day. After we leave the store, we giggle, dipping our heads towards each other as we compare notes about his dreamy eyes and the way his brown hair falls just above them. We know he is too old for us, but it doesn't hurt to look."

Pam's digital story ends, and we viewers all begin talking about things we remember from our childhood summers. "That screen door in the story," says one woman. "I can just hear that. Everybody has been to a store like that."

Many thanks to my graduate students and fellow teachers Pamela Belanger, Patricia Emerson, Kathryn Robertson, and Jennifer Samson-Acker.

Works Cited

Murray, Donald M. 2005. *Write to Learn*, 8th ed. Boston: Thomson Wadsworth.

Porter, Bernajean. 6 July 2006. "Overview of Evaluating Projects." *Digitales*. www.digitales.us/evaluating/index.

16

Composition as Community Action

Writing and Service-Learning

Thomas Deans and Megan Marie

Thomas Deans teaches courses in writing, rhetoric, and literature—many with a service-learning approach—at the University of Connecticut, where he also directs the University Writing Center. He is the author of Writing Partnerships: Service-Learning in Composition, *a comparative analysis of community writing pedagogies, and* Writing and Community Action: A Service-Learning Rhetoric and Reader, *a textbook/anthology designed for college and high school English courses.*

Megan Marie is working toward a Ph.D. in Language, Literacy, and Rhetoric at the University of Illinois at Chicago while teaching community-based writing and women's literature full-time at Malcolm X College. Prior to graduate school, Megan taught high school English in the Kansas City area. Her courses ranged from freshman to senior English, and from creative writing to learning communities for at-risk students.

One day it hit me. I was only half teaching. Devoting hours of time to Romeo and Juliet—practicing iambic pentameter, creating masks for our masquerade ball, writing historically specific articles for a hypothetical Renaissance Newspaper—was sort of cheating my students. I was limiting the power of writing by keeping our writing context and composing work stuck in the fifteenth century. The Capulets and Montagues were no more real to my students than the fictitious audiences for whom the students were writing their Olde Times newspaper articles. I realized I could no longer trap important social issues such as gender, race, class, and violence within a text and time period. Without any idea how, I committed to making the classroom more contextual—to incorporating the communities in which social issues play out every day. My first steps were tiny: we invited neighborhood students to our masquerade ball and each of us chalked the sidewalk with our contemporary interpretations of Romeo and Juliet. But since then, for me, William Shakespeare and teaching have never been the same.

—Megan Marie
Reflections on her first year of teaching freshman English, 1997

For most, it starts with a restlessness with typical writing assignments. Or with a desire to bring long-held activist impulses into one's teaching. Or with a sense of malaise at the prospect of teaching that same Robert Frost poem with that same lesson plan. Or even with the realization that connecting students, as writers, with their communities aligns neatly with the notion that writing is a deeply social process. Whatever the itch, the response, for some, is to connect the English classroom with civic life through service-learning projects keyed to writing.

When engaged in community-based learning, students use writing both to step back and reflect on pressing social concerns and to step up and act on them. Such pedagogies take writing beyond the classroom walls and into local communities. What does this look like? Take the example of Randi Dickson, who opted to connect her ninth graders with elderly people for a unit on poetry. Adopting Kenneth Koch's approach to collaborative creative writing in *I Never Told Anybody*, Dickson paired each student with an elderly resident at a local nursing home. She supplied her students with Koch's prompts and facilitated discussions about the challenges of working across generations; she then took her students to the nursing home so they could prompt, listen, and transcribe the conversations and creations that took place. The students, in collaboration with their senior-citizen partners, generated poetry, edited the poems for publication, and hosted a public reading. Back at school they composed their own poems keyed to some of the same themes they explored with the nursing home residents. Dickson explains, "One day they would be in visiting the nursing homes, and the other they would be in the writing center adding to the files of the person they were matched with as well as refining their own poetry collections" (Dickson 1999, 79). Students also reflected, in journals and essays, on the ways that we as a culture treat our elderly citizens. All of this shuttling—between school and community, youth and experience, action and reflection, listening and composing, creative poetry and critical prose—generated an exciting amalgam of personal, civic, intellectual, and textual engagement.

Or consider the example of Jennifer Kehler's tenth-grade Kincaid Academy students connecting with members of their own communities after having read Stud Turkel's *Working*. Turkel's vignettes challenge readers to consider the "invisible" workers who make our society go round by doing the jobs we never see. Kehler challenged her students to consider why we remain blind to economic realities and to use writing to look at their own neighborhoods with new eyes. Engaging her students in preliminary discussions of class and race, she then asked them to participate in inquiry-based learning through interviewing. The interviews aimed to get students on the streets to find out why certain jobs exist, why some people will work these jobs while others won't, and how implicated every one of us is in our present economy. These interviews then helped shape the district-mandated narrative paper that her sophomore students were expected to write. Instead of assigning the traditional self-focused narrative paper, Kehler took her students into the community to help them see their own lives through the lives of others.

Now consider similar students just a year or two older. A group of high school graduates joined a writing-focused, community-based learning program at the University of Illinois Chicago because they had all done service in high school and wanted to connect their college academic work to community activism. While many of the Chicago students had done volunteer work and some curriculum-based assignments such as those assigned by Dickson and Kehler, none had actually written documents for community organizations. In this instance, students just a few months out of high school were asked to produce written documents for various nonprofit organizations as stipulated by agency directors. Instructors paired the students with agencies, and then the students set to work creating what the agencies asked for, such as fact sheets, brochures, web page content, reports, and so on. Barely eighteen, the students were thrown headfirst into the composing process. They had to discern their writing situation (by working in teams to learn about their partner agency's history, community, and mission); discern the requirements of the rhetorical context in which were asked to write and the genres they needed to use; and discern how to revise, with the guidance of their teachers and community partners, draft after draft until they got it right. These students moved from individuals interested in service to writers engaged in their communities.

These examples reflect different student populations, settings, and enactments of literacy. In each case, however, joining academic study and community action led to powerful student writing.

But What Exactly Is Service-Learning?

As distinct from community service or volunteerism, service-learning is keyed to specific academic learning goals, involves community members in a spirit of reciprocity (not just as objects of study or as deficits to be fixed), and folds in opportunities for critical reflection. In an English classroom this means connecting readings and writings to real-world issues or situations. It might involve reading about the importance of literacy and putting that knowledge to work by having students tutor students in younger grades. Or doing community-based research as part of writing a proposal arguing to convert a vacant lot to green space for one's city. Or students contributing an article to a local nonprofit organization's newsletter. Or establishing an intergenerational pen pal exchange with soldiers stationed abroad. Or reflecting on the experience of working the polls on election day. Adopting a service-learning pedagogy can mean introducing a small community-based component to an existing course or overhauling an entire curriculum. How service gets integrated often depends on the aspirations and constraints of the schools and communities involved. Statistics prove, however, that teachers are choosing to adopt community-based strategies in great numbers: in 1999 thirty-two percent of all public schools featured it somewhere in their curricula, including half of all high schools (Westat and Chapman 1999); in 2004 approximately 4.7 million K–12 students in twenty-three thousand public schools were affected (Stagg 2004). Many high schools, public and private, require service-learning; some states have made it a graduation requirement. Likewise, in higher education service-learning emerged as a national phenomenon in the late 1980s and has been picking up steam since.

While students, parents, and administrators generally laud the idea of service-learning, most gloss over what teachers recognize immediately: that it adds a time-intensive layer of planning, relationship-building, and management to the traditional classroom. Perhaps more significantly, community-based learning demands setting aside safe, prescribed curricula for something more unpredictable and improvisational. So why do it? Deeply held commitments to civic engagement and social justice motivate many teachers, but so does the realization that much of the best learning—and writing—happens on the edge of risk, is embedded in the fray of community life, and is motivated by a concern for others.

In this chapter we focus on English classrooms and the writing process and how both can be connected to community life. We understand that approaches to community-based writing vary from the high school to the university and that every pedagogy must be adapted to the nuances of particular classrooms and institutions. We also understand that most high school English teachers operate in a climate of standardized testing and state standards. Still, we make the case that fruitful academic/community connections can be forged within the constraints of most settings, much to the benefit of novice writers. Our stance is optimistic, maybe even a bit utopist, because we have seen service-learning work powerfully in our own classrooms.

Where Does Service-Learning in Composition Come From?

We can look for the origins of community-based writing in rhetoric, the art of public discourse, which reaches back to the ancient Greeks and Romans. The rhetorical tradition features not only treatises on oratory, persuasion, and style but also an abiding concern with how the use of rhetoric relates to ideals of truth, civic leadership, and the common good. Classical teachers such as Plato, Aristotle, and Quintillian were taken with how language contributed to organizing large groups of people and shaping society. If we jump forward to American history, John Dewey stands out as service-learning's most important predecessor, as his educational philosophy argues for an experiential and democratic conception of schooling, and the titles to several of his landmark works—*Experience and Education, The School and Society*, and *Democracy and Education*—signal his commitment to bridging the very same kinds gaps that service-learning aims to repair. We might also credit the spirit of American civic engagement—marveled at by Alexis de Tocqueville 150 years ago and revisited recently by political scientist Robert Putnam; the inspiration of 1960s civil rights activism; the influence of Paulo Freire's liberatory praxis; and the long reach of various religious traditions.

Community writing pedagogies, then, continue into the twenty-first century with momentum, emerging from several motives:

- The *rhetorical* impulse to position students as rhetors who experience the power of language and as they compose for public audiences. Most school writing is about expressing oneself and demonstrating learning, but community-based writing usually reframes writing as a means of performing tangible social action.
- The *civic* impulse to engage youth more actively in their communities. Students may start with a sentimental posture of doing charity, but effective service-learning

invites them to question one-way conceptions of giving and helping. The reflections of one student illustrate this movement toward a more sophisticated civic stance: "My definition of service has changed from the most basic idea of helping others to a more complex idea of working *with* a community, rather than for one. I have most definitely become more involved in civic affairs and become a more well-informed citizen."

- The *activist* impulse to spur advocacy and social change. Beyond inviting youth to participate more actively in their communities, those taking an activist, sometimes even oppositional or radical stance aspire to change normative assumptions, encourage ideological critique, and address root causes of injustice.

- The *pragmatic* impulse to boost investment in writing and revision by having students take on real-world projects of palpable consequence. Service-learning not only helps young writers to develop a wider repertoire of communication skills but also reinforces a process approach to composing, because students typically revise across several drafts and edit carefully for specific audiences. Indeed, teachers often remark on how students discover—some for the first time—reasons to revise other than a teacher's mandate to do so (Edwards 2001; Gilbert 2001; Graff 2001; Sipe 2001)

Different motives will resonate with different practitioners, and often service-learning's power derives from the ways that various motives reinforce and amplify one another. One thing for sure, however, is that community-based writing quickly helps students see that all writing is not the same, and that when, where, and why students write something does not depend solely on their teacher's whims or a textbook's dictates. Students begin to see that there is a difference between academic and community-based writing (even if some similarities persist, such as the need to edit carefully), and they begin to understand the importance of context in a new way.

Three Kinds of Community Writing

Because local communities and schools are so diverse, the service-learning pedagogies that grow from them assume almost limitless possibilities. Still, three distinct but related paradigms have emerged in English: writing *for* the community, writing *about* the community, and writing *with* the community (Deans, *Writing Partnerships*). Each comes with its own learning aims and ideological freight, as well as its own challenges and rewards.

Writing for *the Community*

With this approach students become writers for local community groups and nonprofit organizations, and they compose purpose-driven documents such as newsletter articles, internal research, profiles of community members, website content—whatever the organization needs and teachers think the students can handle. In this paradigm, the writing is the service.

The Chicago-based students referenced in the opening section illustrate this approach. Students often work in small teams and wrestle with genres that rarely surface in

English classrooms but that are quite common in the workplace. Often described as real-world writing, this kind of community-based work involves students in complex rhetorical situations and gives meaning to key rhetorical concepts (audience, purpose) as well as writing processes (revising, editing) that might otherwise remain abstractions. Most students find writing for the community a challenge, but they experience the power of writing not just to complete assignments and earn grades but also to participate, as writers, in organizations that do good work. And students usually come to recognize that drafting, testing audience expectations, seeking advice for revision, and editing with care are not rules born of the obsessions of English teachers but instead are typical moves for writers who want their texts to get something done in organizations and communities.

Writing About *the Community*

With this approach the community service could be just about anything—participating in an environmental cleanup, staffing a soup kitchen, tutoring—and in response students write to describe, analyze, and contextualize their community outreach experiences. This writing functions as a mode of learning, helping students reflect on the meaning and implications of their community outreach. The service experience functions as a kind of text—in some ways like a literary text—that opens itself to interpretation: students render their own narratives, articulate connections between their lives and what they experience and witness during their community work. Preferably, students also engage in meaningful discussions about the social issues surrounding their experiences (Greco 1992; Herzberg 1994).

Most writing about the community circulates within the classroom rather than in the public sphere, and this approach is particularly appealing to those who wish to make their curricula more experiential and socially aware but value traditional academic genres such as the personal essay, the critical essay, and the journal. Powerful community experiences, especially when married to relevant readings, tend to motivate richly textured narratives and analyses.

Writing with *the Community*

These initiatives emphasize direct collaboration (usually unmediated by nonprofit agencies) between students and local citizens who together use writing to raise awareness on social justice matters, research local problems, give voice to local citizens, and create public art. The ninth graders who composed poetry with elderly nursing home residents were operating in the writing-with-the-community paradigm. So were middle school English students who, after researching the hazardous waste site near where they lived, became environmental activists. The teacher assigned literature keyed to ethical and environmental themes (Ibsen's *Enemy of the People*) and guided students as they did extensive research on health problems in their area, communicated with local governmental and tribal agencies, and launched a public relations campaign to educate citizens about local health risks (Kesson and Oyler 1999).

Other possibilities include oral history projects and place-based writing (Cassell 2000; Gilbert 2001; Winter and Robbins 2005), so long as the resulting texts are ultimately directed toward public audiences and communal purposes. This paradigm also features community-based research—that is, research that actively involves local citizens in setting an agenda for research and carrying it out—and problem-solving initiatives that bring together various community constituencies who have a stake in a common issue to listen, deliberate, and take democratic action. Usually marked by a grassroots sensibility, writing-with-the-community projects foreground the role that writing and research can play in problem solving, advocacy, and social change.

Clearly, there are multiple ways of structuring writing, *for, about,* and *with* the community, all of them deriving from local community and institutional needs, and we do not see any one paradigm as ideal. We think that it is important to make these distinctions, however, so that teachers, curriculum designers, and students are made keenly aware of the various purposes for writing in service-learning classrooms. For example, writing *about* immigration issues in the U.S. demands a different kind of rhetorical work (and teaching) than producing a flyer *for* an agency inviting people to attend an immigrant rights march. Focusing on the role of writing—on what it does in the world—rather than on how community service can or should change the moral or ideological demeanor of our students, helps keep the composing process at the center of our classrooms.

Reciprocity and Reflection

A growing base of research affirms that service-learning, when done well, can improve academic learning, promotes personal development, encourages greater civic engagement, and enhances cultural and racial understanding (Billig 2006; Eyler, Giles, Stenson and Gray 2001). Some research coming out of English studies suggests that the student texts produced in community-based writing courses tend to be more complex and carefully edited than those generated in traditional classrooms (Wurr 2002).

Most service-learning scholarship published to date has been by instructors who render descriptions of their own practice and testify that service-learning works. From both empirical research and teacher testimony consensus on at least a few best practices has emerged. Some recommendations hinge on ethical considerations: initiatives should be planned with community partners from the start to avoid deficit-driven notions of service in which servers define problems and then attempts to "fix" those served. Moreover, programs should, when possible, embrace diversity, prepare students to approach difference respectfully, and build in critical reflection. Other best practices aim to ensure academic integrity: instructors should articulate clear educational goals and include mechanisms for assessing learning outcomes.

A focus on writing calls for a few other practices that are customized to English courses, including journals or writing logs. Journals are, of course, nothing new but they are particularly important in a service-learning context because so much of what students are dealing with is experiential, and journals help learners capture ephemeral experience, converting it into texts that, in many ways, can be appreciated and analyzed much like the literary texts we typically grapple with in English courses.

In their most minimal role, journals can be used to document hours on the job. But just as tallying hours of community service is hardly service-learning, describing the events of one's community outreach in journal entries or emoting about one's experience hardly counts for critical reflection or academic learning. Freewheeling journals or personal essays are usually not enough to engender critical thinking, because even as students use the journal to detail powerful experiences or express heartfelt compassion, their narratives sometimes slip into platitudes about charity or sidestep questions about the larger social context of their service (Anson 1997; Herzberg 1994). For example, when helping with a food drive, students might express authentic compassion for those struggling with hunger but they may avoid, unless prompted by the teacher, reading such texts as Janet Poppendiek's *Sweet Charity? Emergency Food and the End of Entitlement* or Barbara Ehrenreich's *Nickel-and-Dimed: On Not Getting By In America*—and they may not confront the more abstract questions of why people are poor in the first place, why even those who work full-time might need food assistance, and which social, economic and political changes in American culture have led to the exponential growth of food banks over the past thirty years. Likewise, adolescent fiction such as Rob Thomas's *Doing Time: Notes from the Undergrad*, which features stories of students doing community service required by their schools, can raise tough questions about how and why some kinds of service seem shallow and hypocritical.

Journals, at their best, allow students not only to render narratives of their community work but also to invite critical analysis.

Similarly, journals can help students account for some of the complex *communication and writing* issues that surface as students shuttle between academic and community contexts. Consider the following journal excerpt from a student asked to contemplate her recent experience writing a community-based research paper: "Writing a research paper for [my agency] was a new experience for me. Though I had written a research paper before, I felt more pressure writing one for an agency; my argument had to be strong, my evidence had to be thorough, and my sources had to be accurate. My paper could possibly be presented to the public, so I felt more responsibility to produce excellent work." By nudging students toward such metacognition about the composing process, instructors remind students (and themselves) that writing—writing that students and audiences *care* about—remains at the hub of community-based English courses.

Writing for and with Local Organizations: A Few Companion Assignments

Asking students to write *for* and *with* the community triggers a complex set of literacy demands that need to be carefully scaffolded if they are to be successful. The first wave of service-learning enthusiasts who asked their students to get out there and write for local community organizations learned that students are energized by such tasks but often underprepared to handle entirely new rhetorical situations, collaborate with community partners, and compose in unfamiliar workplace and public genres. In addition to orienting students to such issues as racial and class differences, we need to orient them *as writers* to the challenges of writing beyond the bounds of school. This involves prompting students to do good old-fashioned audience analysis: Who is your audience? What do they care about? What do they expect?. We also recommend that teachers consider a sequence of companion assignments to complement projects for local organizations. Below are three experience-tested ones.

Contract or letter of understanding   While typical school assignments are structured by the teacher, community-based projects often change depending on the context for writing and the needs of the community. Thus, community-based writing often demands a more fluid and improvisational arrangement. So that teachers can retain the structure of objectives and assessment, teachers often work out project assignments in advance with participating organizations. However, even then assignments can change when students begin to work with those outside of the classroom.

Students need to align their expectations with those of their community partners. Near the outset of a project, we recommend that students work with their teachers to compose a straightforward *contract* or *letter of understanding* for each project to help keep all stakeholders involved on track. These documents spell out project parameters, due dates, and other details. They can help everyone involved keep the logistics straight, but through writing them students may also begin to see that there is social dimension to the composing process—that successful writing often depends on creating working relationships, on planning, on social as much as sentence-level skills. As one of our students reflected, "Writing [a letter of understanding] helped me decide what I wanted to include in the fact sheet. Moreover, the experience has made me a stronger writer because I was forced to consider all of the factors that are necessary for the completion of a satisfactory document." Questions that students can answer in their letters of understanding include:

- What is the purpose of the project? For whom are you completing it?
- What is the writing goal of the project and what writing situation calls for this document to be written?
- Who is the audience? Might more than one audience read it?
- What kind of language, tone, and style will be most appropriate?
- What is the hopeful consequence of this project?
- How will you begin to write for this project?
- List the steps you will take in order to complete this project, and with your teacher work out a timeline for drafts.
- What kinds of help do you anticipate needing?

Asking these questions up front reduces the opportunity for miscommunication among those involved; answering the questions also helps students clarify the rhetorical situation in which they have been placed.

Agency profile   One of the things that students discover readily when doing service-learning is that many people and organizations in the local community are already doing good work. Part of their writing should be keyed to exploring how those organizations do their work—and if they are paired with one organization, they should investigate it carefully. Because writing is driven by the values, habits, and language conventions of particular contexts and communities, writers need to know something about an organization before they can work and write effectively for it. Through research and interviews, students can learn an agency's history, priorities, programs, and aspirations, setting the stage for successful writing-for-the-community projects. (Student samples of agency profiles can be found in *Writing and Community Action*, by Thomas Deans, on pages 285–337.)

Genre analysis   We must help novice writers attend to genre as they compose using new (to them) formats for workplace writing (such as reports, fact sheets, and request letters) and public writing (such as journalistic articles, letters to the editor, and web content). Students who have written mainly five-paragraph essays or personal narratives have composed mainly for teachers and in school-based genres. Writing for community organizations or public audiences can be worlds apart from school assignments, so time needs to be devoted to alerting students to what writing genres are and how they function. An activity to help students understand, recognize, and compose in an unfamiliar genre is to collect several examples of the genre they are being asked to write and analyze them together. If students approach these examples not as models to follow slavishly but as data to analyze, they can dig for patterns that cut across the examples, plus inquire about how and why some disrupt those patterns. This can feed basic rhetorical analysis as students begin to ask: What do the samples have in common? Which visual and formal features? What kinds of introductions, diction, tone, use of quotations, etc., do we see? Which samples depart from the norm and why? What would our intended audience expect to see as we use this genre? How might they react if we did something different? And overall, how will this genre analysis guide our own writing choices? The point is that students should begin to see genres not as static formats but as tools writers use.

Teachers can find more and more articles on service-learning cropping up in professional periodicals such as *English Journal*; they can also look for resources in a range of places, both in print and on the Web:

- *Community Lessons: Integrating Service-Learning into K–12 Curriculum—Promising Practices*, is online at National Service Learning Clearinghouse (www.servicelearning.org) and includes program descriptions and curriculum guides;
- *Writing Our Communities: Local Learning and Public Culture* by Dave Winter and Sarah Robbins (2005) features lesson plans and teacher reflections for kindergarten through college;
- *Beyond Room 109: Developing Independent Study Projects* by Richard Kent (2000) reveals options and strategies for launching individualized research projects, some keyed to community service;
- *Writing and Community Action: A Service-Learning Rhetoric and Reader* by Thomas Deans (2003) offers readings, assignments, and student samples for late high school through college.

All of these sources can be helpful, and there are certainly many more, but we believe—adapting Tip O'Neil's dictum on politics—that *all service-learning is local*. Projects emerge less from textbooks than they do from the ingenuity of teachers and community partners making the most of local circumstances. So let us end where we began: with a teacher and students in action.

When planning for a unit on the theme of tolerance at her urban arts magnet middle school, English teacher Sarah K. Edwards opted to scrap her earlier habits of arranging activities such as inviting in an African American poet or going on a field trip to the local Jewish community center. Instead she started by assigning fiction and non-fiction, such as Ken Mochizuki's *Baseball Saved Us*, which draws on his family's experiences in a Japanese American internment camp during the 1940s; then she asked her students to reflect, through discussion and writing, on their own experiences with intolerance, plus to gather stories from family members. Edwards reports that "this brought a sense of authenticity to our study of language arts"; it also led them to both interdisciplinarity and service-learning

(Edwards 2001, 41). The students, working under the guidance of their art teacher, created a tolerance-themed mural that featured poetry and visual art, and invitations to the exhibit drew in local schools and the media. Then the students opted to step beyond the bounds of the school to collaborate with a neighboring (but much less privileged) elementary school. Once a week Edwards' eighth graders walked to the other school to act as reading buddies for the younger students, linking most of those readings to the tolerance theme, even using some of the stories that the eighth graders has composed earlier. This brought benefits to both the tutees and the tutors, as Edwards notes:

> Back in our own classroom, we started to talk about reading strategies that 'good readers' use to decode a text. These very same strategies, such as prediction and inference, that I had been fruitlessly trying to teach earlier in the year, suddenly became quite important as my students were now the teachers (42).

Students were eager for more, and word got out about the course, which yielded more community connections. Working at the request of a community food bank and local residents, that same class set to work establishing a community garden. Collaborating with the school's science teacher, students researched soil, water, and plants; they also chipped in manual labor. And on the heels of that project came another, this time sparked by the proposal from a student that the class work on converting some barren school land into a community park. That required students to write letters to school officials for permission and services, to local nurseries and builders for donations, and to utility companies for digging instructions. An area technology school even chipped in, building a ramada to provide shade. Edwards reflects:

> As with any community project, not every student was involved in the same manner. Some students read about similar projects, while others worked on grant writing or newspaper articles to share our progress. This type of writing supported the students' prior experience with process writing, as they continued to edit and revise letters they sent. No longer was writing something that only I assigned and read. It was done to either communicate a desire or share an experience. Isn't that what writing is supposed to be? (44).

Indeed it is.

Works Cited

Anson, Christopher. 1997. "On Reflection: The Role of Logs and Journals in Service-Learning Courses." *Writing the Community: Concepts and Models for Service-Learning in Composition.* Eds. Robert. C. Crooks, Ann Watters, and Linda Addler-Kassner. Washington, DC, and Urbana, IL: The American Association for Higher Education and National Council of Teachers of English. 167–80.

Billig, Shelley H. *The Impacts of Service-Learning on Youth, Schools and Communities: Research on K–12 School-Based Service-Learning, 1990–1999.* W.K. Kellogg Foundation. 15 October 2006. http://learningindeed.org/research/slresearch/slrsrchsy.html.

Cassell, Susie Lan. 2000. "Hunger for Memory: Oral History Recovery and Community Service Learning." *Reflections on Community-Based Writing Instruction* 1 (2): 12–17.

Deans, Thomas. 2003. *Writing and Community Action: A Service-Learning Rhetoric and Reader.* New York: Longman.

Deans, Thomas. 2000. *Writing Partnerships: Service-Learning in Composition*. Urbana, IL: National Council of Teachers of English.

Dickson, Randy. 1999. "Quiet Times: Ninth Graders Teach Poetry Writing in Nursing Homes." *English Journal* 88 (5): 73–80.

Edwards, Sarah K. 2001. "Bridging the Gap: Connecting School and Community with Service Learning." *English Journal* 90 (5): 39–44.

Ehrenreich, Barbara. 2002. *Nickel-and-Dimed: On Not Getting By in America*. New York: Owl Books.

Eyler, Janet, Dwight.E. Giles, Jr., Christine Stenson, and Charlene Gray. 2001. *At a Glance: What We Know About the Effects of Service-Learning on College Students, Faculty, Institutions and Communities, 1993–2000*. 3rd ed. Learn and Serve America National Service Learning Clearinghouse.

Gilbert, Barbara. 2001. "Designing a Town-Based Writing Project." *English Journal* 90 (5): 88–94.

Graff, Patricia S. 2001. "Service Learning Reinforces Language Arts Skills." *English Journal* 90 (5): 19–21.

Greco, Norma. 1992. "Critical Literacy and Community Service: Reading and Writing the World." *English Journal* 81: 83–85.

Herzberg, Bruce. 1994. "Community Service and Critical Teaching." *CCC*. 45 (3). 307–19.

Kehler, Jennifer. 15 June 2006. Personal communication with Megan Marie.

Kent, Richard. 2000. *Beyond Room 109: Developing Independent Study Projects*. Portsmouth, NH: Heinemann-Boynton/Cook.

Kesson, Kathleen, and Celia Oyler. 1999. "Integrated Curriculum and Service Learning: Linking School-Based Knowledge and Social Action." *English Education* 31 (2). 135–149.

Mochizuki, Ken. 1993. *Baseball Saved Us*. New York: Scholastic.

Poppendieck, Janet. 1999. *Sweet Charity? Emergency Food and the End of Entitlement*. New York: Penguin Putnam.

Putnam, Robert. 2000. *Bowling Alone: The Collapse and Revival of American Community*. New York: Simon and Schuster.

Sipe, Rebecca Bowers. 2001. "Academic Service Learning: More than Just 'Doing Time.'" *English Journal* 9: 33–38.

Stagg, Allison. 2004. Fact Sheet: Service-Learning in K–12 Education. *CIRCLE: The Center for Information and Research on Civic Learning and Engagement*. University of Maryland. www.civicyouth.org.

Thomas, Rob. 1997. *Doing Time: Notes from the Undergrad*. New York: Simon and Schuster.

Westat, R. S. and C. Chapman. 1999. "Service-Learning and Community Service in K–12 Public Schools." *U.S. Department of Education Office of Educational Research and Improvement*. NCES 1999–043: 1–16.

Winter, Dave, and Sarah Robbins. 2005. *Writing Our Communities: Local Learning and Public Culture*. Urbana, IL: National Council of Teachers of English.

Wurr, Adrian. 2002. "Text-Based Measures of Service-Learning Writing Quality". *Reflections on Community Based Writing* 2 (2): 41–56.

17

Preparing Students for Life After High School

An Interview Writing Project

Jessica Singer

Jessica Singer is the author of Stirring up Justice: Writing and Reading to Change the World. *Singer is an assistant professor of English education at Arizona State University. Her research and teaching revolve around themes of activism and social justice. She previously taught high school English in Portland, Oregon, where she was also an active member of Portland Rethinking Schools, an activist organization committed to making progressive change in public education.*

> At the very least, the kind of interview I do offers ... an opportunity to learn more
> about someone whose work has moved and delighted us and, perhaps, in some small
> way, altered our perception of ourselves and our world.
>
> —Terry Gross, All I Did Was Ask

Introduction

In my first year as a high school English teacher, I noticed that the students at my school were divided into two groups: honors and regulars. Honors was the name assigned to all classes where students were college bound and earned honors credit. In comparison, regular classes were made up of lower-performing students and moved at a slower pace than the honors courses. The content of these classes was not parallel. I also noticed that the school support programs established for seniors transitioning to college and postsecondary schooling were geared toward honors students and that my regular students, who were talented, intelligent young adults were being left to fend for themselves. My regular students were typically given little to no support in learning about postsecondary options due to low academic performance, socioeconomic status, and second language learning. For example, some counselors visited only honors classes to hand out college and scholarship information. When I discovered this, I went to the counseling office to inquire further into this policy. The counselor explained, "This saves me time. I mean, it's clear that the other kids aren't going on to study. If they were, they would be in honors classes." Scholarship meetings and workshops informing students about how to fill out forms and receive financial aide took place after school when many of my regular seniors could not attend because they had after-school jobs. I grew angry because my students were being excluded from the conversations and support they needed to help them prepare for life beyond high school.

Supporting students in their preparation for the future became my activist project as a high school language arts teacher in Portland, Oregon. I began to think about the ways my school was perpetuating inequity and low expectation with a lack of support regarding post secondary options for students who were not necessarily starting at four-year colleges and universities. I decided to include support for all of my students in exploring postsecondary options within my language arts curriculum. Students needed guidance in learning pragmatic skills, such as filling out financial aid and scholarship forms, researching programs, and writing college admissions essays and resumes. Moreover, they needed models to help them widen their view of their future options. Students had a difficult time thinking about their next steps without exposure to real possibilities for their future life paths connected with their own interests.

The interview assignment described in this chapter represents just one piece of a larger curriculum I created to help prepare students for college and for their adult lives. I wanted to prepare all of my students for higher education and the workplace, regardless of their academic histories. This was not a new idea in education and may seem like an obvious or uneventful act for an English teacher. However, many high school students are left without support during critical life transitions and are often unfairly labeled and tracked (Singer 2002, 16–17). Jeannie Oakes, professor of educational equity at the University of California at Los Angeles, explains the importance of preparing students for life beyond high school:

> I think that schools operate as if we're still in 1954, where finishing high school makes you ready and desirable in the workplace, and it's not true anymore. We haven't kept up in terms of making sure that all of the opportunities that high school students have actually lead them to something beyond high school, some sort of post secondary education, college, or at least a solid vocational program. (Oaks 2004)

Providing opportunities for students to plan their next life steps became my way of teaching for justice.

Writer and educator, Margaret Wheatley, explains the importance of individuals learning directly from others, "In this increasingly complex world, it's impossible to see for ourselves most of what's going on. The only way to see more of the complexity is to ask others for their perspective and experiences" (Oakes 2004, 17). David Pearson, a reading researcher at the University of California Berkley, talks about how "reading and writing are better when they are used as tools to pursue knowledge and not as stand alone goals" (Pearson, personal communication). Both of these educators invite students into projects where literacy is used as a means for gaining new understanding, rather than just a written exercise or technical skill used to fulfill course requirements. There are a number of reasons I chose to include interviews as part of my language arts curriculum, particularly for seniors. First, in the professional world, interviews serve as a gate-keeping device for entry into jobs and higher education. I wanted to demystify the interview process for students before they were interviewed or had to conduct interviews in high-stakes settings. Second, interviews are an important and pervasive form of nonfiction writing and, specifically, academic research writing. Carrying out formal and informal interviews is essential in any form of journalism as well as qualitative research. Finally, interviews are a powerful communication mode and allow students to learn from others through structured dialogue and careful listening.

Interview Examples

As I began teaching this interview project, I searched for various interviews to share with students from magazines, newspapers, books, radio, and television. I found a terrific piece from *The Oprah Magazine* where Oprah interviews her hero and friend, Nelson Mandela, about his life as a political activist in South Africa. I purposely tried to find interviews that focused on individuals taking part in diverse forms of work. Phillip Hooses' (2001) *It's Our World, Too!* is a wonderful collection of essays and interviews with young adults who are committed to working toward positive social change. These examples provided students with expanded options for thinking about life after high school. I also recorded two of my favorite interviewers from radio and television, Terry Gross and James Lipton, to share with students. We listened to Terry Gross' radio show, *Fresh Air*, on National Public Radio and I recorded *Inside the Actor's Studio* hosted by James Lipton. I asked students to bring in interviews they came across in their lives from newspapers, magazines, and television. We collected all of these clippings to store in a class binder, which served as another valuable writing resource. Sharing these examples gave students ideas about how to arrange and conduct their own interviews.

As students read and listened to interview examples, we discussed the diverse questioning strategies we came across. We noticed how some interviewers asked direct and personal questions and how almost all of the questions were open-ended. Before students dove into their work preparing their formal interviews with people outside of the class, I asked them to practice interviewing one another. I provided students with a list of interview tips (see Figure 1: Interview Tips). This rehearsal interview involved creating a set of interview questions, or an interview protocol, as a guide for their brief questioning session. This simple in-class assignment helped students understand that taking time to prepare an interview helps conversation move smoothly and with clear purpose. Allie raised her hand, "Ms. Singer, I just realized the difference between a conversation and an interview. A conversation is spontaneous and sometimes leads nowhere at all, and an interview has a point." Students started noticing some of the complexities and nuances of interviewing. They noticed that it helps having a set of pre-

Here are several interview tips to help you conduct a successful interview:

1. Begin your interview by introducing yourself. Tell the person you are interviewing the purpose of your interview and a bit of information about yourself.

2. Make sure you ask your interviewee for permission to record or take note of the interview, and ask if you may write up the interview as part of a class assignment. Do not proceed with the interview without permission.

3. As you ask questions, take notes to keep track of the interviewee's responses and any important nonverbal reactions (i.e. gestures, shrugs, laughter, change in voice tone).

4. Listen carefully. If you don't understand something or if you want the interviewee to elaborate, then be sure to ask for further explanation.

5. Be spontaneous. If the person you are interviewing says something that catches your attention, but is not a part of your original questioning plan, feel free to let the conversation go in this new direction. Use your prepared questions as a helpful guide but feel free to let the interview become open-ended.

6. Be polite and professional throughout the interview. Try not to interrupt your interviewee as they answer your questions.

7. Ask questions that you really want to know the answers to so that the conversation feels compelling and useful.

Figure 1 Interview Tips

pared questions when questioning a reluctant person. Students also realized that allowing the interviews to steer off course and move in unexpected directions often led to valuable conversation. After students practiced interviewing one another, I provided instructions for the larger interview project. The following is an example of the assignment guidelines:

Interview Assignment

The next step in this project is to interview someone who participates in a field of study that you can see yourself pursuing one day. For example, if you want to be a yoga instructor, you may want to interview someone out in the world who teaches yoga. If you are interested in cartoon animation, you may want to arrange an interview with a cartoonist. Here are the following steps for this interview assignment:

1. Brainstorm people you may want to interview based on your future career or hobby interests.
2. Select a person to interview and contact them to set up an appointment for the interview to take place. (You may do this over via email, telephone, letter, or in person).
3. Create an interview protocol as a way to guide your conversation. This protocol must include at least fifteen open-ended questions.

4. Conduct an interview and take notes or record this process in some way.

5. Write up your interview findings with an introduction, transcript, and reflection.

6. Turn in typed, double-spaced, and spell-checked.

At first, students were skeptical about having to find someone to interview. "Ms. Singer, I don't have any idea what I'm interested in, and I don't know anybody who does anything I want to do in my future," James grumbled. Other students were nervous about asking people to take time out of their busy lives. Brandon blurted out, "Why would anyone want to spend time with me when they could just as easily be doing something more fun?" I wanted to make sure that we worked through these challenges because they are similar to the hurdles that writers and researchers have to face in their careers. As a class, we talked about how the three hardest tasks for anyone setting out to conduct an interview are gaining access and permission to meet with people, finding the time to meet with them, and forming interesting questions. I spent an entire class period helping students brainstorm possible interview subjects and prepare interview questions (see Figure 2: Conducting Interviews). We brainstormed possible questions for our interviews together as a class and individually. Here are a few of the questions we created:

- Was there a turning point when you decided to pursue this career path?
- What advice would you give a young adult interested in this line of work?
- What is the most rewarding experience you have had in your work and what has been a challenge?

I also provided time for students to use the telephone in the counselor's office to make calls and set up their interviews. I helped students like James and Brandon think of ways to make this project work even though they were reluctant. Students crafted email correspondence to communicate with their interview subjects, and I provided time for them to practice their interview questions with me and with classmates.

James decided to interview his neighbor who is an environmentalist because "he lives right next to me and his job is to clean the Columbia River. I want to know how he does that because I want to work outside like he does one day." Adam interviewed the owner of a local bike store because he loves fixing bikes and hopes, one day, to own his own BMX bicycle shop. Koko interviewed her mom's best friend who is a watercolor artist. Koko told me, "I have been interested in art since the first time I played with finger paints in kindergarten. I want to learn more about what a real artist does with her time and if she can actually make a living with her painting."

As students began on this project, I asked them to write a note sharing their first thoughts about their work. This brief writing gave me insight into their progress and ideas about how to support their work.

First Thoughts Letter

Please write me a brief note sharing what you are thinking about your interview project. Who are you planning to interview and why? How is this person connected to a life path you can see yourself pursuing?

Glenda was conflicted about whether or not to interview someone devoted to helping blind people, like herself, or a business person:

1. Make a list of possible interview subjects. Think about the kinds of people who can provide you with information about work and life experiences that interest you.

2. The first step in preparing for an interview is to clearly articulate your purpose. Please write a brief statement about what you hope to gain in through this interview assignment.

3. Make a list of specific questions for one person from your brainstorm list you hope to interview. What about this person's work or experience would you like to learn more about? What specific facts or detail of their work experience do you want to uncover through this interview?

4. Continue your list using open-ended questions you might ask your interviewee. Here are some examples:
   a. In all your experience with _____, what has most surprised you?
   b. What has been the most difficult aspect of your work?
   c. If you had the chance to change something about how you approached _____, what would it be?
   d. Can you share a significant moment in your work?
   e. What do you think is the most common misconception about your work? Why?
   f. Who or what influenced you in your career?

Figure 2 Conducting Interviews

I want to study business, but I am also interested in working with blind people. Perhaps I could talk to someone who has a business that helps the blind? I have always been interested in learning about people with the same disability as me. I want to learn more about how they can overcome the barrier of this disability. I also want to know how this disability has helped them become better people. However, business is also something I have considered studying in my future. My mother wants to open her own business and if I study this field now, perhaps I could be of help to her?

After reading Glenda's note, we met and talked about how she could find someone to interview connected to both of these interests. We brainstormed people who were blind or worked with the blind and who were also immersed in the business field. Through our conversation, Glenda realized that her grandfather fit both of these interests. "My grandfather lives in Guatemala and he is blind, but he has also worked all his life to invent tools for blind people in his country."

Other students, like Ash, shared what they had done to set up an interview. "I only have a basic idea of what this project will look like, but I am lining up an interview with one of the employees of a small independent comic company. The company is responsible for some of my all-time favorite comics, including the Kevin Smith series (the writer and director of several movies)." Ash was a wonderful artist and wanted to pursue his love of drawing as a career. Jessi was a competitive barrel racer, and she decided to interview the previous owner of her horse to learn more about the professional equestrian world. Jessi was already a horse owner and hoped to become a professional horse trainer:

> I am planning to interview Kelly. She is about twenty-one years old and is a college student and a well-known equestrian competitor. She has so much knowledge about horses. This year, she even qualified to go to the Quarter Horse Congress to compete. I admire her because she is so young and has already accomplished so much. My goal in this interview is to get to know Kelly's horse background and find out what helped her get where she is today in competition. I also would like to know what happened to make horses her career instead of just a hobby.

Through these check-in letters, I could see students were invested in the interview process because they were exploring their own interests, some of which surprised me. For example, Phil, unbeknownst to me, was an avid collector of running and basketball shoes and he was interested in becoming a shoe designer. He decided to try to arrange an interview with a Nike employee to find out more about shoe design and production. After trying to set this up over a couple of weeks, Phil grew frustrated and during his reflection writing decided he could interview his friend, Nick, instead. Nick was an employee at an athletic shoe store and shared Phil's interest in shoes. Written reflections like the First Thoughts Letter, served as scaffolding and support for students to check-in regarding their progress.

Connection to Families

I was immediately surprised at the beginning of this interview assignment when several students expressed an interest in interviewing parents, aunts, uncles, or cousins. I am embarrassed to admit my first reaction when students approached me with their interview choices was that they were taking an easy way out" by interviewing family members. I initially thought that because these individuals were close to home and easy to access they were somehow not as important as people students did not already know. Instead of responding to students right away with my doubts, I thought about their request overnight. With more consideration, I realized that my first reaction was ridiculous. I chose to become a teacher, in large part, because my parents are both educators and they have inspired me greatly. My twin brother is a lawyer and was influenced strongly by our uncle David who is a judge. We all have sponsors in our lives who help shape our interests and serve as models for our future life paths. The fact that these people are within close proximity to our lives is exactly why they are such strong influences. I decided to allow students to interview anyone they wanted as long as the person could teach them about a future career interest or hobby they hoped to pursue.

Through students' interview selections, I also learned that it was unfair to assume that family members were easily accessible. Ina chose to interview her aunt who lives in Australia, and she went to great lengths to arrange a conversation with this faraway relative. She called her aunt for a week and could not reach her and then finally contacted her through email. They exchanged information back and forth through handwritten letters and late night telephone calls. Ina's family had moved to the United States from Bosnia only a few years before in order to escape the Bosnian War. She was clearly still processing the loss of her homeland, and used every writing opportunity she could to examine that change in her life and what happened to her family due to war and trauma. Ina chose to interview her aunt to learn about her experience in the Bosnian War. Ina hoped to become a counselor to support war refugees, like the members of her own family. In this excerpt from her interview, Ina shared what she learned through her communication with her aunt:

> I interviewed my aunt who lives in Australia. She is thirty-two years old, and she stayed longer in the war than my family and I. First, I did not know how to proceed with my interview, but then I decided to give her a call. We spent at least one hour talking over the phone. I just can't wait to see the next phone bill! Her life story is unbelievable. The military killed her husband and daughter right in front of her eyes. What I don't understand is how people can be so cold-hearted. She prayed to God every day to keep her family alive and safe, but she lost her lovely daughter and husband in the Bosnian War. What I learned through this conversation is that, no matter what, there are always people who fear something. There are people who just want to stay alive and live happily. I learned that pain can be stuck by your side forever. I learned that it hurts a lot to lose someone, especially someone close to your heart. This interview project taught me that people, like my aunt, still want to do good in the world even though they have suffered greatly.

This interview reinforced Ina's interest in helping people overcome tragedy. Other students, like Glenda, talked to a family member about a subject they had never discussed previously. Glenda interviewed her grandfather over the phone because he lives in Guatemala, and she chose to interview him because, like her, he is blind. Glenda wrote about her interview choice, " My grandfather is coming from Guatemala this weekend, and I have never spent time talking with him about being blind. I want to know how he feels about his disability because, one day, I want to teach students with disabilities like mine."

Nyima interviewed her father, who lives with her at home; however, she expressed frustration because his schedule was so busy and they experienced some difficulty finding a time to sit down and meet. The interviews with family members allowed for a different kind of conversation than what normally took place with these familiar people in their lives. Another unexpected benefit that came along with students' decision to interview family members was that this allowed aunts, uncles, fathers, and grandparents to become involved in our classroom work. Some students learned more about their own histories and their family's homelands through these conversations. The following excerpt from Nyima's introduction to her interview shares what she learned from her father about how he fled Tibet:

> Topygal, my father, escaped from China and came to India with his parents when he was seventeen years old, running away from his own and only country. As I listen to his tragedy that happened back in 1959, I felt what many felt around the world—overwhelming hope and joy because the fact that my father survived is a testament to the power of the Tibetan spirit to overcome hardship. Today, I had the honor of sitting with Topygal and interview him about Tibet and sit with him in his living room. As I asked him questions about his past, I felt like I was in the presence of both grace and loyalty. Even now, I can hardly believe that after leaving Tibet, he still lives happily. He is a peaceful man with a lot of surprising and he also has a good sense of humor. He is a legend around the world because of his brave stand for freedom. What is even more amazing is that he still remembers everything so clearly.

Irene chose to interview her aunt because she is an incredible chef.

Since I was born, I knew my aunt was a great cook. She usually cooked for people's birthday parties back in Russia. Neighbors asked my aunt to cook because they were too busy, and she gladly did it. When she came to the United States three years ago, she decided to keep cooking. She enjoys baking for her husband and she decorates cakes. My aunt also has a great recipe book with different recipes and pictures of food that she made and decorated."

Irene told me that she hopes to apply to the Northwest Culinary Institute in Portland and follow in her aunt's footsteps as a chef.

Another unexpected, yet important, outcome of the interviews students initiated with family members was that these conversations provided an opportunity to see people in their lives with more complexity. Glenda explained how she had held her grandfather on a pedestal before interviewing him, and that learning more about his life through their conversation made her realize that he is a human with flaws. "I was surprised to learn that my grandfather was a different person before I was born. I learned so many things about his life, and I was disappointed in a way, but also so proud of him in other ways because he has come so far with so little help or support. I was disappointed not because he didn't have an interesting life, but because I found out that he is a human being and not the perfect man I thought he was." Providing students with the freedom to choose the people they wanted to interview, family members or not, proved to be a valuable and important part of this project. The insight students gained about people they admired was powerful.

Interview Introductions

One of the reasons I selected sample interviews from sources like *The Oprah Magazine* and *Vanity Fair*, was that I was drawn to particular writing and questioning strategies used in these published pieces. Instead of launching immediately into formal transcripts, each of these published interviews begins with an introduction to the person being interviewed. In Oprah's interview with Mandela, she begins, "This is a moment I will never forget: Nelson Mandela, a man sentenced to life in prison because his fight to end segregation in South Africa, walking away free after 27 years" (Winfrey 2001, 157). In an interview with the rock singer Sheryl Crow the interviewer for *Vanity Fair* begins his piece describing the setting of a dusty music club where he met Sheryl as she was preparing to tour.

After reading a diverse selection of interviews, I became interested in how writers turn conversations into dynamic pieces of writing. I liked the idea of having students use different writing strategies to do more than just report their two-way conversations. We practiced writing an introduction for our interview write-ups in order to provide context and guidance for the reader. Nymia modeled her introduction of her father directly after Oprah's introduction of Mandela. "This is a moment I will never forget: Topygal, a man who escaped China and came to India with his parents years ago. He was seventeen years old running away from his own country." Ash introduced the cartoonist he interviewed through a description of the events of the day the interview took place:

The coffee was brewing and the interview questions were printing in the computer room. Steve was on his way to the apartment. Everything felt a little hurried. I had just stepped in from my Wang-Chung class, and within ten minutes was preparing to interview a man I hardly knew. I wasn't really nervous. I simply wasn't sure what to expect. Steve had always been the supplier for my comic book fix.

Other students, like Carrie, chose a more direct approach: "In this interview with Leah Thurston, I want to reveal her passion for business. Leah has had a wide range of business opportunities, and she shares incredible insight into the business field." Pointing to specific strategies used in published interviews gave students ways of entering into this writing task. Written introductions allowed students to include their own impressions of the interview experience rather than remaining completely neutral or removed from the writing. For their interview write-ups, I required that students set up the interview through their introductions and then they could share their findings, either in a question and answer form or as an essay (see Figure 3: Interview Writing Instructions). Many students, like Ash, chose to write their final interview assignments in essay form, rather than just including an introduction and then following with questions and answers. Ash included his own impressions and reactions to his conversation with Steven, a graphic designer. Here is an excerpt from his final interview essay:

> Steven was born in Klamath Falls, Oregon, thirty-six years ago. About six-months after his birth, his family moved to Portland, where he has lived ever since. As a child, he was not an adamant fan of comics. He had many friends who were, but comics were only a casual pastime for him. "When I got sick, my parents would bring me home a stack of grocery store comics, and I slowly grew more and more interested in this form of writing and drawing."

Students' writing for their interview assignment was dynamic and full of voice. They were invested in trying to capture the essence of their interviews and of the experience as a whole.

Reflection Letters

Before students turned in their final interviews, I asked them to write a letter reflecting on the process. These letters helped me see how participating in these interviews influenced students in profound ways. One of the main things students wrote about in these final reflections was how the interview process benefited the interviewee as well as the interviewer. The following is the prompt I gave students to use as a guide for their letters:

Interview Reflection Letter

I am so excited to read your interviews! Before you turn them in, I would like an opportunity to learn from you firsthand what you learned from this interview experience. Please take time to answer the following questions with thoughtfulness and detail. Thank you.

1. What are your impressions of this interview experience?
2. What did you learn about this person that interested you?
3. What surprised you about this interview?
4. How did you feel as you asked the questions? Was your interview comfortable and relaxed or a bit awkward? Explain.
5. In retrospect, what questions do you wish you had asked that you didn't and why?
6. What do you share in common with the person you interviewed? How are you different?
7. If you could choose one idea or story from your interview what would you share?
8. How did this interview inform you further about your particular interest?

Directions: After you have conducted your interview, please write up your interview to share with others using the following guidelines:

1. Set-up your interview with an introduction. Who is the person you interviewed? Why did you choose this person? When and where did the interview take place? What were your first reactions or initial feelings about the interview? Were you nervous or excited? Explain. This introduction will help guide your reader and gives you a chance to share your impressions of the interview process.

2. Share key pieces from your interview either in a question and answer format or in an essay form. Either way, make sure you interject your thoughts and opinions throughout. For example, if you select an answer to one of your questions that startled you in some way, share this reaction with your reader. This will create an interesting interview to write and read.

3. Include a conclusion that shares what you learned from this interview experience.

Audience: Your classmates, teacher, and I would like each of you to share your final write-up with your interviewee.

Purpose: To learn about career and life choices after high school and to practice conducting and writing interviews.

Your paper must include the following:

1. Title page.
2. Introduction—including setting description and background information about the interviewee.
3. Dialogue—share at least eight quotes from your interview.
4. Your reactions and impressions of the interview process and of the conversation.
5. Share what you learned from this process.
6. Conclusion—this can be a reflection looking back on this experience.
7. Please type, double-space, and spell-check.

Due Date: _____

Figure 3 Interview Writing Instructions

In her reflection, Nyma described talking to her father about fleeing Tibet and his reaction to this conversation:

> I actually think my interview helped my father. I learned, through this experience, that my dad is into politics. Whenever I asked him a question, he would add his opinion about Chinese

1. Students read, watch, and discuss interview examples.
2. Students prepare and participate in a practice peer interview in class.
3. Students receive Interview Project requirements.
4. Students participate in an in-class workshop on choosing an interviewee and preparing interview questions.
5. Students arrange and conduct interviews during class time or on their own.
6. Students write a First Thoughts Letter in class.
7. Students read examples of interview introductions and then write their own.
8. Students receive Interview Writing Instructions and proceed with writing.
9. Students write a Final Reflection letter and turn in their interview write-ups for revision suggestions.

Figure 4 Interview Project Steps at a Glance

politicians and this surprised me. I knew a little about Chinese history, but this interview made me think about what it would have been like to be one of the people who had to leave this country like my parents did. I was a little uncomfortable asking my dad some of these questions because he had to back up and tell me how he felt at this time in his life. He turned pale as he remembered. I tried to cheer him up.

Glenda shared what she learned from her grandfather in their time together:

Talking to my grandfather made me think of all the things I want to accomplish before I have grandchildren. It made me see that what you do in life affects everything and everyone around you. I felt that spending time with my grandfather was the best gift I could have ever given him. This was one of the highlights of my high school experience. I hope that in the future I have more projects like this. This interview was important to me because I had no pressure and it wasn't an order or an assessment. It was something that I actually felt like doing and this was the best part of the whole experience.

Kori wrote about what she learned from her interview with her longtime volleyball coach:

I thought this interview was a lot of fun. I have never really sat down and interviewed someone before, so it was a new experience. I felt that Richard, the person I interviewed, enjoyed this process as well. It allowed us to catch up on old times and learn why he started coaching volleyball. One thing that surprised me is that I never knew that Richard played volleyball himself. I thought he learned how to coach by reading a book. It made me so happy to know that he has felt what I feel when I am on the court. He has felt the joy I feel when I am hitting that ball over the net.

When I asked students to interview a person in order to find out more about a career interest, my intention was for them to gain exposure to people doing real work out in the world. I did not realize that this would also become an invitation to explore a side of their lives that they often left out of their school world. Jenny, for example, had never previously shared her interest in kids and how she wanted to pursue child psychology as a career path.

A RIDE WITH KELLY WEB

"Matt is different than any horse I have every owned . . . he is like a big dog."

It was nine o' clock on a warm spring night and I was feeling exceptionally tired and emotionally drained. I had just driven back to my barn with Zip in tow after a long, grueling drill practice where, once again, I had trouble with Zip. This has been happening for some time because Zip is a "show" horse, not a "drill" horse. Everyone keeps telling me to stop trying to make him do drills because, "showing is what he knows how to do." Maybe it is time for me to find a different horse to use for drill because this is not fun anymore. I am sick of everyone's comments and, that way, I could prepare Zip for the fair and some open shows this year instead of forcing him to do something he is not meant to do.

My mind was in a jumble about this decision when I arrived back at the barn to put Zip away in his stall for the night. I was not overjoyed, as I usually am, to see the owner of the barn walk over my way. He told me that Kelly, his daughter was inside if I still wanted to interview her. I knew I needed to, even though I didn't feel like it in that moment because I was tired and still had a 30-minute drive back to Portland. I followed him into the house anyhow.

Sitting and talking with Kelly relieved my stress. I had never had a lengthy conversation with her, but what I had thought would be a quick interview turned into an hour-long conversation that left me with a smile on my face and hope for my future. Kelly is 21 years old and she is a student at Portland State University. Her parents had horses when they got married and Kelly, as the youngest of four children, became interested in horses "as soon as I was old enough to keep boots on." She was born into riding.

Kelly's older sisters were especially talented at showing their horses. Kelly wanted to be just like them. Her parents bought her a horse named, Poncho, who recently passes away from old age. Kelly rode endlessly trying to be just as good as her sisters. She did not have a trainer, but she went back to Topeka, Kansas, every summer to compete with Poncho. She never had a "normal" summer, as she put it. When Kelly and Poncho competed in their first Quarter Horse Show, it was a huge and exciting event. Any horse circuit is extremely political, so for Kelly and Poncho to enter that ring and walk away winners without a trainer was amazing. This is how Kelly became hooked in the world of equestrian competition.

This hook became her life's work. During high school, and especially during her senior year, Kelly decided to devote all her time after school to horses. She explained, "People think you are crazy when you spend every day riding and you choose it over the American teenager things to do like playing basketball." Kelly didn't care. She knew what she wanted to do with her life.

(Continues)

Figure 5 Interview Example: Student Sample

Two years ago, Kelly's parents helped her purchase, Matt, a red dun horse that can do everything from showmanship, Western classes, and English classes. He is only five years old. When Kelly started telling me about Matt, her eyes lit up and were glazed over all at once. I could tell she was thinking about being on his back. "He's like a big dog. He's different from any horse I have ever ridden . . . he just wants to be with me." When Kelly said this, I knew I had chosen the right person to interview. Kelly and Matt share a special bond that only a horse and rider can have. This kind of connection is hard to explain if you haven't experienced it. Kelly showed me a picture of Matt and I was blown away. I know they are going to go places together.

As Kelly talked about Matt, I became intrigued about showing and competition. I asked Kelly about her favorite kind of show, what events she has participated in, and how she started competing. Kelly could see the excitement mounting in me and laughed. She patiently explained horsemanship and other events she has competed in. I realized that one of the main reasons Kelly has accomplished so much with horses is that she has the support of her family. "They support me as much as they can emotionally and financially." Every family member comes to every show and each person has a different job.

Even though I am not competing like Kelly yet, I wanted to know what her biggest accomplishments had been. Believe it or not, Kelly qualified for the Quarter Horse World Show this November, which is the "best of the best" because you have to win a certain amount of points throughout the year in order to participate. This is the biggest single breed show in the world and Kelly is excited and nervous. I hope I get to watch her!

Talking with Kelly helped me realize that I can make it beyond my open local shows and take Zip and I somewhere important in the world. Through our conversation, I gained a sense of courage and a new attitude. Instead of feeling frustrated with Zip, I keep telling him, "Let's go get 'em!" This is the kind of attitude Kelly has and it has served her well in life. My goal for the next year is to show at breed shows because of Kelly's influence. One day, if I am persistent, I will qualify for the World Show too.

Figure 5 Interview Example: Student Sample (*continued*)

She made it clear, through her writing and interview choices, that she did not just think that kids are cute but that she is intellectually interested in their amazing abilities to learn languages, to play, and be creative. Parker, through his interview with a poet, pursued his interest in becoming an English teacher. "I didn't realize until I talked to Ruth about my writing, that I could actually pursue this as a career path. I love to write, but I had only ever thought of it as a way to vent my anger and emotions. Maybe it will also help me pay my bills one day?"

Not only did students gain from their time with these interesting people, but they were also inspired to think about interests they might pursue in the future. In her interview reflection, Irene wrote about what she learned from her aunt, "I learned that cooking is not just something you learn easily, it is a skill you gain over time through practice. My aunt showed me her recipe books that were all decorated with pictures. I love them. I want to be a cook one day and I want to collect recipes in books just like my aunt." In his reflection letter, Ash looked back on the interview process, "This was, by far, the most important school project I have ever done. The interview allowed me to gain insight into an industry that I plan on affiliating myself with in the future. I plan, more than ever, to pursue my dream and become a graphic designer." Phil shared what he learned through his conversation with his friend Nick about managing a shoe store, "The interview with Nick made me think about how hard it would be to manage a store. You have to worry about everything that is going on and what the employees are doing. That is a lot of responsibility. I admire Nick for taking on this challenge." The reflection writing allowed students to step back from their work as interviewers, and share what they had gained through the process. Many students reflected on how the interview project inspired them to follow their own interests. Glenda wrote, "I have learned more about blind people in the last few months than I ever learned before. It is clear to me why I admire people with disabilities—they are truly incredible. Doing this project brought me closer to who I am and what I want out of life."

Conclusion

The focus of my language arts curriculum for high school seniors is on finding ways for them to use reading and writing to plan and think about their futures. What is typical for seniors who are not highly successful academically is that they receive little guidance about postsecondary schooling or work options. Often, students are provided with very general and basic information, like where and when to get college applications or go to the college fair. This project exposed students to interviews as an important writing and research genre, and gave them an opportunity to collaborate with another person through oral and written communication. Gaining exposure to real people out in the world doing work the students were interested in helped to ground our work together in real possibility. The reading and writing throughout this project was connected to students' own interests and became more than just a scary application process. This interview project was part of a larger curriculum where students wrote college admissions essays, learned to fill out financial aid forms, prepared resumes, and visited a college counselor. Having students first explore a deep-seated interest that they could imagine pursuing in the future as either a career goal or a lifelong hobby made the rest of our work writing admission essays, filing out forms, and preparing resumes take on much more meaning for students. They understood that these tasks were all part of the gateway to a future they wanted for themselves. Supporting students who might not have envisioned themselves having a postsecondary education or career path to explore their interests through interviews was powerful and rewarding. Asking students to take part in this interview project became a way of teaching for justice. I wanted the reading and writing that took place in my classes to help students who typically have little voice and support in deciding their futures.

Works Cited

Hoose, Phillip. 2001. *It's Our World Too! Stories of Young People Who Are Making a Difference*. New York: Farrar, Straus, & Giroux.

Oakes, Jeannie. 2004. *America's Sorting Machine*. http://outreach.thecollegetrack.com.

Singer, Jessica. 2002. "Getting students off the track." *Rethinking Schools* 17 (1): 16–17.

———. 2006. *Stirring up Justice: Writing and Reading to Change the World*. Portsmouth, NH: Heinemann.

Wheatley, Margaret. 2001. "Don't be so sure." *Shambhala Sun*. 10 (2): 17–19.

Winfrey, Oprah April, 2001. The O interview: Oprah talks to Nelson Mandela. *The Oprah Magazine*. 154–226.

18

Writers Reading Local Places

*Field Notes for Writing Outside the Classroom,
or in the Classroom Under the Spell of Beyond*

Kim Stafford

*Kim Stafford is the founding director of the Northwest Writing Institute and author of a
dozen books, including* The Muses Among Us: Eloquent Listening and Other Pleasures of the Writer's Craft *(2003),* Early Morning: Remembering My Father, William
Stafford *(2002), and* Having Everything Right: Essays of Place *(1997). He lives in
Portland, Oregon, with his wife and children.*

> Sound and setting converge, and the wilderness finds a voice.
> —Fiona Ritchie (on Celtic music as a voice for sacred places)

> It is better to do thine own duty, however lacking in merit, than to do that of
> another, even though efficiently. It is better to die doing one's own duty, for to do the
> duty of another is fraught with danger.
> —Bhagavad-Gita, Book 3

What is the singular duty of the individual teacher? I believe it is to transfer the source of
presumed wisdom from the teaching self to the resonant world. What is the unique calling
of the individual student? I believe it is to give voice to something that is "out there" in the
world, and so to find one's place in the human transaction of writing by locating one's discoveries in the "speaking places" of one's own life.

I begin with a wish we should be able to fulfill together: I want a teacher reading student writing to be entranced, stunned by new insights, fed epiphanies. I want the teacher to read such writing as if crossing open ground studded with discoveries—evocative bird calls, luminescent bones, eloquent geology. I want the teacher to learn amazing things from each student—and very different things from each student. I want the teacher to experience that old dream of this calling: a life of reading pleasure. "You mean if I become a teacher I can just keep reading?" Yes. Oh, yes. We will find a way to teach writing so we can read our students' pages with a sense of pleasure and discovery.

How shall we do this? How shall we invite our students to write down the most original, detailed, unpredictable discoveries they can muster—so we may feed on their discoveries with delight?

As one of my students wrote, "I do not write to please but to be pleased." I believe if the student can write so as to be truly pleased, the teacher, reading such pleasures, will be pleased as well. Or as another student taught me: "Don't do what you are good at, but what makes you pay attention." I want us each to write what makes us pay attention: some days this will be a subject in the library, and other days a subject in the field. We will read the landscape and write field notes about what we find there. The teacher will send students forth with tools for seeing in new ways and recording discoveries found abroad. And the student will bring home to the classroom a small museum of emblems, jottings, lists, descriptions, and stories of discovery. For me, one way to invite this gift economy between student and teacher is to empower students to write travel literature—the kind that involves moving on foot, writing by hand, and thinking in such a way that we are free from what we have been taught to see.

What I imagine is a student, or a group of students, settled in a public square, in a coffee shop, at a bench in the mall, or by a river, on a hilltop, at the edge of a clearing, in a garden, under a tree (a tree alone at the edge of a parking lot)—each with a simple field book in hand. The idea of the field book is to record what is found in very simple terms. We might take as our model the canvas Van Gogh is said to have carried into the field, which he would divide into small rectangles for a series of studies in one location. One friend called this canvas "a little museum." So the student field book could be considered an archive for beginnings: lists, short accounts of processes, descriptions in which one tells details about a leaf, stone, seed, bone, or other object or creature until one has said all one can apprehend. This search for what is most resonant in a landscape—what calls to our attention—is akin to finding key passages in a written text (notable features in the spiritual landscape of *The Scarlet Letter*…field notes on *The Red Badge of Courage*).

The advantage of the field book is that it is designed for preliminary findings. It is a tool for keeping the demand for full coherence at bay while in the field. As Van Gogh writes in a letter, "What is drawing? How does one learn it? It is working oneself through an invisible iron wall that seems to stand between what one feels and what one can do" (Van Gogh 1997, 206). A field book should turn this iron wall into an open window: what you see, touch, or consider may be recorded in its native form.

With this goal in mind, let's begin a series of meditations on the practice of reading places and taking dictation on what may offer itself to student writers under the spell of resonant details.

Ecosystem 1: The Neighborhood

First question: Where should I be to write this chapter? What place is currently speaking in my own life? And once there, how shall I read the code of that place in service to my topic? I knew I could not write this essay in my office at Lewis & Clark College where I teach, so I have surrendered to a kind invitation from a tribe of teachers far away....

I am in New Orleans with a group of writing teachers. Our project is called the Writing Marathon, and it's the brainchild of writer Richard Louth and his cronies in the Southeast Louisiana Writing Project. The idea is to fan out, find a place to write with a few friends, pause to share, and then move on to another place. We are reading the French Quarter, and recording what happens when we write there together. The idea is to gather local detail, try to read the signs around you, think about teaching, and see what kind of riff begins when you take up pen or keyboard.

And now I'm sitting at the café called Croissant d'Or, about nine months after the 2005 catastrophe of hurricane Katrina. There's a lot of construction in the neighborhood. New roofs, plywood pried from windows in dark alleys. I love the old clock over the bar, full as a harvest moon, with the name of a Paris café in fading paint on the dial. We're on Ursuline Street, and down the block is the site of the oldest convent on the continent, the cloister now used by local chefs to grow their fresh rosemary and sage, tarragon, chives. Around the corner, they say, is the gloried House of the Rising Sun. And every few feet along the sidewalk is a metal disk which is periodically lifted, I am told, so they can pour poison into the earth to manage the termites.

Carol Bly says an essay consists of an idea, a story, and lots of sensuous detail—in no particular order. So tell me: in the making process, does the idea come first, the story, or the sensory detail? How does this work for me, for you, for your students? Do you sit down with an idea speaking in your mind? Or does this process begin with a story you carry that must be told? I believe either of those approaches may happen sometimes, but for me, writing most often begins with the details. The details are locally available—in a forest, a neighborhood, a book, a conversation, a grief, a journey. Strangely, I find details hard to come by in a classroom. Classrooms are designed to process materials, not to pick them up like a sticky pinecone or a scallop shell, a thorn, feather, bone—or a telling remark by someone you don't know.

Last night at Irene's Cuisine, on Chartres, as we waited for a table, I overheard an interchange that spoke for the local:

> Yankee visitor: Will there be a long wait for a table?

> Southern hostess: You from around here?

Clearly, if one were from around here, it would be considered impertinent, and a foolish mark of missing the easy joys of leisure, to be in haste. And in keeping with this leisure, who should appear but Irene? There was a light around her, or from within her. She was happy, and despite the evening rush, as waiters plucked her sleeve with questions she deftly solved, she lingered to talk with our party where we stood beside the hostess' podium. She was not being polite in brief, but fully engaged for her own pleasure. Soon she was telling a story about the perfect morning: a beautiful café, coffee steaming on the table. Perfect. Then a rat ran across her feet...And before long we were comparing rat infestation remedies: mothballs down the rat burrows in the planter on the balcony, or a glue pot in the attic…

As part of our inquiry in the French Quarter, we are reading *Teacher Man*, by Frank McCourt. The book bristles with writing prompts, especially when we join McCourt's notions with our own:

- Write an excuse note—for being the kind of teacher you are (that is, a manifesto).
- Report one of your humiliations—and one of your miraculous recoveries.
- Describe an encounter with a student you failed to understand—and a part of yourself you have failed to understand.
- Write a critique of your writing style—in the voice of your own most skeptical teacher.

We begin to notice the recurring Frank McCourt process for storytelling—or rather for pedagogical inquiry:

1. a puzzling or arresting moment in class;
2. a recollection of an early experience as a student;
3. some kind of understanding about what's happening in the life of teaching.

And so I bring this experience to bear on the idea of writing in the field: a student writer might take an assigned book to a place outside the classroom and report on the experience of reading that book in that place. The simplest form of place-based writing might be to do school work of any kind in a resonant place, and to explore connections between what the place is teaching and what the text is saying.

I imagine a third-grader reading *Charlotte's Web* in a barn or near a web. A seventh-grader reading her science textbook at the Marine Aquarium (glancing up now and then, wandering, jotting notes). An eleventh-grader reading *House on Mango Street* while sitting on the porch in a lively neighborhood—looking up, writing what's there, weaving what's there in the place with what's there in the text and in your mind, memory, imagination.

And I see these students compiling their field notes in some version of McCourt's sequence:

1. record a puzzling or arresting moment in the reading;
2. write an observation from the place;
3. seek a connective thread between the text and the place, and jot the beginning of your understanding of an idea that begins to speak there.

In a way, the idea is to make a balanced meal of what is often served as a writing assignment protein bar. Write an essay about the reading? Why not read, then remember, then go to a place that will help you summon your understanding?

My student Mariah records such a convergence of reading, place, and discovery, as part of her account of a recurrent experience in her essay, "I Can Hear the World Singing." After reading a novel, caught in its mysterious spell, she drifts out to the greenhouse to join her mother puttering among the seedlings, and there Mariah listens:

The first time it happened it was a sunny day in early summer and I was fourteen. I had spent up until lunchtime curled up in our living room finishing *The Notebook*, by Nicholas Sparks, and I had cried and cried…Still caught in the spell of the book, [in the greenhouse] I tilted my head backward and closed my eyes against the glare of the sun. As I sat there, I just let myself become my surroundings. My senses were acute and I listened to the distant droning of a plane and the more proximate chatter of an upset or overly delighted bird. I smelled the perfume of the nearby flowers and pungent scent of crushed leaves from the rosemary plants I had been cleaning. And in the midst of this meditation, I suddenly could hear the earth singing. It was something far more beautiful than I have ever heard. It was like a mother's voice, comforting and safe. It was like when I would curl up on my father's lap with my ear against his heart and drift between sleep and consciousness while he spoke to his friends. The warm buzz of his voice without distinct words vibrating his chest and the steady thud of his heartbeats brought the feeling of total security.

In this passage the book, the past, and the present place all gather into one hymn of understanding. Without overtly making the connection, the student writer responds to the theme of Alzheimer's in the novel with a hymn of memory and deep connection. The writer, reading, sings.

Ecosystem 2: Landscape

Several years ago I dreamed an odd acronym: PALA. According to the dream-sense, this stands for "place-activated latent aptitude." That is, the mind, the heart, the psyche is filled with what we call in film-based photography "latent images." Light has caused a preliminary chemical reaction in the silver emulsion of the film, but this latent image only becomes visible when the film is developed. The developing agents (developer, fixer, Hypo Clear) make the silver molecules that have been touched by light turn dark, and then the untouched molecules are washed away, leaving the visible image on the film negative. Then a similar process creates latent images on photo paper, which are then developed and made visible.

According to my dream, as I understand it, PALA happens when an encounter with a place brings a certain aptitude or latent knowledge—knowledge that would not otherwise be available—to the surface.

For the writer, the mind is filled with indelible but also unknown images, sensations, impressions, hints, intuitions, story-molecules—and these are only developed when we sit down to write. The non-writer may take these latent aptitudes to the grave—unwritten, unspoken, unknown. But places may, like good teaching, provide a safe and evocative setting for the incarnation of the secret not-yet-known.

As a writer, presented with myriad details in a landscape I see, hear, touch, taste, and am drawn to certain details more magnetically because they begin to summon what is latent in my psyche. In the presence of a thousand stones, I pick up one because it serves as an emblem for something I have to say. A cliff is native Parthenon. The way a river turns at the bend is about my brother. The call of evening blackbirds stands in for an early stage of human reconciliation. And often among friends or strangers, what you overhear is what you are meant to know. (I discuss the process of "professional eavesdropping" in my book *The Muses Among Us*.)

I do not ask students to seek connections in the field, but to write down the fragmentary details in the landscape that present themselves. I think of the objects chosen in these first writings as emblems because they may represent those details in the landscape that promise connections before such connections can or should be articulated.

As Paulus Berenson said in an interview, "a journal was like my workplace, it was like a portable studio...it was soul's kitchen" (Berenson 2003). The student's field notebook records creatures encountered, and details and structures in the natural landscape as beginning points for speculative writing.

The seeking of one's own resonant landscape is a kind of pilgrimage. Just as Chaucer describes his storytellers traveling toward the healing place at Canterbury, teachers might invite students to find a place that offers abundant welcome, consolation, and learning. For an individual student would this be a landscape, a coffee shop buzzing with jive, a concert venue, a hospital waiting room, a hidden place near home, a favorite tree, or the porch at night?

How does pilgrimage work? A pilgrim's narrative consists of episodes and epiphanies, a series of places geographical and spiritual (or perhaps in our terms, place-based and text-based). In the first eighteen lines of the *General Prologue*, for example—the triumphant run-on sentence we rightly celebrate—Chaucer gathers: the season...rain...roots...liquor...virt...wind...inspiration...sun...stars...birds...sleep...son ...night...nature's prick...the heart...human longing...pilgrimage...far travelers...strange places...this road to Canterbury...the martyr...seeking...helping...those in need ..

I imagine inviting students to open their field notebooks and compose an endless sentence like Chaucer's that gathers objects, colors, sounds, textures, associations, and thoughts that arise in one's chosen healing place. In the field notebook, our first step toward coherence is to create an archive of seemingly chaotic abundance.

Ecosystem 3: The Studio of Stories

In my thirty years of writing with students, my perception of writing class has been reversed from what I was first taught about the teacher's role. I used to think the writing teacher teaches students how to write. Now I believe the teacher helps students to use writing to share with each other and with their teacher what they are learning, and by this practice to develop their ability to write. The students are making writing, but the teacher is making writers. And writers are in possession of their own source of learning: their helplessly quirky writing practice.

The purpose of writing class is to make the teacher obsolete. That is, to transfer the source of learning from the teacher to the student's own unfolding experience as a writer. Gravity teaches the river; wind teaches the cloud; the flow of experience at a healing place teaches the writer.

With this in mind, back home at school, I find myself using class time essentially to get our minds out of the building. I sow the seeds of writing prompts, and then we harvest the next round of prompts from student writing shared aloud. In-class time is used to depart from class mentally in search of moments from our lives in the world that embody our best learning.

Over the years, I have gathered a set of examples from this practice. Students write, then we read aloud, and as we read, each writer in the class records resonant lines that may serve as prompts for the next round of writing:

I come from a place so simple it's impossible to describe…

I kept an invisible horse in the barn down the road…

My mother drove me fifteen straight hours, even across Nebraska, so I could see the mountains after my heart was broken for the first time…

Once we hear such lines from each other, we have left the classroom to dwell in faraway times and places.

Dust motes dancing in a finger of light…

We kneeled for a long time and listened to Latin…

I remember living in a leaning maple tree one summer…

I believed the sun would rise over wheat and set over corn…

In his essay, "The Sense of Place," Wallace Stegner (1992) gives his allegiance to Wendell Berry, and his belief that if you don't know where you are you don't know who you are. He is not talking about the kind of location that can be determined by looking at a map or a street sign. He is talking about the kind of knowing that involves the senses, the memory, the history of a family or a tribe. And so we invite student writers in class to read resonant places and their effect on individuals through the lens of memory:

He moves his car from place to place, always legally, but unpredictably, like a cat…

I would spend enough time in Ireland so my father could rest in peace…

The entire soul of my grandmother existed in that one strand of Easter grass…

My mother told me Christmas Eve she had sent my father away…

Ecosystem 4: The Text Itself

Back in the French Quarter, at the club called d.b.a., the walls that survived the hurricane are shaking. Close to midnight, and the dark and smoky air feels electric. Up front, Wolfman Washington and his band are into a line of funk. A wall of sound shifts and weaves. Just when you think there might have been an opening in the music the bass player fills it in, then the sax, the drums, then Wolfman himself smiling behind his shades as his guitar spills out a pocket full of golden change.

In the presence of such rich activity in the world, there is one question that will never occur to me, and it is a question I have come to consider false and impossible: what should I write about? In the presence of the true vibrancy of the world, the only possible response to this question would be, have I been sleeping upright in the presence of events aching for my attention, richly embroidered with detail ripe to hand? In such a moment, the writing hand begins to move.

In place of a deficit model, I want to live by the abundance model. In place of this false question—what should I write about?—I want to ask myself, and invite my students to ask themselves, "What is there? When I am in a lively place, reading a resonant landscape, savoring a promising text, or poised with pen in hand over a ready sheet of paper—what is there? What is around me, in my mind, in memory, in the air? The act of writing, by this approach, is reporting on the actual, not seeking the nonexistent.

By observing what happens for my students when their writing is going well, I begin to see a five-step process for writing anything:

1. Find a place that speaks to you.
2. Notice simple things there—in the world before you, and then also in your mind in the presence of this place.
3. Listen without judgment to these beginnings, and write them down.
4. Notice how you learn more by telling, and then just keep going.
5. See if there may be a thread connecting the disparate things you see, remember, and learn from your mind made present by this place.

In class, we often begin with a compact set of genres for student writing: report, essay, story, poem. In the field, as suggested by emotional response to places, we may try other forms: field notes, meditations, blessings, what Ortega y Gassett called "salvations" (saving a place, a moment—or being saved by what is minutely recorded there), spells, prayers, songs of praise....

This range of place-based genres is exemplified in a number of books that gather episodic accounts of local places. *The Stations of Still Creek*, by Barbara J. Scot, records observations and meditations from a series of recurrent visits to particular streamside locations. A book called *Seven Half Miles from Home*, by Mary Back, provides a similar exercise in recording discoveries from a discrete set of locations in nature. Another example would be *Riverwalking*, by Kathleen Dean Moore. Another would be *Riverteeth*, by David James Duncan. Or perhaps my own *Having Everything Right: Essays of Place*.

Based on suggestions from these and other books on natural landscapes, I would like to offer a series of writing prompts for students in the presence of landscapes as close as possible to home or school, and as rich as possible in processes that are wild and visible:

*   compose an inventory of plants, sounds, textures—in the field, or as you first knew them when young in a place yet vivid for you: "First I remember . . .";
*   draw a map of a place you cherish, and write a key to the map;
*   describe a meeting at the place—with an insect, a plant, a moment (and at some point in the writing, have time stop and the writing go on);
*   interview a plant (Gary Paul Nabhan's assignment);
*   tell the story of an hour at the place or six pages at the end of the road or four seasonal journal entries;
*   inventory kinds of weather at the place (colors, sounds, visual and kinesthetic effects);
*   letter to a former inhabitant with questions or to a future inhabitant with secrets;

- letter to the river (in the rhythm of water) or to the wind (in the word sounds of wind);
- instructions to an artist come to record the place: "I want you to see . . .";
- a story from your own life that should be told at the place: "Friend, let me tell you . . ." (Richard Hugo's assignment);
- an imagined conversation at this place by two people important to you;
- a story for children at this place: "A long time ago…";
- a song to sing at the place (or a work song for labor at the place);
- a story you would tell others so they would protect the place;
- a small family of texts, fragments you could write that are kin to this place;
- favorite published texts you would invite friends to read at this place;
- a secret of your own you could only tell here;
- a blessing for a particular person at a particular time at this place;
- a love letter in the form of a report from this place.

If a student returns from the field with a set of short writings in various genres—a descriptive paragraph about the way the river moves, a little meandering essay on the sensation of cold, a haiku on the ant—this collection may form a ready basis for the kind of multigenre collage that can increase a teacher's reading pleasure. In this case, it may be useful to ask students to do some kind of summative or process writing in which they seek to apprehend the thread that joins their multiple discoveries. Was there a prevailing kind of curiosity that led them to see river, and then the cold, and then the ant blundering through grass? The fancy name for this thread is metacognition—thinking about thinking—but I believe it is simply a beginning of wisdom about the self: how do I see what I see? and how may knowing this help me to see more? To this end, I sometimes share the poem my father William Stafford wrote in the last few weeks of his life:

The Way It Is

There's a thread you follow. It goes among
things that change. But it doesn't change.
People wonder about what you are pursuing.
You have to explain about the thread.
But it is hard for others to see.
While you hold it you can't get lost
Tragedies happen; people get hurt
or die; and you suffer and get old.
Nothing you do can stop time's unfolding.
You don't ever let go of the thread.
            —from *The Way It Is: New & Selected Poems,* by William Stafford (1998, 42)

The thread is the student's own way of seeing things, which will be both a gift to readers, and a student's method for seeking beyond what a teacher can provide.

Practice of this kind will begin a process of engagement that Wallace Stegner identified as essential not just to learning and to writing, but also to residence, and finally to citizenship on earth:

No place, not even a wild place, is a place until it has had that human attention that at its highest reach we will call poetry. What Frost did for New Hampshire and Vermont, what Faulkner did for Mississippi and Steinbeck for the Salinas Valley, Wendell Berry is doing for his family corner of Kentucky, and hundreds of other place-loving people, gifted or not, are doing for places they were born in, or reared in, or have adopted and made their own. (Stegner 1992, 205)

Every student deserves to "own a place in mind," as Thoreau said, and write it into being. In my own experience, the opportunity to write under the spell of a place begins with local practice, but may reach forward into the digital age and outward to the global village. When a friend sent an email from New Zealand, telling me about his efforts to preserve the childhood home of the writer Janet Frame, I was moved to compose a blessing for her house there, and to email this to my friend. The plan is to make this house available as a residence for visiting writers, and I want to bless the creative experience of writers in that place and everywhere. This is what I want the welcoming place to say to a student who comes to read the place, and then to write:

House Where the Road Begins
for Janet Frame

I was the house where dwelt a rare one,
and sky poured through the roof to color
her silence. I was the door that opened then
and let the green path in, come in and coil
friendly by the fire. I was the red fire
who muttered secrets of the dark that burrows
inward like a stone. Stones and potatoes
out from the earth, cries and songs out
from the heart—I was mother to the rare one
then, and whispered songs and stories
humming, brimming up, shining water's lip
for any traveler who fled a cold place
and found in me a haven. I was the house
where a silent one might come to pronounce
what could not be told till then and there.
Friend, here be welcome, and begin.

Suggested Readings

Berenson, Paulus. 1972. *Finding One's Way With Clay*. New York: Simon & Schuster.

Louth, Richard. Winter 2002. "The N.O. Writing Marathon." *The Quarterly*. www.writingproject.org/Publications/quarterly/Q2002no1.htm

Stafford, William. 1998. *The Way It Is: New & Selected Poems*. St. Paul, MN: Graywolf Press.

Stegner, Wallace. 1992. "A Sense of Place" in *Where the Bluebird Sings to the Lemonade Springs: Living and Writing in the West*. New York: Random House.

Van Gogh, Vincent. 1997. *The Letters of Vincent Van Gogh*. Ed. Ronald de Leeuw. Trans. Arnold Pomerans. New York: Penguin.

Works Cited

Back, Mary. 1985. *Seven Half Miles from Home*. Boulder, CO: Johnson Books.

Berenson, Paulus. 1972. *Finding One's Way With Clay*. New York: Simon & Schuster.

———. 2003. Interview on Radio National, Australia, 4 January.

Duncan, David James. 1995. *River Teeth: My Story as Told by Water*. New York: Doubleday.

Louth, Richard. Winter 2002. "The N.O. Writing Marathon." *The Quarterly*. www.writingproject.org/Publications/quarterly/Q2002no1.htm

Mathieau, Paula, George Grattan, Tim Lindgren, and Staci Schultz. 2005. *Writing Places*. New York: Longman.

Moore, Kathleen Dean. 1996. *Riverwalking: Reflections on Moving Water*. San Diego, CA: Harcourt Brace.

Scot, Barbara J. 1999. *The Stations of Still Creek*. San Francisco, CA: Sierra Club Books.

Stafford, Kim. 1997. *Having Everything Right: Essays of Place*. Seattle, OR: Sasquatch.

———. 2003. *The Muses Among Us: Eloquent Listening and Other Pleasures of the Writer's Craft*. Athens, GA: University of Georgia.

Stafford, William. 1998. *The Way It Is: New & Selected Poems*. St. Paul, MN: Graywolf Press.

Stegner, Wallace. 1992. "A Sense of Place" in *Where the Bluebird Sings to the Lemonade Springs: Living and Writing in the West*. New York: Random House.

Van Gogh, Vincent. 1997. *The Letters of Vincent Van Gogh*. Ed. Ronald de Leeuw. Trans. Arnold Pomerans. New York: Penguin.

19

Teaching Writing to English Language Learners

Danling Fu

Danling Fu, professor of literacy and language in the School of Teaching and Learning at the University of Florida College of Education, is a former ESL teacher, and earned her Ph.D. in reading and writing from the University of New Hampshire, where she furthered her studies on literacy for English language learners. Since 1995, she has been working and researching in schools and communities in San Francisco and New York City. Currently she is working with K–12 teachers in thirteen schools from lower Manhattan to the Bronx, which house large populations of new immigrant students. She is the author of My Trouble is My English *and* An Island of English.

In the past decade, I have interviewed hundreds of ESL students in colleges at the undergraduate or graduate levels who studied English either in the United States or in their native countries. Very few could recall if they were ever taught writing in English before coming to a U.S. college. If there were any memories about writing at all, they would be of writing for grammar exercises, such as practicing using past or future tense. In the hundreds of classrooms I visited with English language learners (ELLs)—either in a mainstreamed or self-contained situation at the secondary level—writing instruction rarely goes beyond practicing language skills. Teaching writing to ELLs at the secondary level for communication or self-expression remains an uncharted territory. Though there is much talk among ESL and bilingual educators about ELLs' writing, there is not much study on how to help them develop as both thoughtful and artful English writers. I think the lack of the discussion on this topic results from this puzzle: How can we teach ELLs to write in English before they truly master English language? This chapter first tackles this question, and then moves on to the discussion of writing in content areas.

Before our discussion on teaching writing to English language learners, we need to have an understanding of who these students are in our schools. Among the students defined as ones with limited English proficiency (LEP) and termed as English language learners (ELLs), there are four main categories:

- Students who have strong and adequate first language literacy;

- Students whose formal education is interrupted, with low first language literacy (termed as SIFE ELLs);

- Students who have good or workable communicative skills (oral language), but are unable to read and write well in either English or in their first language (long-term ELLs);

- Students who are mainstreamed in the regular classrooms after passing minimum requirements of the English language test and are still struggling in many other areas of their schooling

The first two groups are usually recent arrivals, and the second two groups often have been in the American school system for quite a few years but still haven't acquired sufficient English proficiency to achieve academic success. All these students, except the last group, are entitled with resource support (ESL service), which varies according to requirements from state to state.

To varying degrees, they are all struggling to learn in our classrooms. The second group often turns into the third group because of lack of a formal educational background or low first language literacy, and the fourth group is often in a sink-or-swim situation due to the lack of support they need in regular classrooms. That is why these students are "approximately three times more likely to be low achievers than high achievers and two times more likely to drop out than their native English-speaking peers" (National Center for Education Statistics 2004).

In secondary schools, due to the lack of budget and resources, we may encounter every kind of the above categorized ELLs in our classrooms. With large classes, multiple sections to teach, and heavy curriculum to cover, teachers can barely spare time to meet the needs of these students, so often they are left treading water on their own. I have often heard teachers say this about having ELLs in their classrooms: "I know if I give them more help, they would make better progress, but I just can't with the number of students I have. They need so much help, I just don't have that much time. I know I ignore them, I feel guilty, but what can I do?"

Teaching ELLs is challenging, but this is the challenge we need to meet head-on, because ELLs in U.S. schools have increased faster than ever. Over the past two decades the number of ELLs in the United States has grown from twenty-three million to forty-seven million, or by 103 percent (Fix and Passel 2003) In fact, in the United States, one out of every five students (twenty percent) resides in a home in which a language other than English is spoken. By the year 2030, this number is expected to double—to reach roughly forty percent of all students. Such data is enough to alert all educators to the urgency of the need for exploration of effective instructional approaches designed specifically to accommodate the unique needs of this ever growing and very diversifying population.

Teaching Writing to Beginning ELLs

In many or most classrooms, the focus in teaching ELLs to write is usually on grammar and word usage. Freewriting, writing workshops, and writing across curriculum rarely exist for ELLs. One of the reasons for this is that many teachers believe that "real writing" can only begin for ELLs after they have mastered basic English language skills. This implies that if these students can write in English, they wouldn't be defined as ELLs anymore. English language learners (ELLs) literally means they are learning the language. But to master a language takes years, so year after year those ELL students never seem ready to do any real writing, and they become less and less confident as writers in English as well as in their primary language. If we let young children speak while learning to talk and let them learn to read and write while learning the language, we should do the same for all ELLs no matter what age they start to learn English.

Writing in Their First Language

Before students are able to write in English, we should encourage them to begin by writing in their first language. To write is to think. When we teach young children to write, we encourage them to write as they speak and to use invented spelling for the words they don't know how to spell. For emergent writers (two to four years old), almost every word they write is invented, of which some are not even close to conventional spelling (scribbles). We accept, foster, and celebrate their act as emergent writers. Based on the same belief, we should encourage our ELLs to continue developing their thinking through writing and to use whatever tool or medium they have to express their thoughts and feelings. If we let them wait until they have mastered the language, their lack of the practice in writing (thinking) will not only affect their cognitive development as a whole, but also hinder their language development. Based on the theory of literacy transference (Cummins 1979), people who are strong in their first language literacy usually learn a new language faster than those who lack such competency.

Adolescents in general are going through a lot of changes physically and emotionally. ELL adolescences face many additional challenges in their new lives in the new world. The loss of their past, identity, and everything familiar is already hurtful enough, yet they still encounter discrimination, alienation, humiliation, and confusion daily in both their school and home lives. Writing could be a way for them to express their thoughts and vent their emotions, to forge their new identity, and to understand their new position and relationship with others around them. They would not be so disconnected, both emotionally and personally, with school learning if whatever they did at school had something meaningful for their present being. It is hard enough for adolescents to learn anything basic such as basic language skills, which makes them feel like helpless young children again. Not only is learning basic skills all day long boring, but this can also be humiliating for them. Adolescents have little patience to tolerate this kind of schooling for too long. Out of frustration many of them may act out, appearing that they don't care, don't want to learn, or can't learn. They refuse to learn rather than fail to learn. As a result, many discipline problems occur among ELL adolescents in our secondary schools.

To let students write in their first language we may puzzle: How can we know what they write when we don't understand their first language? It is unthinkable in our teaching when we don't understand our students' work. But often in a class, we may have ELLs with vastly diverse language backgrounds. To understand the primary languages of all these students is impossible. Here are several ways I have seen teachers solve the problem when they don't understand what their ELLs wrote. They judge their writing according to the length. If they only write a few lines, the teachers would push them to write more. In very rare instances, the students could write nonsense or cheat the teachers. Having observed hundreds of ELLs at different levels in the past decades, I haven't found any that would write to fool their teachers who didn't know their primary languages. They were glad that they were allowed to write in their first language at school. Most were relieved that they could be themselves again, real adolescents, who didn't have to learn to speak, read, and write like young children. Most teachers don't like to stop at just how much the students wrote, and they do want to understand what was written if possible. Usually they would ask a student in class who knew the language of the writer to translate the main ideas of the writing, or ask the writer to draw pictures to tell about the writing. The teacher's desire to know what the student wrote is very rewarding to ELL writers. You could always see the smiles or content, appreciative expressions on their faces when they listen to their peers translating their words to the teacher and catch the teacher nodding and smiling in response. They would try very hard to draw pictures or use any graphic ways to communicate to their teachers about their work. When they see us try hard to understand their work, they try harder to find ways to help us understand it.

Making Transitions from First Language Writing to English

Ninety-nine percent of ESL and bilingual programs in U.S. schools are transitional ones. "Transition" means that after two to three years of studying in these programs, or being served by an ESL program, ELLs are tested out and mainstreamed into regular classrooms, where they study alongside their proficient English speaking peers learning the same curriculum. How do we help ELLs make transitions in writing from their first language to English? My study suggests that there are four transitional moves in ELLs' writing development, which can be identified as moving from "first language usage" to "code-switching" to "trans-language usage," and finally, to "approaching standard English." "Code-switching" here means mixed usage of two languages in writing, such as English writing with the words from the first language or vice versa. "Trans-language usage" suggests a language in between, which appears as English words in the student's first language syntax (see Figures 1a–d).

The transitions ELLs make in their writing development are similar to how people learn a new language. For example, when we travel abroad, we often use one or two words we know, or speak the local language mixed with English words and attempt to speak any way we can to make ourselves understood. In that situation, speaking a broken language is much better than only using gestures or being mute. This represents an initial effort in communication through a new language, or the first stage of language acquisition. That is how we acquire spoken language and use that language for genuine communicative purposes. The results of my study propose that this is also how ELLs acquire the communicative ability in written language.

The ELLs' transitional moves in their writing development also resembles that of the native English-speaking children's as this chart indicates:

Native English-speaking children (from oral to written)	Oral language	Writing with invented spelling	Conversational style and formal writing style combined	Demonstrating mastery of different genre forms in writing
English language learners (from first language to English)	The primary language	Code-switching (Writing with mixed languages)	Trans-language writing (English words in the primary language syntax)	Approaching standard English in writing

We start from where our students are or what they know. For native English speaking children, their oral language is the basis for their writing and for ELLs, their first language is their starting point. To enhance writing development in a new language, we need not only to legitimate each transition in the development, but also to provide support and guidance to enable the students to develop their writing skills in each transitional stage. It is important to recognize that nearly all ELLs live and go to school in a dual language environment. They use their first language at home, among their peers, in the community, and in their bilingual classes. They learn English at school and live in our English-dominant world. Living in a dual language environment, it is natural for them to code-switch in their daily conversation and writing as Callahan (2004) states: "Codes-witching between [two languages] is a natural consequence of a situation of intense daily contact" (121).

Recognizing this, the teachers in the New York City Chinatown middle school where I conducted my research introduced English terminology, vocabulary, and phrases while teaching ELLs content knowledge in their first language. Then, they welcomed the use of English words and phrases in the students' first language dominant writing and accepted code-switching, or the mixed usage of both languages in the students' writing (see Figure 1b). I believe this not only helped the ELLs develop their English language skills, but encouraged the development of the social, cognitive, and linguistic flexibility associated with bilingualism.

I found that the eleven- to thirteen-year-old new English language learners in this Chinatown middle school code-switch naturally as soon as they learn some English vocabulary. They sometimes found that it is easy to use English words to express their life experiences in this country. Those words or phrases tend to be ones that have more condensed or more general meanings in English such as *shopping, have a party*, and *uncle* or *aunt*, or new concepts such as *yard sale* and *flea market*. The translation of these words into Chinese either would require rather complicated language and the loss of general meaning (e.g. Chinese has words meant to specifically distinguish between various paternal or maternal uncles and aunts) or might lead to the loss of the original flavor of words and phrases such as *yard sale* or *flea market*. Such usages not only reflect rather sophisticated bilingual understandings pertaining to each language, but can also lead to insight concerning the importance of word choice and the special voice a language and culture contains.

(a)

(b)

(c)

(d)

Figure 1 (a–d) Stages of Chinese ESL Students' Writing Development

At some point, syntactic transformations, like lexical ones, are evident in the student's writing. Often their written English sounds "broken," because English words were used in the syntax of the native language. This trans-language transformation signals that the writers or speakers usually think in their first language and translate the meaning into English, and the word-for-word translation can sound foreign to native English-speakers (see Figure 1c).

Very often the transitional stages are identified as deficiency, or limited proficiency as English language learners. And we tend to—and often are advised to—only teach ELLs to write in standard English, which is similar to forbidding children to use invented spelling or their dialects during the writing process. That kind of teaching is based on the belief in separating language learning from meaning—making and disconnecting writing from thinking. If we don't value what and how ELLs write in their transitional stages—and only aim at teaching them to write correctly or learn standard English—these students won't develop into writers with depth of thinking and voices of their own. Even when their English becomes proficient, few of them would have confidence as writers of English, which may mean on the surface they speak or write correctly (or close enough to their English-speaking peers), but they still lag behind in their overall literacy skills, as thinkers, writers, and readers. To effectively guide ELLs' writing development to a new language, teachers need to learn to assess their students' work from a developmental perspective, attempting to see the logistics behind language errors and understand the linguistic transitions from one language to another (Fu 2003; Shaughnessy 1977).

When we talk about development or use the terms *stages* or *transitions*, it is easy to interpret the movement as linear and to assume that all ELLs develop as writers from their first language to English along this linear pathway. However, my study found that their progression from the first language to second language usage is not necessarily as linear as the four transitional stages imply.

Looking through the students' writing portfolios, I discovered nonlinear patterns in the ELLs' writing development. Take the students from one seventh-grade social studies class for example. At the beginning of the year, many students began writing in English and their writing was close to standard English. These pieces were about topics related to what they had learned and what they had enjoyed most during the previous year, and what they had done during the summer (see Figure 2a). As the school year moved on, they were assigned to retell and summarize their readings and to make comparisons between the topics under study. For example, they were asked to compare the Revolutionary War with the Civil War. As the writing topics became too complicated for them to express themselves adequately in English, the students chose to write in their first language. Some even wrote their reading responses in Chinese to the English books they read, indicating that they'd understood what they'd read but that their receptive abilities in their new language exceeded their expressive skills (see Figure 2b). In writing, when the teacher stresses on content more than language usage, students move back and forth among the four transitional stages depending upon the complexity of the topics and their particular communicative strengths and needs. This finding suggests that when we stress thinking, content, and ideas in writing, and allow ELLs to move back and forth in between languages until they are able to express what they want to say properly in that language, they will not only become proficient in standard English, but will also have the added advantage of being able

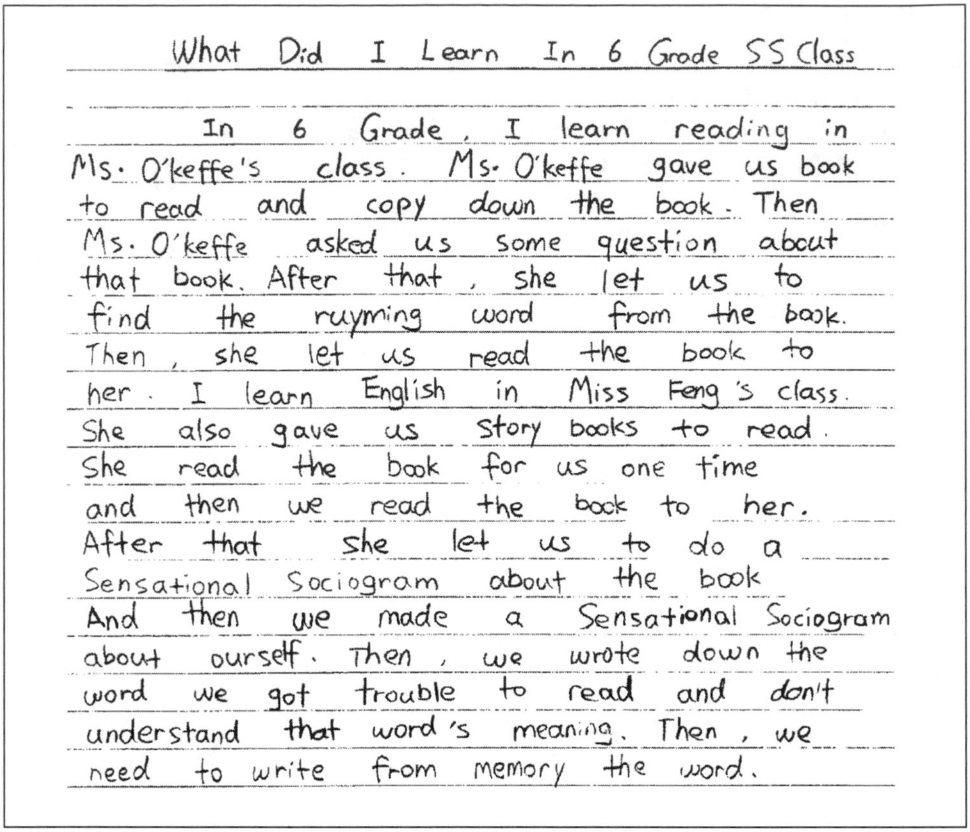

> ## What Did I Learn In 6 Grade SS Class
>
> In 6 Grade, I learn reading in Ms. O'keffe's class. Ms. O'keffe gave us book to read and copy down the book. Then Ms. O'keffe asked us some question about that book. After that, she let us to find the ruyming word from the book. Then, she let us read the book to her. I learn English in Miss Feng's class. She also gave us story books to read. She read the book for us one time and then we read the book to her. After that she let us to do a Sensational Sociogram about the book And then we made a Sensational Sociogram about ourself. Then, we wrote down the word we got trouble to read and don't understand that word's meaning. Then, we need to write from memory the word.

Figure 2 (a)

to make sophisticated choices with regard to expressing a bi-literate voice. Therefore, allowing ELLs this freedom to travel between languages to express themselves in writing enhances their development as bilingual writers.

Teaching Writing to ELLs with Limited First Language Literacy

Among secondary ELLs, about fifteen to twenty percent (depending on the school community, this number can be larger or smaller) of the ELL population who are identified as SIFE students: students with interrupted formal education. Usually SIFE students have limited reading and writing skills in their first language and English. In order to teach writing to these students means that we need to teach them how to write in general, which includes: how to think, to imagine, to organize ideas, to find topics, or to understand the writing process. And most importantly, they need to learn how to use writing as a tool to express themselves. Compared to elementary SIFE ELLs, most of the SIFE ELLs at the secondary level have much better oral language ability with some limited reading and *writing* skills in their first language. Therefore, their oral language and limited first language writing ability should be the starting marker in respect to their writing. However, it is just as we teach our

Reading Journal # 9

1. Title: Corn Mother _____ ☆

2. Author: _____

3. Characters: 造物主, First Mother (Corn Mother), Frist Mother 的丈夫

4. Setting: Northeast Woodland

5. Retell:

     在 Northeast Woodland 那边, 有一个造物主, 他可以创造很多东西。有一天, 滔滔的浪花变成了一个年轻的男孩子, 男孩子和造物主一起创造了很多东西, 后来, 在树叶上的露水掉下来, 变成了一个女孩子, 后来男孩子和女孩子结婚了。造物主走到第二个地方去了, 如果他们有困难的话, 造物主会回来。慢慢的, 男孩子和女孩子生了许多孩子, 女孩子变成了 First Mother。因为人口越来越多, 东西都给他们吃完了。孩子们都走去求 First Mother 给他们东西吃, Frist Mother 因而伤心起来, 她天天都哭, 她的丈夫见到这样, 就走去求造物主, 造物主造诉他, 要照着 Frist Mother 的那个办法做, 结果在第二天中午, Frist Mother 的丈夫把 First Mother 杀死了。她的两个孩子抓住 First Mother 的头发, 把她拖着在土地上走来走去, 直到 Frist Mother 的肉全都脱掉了, 然后把她的 bone 埋起来。过了七个月后, Frist Mother 的丈夫和她的孩子, 人民都回来了, 地面上长出了许多 Corns。从此以后, 人民就有食物, 人民也因而把 Frist Mother 取名为 Corn Mother。

6. Response:

     听了这个故事之后, 我觉得 Corn Mother 很伟大, 她为了人民有食物吃, 就牺牲了自己, 用她的肉和 bone 造造出很多 corn 来, 让她的人民能够吃得饱, 她的那种舍己为人的精神很高贵。我们今后要学 Corn Mother 那样, 不要只顾自己的利益, 也要顾到别人的利益, 不要做自私, 有像 Corn Mother 那样, 这样才会受到别人的尊重。

Figure 2 (b)

emergent writers, we should encourage them to write as they speak, use invented spelling if they can, and coach them to write longer through peer or teacher questions and response. Seeing their own words appear on a page and filling the page can be so new and rewarding for them. This new experience can be exciting and motivate them to go on.

For beginning ELL students, ESL teachers often use pattern books, or books with repetitive language patterns on each page, to develop their speaking, listening, vocabulary, and grammar skills. These kinds of books can also be used for their writing practice. They can model the pattern books and write their own pattern books to express their daily routines, their feelings, and their home lives. Many secondary teachers are hesitant to use books like these, as they fear their ELL adolescents would feel embarrassed by reading and writing such elementary books. It truly depends on how we use these books., which are, after all, written in a simple format, from one or two sentences to one or two paragraphs on a page. If we use these books to teach the concepts or the content of the books, the ELL adolescents will feel insulted. But if we use them to teach ELLs how to use the language to speak, to read with fluency, to write to express their own lives, then they won't feel that those seemingly simple books are babyish anymore. Let's try to put ourselves in our ELLs' shoes. When we learn a foreign language, do we feel insulted if we are taught to read, speak, or write in a new language such sentences as: "My name is…" and "I am…"? We are proud of the simple words and sentences we are able to express about ourselves, rather than feeling awkward by having to learn these basic words and sentences. But if we were asked "What does 'name' mean?" we would feel slighted.

In addition, we should let our ELLs draw or use any graphic ways to express their ideas. Drawing is used as a way for young children to express themselves and is encouraged and assessed as a form of emergent literacy at an early age. But in upper elementary and secondary schools, drawing or artwork discontinues to be valued as a form of writing activity, which implies drawing is only for young children and is only a prewriting tool for their self-expression. We all live in a rich visual art world: digital arts, movies, dances, cartoons, comics, and books with pictures and photos. We go to museums and visit parks. We adults learn so much from the visual arts. If we truly believe that a picture is worth a thousand words, why do our schools devalue drawing as part of the writing activity, especially at the secondary level? The fear that the joy gained in drawing would take over willingness to write using language symbols finds no ground in any research.

In schools I have seen ELL adolescents enjoy drawing strings of pictures to tell about their lives in their home country, and contrast their past lives in villages with green hills and rice patties to their present lives in city ghettos with garbage along the streets and iron bars on the apartment windows. I have seen their published photo books with one word or a phrase captioning each page to express what they have learned during their field trips; and about their families and communities; and their observation of moon, clouds, and city bridges. I have also seen the sculptures the ELLs made from string, clay, and porcelain in front of the school building to express their political views and love for their community. Drawing and artwork have given our ELLs opportunities to express themselves and communicate with others about themselves and what they are learning. From their drawing and artwork, our teachers not only understand these students as individuals, but also learn what language (words or sentence structure) they need to teach them the age-appreciative competency of expression and communication.

Writing in Content Areas and Across the Curriculum

ELLs at the secondary level are just like their peers: they have to learn all the subjects required. Some schools may have bilingual programs, where the ELLs can learn certain subjects such as science, social studies, and math in their first language. Many schools don't have any such bilingual programs or can't provide bilingual programs for all their ELLs, where some ELLs may simply be put in regular classrooms, learning the same curriculum along with their English proficient peers. Every day, they spent three to four or five periods learning in the content areas, the same as their peers. Writing is the essential way for all students to learn the content and the language no matter in what language they are studying the subjects. Unfortunately among the classes I observed at the secondary schools, the content area classrooms require the least writing. Many are still doing workbooks: filling blanks, or answering questions which require yes/no or one word or short phrase responses. ELLs are given hardcover textbooks to read, which they can hardly understand. Though they go through the book chapter by chapter and do all exercises required, they learn little of what has been covered. When they do the workbooks or answer questions after the reading, they basically copy the words from the text to the worksheets with little comprehension.

Studying in content areas not only requires learning different subjects, but also the academic language pertaining to the subjects and topics covered. According to Thomas and Collier (1997), it takes five to seven years to develop academic language proficiency in contrast to two to three years to develop communicative English, in part because the academic language is more abstract and less tied to familiar context. However, ELLs at the secondary level don't have five to seven years to wait; they have to move along with their English proficient peers. Chasing the wind is the metaphor that best illustrates the situation of ELLs learning in content areas at the secondary level.

Most content area teachers at the secondary level don't feel they are trained to teach language, let alone writing. Therefore, feeling helpless on how to reach ELLs, they simply teach the topics and have the students memorize the facts, rules, or formula they barely understand. In order for students to learn the content and develop academic language, they have to write, which means going beyond answering questions, or moving words from the textbooks to the worksheets. Writing in connection to learning of content knowledge will help ELLs not only understand the subjects they are taught but also develop academic English proficiency.

Reading for ELLs in Content Areas

Writing in content areas means writing that is closely linked with what the students read about the subjects covered in class. Most reading in the content areas involves textbooks written in condensed language and packed with solid information. ELLs have a hard time digesting it all. In order for them to write about what they study, they need to understand what they are reading first. The dilemma for content area teachers in secondary schools is that they need to teach the content, but the textbooks they use are designed for students with English proficiency. My study shows ELLs are only able to understand about 30 percent or less of the content covered in these textbooks. Cunningham and Allington (2003) illustrate through their studies that instructional level of a text for readers is at 75 percent of their reading comprehension. When ELLs can hardly understand the text they are assigned to read, it is hard for them to present their learning in writing.

My first recommendation is: put books in the students' hands that they can understand. Very few textbooks at the secondary level are easily understood by ELLs. Therefore we need to go beyond textbooks and search for picture books written on the same topics in the content areas. For example, there are pictures books, information books, and chapter books on social studies and science topics covered in the secondary level such as the Civil War, slavery, historical figures, immigrants, American government, ecosystems, rainforests, and natural disasters.

Many teachers at the secondary level are not comfortable using books seemingly written for elementary children. They think that these books are not giving enough of the information they need to cover, and that to use them puts down the students at the secondary level. Even though an individual book may not provide all the facts and information a textbook does, many of them together can provide a similar amount of information—in rich contexts and communicative language—which are easy for ELLs to understand. If we let students read different books with the same theme or the same topic, they can learn a lot from each other through discussions and book talks. It is also true when we use the books that our ELLs can understand, we may not cover all the topics that the curriculum requires. Ted Sizer (1991) argues that in education less can be more. Through rich discussion of what students read, "we may have 'covered' less, but in the end we will have 'uncovered' more" (Walqui 2006, 178).

When we let our students read different books rather than using one textbook for the whole class, most students don't mind choosing books to read at their level. For adolescents, it is very hard for them if the whole class reads one hardcover textbook, and a few of them are given easy books to read. They would feel so embarrassed that some may prefer not to learn anything by holding the same book as their peers rather than reading the books they can understand. This indicates that they give up their learning for their social images. For a class with students of diverse learning, language, and academic backgrounds, using one book for the whole class throughout the year is not an effective approach in instruction. Many students are victim of our defective instructional approach. It is us teachers that need to revise our teaching, not just for the students' self-image, but for us to help them all learn effectively.

Only when ELLs can understand their reading and are able to share and talk about their learning, writing for them in the content areas can possibly happen. Reading and talking about their reading should be the prerequisite of their writing in the content areas.

Writing for ELLs in Content Areas

Writing in content areas in our schools is usually restricted to a few expository pieces such as book or lab report, a summary of a reading, or short essay-type answers to questions. And the purpose and opportunity for writing in content areas is also limited: simply for a checkup of understanding the topics covered, and two or three short essays in a year. First, for the sake of students' learning in content areas and their language development, they have to write much more frequently: informally and formally and in different formats. I don't think the writing in content areas should be very different from what students do in English or ESL classes, where they are required to write daily or weekly journals, reading response journals where they can make person-to-person, text-to-text, and text-to-world connections, and publish their work in different genres about their learning and lives.

Daily and weekly journals will help ELLs to use everyday language to connect their learning from the classroom with their lives, such as their observation of the environment and their community; their views and opinions of the current events locally, nationally, and internationally; and their response to global warming issues. This kind of free and personal writing related to the topics they learned in class will not only connect their book learning with their personal lives or experiences, but also help them learn more deeply and enhance their cognitive language development.

A reading response journal is much better writing than giving answers to questions or worksheets. The former presents more comprehensive information pertaining to the students' content knowledge and language skills than the latter (see Figure 3). In addition, the reading response gives students freedom on what and how they want to present their reading comprehension. When the students are reading different types of books written in different genres on the topics in the content areas, they should be given freedom to present their learning in those diverse ways. In two New York City middle schools (one Chinese dominant, and one Spanish dominant), I saw ELLs write personal narrative, stories, compare/contrast essays, plays, and poetry to present their learning and inquiries and research in their social studies and science classes. They published their nonfiction books or writing of different genres in magazine formats on science topics and put on their plays on social studies topics. Their publication demonstrated their solid and broad knowledge gained through research on the topics they were studying and also the development of academic English language proficiency. The final publication of their work had gone through multiple drafts, revisions, and layers of editing, and is the result of weeks of research which included book reading, internet searching, note-taking on field trips, and also personal interviews. Most of this published work is the product of two or three students grouped to work on one topic according to their interests.

Assessment of Students' Writing in the Content Areas

Requiring students to write more increases more work for the teachers. But if less work for us means less learning or no learning for students, we have no right to take a less or easy road in teaching. But it doesn't mean we should make our work unreasonably overwhelming and unmanageable. Usually the teachers in the content areas at the secondary level have 120 to 150 students. It is hard to read or grade all the students' writing when writing becomes frequent and in different formats. To read ELLs' writing it is hard, as each piece is packed with errors and non-idiomatic expressions (see Figure 3). Content area teachers can get so frustrated at reading their work, they may just let students write less, do multiple-choice exercises, or simply go back to easy-to-grade worksheets which often require one- or two-word answers.

First, we don't have to read each piece of our students' work. But that doesn't mean we let students write and never attend to it. For daily or weekly journals, we should let students share their writing in groups. This kind of writing prepares students to talk in groups and have something to say which connects their learning with their lives. The teacher can go around and join the conversation from group to group, randomly checking the students' work. We can do the same with their reading response journals. We can group the students who read the same book or different books to do book talks. Their reading response journals ensure their reading, demonstrate their reading comprehension, and prepare them to join the group discussion. The teacher can sit in their discussion, one group at a time. For ELLs, this kind of talk is very beneficial to their learning and language development. For

Spain Explorer 1.

today I in S.S. class learn in
Spain have a Explorer he name is
vasco Nunez de Balboa, Balboa he first
go to Hispaniola, the Hispaniola final
become two place, first is Haiti
海土也, seacond is Dominican Republic
多明尼亚, then Balboa dnot think in
hispaniola this place, he want to 别
的 place, Balboa 躲 in 一舟 船上, this
船 of captain 对 水手 very bad, Balboa
出来 and 水手把 captain 扔进海里, he
oneself do of captain, they 经过了
many swaps and many jungles, they
arrived panama, then panama be
they 战败了, they 互並见 Indina, Indina
tell they if 你们 need to go find 金银
珠宝 need 往西走, they start south
America, then they 发现 一丁 sea, Balboa help

Figure 3

the journal writing, either daily/weekly or reading response, I recommend we don't read each piece or pay much attention to how it is written. This writing is like people babbling and speaking to themselves and will improve gradually through time and intense language contact. I may check it based on whether the students does the writing or how long they write, but nothing else. The opportunities for them to share in groups based on this writing should give them enough incentive to continue, and enough time to improve their work gradually. Kohn (2006) points out "Homework in the best classrooms is not checked—it is shared" (37).

Writing for publication takes time and involves not only content learning, but also reading, research skills, writing, and language development. Sometimes many topics under one big theme are studied as a unit, such as countries and cultures across the world. Different groups would read and research about different countries or cultures, and individual students in each group will take a different focus to do in-depth research and draft their individual work to fit in the collaborative product. Teachers give directions and lessons on general issues and skills; and facilitate the group work through mini lessons, group and individual conference, and class demonstrations.

Usually teachers do two or three long-term projects of this kind in a year. If we give students enough time, if we let them work with each other on their research and help one another with their writing, if we only periodically or selectively read their work, it should be manageable. Since our students are at different levels with their English ability, we should also accept their work with different expectations. Some can write longer, some shorter; some can write to discuss more complicated issues, and some can present simple facts, as long as they all try their best.

I would also suggest content area teachers work closely with the ESL resource room teachers. Let ELLs continue their writing in their ESL rooms or have their ESL teachers help them with revision and editing. This would not only reduce the content area teachers' work considerably, but also make the learning for ELLs between ESL and subject classrooms connected. ESL teachers can assist ELLs to revise and edit their work and help them finalize their products. I highly recommend the collaboration between classroom and ESL teachers, such as sharing each other's curriculum and the students' progress. Usually there is a disconnect between ESL and classroom teaching, which results in a discontinuity of ELLs' learning that slows down the overall progress of ELLs' learning.

The errors in ELLs' writing can be overwhelming, especially to content area teachers as they are not used to reading writing packed with errors and strange expressions, which include ungrammatical sentence structures, spelling mistakes, improper word choices, and non-idiomatic expressions. The overwhelming errors can block our mind from reading on or even trying to understand what the students are writing. Working with ELLs, we do need to learn to read through that "broken" surface structure, to understand the meaning the ELLs are trying to convey (Fu 2003). Otherwise, it is impossible for us to focus on the idea or content of their writing when we read their beginning drafts. It is like listening to a person with a limited English proficiency, if we don't try hard to understand what he tries to say, but focus on correcting how he speaks, the speaker will stop speaking or communicating with us completely. If we give our attention to errors in ELLs' writing during the draft stage, the students would focus their attention to producing correct English, which would turn writing into language practice exercises, rather than writing for content presentation and self-expression.

It doesn't mean we should ignore all the errors. I had an interview with an ESL teacher when I saw a final copy of one of his beginning ELL's work, which was corrected from the first draft but still has many grammatical errors (see Figure 4a and 4b). Here is his explanation:

> When I work with my beginning ELLs, I pay much attention to what they try to say, and I help them to get the meaning uncrossed. When I help students edit their work, I don't help

them correct all the errors, which would rewrite every sentence for them, but only enough to be understood.

For this student, this was the first piece he ever completed in English, and it took him quite a long time to finish this piece. For the final copy, I helped him edit a few basic things, such as capital letters, verbs, and possessive pronouns, and leave alone tense, plural forms, and even certain sentence structures. Or I will rewrite everything for him. I want him to continue to write and take the risk.

Seeing the difference between the draft and the final typed copy, I understand what this teacher meant by not correcting all the errors. We propose in our writing instruction: teach writers rather than simply teaching writing. This teacher certainly holds this view in his teaching practice. Usually by working through many drafts and sharing their work repeatedly with their peers, many ELLs should have made their work better understood with fewer errors than the beginning draft. For editing, which may take a lot of time, it can be a good opportunity for ELLs to work on their English skills. I would recommend we let students help each other edit their work as much as possible and continue their editing work in the ESL room, which is contextualized language learning. Just like improving English speaking, by writing frequently, the students will improve their writing and language skills from one piece to another. Making every piece perfect doesn't always produce good writers, but may inhibit students to take risks in learning.

Writing and Language Development in Content Areas

Writing, as one of the language skills, is well connected with reading, speaking, and listening ability. It is hard for a person to write well in a language which she can barely speak. But the challenge for ELLs, especially at the secondary level, is they have to develop all these language skills spontaneously while studying all the subjects required. We need to help them develop all the language skills in the context of learning subject knowledge. In the content areas, rather than specifically teaching the language skills, we should provide plenty of opportunity for ELLs to speak (listening is part of speaking activity), read, and write. Talking about their work not only helps them learn and write better, but also provides a good language practice opportunity for them to use language in rich and purposeful contexts. Any writing ELLs have done should be used for part of their reading and speaking activity. They should read fluently whatever they have written and share it in small groups or in class. Since we have limited class time, they should practice this reading and speaking as part of the homework before they do it in class. English in content areas tends to have special terminology and formal language, and ELLs need plenty of practice before they are able to speak and use it in their writing.

Usually content area teachers don't think they can teach language or are responsible for their ELLs English language development. Language is the tool to learn and write. If we don't help them develop this tool, we cannot teach them either the subject knowledge or writing. Instead of giving specific grammar lessons or other language instruction, we should purposefully link writing with reading and speaking depending on variation among individual ELLs. Their writing prepares their reading and speaking, and their reading and speaking will help them write better. This cycle is not just a language learning cycle, but an interactive teaching/learning approach: a student learns through repeatedly listening to, speaking, reading, and writing, which is a cognitive process of internalization and individualization of a new

My first time see look like dog big mouse
run for street I and my father was very shocked . It teeth
have 3 inches long. It tail have 20 inches lon
It 4 lege have 5 inches long. It eyes has red
color and one people run for this mouse. My
Father walk for this people talk this people and I run to
this people list. My father say "this big mouse or
day eat who many Food". this People say this mouse one d
eat 15 pound for food. My father say "this big mo
1 hours run who long". this people say th
mouse 1 hours run 80 miles look like a
van rental. I say "this mouse live in where"
This People say "live in dog home". I and my fat
to this people talk so long. This people go home
I and my father walk to home. I say "My fir
time see this big mouse."

(a)

My first time

My first time see look like dog big mouse run for street I and my father was very shocked.

Its teeth are 3 inches long, Its tail are 20 inches long, Its 4 leges are 5 inches long. Its eyes are red color and one people run for this mouse. My father walk for this people talk this people and I run to this people listen my father say, "This big mouse one day eat who many food." This people say, "This mouse one day eat 15 pound for food." My father say, "This big mouse 1 hours run who long." This people say, "This mouse 1 hours run 80 miles look like a car the miles." I say, "This mouse live in where." This people say, "This live in dog house." I and my father to this people talk so long.

This people go home. I and my father walk to home, I say, "My first time see this this big mouse."

(b)

Figure 4(a–b)

knowledge. ELLs need stronger doses of this cycle but may have a different order than their English proficient peers such as from writing to reading to speaking (listening).

In summary, teaching ELLs to write, we need to:

- Provide them with plenty of writing opportunities in every subject area
- Let them write in their first language as the starting point
- Understand their writing moves transitionally and learn to appreciate their code-switching or " broken" English
- Help and guide them to make the transitions
- Link writing with other language skill development

Writing is the most challenging skill for ELLs, and it is the least taught to them. From elementary to graduate school, I have heard frequent complaints from instructors that their ELLs just can't write. But we rarely ask if they have ever been taught to write, or how they have been taught to write, or if they have had any teacher in their schooling that helped them express what they wanted to in writing through English. We must take the time to teach writing more seriously to English language learners. When this happens, our students will grow as writers and as people.

Works Cited

Callahan, Laura. 2004. *Spanish/English Codeswitching in a Written Corpus*. Amsterdam, The Netherlands: John Benjamins Publishing Co.

Cummins, James. 1979. "Linguistics Interdependence and the Educational Development of Bilingual Children." *Bilingual Education Paper Series* 3/2 (ERIC Document Reproduction Service, No. ED 257 312).

Cunningham, Patricia and Richard Allington. 2003. *Classrooms That Work*. 3rd ed. New York: Pearson Education, Inc.

Dyson, Ann. 1993. *Social Worlds of Children Learning to Write in an Urban Primary School*. New York: Teachers College Press.

Fix, Michael and Jeffrey Passel. 2003. "U.S. Immigration: Trends and Implications for Schools." Paper presented at the National Association for Bilingual Education's NCLB Implementation (New Orleans, LA, January 28–29).

Fu, Danling. 2003. *An Island of English: Teaching ESL in Chinatown*. Portsmouth, NH: Heinemann.

Kohn, Alfie. 2006. *The Homework Myth*. Cambridge, MA: Da Capo Lifelong Books.

National Center for Educational Statistics (NCES). 2004. *The Condition of Education, 2004*. Retrieved July 16, 2004, from http://nces.ed.gov/programs/coe.

Shaughnessy, Mina 1977. *Errors and Expressions*. London: Oxford University Press.

Sizer, Theodore. 1991. "No Pain, No Gain." *Educational Leadership*. May: 32–34.

Thomas, Wade and Virginia. Collier. 1997. *School Effective for Language Minority Students: NCBE Resource Collection Series, No. 9*. Washington, DC: National Clearinghouse for Bilingual Education.

Walqui, Anita. 2006. "Scaffolding Instruction for English Language Learners: A Conceptual Framework." *The International Journal of Bilingual Education and Bilingualism*. 9 (2): 159–180.

20

Boys and Writing

Michael Smith

Michael W. Smith is a professor at Temple University's College of Education. He joined the ranks of college teachers after eleven years of teaching high school English. He has won awards for his teaching at both the high school and college levels. His research focuses on understanding the knowledge, skills, and dispositions of experienced readers and writers; how to help students develop those prerequisites for success; and what motivates adolescents' reading and writing outside school. His publications include "Reading Don't Fix No Chevys": Literacy in the Lives of Young Men *for which he and co-author Jeff Wilhelm received the 2003 David H. Russell Award for Distinguished Research in the Teaching of English.*

The dawn of the twenty-first century has been marked by an unprecedented attention to what for many is a totally unexpected achievement gap: Girls are outperforming boys on a variety of measures of educational attainment. The alarm sounded by educational researchers has reverberated in the popular press. A *Newsweek* cover proclaims "The Trouble with Boys: They're kinetic, maddening and failing at school."

The cover story begins with a profile of one of those failing boys:

> Spend a few minutes on the phone with Danny Frankhuizen and you come away thinking, "What a *nice* boy." He's thoughtful, articulate, bright. He has a good relationship with his mom, goes to church every Sunday, loves the rock band Phish and spends hours each day practicing his guitar. But once he's inside his large public Salt Lake City high school, everything seems to go wrong. He's 16, but he can't stay organized. He finishes his homework and then can't find it in his backpack…Last year Danny's grades dropped from B's to D's and F's. (44)

My research with Jeff Wilhelm establishes that Danny Frankhuizen is not alone. Young men who are labeled as failing because they are having difficulties in school almost always have areas in their lives in which they are a success. If Danny brought the same kind of engagement to his schooling that he did to his music, he wouldn't be in trouble in school at all.

The premise of *"Reading Don't Fix No Chevys": Literacy in the Lives of Young Men* (Smith and Wilhelm 2002), our study of young men's literate lives both in and out of school, is that if we understand why boys like to do what they like to do outside of school, we can use that understanding to reimagine what things might be like inside school. In that book we draw on Mihalyi Csikzentmihalyi's description of flow experiences—those in which we are "fully involved" (2) with what we're doing, so involved that while we are so engaged nothing else matters—as a lens to understand why the boys in our study liked to do what they liked to do. Our most compelling finding was the importance of competence. That is, like most of us, the boys in our study became fully involved only in activities in which they had a feeling of competence. Unfortunately, I'm afraid that the dominant models for teaching writing do not do a very good job helping students feel they are competent before they are asked to write. The purpose of this chapter is to present an alternative model, one grounded in the work of George Hillocks, Jr., that has the promise of making writing a flow experience for more students. But first, let's take a look at the scope of the problem and what the boys told us that suggested a possible solution.

The Scope of the Problem

Even a quick look at research on writing achievement establishes that boys underperform girls on measures of writing. The 1985 International Association for Evaluation of Educational Achievement investigated writing achievement across fourteen countries and found that "gender by itself or in combination with certain home variables was the most powerful predictor of performance, particularly with academic tasks" (Purves 1992, 201). The *ETS Gender Study* reports that the gap in writing between eighth grade males and females is over six times greater than the differences in mathematical reasoning (Cole 1997). In the NAEP writing assessment for 2002, twenty-one percent of eighth grade boys scored at or above proficient, while twice as many girls (forty-two percent) reached this standard. The gap is even greater at twelfth grade: fourteen percent of boys scored at proficient or advanced compared to thirty-three percent of girls.

Hedges and Nowell (1995) studied gender differences in a variety of tests and came up with this troubling conclusion: "Average sex differences were small except for writing, in which females performed substantially better than males" (44). They view this situation with concern: "The large sex differences in writing ability suggested by the NAEP trend data are alarming. The data imply that males are, on average, at a rather profound disadvantage in the performance of this basic skill" (45).

Some researchers have suggested that some of these disparities might be because the tests themselves are biased against the kinds of writing that at least some boys tend to do, an artifact of the assessments themselves. Peterson (1998), for example, argues that girls' narrative writing was privileged during the Canadian provincial assessment she studied. If boys tend to write action stories and if action stories is a genre that is not rewarded on large-scale assessments, poor scores may be a function of evaluation bias and not actual performance.

Newkirk (2002) makes a similar argument, though his focus is classrooms rather than high-stakes tests. He argues that the kind of literacy work that boys find most pleasurable is undervalued in school: jokes, comic books, adventure stories, and so on. The stakes of the game are quite clear to Newkirk. He writes "We must resist those forces that would narrow the range of writing…allowable in school. Such restrictions will invariably most hurt students outside the mainstream, those who draw their inspiration from low-status cultural sources" (186).

The data from a wide variety of tests coupled with the arguments of Peterson and Newkirk make it clear that many young men have no reason to feel that they are competent school writers. Yet our research clearly established that a feeling of competence was crucial to young men's motivation. It's to that research that I now turn.

The Importance of Competence

When we asked Guy why lacrosse was his favorite activity, he responded in a way that could summarize the attitude of all of the boys in our study: "I just like being good at it." What the boys in our study were good at varied widely, but one thing remained the same: Competence was key.

Buster makes the importance of competence clear when he talks about his biking:

> See, for me actually, the sports I like are kind of different from a lot that other people like. A lot of people like basketball, baseball. I'm a little bit different; I like individual sports and probably my favorite is mountain-biking. It's something I'm decent at, you know. I've got to see different parts of the country traveling throughout and you know it's something that I've really…it's something that I've been, it's something that I can always work towards, and it's just…it just gives me a lot of motivation.

If he didn't feel competent in an activity, he tended to reject it:

> I don't know, something about computers, I'm really not all that. I mean, I like the communication aspect of computers, but I'm really not…I don't know, something about them that I'm not—first of all I'm not all that computer literate, and second of all there's just something about them that I'd rather…they're too complicated for me I guess.

On the other hand, a feeling of competence was crucial to Buda's motivation to do computer-related work:

> Well, I'm actually the only computer literate person in my house pretty much because my…I'm very good with computers like I know my way around computers, and I know what to do in situations if something happens and my parents and my brother don't; and they're always asking me, what does this do? and how do you do this? and ah, it's just fun.

But if Buda didn't feel competent, he rejected an activity. Such was the case with drawing: "Drawing is boring because I have pretty much no talent in drawing."

On the other hand, Maurice loved to draw. His feeling of competence is clear as he explained why:

> Well, I like to draw graffiti, design headbands like bandanas. I buy a plain white bandana, and I'll get some markers and I'll draw a couple words or a nickname or what part of town I come from and I'll put it on the headband; and you can sell them for like four dollars a piece or whatever. Make a little profit. So you can have fun and make money at the same time.

Any teacher of writing knows that becoming a writer takes hard work. But the boys in our study told us that unless they felt competent in an activity they were reluctant to engage in it. If that feeling of competence didn't come, the boys rejected the activity, as Clint explained:

> Like I try and do new stuff, but I usually stick with what I already know. Like if I try and do something new, and I'm no good at it like I won't just try something for a minute and then say I don't want to do it because I'm no good at it. I'll try it for a long period of time, but if I don't get better at it, I'll just stop.

Interestingly, this ethic applied even in areas in which they boys had had some success. Bodey was a gamer, yet he would give up games that proved too difficult, as he indicated in a conversation with Jeff:

> BODEY: I look for in a game I would say that they are fun, they aren't…um…like extremely hard, and they're possible to play.
>
> JEFF: What do you mean by not extremely hard and possible to play?
>
> BODEY: Um, I rented one game and it was Superman. It was about Superman and, ah, you really couldn't fly him that well in the game and it really didn't set up the buttons that well for what he did, and it therefore made it harder to do and it made you want to quit it and not play it.
>
> JEFF: So when you play a game, you want to be adept at it from the start.
>
> BODEY: Right.

A Look at Traditional Instruction

Unfortunately, much of the writing instruction students receive is not designed to help them develop a feeling of competence. Think back on how you were taught writing. My bet is that most of your teachers used the assign and assess method. That is, your teachers assigned writing, often about the literature you read in class, and then graded it, providing comments both as a way to justify the grade and as a way to provide instruction for future work.

It's easy to see that the assign and assess approach doesn't fulfill the conditions of flow experiences, no matter how engaging an assignment might be. Not long ago, I was hired as a consultant to evaluate a school that was rated by a national magazine as the very best high school in its state. As part of my evaluation I did focus group interviews with groups of ninth- to twelfth-grade students. The students were outspoken in their affection for their school, an affection that was manifest just walking up and down the halls. But there was one common complaint: the way writing was taught. Student after student told me of the shock he or she received upon getting back the first paper assigned in ninth-grade English, regardless of the ninth-grade teacher involved. Students used to getting As got Bs or Cs or worse. And very often the first set of papers was returned with some version of the following complaint: what did those middle school teachers teach you anyway? The students praised their teachers for being willing to work with them outside of class to learn how to write the kind of essay that they would be asked to write in high school. And after some time, most of them figured things out.

The problem here is two-fold. The students worked hard and wanted to please their teachers but they didn't know how. (Less conscientious students and students with less of a history of school success might not have sought out the extra help teachers were willing to provide.) And the teachers were frustrated, in large measure because of all of the hours they had to commit to responding to papers and to meeting students in conferences There has to be a better way.

But I'm afraid that providing rubrics or model texts, two common approaches teachers use to clarify their expectations and communicate them to students, isn't the answer. Although both provide a target students can aim for, they don't help students hit that target. Knowing that descriptive detail or support is worth twenty points out of one hundred doesn't help students develop the writing skills they need to create compelling descriptions or well-reasoned arguments.

Models are plagued by a similar problem. Let's do a thought experiment: think of how many novels you've read in your life. Now ask yourself whether you feel ready to write one. Knowing what you're supposed to do doesn't mean that you can do it. It takes something more.

An Alternative Approach

George Hillocks has convinced me that what it takes is practice. He has demonstrated that activities that engage students in developing the skills they need to write a particular kind of text, what he calls procedural knowledge, hold the most promise for helping students become better writers. According to Hillocks, students need to know more than the formal features of the texts they are trying to write. They need to know how to achieve those features.

But asking students, especially students who don't consider themselves writers, to practice by producing whole texts does not provide the motivation the young men in our study seemed to need. Hillocks explains that teachers can most effectively support their students by doing a task analysis of the writing they want them to do, and then devising what he calls "gateway" activities that provide extended practice with each of the aspects of the task. I've come to call this approach providing practice in miniature. The key is to devise engaging gateway activities to provide that practice, and there's no formula for doing so. Hillocks writes,

> What are the key production strategies for generating activities that will enable students to learn production strategies for various writing tasks? That is the key question. Every year my students set out to invent these key activities and many have subsequently published them…However, I can never tell them how to do it exactly. The best I can do is indicate general strategies that have proved useful in devising successful gateway activities. (Hillocks 1995, 150)

I'm one of those students, and I've experienced the same frustration that he describes above when I work with my own students to design the kinds of prewriting activities that George calls for. One of the things that has helped me articulate "how to do it exactly" is the voices of the boys in our study. Asking myself how I can help students feel adept right from the start and how I can help them experience noticeable improvement relatively quickly helped me generate a heuristic that has proven useful. I've had the most success with practice in miniature when it moves in at least one of the following directions:

- From the immediate to the imagined
- From the short to the long

- From the oral to the written
- From the scaffolded to the independent
- From the social to the independent

Moving from the Immediate to the Imagined

A task analysis of narrative writing will reveal that writing about some kinds of experiences requires attention to a character's bodily sensations. A writer can't communicate the thrill of a roller coaster ride or the trepidation of sitting in a dentist's office just with sight and sound details. To help students understand how to turn their attention inward, what I call developing an inner eye, I used to ask them to do a series of exercises: holding their breath, running in place, and so on. After each exercise students would write. As they were writing, I'd circulate so I could praise their efforts. Then we'd share so we could all appreciate each other's work. Because they had just experienced the sensations, they were able to write about them far more easily than they would have had I asked them imagine a sensation and to write about it.

Moving from the Short to the Long

Moving from short writing exercises to longer ones is another way to help students develop their feeling of competence. A task analysis of narrative writing makes it clear that writers must be able to employ descriptive details. Asking students to show and not tell in a narrative is far more daunting than asking students to write a series of descriptions of particular scenes. Playing recordings of a roaring crowd in an arena, a construction site, and so on and asking to students to describe what they heard provides both immediacy and the assurance that you're not asking them to do more than what they are willing to try. Repeated practice in miniature also allows you to identify particular techniques students employ, for example, using figures or describing a sound based on the feeling it creates.

Moving from the Oral to the Written

If your students are like my students, most of them are far more accomplished talkers than they are writers. Moving from the oral to the written, therefore, increases their feeling of competence. Any task analysis for narrative is sure to include the importance of realistic dialogue. In my experience, asking students to role-play particular scenes and then have them write what they acted has always been more effective than having them act out what they've written. After all, students have been engaging in dramatic play for most of their lives. Tapping their oral abilities helps them to see themselves as composers.

Moving from the Scaffolded to the Independent

My students seemed to profit from practice in miniature that moved from the scaffolded to the independent. For example, as a way to practice physical descriptions of characters, another element of my task analysis for narratives, I used to show pictures that created a very strong impression. We'd talk as a class about the feelings the photos evoked, and then we would write the details that gave rise to those feelings. As I circulated, I could ask students questions or direct their attention to one aspect of the photo or the other. As we wrote about other photos, I could begin to fade into the background.

Moving from the Social to the Individual

Finally, my students always profited from moving from the social to the individual. That is, during all of the activities students worked with their classmates, sometimes doing collaborative planning, sometimes by doing collaborative writing, often by providing each other an immediate audience.

Hillocks (2006) details a sequence of lessons that inspired the teaching I described above. Sharing the kind of meticulous planning that he provides is clearly beyond the scope of this chapter. What is within the scope of this chapter is demonstrating how activities that provide practice in miniature help students develop a feeling of competence before we ask them to do extended writing and illustrating; how thinking about moving from the immediate to the imagined, from the short to the long, from the oral to the written, and from the scaffolded to the independent has helped me generate those activities.

Of course, a heuristic is of limited utility if it can only be used to generate activities for one kind of writing. So let's try it with another kind of writing: fables. When I taught ninth graders, I worked with them to write fables. I thought that doing so would be a great way to build bridges between our reading and our writing, for casting students as creators of symbols would, I thought, surely help them develop as interpreters of symbols.

But I'm afraid I didn't have tremendous success with that writing. We read fables together and talked about the characteristics of the genre. I guess I thought that knowing the formal features of fables would be enough for them to write them, as fables are much less complex than narratives. But I was wrong. My students turned in writing that resembled fables. The central characters were animals. But instead of behaving like real animals with the exception of the fact that they could talk, many of my students' characters behaved like cartoon animals, that is, completely anthropomorphized. And instead of having fables that satirized human foibles, many of my students wrote fables that offered such innocuous advice as "Look both ways before you cross the street," or "Make sure that you brush your teeth after every meal." I think I mistakenly took for granted that my students had a better understanding of fables than they really did.

One of George's most significant influences on me was his profound belief that virtually all students can be successful if they get the appropriate instruction. I have always believed that if my students didn't do well, it's my fault and not theirs. Obviously, in this case I was doing something wrong. The heuristic that I shared above points the way to what I could have done. Had I thought more carefully about fables, I would have realized that the heart of the matter is identifying the human foible one wants to satirize. I could have moved from the oral to the written by having a discussion about the kinds of things that really bother us about others. It would have been good fun to make a list of our pet peeves.

Then we could have thought about what kind of animals would best represent those traits we wanted to satirize. Perhaps I could have brought in videos from the Discovery Channel of an animal or two in its habitat. Doing so would help students see how an animal's characteristic behavior could be a springboard for developing a plot. Then they could move from the immediate to the imagined by working together to select animals that might be appropriate for a fable that targeted the pet peeves we had identified.

I could have given my students practice in writing memorable morals by giving them a set of unfamiliar Aesop's fables, with the morals removed, and asking them to write morals for them. Such an activity is scaffolded in that they only would have had to concentrate on writing the moral, as the rest of the story was provided. And having experienced success in writing such an important feature of fables would surely motivate students to engage in writing an entire fable. And when they did, they'd be moving from the short to the long. George sketches out a similar sequence as one of his illustrations of his approach (Hillocks 1995, 151–155). Although he provides powerful illustrations, he notes that he "cannot be more specific about the invention of the activities" (Hillocks 1995, 169). My contribution to George's thinking, then, is in trying to be a bit more specific about how to generate gateway activities and in providing additional support for his ideas in the research Jeff and I did about boys.

Any kind of writing you want your students to do is amenable to the kind of analysis I've shared here. A job application letter? Well, one key would be thinking through the kinds of attributes and experience that employers might find useful. I could go from the oral to the written, from the short to the long, and from the social to the independent if my students began by working in groups to list the two or three most important qualities different kinds of jobs require.

How about screenplays? Well, I know that what distinguishes screenplays from other kinds of writing is that writers have to detail directions for music, camera angles, and so on. We'd probably have to start by looking at a few, but models alone aren't enough. I could move from the immediate to the imagined, the social to the independent, and the short to the long if I showed the first two minutes of several films and had students work together to write the technical directions.

Haiku? Hmm. I know that a key is being able to develop a figure. Maybe we could read some, and then I could ask kids to write one or two using a first line I provided that contains a metaphor. That's moving from the scaffolded to the independent. Then I could show a picture of something in nature and kids could develop their own figures. Then they could write their own haiku about scenes they picture themselves. That's moving from the immediate to the imagined.

Research papers? Well, my students always had problems explaining how the evidence they cited related to the claims they made. So before my eleventh graders did their own research papers, they wrote one using research that I did. Since we were reading *The Catcher in the Rye*, I put together a packet of material from adolescent psychologists and asked them to write a research paper in which they took a position on whether Holden was a typical or pathological adolescent. I scaffolded their citing and explaining evidence because that's all they had to focus on. I had done the research.

A sonnet? Knowing the form of a sonnet is certainly not enough. Writing fourteen lines of iambic pentameter won't seem so daunting once kids have worked on revising a line or two to make them fit the form. So, for example, say I provide these ideas: "I often think about all of the bad things you've done to me, especially when it's late at night. I wonder if you do too." I could then help my students move from the short to the long, from the scaffolded to the independent, and from the social to the individual if I divided them into pairs, and asked them to work together to come up with lines that express the same sentiments but that fit the meter. Here's my first attempt: "In dark of night I think upon the hurts / And wonder if your night has passed just so." I have to admit that it took me some time to come up with an example that scanned (even an example that's not very good), and I'm fifty-two and write all the time. Imagine what your students face if you just assign them to write an entire sonnet!

Jeff and I spin out our ideas on the implications of our research much more fully in *Going with the Flow: How to Engage Boys (and Girls) in Their Literacy Learning*. You can see how a host of George's students apply his ideas in *Reflective Teaching, Reflective Learning* (McCann, Johannessen, Kahn, Smagorinsky, and Smith 2005).

Back to the Boys

One of the things Jeff and I are asked most often when talk about our work is whether we see the gender of the teacher as a crucial factor in the success of young men. One argument for the reason boys underperform girls is that they see literacy as feminized, in part, because the majority of their literacy teachers are women. We did hear complaints about having to read "girlie" books in school from some of our participants, but their complaints about the books did not extend to the teachers of those books. We combed our data looking for such a sentiment, but we didn't find any instances of its occurrence.

Although the boys in our study didn't make a distinction between men and women teachers, many of them did make another distinction: the teachers versus the assigners. That is, the boys believed that most of their teachers simply assigned work in the belief that doing the work was enough to help students get better at it. They embraced those few teachers that they saw providing active assistance. Wolf was the most articulate spokesman for such a view:

> I mean you are a teacher, I assume that you teach, I am going to assume. Obviously you have some amount of homework, that there is going to be some amount of homework involved in teaching no matter what happens. That is a given, but my teachers will just give out thousands and thousands of pages of homework and expect that to teach you. They don't teach. It is just like do chapters, questions 1–5. And then they are going to assume that you know it because you do the questions 1–5, and even if you talk with somebody, you aren't going to know it. But if you actually get up there and teach it to people and ask questions they are going to know it. That is why America is stupid.

Kent (2002) made a similar finding. None of the twenty boys in his study commented on the gender of the teacher when they were discussing the qualities of an engaging English language arts teacher. But all of them applauded teachers who work "personally with students." All of them praised teachers who are "helpful." All of them noted that a "hard teacher can be a good teacher" if that teacher helped students successfully meet the challenges he or she set before them.

The Assign and Assess approach doesn't provide the kind of instruction that Wolf and Rich Kent's participants are looking for, no matter how engaging the writing prompt. Models don't either. Showing a model is not unlike referring students to the correct answers at the end of the math book. A model tells you where to go but doesn't help you get there. On the other hand, the kind of gateway activities that Hillocks calls for do seem to meet the standard of being a teacher and not just an assigner. They provide the feeling of confidence and the experience of success that the boys found so motivating.

Other models of writing instruction also move beyond Assign and Assess, but none that I know of have the power of the approach I advocate here. For example, a workshop approach provides an opportunity for instruction in two ways: through mini-lessons and through coaching students as they write. I worry about an exclusive reliance on this approach, though, for a number of reasons. In the first place, mini-lessons, even long ones of twenty minutes or so, just aren't long enough to help students develop complex procedural understandings. To be sure, you could illustrate the difference between showing and telling in a mini-lesson. You could do a think-aloud while working on showing the feelings you experienced during some meaningful event in a mini-lesson. But you couldn't give the kind of repeated practice that kids need to develop their own ability to create evocative descriptions.

In this way, writing is like most other human activities, at least according a compilation of research on expert performers in a variety of domains, which will appear in the *Cambridge Handbook of Expertise and Expert Performance. The New York Times Magazine* recently reported that the studies, which include investigations of such different activities as "soccer, golf, surgery, piano playing, Scrabble, writing, chess, software design, stock picking and darts" (par. 7) make

> a rather startling assertion: the trait we commonly call talent is highly overrated. Or, put another way, expert performers—whether in memory or surgery, ballet or computer programming—are nearly always made, not born. And yes, practice does make perfect. (par. 8)

But not all practice is the same, according to the article:

> Deliberate practice entails more than simply repeating a task—playing a C-minor scale 100 times, for instance, or hitting tennis serves until your shoulder pops out of its socket. Rather, it involves setting specific goals, obtaining immediate feedback and concentrating as much on technique as on outcome. (par. 6)

Gateway activities provide this kind of deliberate practice in a way that mini-lessons can't. (My thanks to David Neuschulz for sending me *The New York Times Magazine* article as I was composing this chapter.)

The kind of instruction I'm advocating also differs from the kind of instruction provided in conferences. In writing about conferences, Nancie Atwell argues that "they call for teachers who know something worth saying after we sit down next to our kids and ask, 'How can I help you?'" (Atwell 1998, 261). Her examples detail how effectively she responded to her student writers' needs. Certainly, being an effective teacher of writing requires one to observe one's students to identify what they need to learn to overcome the difficulties they encounter as they write. But as powerful as that kind of responsive teaching is, I think it would be even more powerful if it were coupled with anticipatory teaching. That is, by thinking hard about the kinds of demands different writing tasks place on students, I can anticipate the difficulties they may encounter and devise instruction so that students are less likely to encounter the difficulties in the first place. The young men in our study told us how important it was for them to feel competent if they were going to engage in an activity. They told us how quickly they would quit if they didn't gain that feeling of competence. Providing plenty of practice in miniature seems to meet those requirements.

That's not to say that the Hillocks-style instruction cannot be combined with a workshop. I could imagine having a story-writing workshop once a class has completed the sequence on writing narratives that I described earlier, for example. But it is to say that some approaches to writing workshops may be less effective in helping students develop the expertise they need to be successful than would sequences of gateway activities.

One more word in closing: although I did not study girls, I am the father of two teenage daughters. My kids seem just as interested in demonstrating their competence as the young men in our study. That makes sense, for Csikszentmihalyi's analysis of flow experiences is built on data drawn from both men and women. Writing instruction that appeals to young men does not have to come at the expense of young women. I am convinced that if we do a better job of teaching our young men we will do a better job of teaching our young women as well.

Works Cited

Atwell, Nancie. 1998. *In the Middle: New Understandings About Writing, Reading and Learning.* Portsmouth, NH: Heinemann.

Cole, Nancy. 1997. *The ETS Gender Study: How Females and Males Perform in Educational Settings.* Princeton, NJ: Educational Testing Service.

Csikszentmihalyi, Mihaly. 1990. *Flow: The Psychology of Optimal Experience.* New York: Harper & Row.

Dubner, S., and Levitt, S. 7 May 2006. "Freakonomics; A star is made." *New York Times Magazine.* www.nytimes.com/2006/05/07/magazine/07wwln_freak.html?ex=1147838400&en=7265a5e 2cf70a87&ei=5070&emc=eta1.

Hedges, L. V., and Nowell, A. 1995. "Sex Differences in Mental Test Scores, Variability, and Numbers of High-Scoring Individuals." *Science* 269: 41–45.

Hillocks, G., Jr., 2006. *Narrative Writing: Learning a New Model for Teaching* (WT). Portsmouth, NH: Heinemann.

———. 1986. *Research on Written Composition: New Directions for Teaching.* Urbana, IL: ERIC and National Conference for Research in English.

———. 1995. *Teaching Writing as Reflective Practice.* New York: Teachers College Press.

Kent, Richard. 2002. "The Guys: Boys, School, & English Class." Unpublished doctoral dissertation. Claremont Graduate University, Claremont, CA.

McCann, Thomas, Larry R. Johannesson, Elizabeth Kahn, Peter Smagorinsky, and Michael W. Smith, eds. 2005. *Reflective Teaching, Reflective Learning. How to Develop Critically Engaged Readers, Writers, and Speakers.* Portsmouth, NH: Heinemann.

Newkirk, Thomas. 2002. *Misreading Masculinity.* Portsmouth, NH: Heinemann.

Peterson, S. 1998. "Evaluation and Teachers' Perception of Gender in Sixth Grade Student Writing." *Research in the Teaching of English.* (33): 181–206.

Purves, A. 1992. *The IEA Study of Written Composition II: Education and Performance in Fourteen Countries.* Oxford: Pergamon Press.

Smith, Michael W. and Jeffrey D. Wilhelm. 2006. *Going with the Flow: How to Engage Boys (and Girls) in Their Literacy Learning.* Portsmouth, NH: Heinemann.

———. 2002. *"Reading Don't Fix No Chevys":* Literacy in the Lives of Young Men. Portsmouth, NH: Heinemann

Tyre, P. 2006. "The Trouble with Boys." *Newsweek,* 147 (5): 44–52.

Alexis Martin, Kate Sullivan, Jabari Mahiri

21

Exchanging Writing and Difference

Jabari Mahiri, Alexis Martin, and Kate Sullivan

Jabari Mahiri is an associate professor of education at the University of California, Berkeley. He is codirector of the Center for Urban Education and a Senior Scholar for the National Urban Alliance for Effective Education. His research interests include effective teaching and learning practices for urban youth, writing development across textual mediums, and connections between digital literacies and youth popular culture.

Alexis Martin is a doctoral student in Social and Cultural Studies in the Graduate School of Education at the University of California, Berkeley. Her research interests include out-of-school literacies, popular culture pedagogy, student experiences of small high schools on shared campuses, and the translation of critical education theory into practice.

Kate Sullivan is a high school English teacher at the Media Academy, a small school on the Fremont High School campus in Oakland, California. She graduated from the University of Kansas with degrees in English and American studies.

Exchanging Difference

Sinh Le, a seventeen-year-old Vietnamese American girl born in the Philippines, was a writing exchange partner for four months with Denise Lew, a twenty-four-year-old Chinese American woman born and raised in San Francisco. Sinh was a student in one of two participating senior English classes at an urban high school, a new small school that was one of the reform efforts in an older, magnet high school that had a long history of low achievement. Denise, a third-year doctoral student, was one of 44 students in a graduate class on urban education during the fall semester of 2006. Fifteen of these graduate students were preservice teachers.

Over the course of the semester, Sinh and Denise as well as all of the other high school and graduate students exchanged letters, essays, and personal reflections. "I'm so excited to begin our writing exchange," Denise wrote in her first correspondence. "I think it's a great way to meet others in the community and to improve our writing skills." Individuals in the partnering groups had significant differences in age, ethnicity, socioeconomic status, neighborhoods of residence, and cultures. Yet, as Denise's statement suggested, the graduate students felt they could learn as much from the exchange as the high school students. The high school students felt similarly, as reflected in comments like the one sent by Cynthia Fausto, who works evenings at K-Mart. She wrote, "I gladly answer your letters because this kind of helps me develop my writing skills, and I also get to know college graduates." Her classmate Marcelina Perez added, "I feel good that we did this exchange because living in an urban area it's not easy to talk or even write to college students."

"It doesn't take long," Kate Sullivan (the collaborating high school teacher) noted, "for a casual observer in a secondary English classroom to understand that few students approach teacher-assigned writing tasks with the kind of investment and attention to detail that are essential if they are going to improve at academic writing." She continued,

> The yearlong writing curriculum in a standard high school English class appears as a parade of irrelevant words and equally extraneous tasks—*Expository! Narrative! Persuasive!*—and even when the subject is captivating or self-selected, students complete the task as if a chore, cutting corners as long as the job is basically done. But in other realms of their lives that require writing—from text messaging, to email, to notes exchanged between friends—that ennui is nonexistent. The writing exchange has allowed my students to bridge the gap between academic writing and writing as communication with (relative) peers. In writing for strangers, they felt a sense of responsibility to write well grammatically and conceptually, and to really commit themselves to this exchange out of respect for their partners. This unparalleled sense of responsibility and commitment to a writing assignment developed easily when it was clear from the college students' first letter that they really cared about the backgrounds and successes of their high school counterparts. My students met every new letter thereafter with eager anticipation and produced multi-page responses by the end of the class period. It is to date the most productive and beautifully loquacious that they have ever been.

We also feel that this writing exchange offered insights into individual writing processes, as well as viable writing strategies for developing academic writers that contribute to the conceptual framing and practices of teaching writing. We discuss how a writing exchange, when effectively designed and organized, can address a number of things that often work to impede academic writing development, particularly for struggling writers. From their writing for real purposes and real audiences, we used the work and words of the writers themselves to reveal how this exchange increased student motivation to write; how it facilitated students sustaining their practice of writing and revising; how it provided a systematic sequence for writing development from structured personal writing to argumentative essays; how it contributed to the generation of ideas for writing; how it allowed for honest engagement of difficult topics like racial, ethnic, gender, generational, and geographic differences; how it enhanced interpersonal connections and a sense of community; and how it provided a level of in-depth analysis of student writing that would be virtually impossible under normal classroom circumstances. As high school student America Rodriguez wrote, "I didn't really think that I would benefit from it, but I did, a lot. I'm more into writing even if I'm still a bad speller."

Leslie Plettner originated the idea for our writing exchange. She was the Bay Area Coalition for Equitable Schools' (BayCES) coach for the small school that partnered with a graduate, urban education class. Jabari Mahiri (the professor for the graduate class and a board member of BayCES), Alexis Martin (a doctoral candidate and graduate student instructor for the class), and Kate Sullivan (the high school teacher) collaborated to develop and implement the idea. With permission, we have identified the students by name when quoting from their writing, comments, or interviews. Four rounds of writing exchanges were completed that produced more than 350 pieces of varied genres of writing during the fall semester of 2006. Copies were made of each piece of writing, and our analysis of these, along with email exchanges and taped interviews of some of the participants is the basis for the discussion in this chapter.

"Because this exchange comes at a time when these students are confronting huge decisions, from finishing high school to working full-time to attending college," Kate reflected, "it really helped them see that the doors are open, and that they *can* succeed in the ways they want, particularly if they learn to master written communication." The overall spirit of the exchange was consistent with the comment of graduate student Megan Spevek who noted, "young people could really get to know college students on a personal level [creating] human connections that may help them discover that higher education can be their reality." The writing exchange sought to acknowledge difference, but also to discover human connections beyond difference or indifference.

Developing Writing

Freedman and her colleagues created a writing exchange that became a trans-Atlantic dialogue between middle and high school students in the San Francisco Bay Area and students in London. In part, she was interested in ways that the writing exchange could facilitate the study of cultural boundaries. Her framework of teaching through social dialogues, theorized through the work of Vygotsky, Wertsch, and Bakhtin, was useful for conceptualizing the kinds of practices we included in our writing exchange.

Like Freedman, we wanted to explore how intellectual and skill development of student learners could be enhanced through communicative and social interactions with more expert writers. In our case the more expert writers assisting interactions within the Vygotskian (1978) "zone of proximal development" were the graduate students in the urban education class. In commenting on these communicative and social interactions, Denise actually echoed Vygotsky's "buds" or "flowers" being assisted to "fruit" metaphor of the learning process (86). Vygotsky by saying she saw her high school writing partner "like a budding rose, barely opening up to the world," but added that she "sees a lot of herself" in her partner too.

Following Delpit (1991), we felt the exchange could help make the codes of writing in academic discourse, the "processes or procedures that literate people consciously control which enable them to comprehend and compose text" (541), more explicit for the high school students. We designed the assignments for the early writings such that they could provide, or be revised toward, clear models of specific techniques used by competent writers of academic essays. We were also attempting to stimulate more of a college-going culture by revealing and providing cultural modeling activity through asynchronous communication and social engagement (Lee 2001).

As Gee noted, control over a discourse, any of the numerous varieties of academic discourses, required the appropriation of an "identity kit" that included "ways of using language, of thinking, and of acting" that would get one recognized as a member of a particular discourse (1991, 3). For example, researchers from the nonprofit Editorial Project in Education Research Center in Washington, D.C., found thirteen distinct measures highly associated with young people's academic success including having parents who earned at least a mid-level income, completed college, held full-time jobs, and spoke fluent English. According to this study, California, the state in which our writing partners lived, had by far the nation's lowest percentage of children whose parents spoke fluent English—sixty-two percent (Asimov 2007).

Finally, the exchange addressed specific considerations for developing writing from Mahiri (1998). These included increasing the understanding of both writing groups that a key aspect of the social practices associated with academic writing as reflected in the idea of "edited texts." Mahiri noted:

> As we acknowledge and honor the validity of ways that students may be comfortable speaking and writing in culturally specific contexts, we can also make explicit and accessible the conventions, strategies, and skills that attend to edited texts…[the] intense, dynamic, and often collaborative activity…required to produce each piece of edited English (60).

Exchanging Writing

The writing exchange had five phases. First was an introductory essay-styled letter exchange. Next was a follow-up letter exchange to extend the process of the writing partners getting to know each other. Then the high school students wrote argumentative essays based on an SAT-styled prompt, and the graduate students wrote responses in essay form to these arguments. In the last writing exchange, the graduate students sent letters, along with copies of their personal statements for college to the high school students who then wrote and sent drafts of their intended personal statements back to receive the graduate students' last written response. Finally, a party was scheduled at the end of the semester that brought the high school and graduate students together on the university's campus to meet and further share their experiences.

In an attempt to increase the comfort level for the initial exchanges, high school and graduate students were matched by gender and racial or ethnic background to the greatest extent possible. As a result over ninety percent of the students were paired with a partner of the same gender, and a majority of those partnerships also shared something in common regarding racial or ethnic backgrounds. In this regard high school student Angelica Luna-Acosta noted, "I felt like my partner was matched with me for a reason. She helped me gain confidence in my writing and treated me like an individual, not a child or some 'random teen' who she was just writing to so she can pass her class. Every letter was sincere and helpful with much advice."

Replicating this type of exchange would not be difficult; the first step for a high school teacher would be to contact an instructor for preservice teachers at a local college or university. Because the exchange proved so beneficial in assisting future teachers and other graduate students in getting to know and work with local students in a nontraditional manner, we believe that most teacher preparation instructors would be interested in implementing such an exchange. Though we held two meetings to set everything up, most of the ongoing logistical dialogue was done via phone and email. Our first meeting was to discuss the goals and mission of the exchange, as well as agree on dates throughout the semester when letters and assignments would be due. About halfway through the semester, we met again to check in with each other and to plan the end-of-semester party. Kate and Alexis met at mutually convenient times and locations to give each other the stacks of letters and essays. We did not discourage either group of students from exchanging contact information; in fact, several exchanges were facilitated via email. However, they were not to meet each other until the final end-of-semester party.

Structuring Introductions

To start the exchange, the graduate students were asked to write initial, essay-styled letters to introduce themselves to the high school students. There were two additional purposes for these initial writings. The first was to provide clear models that contained essential elements of an academic essay, even though it was in the form of an introductory letter. Kate then had her high school students emulate some of these elements in their written responses to their newly identified writing partners. The second purpose was to introduce and describe a multi-textual identification project that the graduate students had done to build community in the class, and that the high school students also were going to do.

Based on work of Mahiri, we felt that the selection of particular types of texts for models, joined with appropriate pedagogical strategies, could be highly effective in helping students practice and develop specifically targeted writing strategies. He had found that struggling writers were able to replicate complex stylistic devices, specific grammatical structures, and sophisticated rhetorical strategies that they were guided to practice in conjunction with selected writing models (Mahiri 1998, 78–82).

The graduate students were given an assignment sheet that specified how the first correspondence was to be structured and thematically focused. They were asked to handwrite it to make it more personal for the high school students. It was also to be exactly four paragraphs, with each paragraph being focused and written as a model of coherent paragraph development. The first paragraph was to provide a personal introduction that included discussion of interest in the writing exchange and announcement of the multi-text identification project that each graduate student had done. The second paragraph was to provide a detailed description of a class project. The third paragraph was for each individual to reflect on why they constructed their project the way they did, the choices they made for texts and foci, and the essence of identity that they wanted to communicate to others. The fourth paragraph was to model a well-developed conclusion and to also invite the high school partners to write a response that revealed how they would do a project like this to introduce themselves to classmates and their teacher.

Kate had coordinated the timing of assignments in her English class to include a similar project. She announced it right after her students received their first correspondence so that they could use ideas and models from the graduate students for their own projects as well as for their first letter responses. HiHiInterestingly, high school student Adrian Ambriz responded in a way that made it seem as if this structured connection was a bit mysterious. "I think it's cool that we get to write to each other too. But anyway, for some reason my class had to do that same project about ourselves."

In attempting to facilitate a community of learners and as a way to begin exploration of multiple literacies revealed in multimodal texts, both the high school and graduate students were asked to develop a creative way of presenting themselves to their respective classmates in a multi-textual format, an idea that came from former graduate student instructor Dawn Williams. Some students chose to use computers to create their projects, but it was made clear that other textual mediums were as viable and as valued. This helped students like Phil Miller who noted, "I'm not a very 'computery' type person." In addition to Power-Point slide shows and web based presentations, high school and graduate students created mini-movie DVDs; revamped cereal boxes, hat boxes, fish bowls, and other artifacts with personal pictures and messages; baked and shared cookies, cakes, and other foods; played musical instruments; and performed original poems, songs, skits, and dances.

Excerpts from Lara Hale's first correspondence to her partner provides an example of one of the nondigital projects:

> I chose something that was already part of my life: a pair of old, patched-up blue overalls. My mom wore them before I was born, and handed them down to me when I was in high school. Each piece of fabric reminds me of a piece of clothing that someone in my family once wore...Each of the patches reminds me of a story about them—patching [was] as a way to show my history.

Cynthia achieved a similar affect with her high school class with bracelets. "I wore more than 20 and explained [how] each and every single one of them represented my family and friends."

The emotional and creative qualities of making and presenting the projects were expressed by many students. Michelle McConnell noted, for example, "that as I shared 'My Life in a Fishbowl' with my classmates...I had to fight back tears." After describing her "memory box," Emma Katznelson told her partner that the "assignment was a really terrific way to get to know the people in my community. I was amazed at how creative and inventive everyone was." Robyn Gould actually invited her writing partner to view the project that she created online on MySpace. "As the main site for meeting new people," she wrote, "it seemed an ideal medium for introducing important people in my life to my classmates...and I became a pro at creating MySpace profiles!"

The high school students' responses to these introductory letters showed that they were usually able to replicate the structure as well as elements of paragraph development in their own writing as these features had been modeled by the graduate students. They also showed that from the very start of the exchange, the high school students were highly motivated and excited by writing to real audiences. The personal identification projects that they presented to their classmates, and wrote about to their exchange partners, reflected similar creativity and emotional content to those completed by the graduate students. Lydia Deflorio noted to her high school partner in one correspondence that "Your enthusiasm and energy were contagious and I found myself smiling a lot as I read [about your project]."

In another example, high school student Marcelina Perez wrote, "I learned many things about my classmates, and how life is a struggle and things I didn't know about them and how hard it is. There was crying and a lot of emotion in response to my classmates' projects." High school student Stephanie Chao had written that "One of the girls sang [a song she wrote for her deceased grandmother] and I started really crying because it was touching but that was weird because I am not that sensitive…[But] four of the students started crying and man did I tear up." She continued saying, "After this project I started really thinking deep as to what I want to do. I'm a senior in high school and I know the real world is right around the corner…and I'm afraid to admit it, but I'm actually really scared!" Stehpanie's partner, Jill Antal, wrote "I think we don't often get a chance to really show people who we are on the inside, and that experience can be very powerful and moving. It seems we spend a lot of energy projecting our 'outer selves' to the world, but we only let a few people close enough to see us as we really see ourselves."

Extending Connections

The second writing exchange was not tightly structured like the first, but it had the goal of continuing to build relationships between writing partners through written discussions of their points of similarity and difference. After the initial personal contact had been made, both groups were told they could type their subsequent responses. Both were surprised to see that beyond generational, geographic, racial, ethnic, and cultural differences, they found many interesting points of connection. We felt this phase was crucial because the future exchanges involved the graduate students offering direct suggestions for the high school students to strengthen their writing of SAT-styled essays and personal statements for college. The way the high school students responded to these suggestions, we felt, would be determined by the kind of personal relationships that were emerging.

There were numerous ways that connections were made. Like Stephanie, many of the students opened up personally, and honestly discussed some of their struggles and vulnerabilities. Jacqueline Bermudez talked about how her writing partner "helped me through my hard times," but that she also "helped me understand that I need to go to college to get ahead in life. At first I was skeptical about going to college or what I would study, money and housing. [She] helped me find colleges that would help me in all of that." Kelly Middlebrook and Viet-Ly Nguyen were among those who shared that they were very shy in class and having to make oral presentations made them extremely nervous. They both admitted that they had designed projects that would not require them to do much talking.

Kelly went on to talk about her racial identity "which is biracial—American Indian and Irish—and [she] discussed the implications of looking white in a minority community." In response to a consideration from her writing partner about being bi-racial, Katie Schmidt wrote that she had often dated interracially and at times had thought that she might "have beautifully mixed children." Her writing partner, Peter Roth, had noted that he had been "raised in a Mormon and Buddhist family" and that he was "very mixed" and didn't identify with a single culture. But he had a theory that "the more mixed people in our society the less racist we will be."

Race came up frequently in the exchanges. Martin Smith wrote about how he had challenged stereotypical beliefs from other black teammates in college basketball "by explaining that conceding that black people are inherently better athletes means that it is alright to assign specific biological characteristics to an entire race." Denise shared with her partner that as a Chinese American attending a private Catholic school, she was continually "around a lot of wealthy, religious, white kids form the suburbs." She later commented, "I always perceived myself as inferior to my classmates   all I wanted as a young girl was to be 'white' like the other girls in my class; I just wanted to be like them so I could be 'happy.' Isn't that sad? My ethnic and familial shame lasted for years until I traveled and studied in Asia when I was twenty. I admit that I still struggle with it now."

The writing partners found many other similarities and differences. Helen Salcedo learned that she and her high school writing partner both had parents from Mexico. When graduate student Zoe Segnitz learned that her writing partner was fluent in Spanish, she wrote back to her in Spanish for about one-third of the next correspondence. Jordan, a graduate student who described himself as Filipino/Chicano, compared experiences with his writing partner who was Guatemalan/Jewish. Martin found that he and his high school writing partner were both from large families with lots of children. Sam Stevens talked about growing up on the Navajo Indian Reservation in New Mexico and earning a B.A. in Anthropology from Arizona State University. Melike Acar wrote about being born and raised in Turkey and recently coming to the United States to attend graduate school, while high school student Julie Garana wrote of being born and raised in the Philippines and of her experiences coming to the United States just last year. "At first, it was a challenge for me to speak English, and until now, I'm still learning how to speak it. My family and I are now living in [what] I consider as the most dangerous city I've ever been to."

Julie's classmate, Lalo Navarro expressed a different view of the same city to his graduate student writing partner, Oscar Medina. Lalo wrote, "I find it very interesting how you grew up, it's kinda similar to how I grew up also." He went on to say, "I found out that we were like the same person. We come from the same type of neighborhood, had the same type of problems when we were growing up, and to see someone like him go to Cal coming from the neighborhood that he came from only let me know that I can do it also." Oscar had responded, "the reason I go to class is to learn from *them* and their segregated lives. From your writing," Oscar continued, "I can tell you are a multilingual, multicultural, and multi-talented individual."

The intensity and honesty of the writing partners allowed them to express what they knew and explore things that were new. They were forming interpersonal connections and a sense of community that allowed for the engagement of difficult and, at times, provocative topics. These were some of the reasons that the partners were motivated to sustain and develop their writing beyond the use of things like grades for motivation.

Responding Persuasively

Kate assigned her high school students' to write an argumentative essay that responded to an SAT-type prompt. The essays were sent directly to the graduate student writing partners for their responses on how to strengthen both the arguments presented and the overall writing of the papers. The graduate students were given considerable latitude on how to formulate their responses, but they had to include a least a one-page discussion on a separate sheet that first pointed out the strengths of each paper, and then things that could make it stronger. Angelica talked about how it felt to receive her writing partner's response:

> My favorite exchange was when we wrote a persuasive essay on the question: 'Do circumstances rule men or are men architects of their own destinies?' It's my favorite because it was a topic I strongly agreed and disagreed with and I think it's the only essay I've ever been happy to write. But I remember when I got my partner's letter back and saw that my essay needed corrections. At first, I felt discouraged because I felt as if I've never written an essay before. But then I realized that my partner truly wanted to help me improve my writing and not tear me down.

A few examples are provided to represent the extensiveness of the graduate students' responses. Although personal connections had been made for two months through the earlier essays, and through the fact that the two groups had began to exchange emails and visit each other's websites on their own, considerable attention was paid to the preparation for and tone of the responses. In responding to the persuasive essays, the graduate students challenged themselves to respond persuasively, or in other words, in ways that would help ensure that the high school students actually took their advice. Kelly, for example, started by saying, "I love the idea of collaborating with other students, so I'm really excited to have this opportunity to work with you. Throughout every step of my education I have had friends, family, and mentors who helped me to realize my potential as a writer. It's really wonderful to be given the chance to work with you in the same capacity as my mentors worked with me." Using herself as an example, Kelly was attempting to help her writing partner see that everyone's academic writing goes through an editing and revising process and that this should be seen as a natural part of writing.

The technique of using one's self as an example of the considerations that were being made for the high school writer to improve his or her work permeated graduate student responses. The following one by Katie exemplified this and other strategies.

> While I definitely understand your persuasive argument…there are some things you could do to make it even stronger. First, in the opening paragraph, you eventually want to lay out a 'sneak preview' of everything that is to come…Another thing to work on is your transitions, which is an area that I always struggled with in high school (and still do)…Finally, have a few friends read your paper over to help you catch [grammatical errors], or read it aloud yourself a few times…You will also see where you have fragments that need to attach to the sentence before or after.

Often, the graduate students also sensitively challenged the ideas and thinking in the persuasive essays. After Kate Walsh-Cunnane talked about the strengths in her writing partner's argument, she responded directly to the logic of some of the ideas. In part she wrote:

> I thought the idea to use *Of Mice and Men* was great because I think it fits in well with your theme. But the example you used is where George kills Lennie so that he can go his own way. Do you think this is right? You might want to think more about if George killing Lennie represents him taking control, or if it represents him feeling powerless to help or change Lennie.

Similarly, when Jeremy Brett felt his writing partner was putting forth a provocative example without sufficient substance, he offered the following alternative insights:

> I agree that Hitler made his own life course. But what about all the people who died in the Holocaust? What happened to their lives? I mean, in some way they weren't free to choose their life courses, but were victims of the Nazi regime.

Our belief was that graduate students would be able to go to some lengths to offer revision suggestions, and even conceptual challenges, because personal relationships had been build first. Additionally, the level and depth of analysis and response that the graduate students provided for each of the essays would be nearly impossible to achieve under normal classroom conditions by a single teacher. Kate felt that the dialogues around the persuasive essay were extremely helpful to her students in their continuing work to develop the quality of their papers based on the ideas they received. Even through critique, the strength of the interpersonal relationships was preserved and reflected in the overall substance and affirming tone of the responses. They seemed to have gained each other's trust as reflected in Zoe's closing statement to her partner. "Thank you for trusting me with your paper. I loved reading it. I can't wait to read more." And the academic effects went beyond the writing. As high school student Mercedes Saeteurn noted, "I think the experience has changed me. I'm more talkative in class than before. It was weird, because when I first started talking to my partner, I had no idea what to say, but the more we talk the more it seems like we (have) known one another for a very long time."

Getting Personal

The final formal exchange of writing involved the graduate students sending letters along with copies of their personal statements for college to the high school students. As Lara wrote, it was "a personal statement that I wrote in twelfth grade when I was applying to college." In addition to providing successful writing models, this exchange also had the effect of providing exchange partners with additional information, particularly with respect to how the participants viewed their strengths and saw their goals for the future.

Kate had assigned her high school seniors to review the statements they received, and then to write a draft of their own personal statement for college to share with the graduate students. They in turn wrote responses back to the high school students, acknowledging strengths and suggesting ways to revise and improve the statements. Again, the graduate students were asked to write a letter response along with making direct notations for revising on the high school students' drafts. Amazingly, some of these letter responses were two or three pages of single-spaced type. Graduate students used these accompanying letters to talk about considerations for going to college and for going through life that went far beyond guidance on the writing of personal statements.

For example, Lydia shared her views regarding larger considerations of the admissions process. "I going to be really honest with you," she told her writing partner…I believe that in many ways [the admissions process] was designed to keep certain people out of college…But, I also believe that college is important—especially for the people they are trying to keep out. For me, college is where I learned to think…skills I acquired in college carried over into every part of my life in very important ways, and I am now in a position where I can sometimes force people in power to take me seriously and listen to what I have to say."

David Watts actually shared part of his original rejection letter to the university— "After careful review, we are sorry that we are unable to offer you admission for the fall semester." His point to his writing partner was that even though he had to start his fresh-man year at another school, he stay poised and eventually gained admission to his first choice school. Megan Low reminded her writing partner that the personal statement, like the previous essay, also had to be considered a persuasive essay. "You really want to be per-suading your readers as to why it's possible for you to do whatever you want to do" in terms of higher education. Megan had been a professional dancer with the San Francisco Ballet before returning for a graduate degree. She told her writing partner that she had to also do some persuading in order to get back into college because "there are many stereo-types associated with ballet dancers. Many people think that we are just a bunch of skinny girls who do a lot of dancing and not much thinking...I've attached an essay of my own to this letter so that you could read a sample of my writing. This is the essay I used to get into graduate school."

In the end, the high school students received the kind of guidance and response to their personal statement drafts that may not have been available, even from the most well intentioned college and career counselors.

Meeting Partners

A party was scheduled at the end of the semester that brought the writing partners together on the university's campus to meet and further share their experiences. Kate had secured parental permission to bring her students to the university for the event, but noted that "Even the most outgoing of them were feeling some trepidation as we trekked to the cam-pus. Yet, the time spent talking with their partners in person and connecting on a different level really confirmed for them that they had a support system if they wanted it, and that college had provided the graduate students with many opportunities that my students could have too if they wanted it."

Everyone provided food, and there was music. There was almost 100 percent atten-dance, so there were over 90 people in the room. Initially, the writing partners had to find each other in the cacophonous crowd. After socializing for a while, several high school and graduate students volunteered to present their multi-textual identification projects. There were brief discussions about a redecorated cereal box and a decorated Styrofoam head. Then, America sung her emotional tribute to her grandmother entitled "Angel Above" that she had earlier performed for her high school class, and everyone clapped along to keep time.

Toward the end, a number of people talked on audiotape about the significance of the exchange. High school student Angelica commented, "This experience was very impor-tant to me...I decided to completely go into it, and I met a wonderful person, and her name is Helen. With my friends, I'm very open, but it's hard to open up to strangers. And having someone open up to you kind of encourages you to do same...Yeah, I grew a lot from this experience." Interestingly, Jacqueline, another high school girl, found it actually easier to write to strangers. She said, "the writing exchange is like someone to talk to that doesn't know anything about you. So it's like a third party...If you are talking to a total stranger, it's like they might have a different point of view that you wouldn't get from your friends or parents. It was like a friend that doesn't know you, but in a way they do know you. So, I liked it."

High school student Jose said, "To me, I thought it was a good thing. Like in school the teacher would give us something, just a topic to write about, and I would just have to sit there and try to think about stuff to write. But with my partner, I was just writing to him, and I wasn't stressing or anything. So it was like a better idea." Sam was Jose's partner, and he responded to him once again by saying, "Yeah, this was pretty cool. I've never done anything like this, like hang out with a high school student…And then meeting him was really weird because when I saw him walking this way, I thought that's probably the guy right there. Then I saw his name tag, and I said like whoa…It's surreal almost. It's kinda like hanging out with one of my brothers."

In their own words, students expressed ways that writing had been approached as a human endeavor with real purposes and real audiences. With a systematic design and effective administration, writing exchanges can also have real developmental consequences for writers who want to increase their facility with essential aspects of academic discourse. They can provide motivation, idea generation, and sustained engagement and practice with different academic genres. They can also work in ways that sustain engagement with difference.

In talking about her students' reaction to the exchange at the final party, their teacher Kate, said, "I will say that this has been amazing. I have never seen you guys get so into writing than when I'm giving you your next letter, you just tear it open! Yeah, they do. They just really get into it." Her student, Cynthia Fausto, provided a final expression of the hopes that all of the participants had for this experience. "This writing exchange inspired me into majoring in linguistics because we have so many people in the state of California that don't know how to speak English that need help, as well as others that would like to learn other languages…One thing I know for sure is that I would definitely do the writing exchange again, and maybe next time I will be the college student."

Works Cited

Asimov, Nanette. 2007. "State's Children Less Likely to Succeed: California 34th in Nation in Study of Criteria that Help Identify Chances to Excel." *San Francisco Chronicle* (January 4): 1, 13.

Delpit, Lisa. 1991. "A Conversation with Lisa Delpit." *Language Arts* (68): 541–547.

Freedman, Sarah W. 1994. *Exchanging Writing, Exchanging Cultures: Lessons in School Reform from the United States and Great Britain.* Cambridge, MA: Harvard University Press (and NCTE Press).

Gee, James. 1991. "What is Literacy?" In *Rewriting Literacy: Culture and the Discourse of the Other.* Ed. Candace Mitchell and Kathleen Weiler. New York: Bergin and Garvey: 3–11.

Lee, Carol D. 2001. "Is October Brown Chinese? A Cultural Modeling Activity System for Under-achieving Students. *American Educational Research Journal* 38 (1): 97–141.

Mahiri, Jabari. 1998. *Shooting for Excellence: African American and Youth Culture in New Century Schools.* New York: Teachers College Press (and NCTE Press).

Vygotsky, Lev S. 1978. *Mind and Society: The Development of Higher Psychological Processes.* Cambridge, MA: Harvard University Press.

22

Students with Special Needs

Richard Kent

Richard Kent is director of the Maine Writing Project, a site of the National Writing Project, and an assistant professor of literacy at the University of Maine. After twenty-one years of teaching and coaching in a small town in Maine, he moved west to pursue a Ph.D. and work as a teacher educator in the high schools of Los Angeles. Kent is the author of two young adult novels, a chapbook of poetry, and three books focused on secondary English teaching. A Maine State Teacher of the Year and National Educator Award recipient, Kent researches writing to learn in athletics and serves as a consultant to athletes and coaches as they develop training programs and utilize Athletes' Journals and Team Notebooks.

Everybody is talented, original, and has something important to say.
—Brenda Ueland, If You Want to Write

Six years into this new century, the national news featured the story of Jason McElwain, a seventeen-year-old high school senior from Rochester, New York, who for several years had served as the manager of the boys' varsity basketball team. But in the final home game the coach added Jason to the roster and gave him a uniform so that he could sit on the bench as a player. With the game well in hand and four minutes left, the coach pointed to the boy who previously collected towels and shagged errant foul shots for his teammates. In that moment, Jason's dream came true: he was playing varsity ball. Six three-point baskets later pandemonium erupted. Hoisted onto the shoulders of his teammates and surrounded by hundreds of screaming fans, Jason was carried from the court. The story is extra special, as you may know, because Jason lives with autism.

When I grew up in the 1950s and 1960s, kids like Jason didn't go to school with us. Cloistered in large institutions or kept at home, children with disabilities of all kinds were

(1) That to the maximum extent appropriate, children with disabilities, including children in public or private institutions or other care facilities, are educated with children who are non-disabled; and (2) That special classes, separate schooling or other removal of children with disabilities from the regular educational environment occurs only if the nature or severity of the disability is such that education in regular classes with the use of supplementary aids and services cannot be achieved satisfactorily. [20 USC 1412 Section 612 (a) (5), and its implementing regulation found at 34 C.F.R. ß300.114(a)].

Figure 1 Individuals with Disabilities Education Act (IDEA)

RESOLVED, that the National Council of Teachers of English support curricula, programs, and practices that avoid tracking, a system which limits students' intellectual, linguistic, and/or social development;

that NCTE urge educators and other policy makers to reexamine curricula, programs, and practices which require or encourage tracking of students in English language arts;

that NCTE support teachers in their efforts to retain students in or return students to heterogeneous language arts placement; and

that NCTE expand its efforts to educate the public about the effects of tracking.

NCTE Committee on Tracking and Ability Grouping in the English Language Arts Classrooms, K–12

Figure 2 NCTE's Opposing Tracking

not included in mainstream society. Our great loss. But thanks to IDEA, the Individuals with Disabilities Education Act (Figure 1), and backed by statements such as NCTE's opposing tracking (Figure 2), today's classrooms welcome a wide variety of learners. Although not everyone agrees with mixed groups, my experience has been that including everybody adds richness to our classrooms and schools.

Managing a twenty-first-century language arts classroom that welcomes diverse writers—as well as a variety of readers, speakers, listeners, artists, musicians, athletes, mathematicians, and scientists—is tricky. There's no single formula, template, or textbook to guide us in this work. Our students arrive, each one with an assortment of gifts and challenges as writers, learners, *and* as people, and that's where we begin.

In the next section of this chapter, you're faced with a single-spaced manuscript, "During Christmas vacation and The other Vacation's". Your assignment: Read the story.

During Christmas vacation and The other Vacation's, On Christmas eve morning me and my dad went up in the woods to go make a couple of hitches. When we got there we tried to start up the skitter after a while we got it started we put the chokechains on the back of the skitter. After I got done putting the chokechains on I put my chap's on and got onto the skitter and went to go get a hitch of tree's. When my dad cut's down tree's I have to hitch them up and if I feel like I limb the tree's sometimes. Around 12:00 we ate lunch and headed back up to get more hitches of wood when we went back down to the yard the pulp truck was there so I unhooked the log's and went to park the skitter. About 3 minutes later my dad's boss showed up. We had to pull the pulp truck up into the yard. When we got it up there we un hooked the pulp truck from the skitter and he started loading the truck up. My dad was up in the back of the trucks body piling the wood right so it would'nt fall out. My dad's boss went to start up the skitter to fuel it up and oil it. the fuel was down in his truck so he brough the skitter down there and fueled it up. When we got done we parked the skitter by my dad's truck well not to close. When we got done loading the pulp truck we picked up to go home when we got home we changed and I went down stairs to go see what my grandfather was doing he said nothing so I went out side and Chris came over and we went on the back trail to clean the tree's out of the way we're not done yet. When we have time we're going to finish it When I got home we went to a friends house his name is Leelin he is probably 56 years old he is a real friend to us. When we went home me and Chris played Super Tecmo Bowl and Street Fighter II. After I went home and ate supper. And after I went down stairs because we had a Christmas eve party my aunts and uncles and all of my cousins and my grandparents. Well it was there house we had it in I live up stairs from them. We have a it every year down there. After I went up stairs because we had company to then we had a little Christmas ever party to my parents went out and I went to East Andover with my grandmother to go get my cousins Regine 10 years old and my other cousin Eric 7 years old. I stayed down down my grandparent's house for the night. The next me Eric, and my other cousin Robert. A week later I went up in the woods with my dad and my grandfather when we got up there we tried to start up the skitter but it wouldn't start so my dad said forget it so we cut some boat wood up and loaded up the three trucks I had one my dad had one and my grandfather had his well I had my grandfathers scout four wheel drive. After we got done loading up the trucks we got in them and headed for home we drove the galond pond road over to my house the when I got home I seen my cousin Robbie running back and forth over to my uncles house across the road from my cousins house and my uncle lives next door to me. Anyway I went over to see what was wrong I went into the house and it was full of smoke so I called the fire Department because it was a fire. Anyway the house burnt flat down I helped hold the water hose. What a New Year he had huh. Right now they are making out good. Anyway he had good Insurance. After it was done I went home and brought up wood and ate and them I left

The End

Peter Stryker

Peter's Story: Another Way of Seeing

When I first began to read "During Christmas vacation and The other Vacation's," the corrector in me surfaced. I scoffed at the title and how it ran into the text. The single spacing annoyed me. I began inserting commas, changing constructions, and figuring out how I could fix all of the run-ons.

I'm not sure exactly what made me stop dead in my correcting tracks. Part of it must have been the guilt I felt for marking up Peter's story without his permission, a courtesy I automatically afforded all writers. Did I take Peter's writing less seriously because he was a student with special needs? Then the echoes from the previous summer reverberated. My teacher Michael Armstrong at the Bread Loaf School of English asked, "How do we represent to children the quality and potential of their thinking? The first requirement is to recognize the authority of children's texts."

The authority of children's texts.

Peter's resource room teacher, John Jamison, had handed me the story early one morning. "Got any suggestions?" I sensed John's frustration, but admired his patience and his gentle manner. He believed in his students, he respected them.

Again, from my Bread Loaf class, Michael Armstrong's voice cut through the haze. "To teach writing, in a sense, is a way of teaching people to tell the stories of their lives." I put the pencil down and started to read Peter's story again, from the beginning. This time I read like a writer, a coach, and a caring friend. I looked for the power and the potentiality of Peter's story.

I didn't have to look far, and here is what I wrote back to his teacher:

Dear John,

Peter's retelling of his holiday is fascinating. The expressive nature of the piece makes it most engaging. There are no pretensions, no ambiguities, and nothing self-conscious about the writing…what we see is what we get. The honesty behind such a piece is rich, warm, and refreshing—I felt as if I were being invited into Peter's family and into his life. At the end I felt trusted and honored to have been included.

Peter is most detailed in his opening few lines about his Christmas Eve work with his "dad" and the "skitter." From his writing I feel a sense of understanding and maturity on Peter's behalf when it comes to work in the woods.

In the woods Peter is capable, confident, and knowledgeable. There, he would be my teacher.

It's obvious through his retelling that Peter is trusted by his father. Their relationship sounds wonderful—father and son working together in the woods—what a healthy and sound relationship to read about. I don't hear anything about Peter being ordered into the woods to work with his father: "…me and my dad went up in the woods to go make a couple of hitches."

Peter's voice throughout is even tempered and kind. He never assumes, he never pushes. What I truly loved was that the "work" didn't sound like labor. To the contrary, Peter and his dad joined in celebration of sorts…listen to the relationship:

"When we got done we parked the skitter by my dad's truck well not to close. When we got done loading the pulp truck we picked up to go home when we got home we changed…"

For most of this expressive piece, Peter is deeply involved in relationship. He talks about himself briefly, but the mainstay of his writing is involved with others. People matter to Peter.

"…we went to a friends house his name is Leelin he is probably 56 years old he is a real friend to us."

The more I read the piece, the deeper I listen to Peter, the more I come to know how wonderfully warm he is as a person. He identifies his cousins by name and age. This detail shows respect for the reader and, undoubtedly, for his cousins. They're not just names.

The precision of Peter's description brings life to the piece. It's not just a truck, it's a "scout four wheel drive." It's not simply Nintendo, it's "Super Tecmo Bowl and Street Fighter II." It's not wood, it's "boat wood." Detail after detail shows Peter's force as an author and as a storyteller. In its purest form, this writing has a kind of brilliance within it that the average reader might lose if bothered by the lack of "correctness."

If I were to grade the variety of sentence structures in this piece, Peter would receive high marks. His writing is rich with diversity—a pleasant combination of variety. Many young adult writers struggle getting beyond noun-verb-complement sentence structures. Peter has avoided the trap of "I went to the woods...I drove the skidder...I ate lunch."

His is an active piece that is filled with phrases and clauses and literary techniques that usher the reader into and through the story. Listen:

"When we went home..."

"On Christmas eve morning..."

"Anyway I went over..."

"Well, it was there house..."

"A week later I went up..."

In the last few lines we hear the conclusion building. The house didn't just burn, "the house burnt flat down and I helped hold the water hose." Details, always details. And then the personal side—back to considering the reader: "What a New Year he had huh." He speaks directly to us. Again, no pretension, no showboating, no melodrama.

Peter's piece ends simply and honestly. "After it was done I went home and brought up wood and ate and them I left."

Peter is an author. He has developed an engaging story that skillfully takes the listener through a ten-day period with the kind of detail that all fine writers aspire to. Once the reader allows him- or herself to get beyond the technical differences of Peter's style compared to what most consider as acceptable, this young man's writing creates music with its rich and wonderfully composed descriptive passages.

Warmly,
Rich

"Now I see," said John.
So did I.
Peter wrote many stories that year. The next one had the same number of "grammaticals" as his Christmas story, but it was double-spaced. John had convinced him of that. When Peter brought it to me to read, I took a chance. "This is really interesting. I like it as much as your Christmas story. I'm curious about one thing, though. Listen to this." I read him the first line that had a missing word. "Duh!" he sounded, slapping his forehead in mock disgust. "Left out a word."
"After I write something it helps me to read my stuff out loud," I explained. "I catch the little mistakes."
Both John and I continued to encourage Peter. He loved coming across the hallway to share his stories with me. He especially enjoyed coming in when my room was full of students. It was not difficult to figure out why. Peter suffered from fetal alcohol syndrome

(FAS). All his life he had been relegated to special education. Now, his work—and, in a real sense, he—had busted loose.

Peter never seemed inhibited when he came to visit. Each new story showed a bit of growth. Each had the sign of an author struggling to find those best words. In time, he began to edit pieces with Mr. Jamison and keep the drafts in a folder. Whenever I saw him—in the hallways, down in the cafeteria, at sporting events—Peter would talk about his writing. "I'm doing one on the speedway up at Oxford." "I'm writing about snow machining with my uncle and cousins."

Talking with Peter about his writing had the same feel as talking with my adult writer friends. "I get stuck here after I tell about winning the race." "Sometimes the words don't come." Unlike many of my student writers, Peter's focus stayed on the story. We never diverted, chatting about the Red Sox or Celtics, spring break or summer plans. It was the story, plain and simple. His story.

If I offered even the smallest suggestion about content, Peter would adamantly reject it. He had a definite sense of the story because he had lived it. "I can't say that. That's not the way it happened."

Most times when I passed Mr. Jamison's room and glanced in, Peter sat poised at the computer, composing. In every sense of the word, he lived a writer's life. He kept regular hours. He had an editor, a readership, and a portfolio of work. He always talked story: the essence of plot, the development of character, and the elusiveness of words. Peter possessed a powerful presence as a writer.

John continually complimented me on my work with Peter. However, it didn't take long to find out exactly who, besides Peter himself, deserved credit.

After reading his third story (he cranked out two a week), I called a friend at the middle school who worked in special education. I wanted to know Peter's history as a writer. His file in the high school office had a wad of papers on disciplinary actions and a series of documentation about his FAS diagnosis, but no significant writing samples.

My friend's words are still with me: "Peter never wrote more than three lines in middle school."

Epilogue

At the end of the year, John Jamison packed up the contents of his desk and his country home. He moved to the Pacific Northwest, where he teaches today. During the last few weeks of the year, John came into my room a number of times. Before leaving, he spoke passionately out of concern for his students. "I don't think some people see what I see in these kids. They have so much to offer."

The following August, I handed the new teacher Peter's portfolio. "I thought you'd find Peter's stories fascinating. Let me know if there's anything I can do to help." She smiled. "Oh great. I can't wait to read them."

That year, Peter stopped writing altogether. The new teacher lost the collection of Peter's stories, and later, she lost her job.

Our Special Education Colleagues

Peter made out just fine. He still works in the woods cutting pulpwood for the local paper mills. He's married, and his own kids are "writing their faces off" in elementary school.

When Peter talks about his experiences back in high school, he shares stories about Mr. Jamison and Mr. Young, two of his special education teachers. These teachers helped Peter make sense of school.

Each year in my writing methods class at the university, our talk turns to students with special needs. We make a list of the various learning disabilities their future students may have and talk through accommodations they've learned about in their special education coursework (e.g., reading written information aloud, allowing extra time on exams, recording mini-lessons, providing a scribe, or using various technology). We talk about how IEPs and Section 504 plans can guide lesson planning with all kids in mind. Someone mentions web-based resources like LD Online, and another reminds us of the *International Journal of Special Education* (use your favorite search engine to find it). Just when I begin to see that frazzled look of *this is a lot to handle*, I remind them, "As a classroom teacher, you're not in this alone." For starters, look to the special education teachers or Ed. Techs. They're your number one resource.

Ms. Martel & Joshua

Cindy Martel worked closely with Joshua; she was his Ed. Tech. In class, when Joshua would buddy up with his pal Anthony, Ms. Martel moved around the room to see if anyone else needed help. She kept daily contact with Joshua's parents—they traded letters, phone calls, and more than a few laughs. (Joshua's claim to fame: Elvis impressions.) Cindy and I discussed adapting the portfolio requirements to fit Joshua. For example, he would write forty-eight journal entries per quarter, but most wouldn't be the standard class requirement of 150 words. We agreed that a variety of journal subjects motivated Joshua, and we would let the five quarterly portfolio papers serve as his in-depth pieces.

During the mid-year assessments, I asked students to write on the following prompt during a timed writing period:

> One of the purposes of education is for us to come to know ourselves and our emerging selves. Write a letter to your future college roommate or apartment-mate explaining "you." Be detailed and honest. You might use a story to help the person come to know you. Please write out your notes on the first page and your first-draft letter on the second page.

During the exam period, Cindy guided Joshua through the note-taking phase of the exercise by helping him make a list of his attributes as a person (Figure 3). First, she adapted the page setup of the examination—I had not included lines or numbers, so Cindy did. Lines kept Joshua's sentences from drifting about and, as Cindy knew, the increasing numbers motivated Joshua. Next, she helped Joshua flesh out fourteen of his traits.

Cindy framed up Joshua's letter (Figure 4) with the "To-From" and "Dear Roommate." Joshua's opening and closing sentences reveal an acute understanding of letter writing. He explains what he's writing about ("I am looking for someone to share an apartment with") and he ends by suggesting they "talk soon." Cindy provided sound advice. Additionally, notice the closing and how the boy had crossed out "Your." Joshua always signed his letters "Your friend"; in this case, however, Cindy explained mid-signature that he didn't know this future apartment-mate, so he should use "Sincerely."

Cindy and Joshua's relationship revealed the very best of what IDEA promotes. As for Joshua's relationship with his classmates?

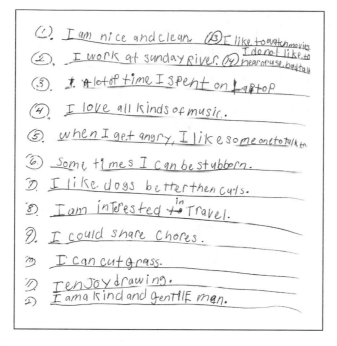

Figure 3 Joshua's Prewriting Activity

Having Josh in English class was probably one of the most valuable experiences in my high school career. In every other course I took, I saw the same 'honors' people. I pretty much spent the whole day with them. Josh was a reminder that people ARE different, and that a student with Down's Syndrome can get just as much out of the same class as an advanced placement student. Joshua's comments gave me a new perspective on most things…[A] major flaw in the educational system is the amount of segregation in courses. It encourages students to exclude each other and perpetuates limited relationships. Being in an integrated classroom helps students understand that everyone has something to give. (Josie Bray, email, October 8, 1999)

For "Stage 109," our acting segment of class, Joshua needed absolutely no accommodations. During the third quarter of the school year, students were assessed on the following presentations:

Introduction of person

Show 'n Tell presentation

Poetry reading

A reading from a novel or short story

Solo improvisation

Group improvisation

Group play

> To: My future roommate
> From: Josh Austin
>
> Dear Roommate:
>
> My name is Josh. I am looking for some one to share an apartment with.
>
> I am nice and clean. I pick up my messes. I will share the chores.
>
> There are some things that I want you to know about me. When I get angry, I like to have someone to talk with. Some times I can be stubborn.
>
> I like dogs better then cats. Drawing is my favorite thing to do.

(a)

> Movies are something I enjoy.
>
> music is one of my Passions.
>
> I am kind and gentle man.
>
> travel interests me.
>
> 0   Other things you might want to know!"
>
> 1   I can cut grass.
> 2   I spend a lot of time with my laptop computer.
> 3   I do not like to hear or use be talk.
>
> 4   Thank your time. I hope
> 5   We can talk soon.
>
> 6   your
>   Sincerely,
> 7   Josh Austin

(b)

Figure 4 Joshua's Letter

The Solo Improvisation unnerved many of us. Yes, I participated, too. Here's how the activity went: I collected thirty items and placed them in paper bags. These were items commonly found in the home, school, or workplace, such as jewelry, a baseball, a gold-colored pen, or a feather. The student picked a sealed bag, opened it, and immediately performed with the item for ninety seconds. Let me tell you, a minute and a half feels like six weeks when you're standing in front of twenty-five teenagers holding a peacock feather.

But not for Joshua. We all have our gifts.

Accommodations: Adapting the Multigenre Paper

Tom Romano's multigenre paper (Chapter 9) challenges and delights most writers. However, for some writers with special needs, there could be any number of barriers to creating this tapestry. What ways could we adapt this project to accommodate diverse student writers? As you've read in Tom's chapter, he assigns the genres required for students' multigenre research papers:

- Brief expository piece, 250–350 words. Make this vivid and informational. Explain, explore, argue. This piece can appear as a mini-essay, or you can drop the exposition into a form that fits your multigenre project.
- Preface/Introduction/Dear Reader
- Prose poem
- Flash fiction
- Poetry in contemporary free verse style
- A visual element
- Bibliography
- Note page
- Unifying elements

We could view Tom's list of required genres as an accommodation. And within this list there are some choices for the writer (e.g., a visual element, unifying elements). Providing a required list of genres with such options is a welcoming approach, one that allows students a certain level of freedom while at the same time eliminating some of the anxiety brought on by having to compose more than several genres on one theme.

When I use multigenre papers, I do not assign the specific genres. I also ask students to take a chance by trying out several new genres. How would you accommodate those writers who struggle with this assignment? I supply a list of genres from which to select (Figure 5). As a follow-up in class, I ask students to think of more genres to add to this list. (You'll be pleasantly surprised by the suggestions.) This extensive list could be overwhelming for writers with or without learning disabilities. One way to help some writers organize their drafts is with a graphic organizer (Figure 6). This drawing or outline helps student writers see the larger picture of the project and gets them moving forward. It is always amazing to me how such a small organizational tool can provide such reassurance and assistance.

Advertisement
Affidavit
Application (jobs)
Application (college)
Application (scholarships)
Annotated bibliography
Autobiography
Autopsy
Bank balance
Bills, receipts
Biography
Birth certificate
Book cover
Book dedication
Book review
Brochure
Business letter
Caption
Calendar
Cartoon
CD Cover
Collage
Commentary
Commercial
Compare essay
Contrast essay
Condolence letter
Contract
Credo
Critique
Crossword Puzzle
Day Planner entry
Database
Diagnosis
Diagram
Dialog
Diary
Dictionary List
Digital Story script
Directions
Doodle
Drawing
Dream sequence
Editorial
Encyclopedia article
Epigram
Essay

Eulogy
Evaluation
Facebook page
Facebook wall-to-wall
Feasibility study
Flash Cards
Graffiti
Grant
Graphic Novel
Grocery List
Historical fiction
Horoscope
IM Transcript
Interview
Joke
Journal
Knitting chart
Letters w/ envelope
Letters of introduction
Letters of complaint
Literary analysis
Literature Review
Loudspeaker announcement
Magazine ad
Magazine feature article
Manual
Marketing analysis
Memoir
Memo
Minute
Mission Statement
Movie ticket stub
MySpace Page
Multigenre in a multigenre
Narrative report card
Newsletter
News article
Newscast
Novella
Nursery rhyme
Observation
Oil painting
Outline
Pamphlet
Philosophy of life
Play
Poem

Political speech
Pop-up scene
Portfolio
PowerPoint Model
Proposal
Quilt
Reading log
Research paper
Request
Response
Response to literature
Resume
Rule
SAT Prompt & Essay
Science Lab
Scientific Research Report
Screenplay
Script
Self-evaluation
Self Portrait
Sketch
Song
Sound Track
Speech
Sports article
Slideshow
State Writing Assessment
Sticky Note
Story
Summary
Survey
Synthesis
T-shirt art
Table/Chart
Technical Report
Toast
Top Ten List
Traffic Report
TV script
Video script
Voice mail transcript
Watercolor
Weather report
Webpage
Webpage pop-up
White paper

Figure 5 Models of Writing, Technology, & Art Genre for Multigenre Papers

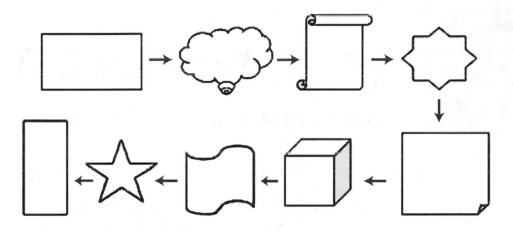

Figure 6 Multigenre Paper Outline

Naturally, there are as many accommodations as there are students. Depending on the specific students and their learning disabilities, a teacher may want to suggest a writing buddy or provide adaptive technology (e.g., screen magnification through ZoomText, a speech synthesizer). You may wish to keep a selection of model multigenre papers from previous years in your classroom files. (If this is your first time with this assignment, you'll find models online or from a colleague.)

Call it a teacher's or writer's intuition, but I don't immediately give out these models to students. I ask them to think about the possibilities of their own papers, to look over the list of genres supplied, and to experiment with as many graphic organizer sheets as needed. But I'm up front about the models: "I've got them, and if you think you'd like to look through some, that's fine."

You'll see, as I did, that several of your students will ask to look at model multigenre papers. That's how they work, and really, how they learn. But that's not so for everyone. And that's the nature of the classroom that welcomes every writer.

Works Cited

Armstrong, Michael. 1980. *Closely Observed Children: The Diary of a Primary Classroom*. London: Writers and Readers Publishing Cooperative Society.

———. 1992 "Conversations at The Bread Loaf School of English." *The Invention and Discovery of Meaning*. Lincoln College, Oxford University.

Kent, Richard. 1997. *Room 109: The Promise of a Portfolio Classroom*. Portsmouth, NH: Heinemann.

Writing 2.0

Developing Students' Textual Intelligence

Jim Burke

Jim Burke teaches English at Burlingame High School. He is the author of numerous books, including The English Teacher's Companion, Writing Reminders, Tools for Thought, Illuminating Texts: How to Teach Students to Read the World, Reading Reminders, *and* I Hear America Reading: Why We Read & What We Read, *all of which are published by Heinemann. He is also the author of* The Reader's Handbook *and* Academic Workout. *His latest book is* 50 Essential Lessons for Teaching English Language Arts, *published by Heinemann firsthand. He has received numerous awards, including the NCTE Intellectual Freedom Award, the NCTE Conference on English Leadership Award, and the California Reading Association Hall of Fame Award. He served on the National Board for Professional Teaching's Standards Committee on Adolescence and Young Adulthood English Language Arts Standards and the National Adolescent Literacy Coalition. For more information visit his website at www.englishcompanion.com.*

A few years back I worked with a big technology company that wanted to create a personal education tool. It would have been something like a cross between a graphic calculator, a Personal Digital Assistant, and a voice recorder. My job, which I enjoyed, was to dream out loud about what it should do and how kids would use it. I even asked my freshmen to draw what they thought it should look like, an assignment they relished. In fact, they came up with such interesting ideas that the engineers at the company tacked these drawings on the walls of their design lab. It was all good fun, but took a profound turn when I proposed that the device have voice recognition software that would allow students with writing difficulties to speak instead of write their papers. They could, I suggested, upload the file to a computer where it would appear as a text document they could then revise. This was the first time I can remember wondering what it would mean to write in the twenty-first century.

Not long after, I had a friend who was hired to travel to China where he was to make a video travel guide of all the major sites. I asked him how people would watch and access such a visual guide while traveling around. "They plan to format it for cell phones so you will be able to call up whatever part of the guide applies to the site you are visiting. It's all interactive," he explained. In the intervening years since that discussion, I have used and, on occasion, created other forms that previously existed only as writing: video documentaries, digital photo essays, and multimedia presentations that incorporate words, images, and sounds in order to explain, persuade, or describe. To the more technological means of conveying information we could add infographics: charts, graphs, and visual explanations that incorporate elements of both as well as other, more unique features.

As a high school English teacher—one committed to the power of the word, the value of reading books, the importance of learning to write well—I could no longer ignore the trends, the realities. After thinking about the changing nature of texts, I developed the notion of "textual intelligence" which I defined as follows:

> TI (Textual Intelligence) is all about how texts are made, and how different grammatical structures create meaning for or affect the reader. Writers use their TI when they do everything from choose the format (poem vs. prose vs. play) or the purpose (to entertain vs. to inform) or the structure (narrative vs. expository), or the medium (word or image, page or screen). They make TI decisions as they choose the point of view, the tense of the story (past tense, present tense), the use of foreshadowing or flashbacks, the organizational structure (linear or episodic). All these choices come from, in part, the writer's understanding of how texts and language work. Therefore, the more a student understands these structures, the more options he or she has when they write.

We face daunting challenges when it comes to teaching writing in the twenty-first century. On the one hand, the very nature of text is changing, challenging us to make room for blogs and threaded discussions, PowerPoint slides and videos alongside the more traditional forms such as essays or stories. Lanham (2006) would argue that text is changing because we are overwhelmed by the volume of information, especially within the "digital expressive space":

> We are drowning in [information]. What we lack is the human attention needed to make sense of it all. It will be easier to find our place in the new regime if we think of it as an economics of attention. Attention is the commodity in short supply (iv).

In other words, the nature of our language, and the way we organize and format that language, must change if it is to succeed in the competitive environment of the marketplace for our attention. Essays will always be with us; expository writing will endure; but as Tom Romano shows, it must adapt to the evolving needs of those who will read and want to communicate. Yet all this talk of economics and efficiency raises one more issue that troubles English teachers at the start of the new century: the need for personal writing, expressive writing, contemplative and reflective writing in an era that is becoming more obsessed with writing on demand (for the SAT and exit exams) and testing (instead of writing). Thus twenty-first-century English teachers are called upon to teach an increasingly diverse group of students the fundamentals; at the same time they must teach these students the more advanced forms and functions that will enable them to succeed in the colleges and the global economy for which we are preparing them.

As technology advances, I cannot help but wonder how writing will evolve and what that evolution will mean for English and writing teachers. It seems that writing by hand, whether with pen or keyboard, will become a preference, the way writing by pen is now for those who might otherwise compose on a computer. Such digital composition will allow texts to be translated—for improved and efficient global communication—into other languages at the stroke of a key and transformed into writing for those who will read them, though in such a digital realm, *read* might well mean asking the computer to read it to you in a familiar voice, one that sounds like your favorite uncle.

Thus I conclude that thinking will emerge as the heart of the writing curriculum— and for similar reasons, the reading curriculum, too. In his essay, "How to Speak a Book," novelist Richard Powers (2007) writes:

> Except for brief moments of duress, I haven't touched a keyboard for years. No fingers were tortured in the producing of these words—or the last half a million words of my published fiction. By rough count, I've sent 10,000 email messages without typing. My primary digital prosthetic doesn't even have keys. I write these words from bed, under the covers with my knees up, my head propped and my three-pound table PC—just a shade heavier than a hardcover—resting in my lap, almost forgettable. I speak untethered, without a headset, into the slate's microphone array. The words appear as fast as I can speak, or they wait out my long pauses. I touch them up with a stylus, scribbling or re-speaking as needed. Whole phrases die and revive, as quickly as I could have hit the backspace. I hear every sentence as it's made, testing what it will sound like, inside the mind's ear (1).

This sounds like the way we want our students to work when they write, which is to say how we want them to think.

Many will turn toward the forms and functions of the past for the simple reason that they are familiar. Those who want to insist on response logs instead of letting students write blogs and threaded discussions, forms that have shown strong gains in performance and engagement, ignore the rich, evolving literacies students already have. Schools in the twenty-first century will require teachers who have not only the traditional knowledge and skills for writing expository prose, but the design sensibilities and technological literacies essential for writing, composing, and creating twenty-first century content, the sort the world will expect students to have upon entering the workforce. Writing in this new era will be for the 8.5 × 11 inch page and screens ranging in size from 2 × 2 inches (cell phone) to 15 inches (computers) to 10 feet (presentations); it will need to be succinct but sophisticated, saying with clarity and grace in a sentence (or with an image) what we could take a paragraph to say in the past. Such textual intelligence will ensure students' success so long as we cultivate our own, looking not to the students but the world outside of school for guidance.

We must look elsewhere, too, for such guidance. We must look within ourselves, examining the reasons we write in the first place. Throughout this book, we see the rich tapestry of writing, reminders that we must write not only for the world outside, but about the one inside ourselves. Writing has, after all, always served both public and private ends. We write to learn about and discover the environment within which we live, as Kim Stafford says, but also the "movement of the mind" that Gretchen Bernabei refers to in her earlier essay. What moves through all these essays, and through writing itself regardless of its form or function, is the individual's voice. What moves me most about teaching writing, and what inspires me most about these collected essays, is the affirmation of that voice and our role in helping students learn to use it to shape and explain their world.

Works Cited

Burke, Jim. 2001. *Illuminating Texts: How to Teach Students to Read the World*. Portsmouth, NH: Heinemann.

Lanham, Richard A. 2006. *The Economics of Attention: Style and Substance in the Age of Information*. Chicago, IL: University of Chicago.

Powers, Richard. 2007. "How to Speak a Book." *New York Times* online edition. http://query.nytimes.com/gst/fullpage.html?res=9900E3DC1F31F934A35752C0A9619C8B63.